WRITERS & THEIR CONTEXTS

Series editor John Spiers, Senior Research Fellow, Institute of English Studies, School of Advanced Study, University of London

1. John Sutherland, *The Secret Trollope: Anthony Trollope Uncovered.*
2. Edward Guiliano, *Lewis Carroll: The Worlds of His Alices.*
3. Albert Rolls, *Thomas Pynchon: The Demon in the Text.*
4. Jo Brantley Berryman, *Ezra Pound's Aesthetics and The Origins of Modernism.*
5. William Pratt, *A Faulkner Profile: The Man and The Writer.*
6. Ann Erskine, *The Sexual Politics of Jane Eyre. Representations of Fear and the Construction of Text in Charlotte Brontë's Jane Eyre.*
7. Terry Scarborough, *Bite The Hand That Reads. Dickens, Animals and Sanitary Reform.*
8. Camilla Del Grazia, *No Ghosts Need Apply. Gothic Influences in Criminal Science, the Detective and Doyle's Holmesian Canon.*
9. Ceylan Kosker, *Violet Fane. The Literary Identities of the 19th Century Poet and Novelist.*
10. Robert C.G. Gamble, *Mrs. Gaskell's Personal Pantheon. Illuminating Mrs. Gaskell's Inner Circle.*
11. Frederick Nesta, *Gissing, Grub Street, and the Transformation of British Publishing.*
12. Alina Ghimpu-Hague, *Consuming Strangeness. Nonsense and Mass Culture in the Nineteenth Century.*

WRITERS & THEIR CONTEXTS
No. 5

A FAULKNER PROFILE
THE MAN AND THE WRITER

A Faulkner Profile
The Man and The Writer

William Pratt

EER
Edward Everett Root Publishers, Brighton, 2020.

EER
Edward Everett Root, Publishers, Co. Ltd.,
30 New Road, Brighton, Sussex, BN1 1BN, England.
www.eerpublishing.com

Full details of our overseas agents and how to order our books are given on our website.

edwardeverettroot@yahoo.co.uk

A Faulkner Profile
The Man and The Writer

William Pratt

First published in Great Britain in 2020.

© William Pratt 2020.

This edition © Edward Everett Root 2020.

ISBN: 978-1-913087-15-9 Paperback
ISBN: 978-1-913087-09-8 Hardback
ISBN: 978-1-913087-10-4 ebook

Writers and Their Contexts series, volume 5.

William Pratt asserted his right to be identified as the author of this Work in accordance with the Copyright, Designs and Patents Act 1988 as the owner of this Work.

All rights reserved. No part of this publication may be reproduced, stored in a retrieval system or transmitted in any form or by any means, electronic, mechanical, photocopying, recording or otherwise, without the prior permission of the copyright owner.

Cover and book design by Pageset Limited, High Wycombe, Buckinghamshire.

Brief Biography

William Pratt is Professor of English Emeritus at Miami University in Oxford, Ohio, and author or editor of twenty books in the field of modern literature, including *The Imagist Poem: Modern Poetry in Miniature; The Fugitive Poets: Modern Southern Poetry in Perspective; Singing the Chaos: Madness and Wisdom in Modern Poetry;* and *Ezra Pound and the Making of Modernism.* From 1991–2005 he served as Secretary of the Ezra Pound International Conference, and in 2015–16 he was President of the Literary Club of Cincinnati, founded in 1849, the oldest literary club in the USA.

DEDICATION

TO MY WIFE AND MY FIRST READER
ANNE CULLEN RICH PRATT

CONTENTS

LIST OF ILLUSTRATIONS — vi
ACKNOWLEDGMENTS — vii

PARTS

I. PROLOGUE: MEETING FAULKNER — 1
II. FAULKNER THE MAN — 13
III. FAULKNER THE WRITER — 141
IV. EPILOGUE: READING FAULKNER — 251
V. APPENDIX — 259

LIST OF ILLUSTRATIONS

Faulkner portrait: letter x
Rowan Oak, Faulkner's Home 17
Faulkner & Bertrand Russell at Stockholm for Nobel Prize 18
The Old Colonel William Clark Falkner 29
Old Colonel's Statue in Riply MS cemetery 32
Faulkner birthplace in New Albany MS 37
New Albany MS Train Station 38
Self-portrait sketch in college 49
Ole Miss Post Office Faulkner managed 1921–24 51
Lafayette Co. Courthouse & Mr. Ike Roberts, hunting companion 56
Gathright-Reed Drugstore on town square of Oxford MS 57
Mac Reed & Bill Faulkner in Drugstore 57
Plaque in Pirate's Alley New Orleans 59
Faulkner outside window of Drugstore 65
Faulkner emerging from Drugstore 67
Faulkner's grave in St. Peter's Cemetery 83
Phil Stone & Bill Faulkner 89

ACKNOWLEDGMENTS

This book has been in the making for many years and comes from a variety of sources, published and unpublished. Unpublished sources are listed in "Faulkner the Man." They are personal conversations with Faulkner himself and with those who knew him in his native Oxford, or in New Orleans, Hollywood, Charlottesville and other places where he lived. Published sources are books by and about Faulkner and articles written about him. Quotations and excerpts from them are taken from the public domain or from books, within the Fair Use provisions of United States copyright law for scholarly books.

> Murray Ll. Goldsborough
> Portraits
>
> 722 Parkhill Avenue
> Lakeland, Florida
>
> This is the original charcoal sketch that I made of William Faulkner, preliminary to painting his profile portrait in March 1962 -- just three and a half months before his death.
>
> Mr. Faulkner seemed fascinated by this drawing and said it was a "remarkable likeness."

Faulkner portrait: letter

Prologue: Meeting Faulkner

In New Orleans in the early 1920s, when William Faulkner and Roark Bradford were young writers trying to make their mark in the world, Faulkner told his friend, "I hope to be the only unregimented and unrecorded individual left in the world." It was his ambition to be forgotten as a man and to live only in his work. He held to that ambition for a long time, evading publicity and giving misleading answers to interviewers who sought him out, but fame caught up with him eventually, and forced him to acknowledge that readers interested in his work would naturally want to know more about the author. He might prefer anonymity, but he could not escape fame. For years he struggled to earn a living as a writer, and only when his books began to sell did he realize that his originality as a writer would lead readers to seek the source of it, to be curious about the personality of the man who possessed such an astonishing command of words.

Always reticent as a man, Faulkner was eloquent as a writer. From the start, he cultivated a style that was elusive and difficult, consciously original in technique and intellectually challenging, choosing his words carefully in ways that were baffling to many readers, yet he succeeded to an astonishing degree in appealing to a wider and wider circle of readers. He did so by becoming a major participant in the movement that dominated twentieth century literature. It was the Age of Modernism.

In English literature, Modernism was chiefly the creation of three major poets and three major novelists. The poets were Yeats, Pound, and Eliot, and the novelists were Joyce, Hemingway, and Faulkner. Together, they fashioned a new literary style out of a variety of personal styles. Through collaborating or interacting with each other they produced, in the first half of the twentieth century, a series of masterpieces in poetry and fiction. Hemingway and Faulkner were the youngest and last to acquire a world audience. What they learned from the older Modernists was how to intrigue, mystify, and induce readers to enter into a poem or story so deeply that they would experience what the French Symbolist poet Stéphane Mallarmé had earlier called "the delicious joy of believing he is creating" the very work he is reading.

Hemingway did it by combining the colloquial American style of Mark Twain's fiction with the compact Imagist style of Ezra Pound's poetry, to create in the early 1920s what is called The Hemingway Style: brief, realistic fictional dialogues. Faulkner did it by combining the American colloquialism of Twain with the poetic prose of James Joyce, to make extended, rhapsodic interior monologues.

Faulkner eagerly embraced the new Modernist techniques, introduced into fiction by Joyce, which many readers found too complex and obscure to be easily understood. It was in 1922, with *Ulysses*, that Joyce had broken new ground by means of dreamlike sequences inside the minds of his characters, inventing a new narrative technique which came to be called the stream of consciousness. In 1929, Faulkner employed this technique brilliantly through the minds of very different characters in *The Sound and the Fury*. These two novels, published less than a decade apart, struck some critics as masterpieces, but struck a majority of readers as too difficult to comprehend, and so fame eluded Faulkner as a writer until late in his career. As a man, however, Faulkner was never anyone but himself, a unique human being who followed no pattern of behavior except his own.

In time Faulkner became the writer he was by being the man he was, and late in his life he became a writer for the world, not just for his own kind. He was always unmistakably a Mississippian, a Southerner, and an American, but he gradually discovered how much could be made of those discrete identities. He did so by obeying, as all great writers have, the simple truth that the Greek oracle asked of Socrates: "Know thyself." By seeking self-knowledge Faulkner was led, story by story, into ever deeper knowledge of human nature. His uniqueness as an individual matched his genius as a writer, but it took him a long time to make them coalesce.

To know Faulkner the man is as challenging as to understand Faulkner the writer, but his two identities were linked, though most of those who knew him well are no longer with us. I was not in his circle of intimate friends and family, but I did get to know some of them, and it was my good luck to meet him in the flesh, if only for a few brief moments--moments of paramount importance to me though I am sure they mattered very little to him. They mattered to me because I was one of the millions of readers for whom Faulkner's work had the force of a revelation, not simply the work of a gifted writer, but one of the greatest. My admiration of his work led me to want to meet him as a man, and when I finally did, I saw that he really was what he told Roark Bradford he wanted to be, if not "the *only* unregimented and unrecorded individual left in the world," a man whose singularity as an individual destined him for the greatness he eventually achieved as a writer.

I remember seeing William Faulkner for the first time in the fall of 1937, as he was making his way homeward along a sidewalk in Oxford, Mississippi, his home town. The sidewalk ran beside Lamar Street, named for Lucius Quintus Cincinnatus Lamar, Mississippi Senator, Secretary of the Interior, and Associate Justice of the United States Supreme Court. In the period just after the Civil War, Lamar had been a forceful spokesman for reconciliation between the North and the South, and the best known citizen of Oxford before Faulkner lived there. I was strolling toward the town square with my uncle, only a few blocks away from my uncle's drug store, a place where Faulkner often went for household items, bought tobacco for his pipe, browsed through books on the drug store rental shelf, or leaned against a window to observe the behavior of his fellow citizens.

My first brief glimpse of Faulkner was fortuitous. I was only ten, a generation younger than he was, a small boy walking beside his uncle on the way to town. Faulkner was forty years old, a mature writer who had by then published most of his fictional masterpieces, though they were unknown to me and to much of the rest of the world at that time. It would be another thirteen years before Faulkner would become world famous as a writer. My uncle and I were walking along Lamar Street towards my uncle's drugstore on the town square when we saw, across the street, the slight figure of a man going in the opposite direction. He seemed lost in thought, ambling along, oblivious to the world around him. He did not see us, but we saw him, and my uncle bent down to me and said, in a low voice, "That's William Faulkner. He's a writer." Mac Reed was an old friend of Faulkner, a fact I didn't yet know. I was too young even to know what a writer was, but Uncle Mac spoke in a serious tone, and I made up my mind I was going to find out some day what he meant.

It took me much of the rest of my life to make good on that boyhood promise. In the decade after I first saw him, I had read almost everything Faulkner had written, and I felt able to grasp what Uncle Mac had in his mind when he told me Bill Faulkner was a writer. By then, I had confirmed to my satisfaction that not only was he a writer, he was one of the best. My first glimpse of Faulkner the man led me toward finding out just how much there was to learn from Faulkner the writer, and it prepared me for meeting him in person years later.

I did meet him, exactly thirteen years later, on Easter Sunday of 1950. Looking back to that far-off day, I am glad I first met Faulkner when he was in his prime, before he had gained world fame, because none of the citizens of Oxford who knew he was a writer could have believed he would someday be the recipient of a Nobel Prize for Literature and would make his home town world famous. I met him by the good luck of having a family connection. I was not a native of Oxford, or even a native of Mississippi, as my father was. My father had been born and grown up in Mississippi, before moving to Oklahoma where I was born. He was born in 1895 in the village of Walthall in northeastern Mississippi, not far from New Albany, the small town where Faulkner was born two years later, in 1897. Faulkner moved to Oxford with his family in 1902, when he was a little boy of 5, while my father moved to

Shawnee, Oklahoma, in 1911 when he was only 15. He had completed his education, all ten grades of it, in the public schools of Houston, Mississippi, where his father was town marshal, and his older sister, Mabel, had married a graduate of the University of Mississippi who became a druggist in Oxford after college. The druggist was William MacNeil Reed, my Uncle Mac, who had invited me as a boy to come to Oxford, all on my own, aboard a train, to watch a football game between Ole Miss and Mississippi State, chief rivals for the state championship.

I had come to Oxford to see football, not to see Faulkner. But that was before I knew my uncle happened to be an old friend of Faulkner, that he had stood by him early and late, in bad times and good, before his peculiar genius had made its mark in the world. Uncle Mac was a few years older than Faulkner, and he was the kind of solid citizen Faulkner needed for a friend, since Uncle Mac was a graduate of Ole Miss, and was educated enough to appreciate Faulkner's literary talent when few citizens of Oxford did. Faulkner was grateful for Uncle Mac's support, and acknowledged it in many ways, even signing new books for him as unsolicited gifts, books that dedicated readers of Faulkner would have given a fortune for him to sign. It would not have surprised Faulkner to hear Uncle Mac insist, when I later became professionally interested in Faulkner's work, that he was not a serious student of Faulkner's work, that he was just his friend. Their friendship was solid enough to start me on the way to a professional career, in which Faulkner would be at the forefront of the writers whose work I studied. I am sure that my first chance encounter with the man my uncle knew so well led me eventually to a life of studying, teaching, and writing about modern literature in general, and Faulkner's work in particular.

As I look back now on what would turn out to be a moment that would change my life when I was only ten, I would venture to guess that Faulkner's mind was far away, probably already working on his next novel, *The Unvanquished*, which he would publish in 1938. To Faulkner, the unvanquished were not the Confederate soldiers who had fought and lost the Civil War; they were the women who had stayed behind and who had never given up. Many of the men either had not come back, or had surrendered after Appomattox, but the women had refused to accept defeat. It was the women who remained defiantly unvanquished, who preserved family loyalty and honor despite the humiliation of suffering defeat in a lost cause.

The Unvanquished was not Faulkner's first novel about the Civil War. The first was *Absalom, Absalom!*, which he had published two years earlier, in 1936. Faulkner's name was nationally known by then, but it was not yet a household word. His two Civil War novels had not helped much to spread his name, since they were published just before and just after Margaret Mitchell's *Gone with the Wind*, a longtime bestseller, had virtually cleared the field for Civil War fiction. Neither of Faulkner's novels ever rivaled hers in popularity, though they were far better artistically. They did not become bestsellers until much later, when everything he wrote was a bestseller, nor were they made into Academy Award-winning movies, as hers was, but they did mark a major turning point in his career.

When I was old enough to read both novels, I came to see that *Absalom, Absalom!* was tragic; it dramatized the Civil War as a tragedy that the South had brought on itself and that it deserved to lose, even if heroically. Faulkner was a realist who was both the South's greatest writer and its most severe critic. He believed that the American Civil War had been caused by grave faults of which the South was guiltier than the North, though there was plenty of guilt to go around. He thought Americans in general, and Southerners in particular, had been guilty of exploiting both man and nature. They exploited man by importing and enslaving African Negroes, and exploited nature by driving the Native Americans out and destroying the wilderness, converting it to their own purposes. His first novel about the Civil War, *Absalom, Absalom!* was a tragic vision of human ambition and greed, ending inevitably in death and defeat. His second novel about the Civil War, *The Unvanquished,* was not tragic but broadly comic; it viewed the Civil War as proof of the loyalty and bravery and willing sacrifice of Southerners, even though they were clearly doomed to defeat, and it ended with the deliberate renunciation of violence.

Though his two Civil War novels were published just two years apart, they revealed a seismic shift in Faulkner's viewpoint toward the South, toward America, toward the whole human race. I think that when I first saw him, his mind was in transition, moving from his Tragic Phase to his Comic Phase. Katherine Anne Porter, a Southern writer who ranked Faulkner first among her contemporaries, thought all his work was on a hairline between tragedy and comedy, with either outcome possible in any given work. Certainly there are comic moments in *Absalom, Absalom!*, and tragedy hangs over every chapter of *The Unvanquished*. Nevertheless, the first is definitely tragic, a great novel by any measure, and the other is ultimately comic, taking a more hopeful view of life in the mythical kingdom of Yoknapatawpha County, Mississippi, which Faulkner created and gave to the world.

A few years later, in *Intruder in the Dust,* Faulkner would write that "For every Southern boy fourteen years old, not once but whenever he wants it, there is the instant when it's still not yet two o'clock on that July afternoon in 1863"--and he fights the Battle of Gettysburg over again in his imagination. When I first saw him, in 1937, I think Faulkner must have been re-enacting the Civil War in his mind, but making his mind up to laugh rather than weep at human folly. Shakespeare's plays embrace both tragedy and comedy; so does Faulkner's fiction.

By the time I actually met him, in the spring of 1950, I had begun to understand what kind of writer he was. I was 22 by then, and had graduated from the University of Oklahoma, forty miles west of my home town, then had gone a few hundred miles east to Vanderbilt University in Tennessee to do graduate work in English literature. I wanted to be an English professor someday, and Vanderbilt had been strongly recommended to my father by a Methodist bishop whose opinion he respected. Since my father had been born in Mississippi and my aunt and uncle still lived there, I took a natural interest in Faulkner. In the summer of 1948, before my senior year in college, I had the good fortune to land a job with the U.S. Forest Service in Yosemite National Park. Packing for the trip to California, I included a pocket-size Modern Library dual edition of *The Sound and the Fury* and *As I Lay Dying*, two novels I had yet to read. The natural beauty of Yosemite was the perfect place to spend a summer, and Faulkner's two short, complex novels were exactly suited to careful reading underneath the giant sequoia trees. My choice proved to be decisive.

I found both novels mystifying and beautiful, like everything Faulkner wrote, and I began to think that if I studied his writing more closely I might understand why I was so captivated by it. So in 1949 I chose to write a Master's thesis at Vanderbilt on *The Sound and the Fury*. My mentor was Donald Davidson, one of the Fugitive poets, who as a critic wrote one of the earliest favorable reviews of Faulkner's work. I was working on this project when I went to visit my uncle again in 1950, during the Easter vacation of my first year at Vanderbilt. My Uncle Mac was a graduate of Ole Miss, and though he did not share my literary interests, he approved of them, and he set it up for me to meet his friend Bill Faulkner. He knew Faulkner was an important writer but didn't fully understand why: "I'm not a deep student of his work," he would always insist, "I'm just an old friend who has known him for a long time." He said Faulkner had given him several autographed books over the years which he hadn't had time to read. In one of them, Faulkner had scrawled a handwritten dedication: "For Mac Reed, old friend, by damn." Uncle Mac didn't know, and neither did I, that Faulkner would receive the Nobel Prize for Literature later that year.

And so, on a sunny Easter Sunday of 1950, Uncle Mac drove me in his comfortable Plymouth sedan out to Rowan Oak, a few blocks from his house, where his friend Bill Faulkner lived. We drove into his spacious domain of Bailey's Woods, through its wooden entrance gate marked "No Trespassing," down the potholed gravel road leading to his fading white-columned mansion, the sort of house a Southern writer ought to live in. It had been called The Old Sheegog Place before he bought it, but he renamed it Rowan Oak—not for the Virginia town of Roanoke but for a Scottish superstition that rowan trees ("mountain oaks" Americans call them) were lucky.

He had bought the antebellum mansion in 1930, before breaking into commercial success with his most sensational novel, *Sanctuary*, published in 1931, which he later said he wrote to make money. He succeeded so well that it embarrassed him, because in his view making money was not a worthy aim for a writer. He was not entirely honest in that view, because he did a lot of writing for money, especially when he willingly wrote screenplays in Hollywood, but *Sanctuary* happened to be the first novel by Faulkner I had read, and in spite of the author's low opinion of it, I found it fatally attractive. It hooked me once and for all on Faulkner.

I had heard many anecdotes about Faulkner before I met him, because his eccentricities were legend. An early interviewer quoted him as saying flatly, "I was born male and single at an early age in Mississippi...of an Indian slave and an alligator..." Faulkner had a wicked sense of humor and was fond of saying that writers were born liars; he was equally fond of proving it.

As an undergraduate at the University of Oklahoma, I had gone to a lecture by Hodding Carter, then widely known as Editor of the *Delta Democrat-Times* in Greenville, Mississippi, who told some outrageous stories about Faulkner from his own experience. As my uncle and I drove up to Faulkner's house, I remembered one of Hodding Carter's anecdotes. He said that Faulkner was fiercely protective of his privacy and hated intruders. Not only did he make a practice of digging holes in his gravel driveway to discourage casual visitors, but once, on the porch of Rowan Oak, he became so annoyed at the approach of an uninvited stranger that he stood up, opened his fly, and said, "Well, he's come to see me and I'll give him an eyeful," and calmly urinated into the bushes. I was half afraid he might welcome us in some equally shocking way, but my uncle was an old friend, and Faulkner was on his best behavior the whole time we were with him.

We parked in front of the house and walked through an alley of tall old cedar trees to the front door, where Faulkner greeted us very politely. To my surprise, despite having seen him once before when I was a little boy, I found myself being introduced to a short, slight man with a high squeaky voice. I had imagined from reading his books a tall, imposing figure with a deep voice. My first real encounter with Faulkner taught me something important, that the author and the man are never exactly the same, that the imagined voice of a writer can be quite different from his actual voice as a man. The difference between Faulkner the man and Faulkner the writer were obvious as soon as I met him. Though he was formidable as a writer, as a man he was deceptively shy.

In his polite but diffident way, Faulkner invited us to come in, and then walked us through the dark hall of his mansion to the back door. I noticed as we passed through the main hall that the rooms were sparsely furnished and the walls mostly bare, but I spotted a small niche in the wall for the telephone, next to which he had penciled some phone numbers, including one for Gathright-Reed, my uncle's drugstore. He took us all the way through the house and out to his back yard, where he offered us seats on the bench of a plain wooden picnic table and began talking to my uncle. I was an outsider, and took little part in the conversation between the two men, which mainly concerned people in town they both knew and I didn't. Though he had lived in Oxford most of his life, Faulkner had always seemed disinterested in the daily life of the town, but I found he was aware of almost everyone and everything that went on there, and took as much interest in it as my uncle did. They enjoyed gossiping about their neighbors, and I listened quietly as they talked about people who were strangers to me.

Faulkner also took great interest in the natural world, and was keenly aware of his surroundings in the Mississippi woods, being a farmer, a hunter, and a dedicated conservationist as well as a writer. As we sat there, he pointed to a pear tree which had fallen on its side near the picnic table, which in April was loaded with blossoms. He explained that he had given his yard man strict instructions never to cut down a living tree. Then he went on talking with my uncle about Oxford citizens they knew, who meant little to me.

Once I made a clumsy attempt to enter the conversation by asking about a new book I had heard he was writing, called "Notes on a Horse Thief." It would become an episode of a longer novel called *A Fable*, which he published in 1953. The novel was about the First World War and was set in France, but the horse thief episode took place in his mythical Yoknapatawpha County and was better than the rest of the novel. His reply quickly cut me off. "I don't know much about books," he said. "A book's a book to me, and they're all too durned expensive." I knew it was a lie, and he knew it was a lie, but it was the sort of disingenuous answer an expert might give to a novice to keep him from asking further questions. I kept quiet after that. Later that year I would buy the book at my favorite bookstore in Nashville, after it had been published by Hodding Carter's Greenville Press, in a run of a thousand copies numbered and signed by the author. I still have it in my library. It was Copy 148. I bought it for $15 in 1950; fifty years later, I had it appraised for $1,189.

Although Faulkner was a professional writer, and his income came almost entirely from his publications, he seemed to take little interest in their success or failure and did not care to discuss them. In his early years, he had struggled for recognition, and most people in Oxford regarded him as a ne'er-do-well, though the Falkners (the rest of his family spelled the name without the "u") were a prominent family in Mississippi. His great-grandfather, the first William Falkner, had been a Confederate colonel, a railroad builder, a state legislator, and a writer of popular novels, and Faulkner as a schoolboy said he wanted to be a writer like his great-grandpappy. He did not mean he wanted to write in his great-grandfather's old-fashioned style, which he later criticized as excessively romantic, but he hoped to become a published author in his own inimitable style, which would combine the starkly realistic with the colloquially poetic.

In spite of his boyhood ambition to be a writer, Faulkner was never a diligent student and often played hooky from school. Later he would call himself "the world's oldest living sixth grader." That was no lie; it was close to the truth. He never really finished high school, and though he took a few courses at Ole Miss, where his father was the Business Manager of the university and the family lived on campus, he never finished college. As a young man he had no steady job, working for a time in his grandfather's bank but preferring to paint houses or shovel coal in the university power plant. He wrote one of his best novels while working at night in the power plant. It was *As I Lay Dying*, and he said it was the easiest novel he ever wrote, because the humming of the dynamo was soothing to his ears.

Everyone in town knew that Bill Faulkner wanted to be a writer; but it took him a long time to make it a paying profession. When he returned to Oxford in 1918 from brief service as a cadet in the Royal Canadian Air Force (he was too short to qualify for the US Army Air Force) he wore an officer's uniform with wings and sported a swagger stick. Understandably, most of the people in town saw his pretensions as a pose, and started calling him "Count No 'Count," expecting nothing serious ever to come from him.

Their disdain turned to awe in the fall of 1950, when Faulkner won the Nobel Prize for Literature. It stunned the town, and though it pleased Faulkner to get the news, he went out hunting with some friends when he received the phone call from Sweden, and would have preferred to accept the honor in absentia. It took his daughter Jill to persuade him to go to Stockholm and receive the award in person. She was the editor of the high school newspaper, and it was a golden opportunity for her to cover a news story of international significance. He doted on his daughter, who was his only child, and agreed to fly to Sweden with her.

On the way, he took the time to write the acceptance speech that turned out to be the most famous ever given by a winner of the Nobel Prize. Nobel Prizes for Literature had been given to writers as gifted as William Butler Yeats and George Bernard Shaw and T.S. Eliot and Winston Churchill, but their acceptance speeches were largely forgotten afterwards, while Faulkner's address was the only one widely quoted long after it was given.

Sentences from it are carved today in stone on the wall of the Ole Miss library, which houses a Faulkner Collection that is its main claim to fame: "I decline to accept the end of man," he had said in Stockholm to an international audience, "I believe that man will not merely endure, he will prevail." These words astonished the world, which was trying to live in the shadow of the nuclear mushroom cloud that exploded over Japan in 1945. Many felt that it was just a matter of time until the human race obliterated itself. Faulkner felt otherwise and was openly optimistic about the future of man, declaring that "He is immortal, not because he alone among creatures has an inexhaustible voice, but because he has a soul, a spirit capable of compassion and sacrifice and endurance. The poet's, the writer's duty is to write about these things."

That was what he said in his Nobel Prize Address of 1950, fusing his individualism with his new universalism. Having at last arrived at the peak of his fame, he chose to talk about how he had tried in his work to be true to the essential nature of man, and his words resonated with those he had expressed in the novels and stories that had earned him a world audience. Many readers had taken him to be a pessimist, even a fatalist, whose work dwelt more on human weakness and destructiveness than on moral strength or heroic ambition, and he was sometimes criticized for creating characters more memorable for their vices than their virtues. But Faulkner at that decisive moment in his career gave the world a surprisingly uplifting and inspirational message, which brought many readers to view his whole literary achievement in a new light, aware that they had been missing a steady light in the darkness of his vision. His belief that man will endure despite his often self-destructive character is at the heart of the paradox that Faulkner's fiction presents.

He wrote those stirring words just a few months after I met him. They were not what he said to my uncle and me as we sat at his picnic table in the back yard of Rowan Oak on Easter Sunday of 1950. He talked informally and easily about the hunting trips he enjoyed with friends, in the deep woods of the Mississippi Delta, about farming a patch of land he owned near Puskus Creek, not far from Oxford, and about riding his favorite horse, Stonewall. Stonewall later threw him and precipitated his untimely death in 1962 at the age of 65. All he said to my uncle, as we got up to leave, was "Mac, you don't come out to see me often enough." Then he got up from the picnic table, led us back through the house to his front door, and said goodbye with a courteous old-fashioned bow.

I had only one more brief visit with Faulkner. That was in the fall of 1953, when I was finishing my Master's degree in English at Vanderbilt. Anne and I were engaged, and we were invited to spend a weekend with my Aunt Mabel and Uncle Mac in Oxford, an invitation we readily accepted. Again Uncle Mac was the intermediary. He had arranged to have a showing of a CBS video that was a visual account of Faulkner at home in Oxford for its Omnibus series in 1953. Faulkner hadn't yet seen it, though the film had been stored in the safe of the Gathright-Reed drug store at Faulkner's request. Uncle Mac thought it was time Faulkner had a look at some of the compliments people were finally giving him. He asked the principal of the Oxford high school if he had the necessary room and equipment that would allow Faulkner to view the video for the first time. The principal was glad to say he did, and Faulkner agreed when invited that if "Bill and Anne" were coming all the way from Nashville for a visit, he would be glad to share the video with them. On the day appointed, Uncle Mac escorted us to the high school classroom and we waited for Faulkner to appear for the showing. We heard a light knock on the door of the classroom, and my wife, who was nearest the door, opened it. She had not met Faulkner, and when she opened the door, she was astonished to see a small man standing in a raincoat that looked too big for him. She wondered if this could be the famous author who had written those remarkable books, but she quietly ushered him in. Faulkner entered the room with a gentlemanly bow to her and sat down. Uncle Mac quickly introduced him to us, and the film began rolling on the screen. It presented a highly complimentary view of Faulkner, opening the door of Rowan Oak, riding a tractor on his farm outside Oxford, playing the role of a world famous writer who preferred to be called a farmer. Faulkner sat beside us, showing little emotion, watching and listening silently to the film about him. As soon as the film had finished rolling and the lights were turned on, he put on his raincoat and immediately started for the door. We stopped him long enough to ask if he liked the image CBS had made of him. "It was done up all right" was his only comment. Uncle Mac thanked him for coming and we bade him goodbye. We wanted to ask him about his books, about his Nobel Prize and the acclaim it had brought him, but he didn't pause for any questions. He quickly made his exit out the door and was on his way. That was the last time I met him in person.

PART I

Faulkner the Man

The Sources

1. Meeting William Faulkner twice, in 1950 and 1953

2. Conversations with close relatives of Faulkner:
   Jill Faulkner Summers, his daughter;
   James Faulkner, his nephew;
   Dorothy Oldham, his sister-in-law

3. Conversations with others who knew Faulkner:
   Mrs. Sallie Elliott, Phil Stone's secretary and Faulkner's typist
   William McNeil Reed, druggist and longtime friend (my uncle)
   Byron Gathright, co-owner of Gathright-Reed drugstore
   Aston Holley, who worked for Gathright Reed as a young man
   Louis Cochran, Faulkner's first editor, later an FBI agent
   Hodding Carter, Editor of the *Delta Democrat-Times* and publisher of *Notes on a Horse Thief*
   George Healey, Editor of the *Ole Miss Magazine* and later of the *New Orleans Times-Picayune*
   J. R. Cofield, photographer and friend
   Dr. Felix Linder, schoolmate and physician
   Dr. Dewey Linder, schoolmate and dentist
   Marjorie Fox, wife of Ole Miss Professor, friend of Faulkner's mother
   Peggy Whitehead, friend of Faulkner in a youthful group called "The Bunch"
   Dr. and Mrs. Ashford Little, neighbors and friends
   Christine Drake, teacher and friend of Faulkner's mother
   Andrew Price, Negro helper and groom of his horses
   Bramlett Roberts, hunting companion
   John Cullen, hunting companion
   Charles Nelson, aspiring writer who sought Faulkner's advice
   J. D. Roach, Faulkner's assistant Boy Scout master

> Calvin S. Brown, boyhood friend of Faulkner, later Professor of Comparative Literature at the University of Georgia
> Mildred Murry Douglas, friend of Jill Faulkner
> Mrs. Will Lewis, a friend of Faulkner since school days
> Mr. Matthews, longtime resident of Oxford
> Mrs. Duncan, longtime Oxford resident and friend
> Carvell Collins, Faulkner scholar
> William Boozer, Faulkner scholar
> Joseph L. Blotner, Faulkner biographer

4. Faulkner interviews published by Marshall Smith, John Malcolm Brinnin, and Jean Stein

5. Faulkner as a screen writer, televised comments by Howard Hawks, Hollywood director who hired Faulkner to work on several of his films

6. Books by Faulkner's mistresses: *A Loving Gentleman* by Meta Carpenter
   A Winter Love by Joan Williams

Faulkner and Oxford

William Cuthbert Faulkner was a citizen of Oxford, Mississippi, and a writer of genius. They were two sides of the same man but there was a distance between them. How Faulkner managed to become a writer of world renown while remaining unfailingly loyal to his home town remains a mystery. Oxford, a college town in the Deep South, was his home most of his life, though it was not his birthplace. He was born on October 25, 1897, in New Albany, and moved with his family to Oxford in 1902, when he was five, the eldest of four brothers. New Albany was a stop on the railroad line built by Faulkner's great-grandfather, the first William Falkner, while Oxford was an American college town named for an older college town in England, and the site of the University of Mississippi, better known by its nickname, Ole Miss. The nickname was a relic of the plantation society which had flourished in the South before the Civil War, a time when the planter was called Ole Marster, and his wife Ole Miss. The University of Mississippi, however, was founded to be a beacon of learning independent of the society around it, and it was the main source of Oxford's fame until Faulkner lived there. By the end of his life, Oxford had become better known as the home of William Faulkner.

This book is about what I discovered the first time I met Faulkner, which was the difference between Faulkner the Man and Faulkner the Writer. I met him in person after years of reading and studying what he had written. I knew that his strong regional identity, as an American and a Southerner, had not kept him from reaching a larger and larger audience, most of them neither Southern nor American. What I found to my surprise was that he could be thoroughly provincial as a man while being universally admired, even loved, as a writer. Meeting him confirmed that the difference was real and worth investigating. This book is the result of that investigation, which has lasted most of my life. While Faulkner the man remained provincial, Faulkner the writer became more and more cosmopolitan, a writer with a world audience far beyond his native South.

Faulkner knew that to become a professional writer meant to make some major changes. The first change he made was in the spelling of his name. He had grown up as Falkner, but by the time he began to publish his writings, he had added the u, a concession to the commoner spelling of his name, which was Faulkner. Faulkner changed much more than his name. He made far more significant changes through his work, gradually transforming his home town of Oxford, Lafayette County, Mississippi, into Jefferson, Yoknapatawpha County, Mississippi, the imaginary setting of most of his stories and novels. He succeeded in making his native region more than a place on the map; he transformed it into his Mythical Kingdom, a feat of imagination only the greatest writers achieve. He began his transformation from fact to fiction by changing the college town of Oxford, county seat of Lafayette County, into Jefferson, the county seat of his fictional Yoknapatawpha County, moving the university forty miles away from Jefferson, which made Jefferson a more typical Southern town, more social than intellectual in its activities. Most of his life, Faulkner the man consciously distanced himself from the academic life of his native Oxford, being more comfortable in the company of hunters and farmers and ordinary townspeople than among college professors and students, the kind of serious readers who increasingly hounded him with questions about his books. He liked privacy and solitude more than social engagement, and spent much of his life avoiding publicity rather than seeking it. As a man, he needed solitude to write, but for his livelihood as a writer, he needed people to buy his books. Thus he reluctantly found himself becoming a more and more public figure in the larger world outside Oxford and Mississippi. Faulkner the man was a reclusive resident of an American small town, but Faulkner the writer succeeded in becoming one of the most celebrated writers of his age, a living paradox of reticence and renown. The reticence died with him; the renown survived, and thrived as his work gained readers and admirers all around the world.

Until he won the Nobel Prize for Literature in 1950, William Faulkner was not a hero in his home town. Everyone in town knew him, because he had grown up and lived most of his life in Oxford, Mississippi, but most of his fellow townsmen thought of him as little more than a lone drifter, who played hooky more often than he went to school, and who never graduated from any educational institution. Most of the respectable citizens in Oxford regarded him as an idler who would often appear in town barefoot and ragged, looking more like a tramp than a dignified citizen Though his grandfather was president of the bank and his father was business manager of Ole Miss, he seemed indifferent to his reputation. He knew what people thought of him and ignored their disdain, until he came home from Sweden after receiving the Nobel Prize. Then he knew his hometown reputation had changed for the better. "The tramp has become famous," he acknowledged to a friend. He added that it had not made him any happier.

Until his moment of fame arrived in the fall of 1950, few people in town read his books, and many consciously avoided them. They knew that his first book had been published at his own expense, with the help of a few friends who were aware of his talent. Published in Boston in 1924 when he was twenty-seven, his first book showed little promise for a writer intent on a professional career. It was no more than a slight, fanciful narrative poem called *The Marble Faun*, seldom read today, hardly a harbinger of the brilliantly original novels that would later make him famous. Thus in his early days in Oxford, he passed for a would-be writer of limited talent, whose books did not sell and were mostly given away to friends. Then in 1931, after publishing two masterpieces, *The Sound and the Fury* and *As I Lay Dying*, he published *Sanctuary*, a shocker which woke his fellow townsmen up. They began to regard him as a sensational novelist willing to blacken the reputation of the town for money, the black sheep of a reputable family. He had attracted their attention earlier when he enlisted in the British Royal Air Force in Canada in 1918, and returned in uniform with a swaggerstick, claiming to be a combat veteran who had flown missions in France in the First World War, and had been shot down and suffered a head injury. It was one of the many lies he told on the way to becoming a fully accredited writer. He had in fact been an air force cadet in Canada, who crashed in a training flight, a truth he barely concealed. He was still trying to redeem himself as a genuine writer when, in 1930, he bought a white-columned antebellum mansion known as the Old Sheegog Place, in Bailey's Woods off Old Taylor Road, a few blocks away from the town square. He had lived with his family in several different homes growing up, but there he settled for good, choosing to live for the most part in guarded privacy, posting a No Trespassing sign at the entrance to keep strangers at a distance. He was known best to his own family, or to a few old friends in town like Phil Stone, the lawyer, and Mac Reed, the druggist, and others willing to drink with him at private parties as long as Prohibition was in force. He especially liked to join some rather rough and ready hunting companions for expeditions into what remained of the wilderness, often going off with them as far as the Mississippi Delta to hunt wild animals for sport and food for the table.

Rowan Oak, Faulkner's Home

A dramatic change occurred in the town's opinion of Faulkner when he won the Nobel Prize for Literature in 1950, at the age of fifty-three. Their former doubts turned into open admiration. By the time of his death twelve years later, he had become the most honored citizen of a quintessentially Southern college town, proud of its resemblance to the older English college town for which it was named. Faulkner came to be revered as a home town hero, a local boy who made good, whose bronze likeness now sits on a bench beneath the courthouse on the town square, and whose continuing presence has a magnetic attraction for foreign as well as American visitors, especially older scholars and younger writers eager to breathe the air that inspired him to write his stories and novels. He renamed his home, the Old Sheegog Place in Bailey's Woods, Rowan Oak, symbolic of good luck. The name held true after his death, when Rowan Oak was purchased from his family to become a major attraction on the Ole Miss campus, a principal place of homage for most visitors. Faulkner's white-columned mansion has a less rundown look than it did when he lived there. It has been restored handsomely by the University of Mississippi and opened to the public. The house was purchased from Faulkner's daughter, Jill Faulkner Summers, to be maintained as a place of pilgrimage for Faulkner readers, who may and do come from anywhere in the world. The man once shunned by the more respectable citizens of the town has become its principal claim to fame, announced by a sign on the way into town proclaiming that Oxford is the home of William Faulkner. Honor in his hometown was late in coming, but it did finally come. Faulkner the writer had been admired in the outside world, especially by French readers, long before he was admired in his own home town, proof of the Biblical saying that a prophet is not without honor save in his own country.

Faulkner & Bertrand Russell at Stockholm for Nobel Prize

Faulkner turned out to be a true prophet, even in his home town, but it took him a long time to find himself as a writer. He started out writing poetry before he settled for writing prose. He would later call himself "a failed poet," because he believed that poetry was the highest form of literature, expressing beauty and truth in the fewest possible words. Faulkner soon recognized his attempts at poetry fell short of his high goal, and he would later treat them as "a youthful gesture I was then making of being 'different' in a small town." Being different was his natural style. He cultivated it all his life, since he was customarily aloof, seldom openly greeting or smiling at others. His demeanor was rooted less in arrogance than in shyness, because he was always conscious of his lack of formal education in a college town proud of its intellectual identity. He would candidly admit that he never liked school, and proved it by never graduating from high school or college. Ironically, of course, Faulkner did more for the intellectual reputation of Oxford than any of its graduates. No American writer has ever been more loyal to his home town than William Faulkner, but he instinctively valued privacy more than fame. When a reporter tried, early in his literary career, to elicit some facts about his life, Faulkner made the ridiculous claim that he was "born at an early age in Mississippi of an Indian slave and an alligator, both named Gladys Rock." He would later justify this self-mockery by saying that writers are born liars. Such self-criticism helped him maintain a distance from others, giving him the space to write "of the human heart in conflict with itself," which, he declared in his Nobel Prize address, should be the ambition of any really serious writer. His eccentricities were legend in Oxford, where everyone knew him, whether drunk or sober, obscure or famous, and everyone talked about him, giving him a protective cover that left him free to write as he pleased, transforming the realities of his own place and time into universal truths about human nature. His peculiarities as a man served to set him apart, enabling him to become what he was destined to be, a writer in the high tradition of world literature.

Impressions of Faulkner ourside Oxford

Early interviews barely scratched the surface of Faulkner's complex personality. Marshall Smith, his first interviewer, reported in 1931 that people down in Oxford, Mississippi, where he lived, did not think he was a great man. Mr. Faulkner in fact told him that most of the townspeople thought him merely lazy. "A lot of them don't know I write books," he said, "and they think I don't do anything at all. The bookstore in Oxford only sells school-books. The drug store down there has some of my books—some times." In that same year a "Talk of the Town" column in *The New Yorker* confirmed that "Only a few of the townspeople know he writes at all; most of them think he's lazy. The local drugstore ordered several copies of his last novel but didn't do very well with them. His mother reads every line he writes, but his father doesn't bother and suspects his son is wasting his time."

When Marshall Smith visited Faulkner at Rowan Oak in 1931, bent on finding out all he could about this virtually unknown writer of a scandalous book called *Sanctuary*, he reported that as he arrived, Faulkner was making home brew with the help of a Negro man. When questioned, Faulkner was dismissive about his books, saying he liked to "Read a book and let it go at that," and that "the public expects too much of present-day novelists." He had written some of his greatest novels by then, but claimed "I haven't written a real novel yet." Smith reported finding to his surprise that the office where Faulkner did his writing was littered with guns and books about hunting, rather than by literary classics. His sole equipment for professional work was a home office containing a chair, a portable typewriter, a table, a cot for taking naps, and a filing cabinet where he stored his writings. Smith's interview, published in *The Bookman*, in Dec., 1931, was the first public account of William Faulkner as a serious writer beginning to make his mark in the world, and it was hardly flattering.

John Malcolm Brinnin added to Faulkner's growing reputation as a professional writer with a personal interview he published in *Harper's Bazaar* in the later 1930s. He gave a detailed impression of Faulkner's appearance and behavior, observing his "compact strength" and noting that "his eyes—steady, almost expressionless—are most memorable." He said Faulkner seemed capable of "continuous concentration" and from time to time "his eyes glow with instant warmth and illumination, like a gust of wind or fires banked deep." Brinnin interviewed Faulkner in the library of Rowan Oak, where he was surprised to see that the writer chose to surround himself, not only with books, but with saddles, shotguns, a portable typewriter on which he wrote, and the pipes he liked to smoke. Faulkner was so pleased with Brininin's interview when it was published that he sent it to his mother, "Miss Maud," his chief fan all her life, as a gift from her devoted son.

Faulkner had a way of seeming indifferent to others, but whenever he chose, he could be polite, even sociable. In his younger years, he had been happy hunting deer on foot in the woods of rural Mississippi with his hunting cronies. In his later years, he could be just as happy, dressed in coat and tie, hunting foxes on horseback in the hills around Charlottesville, Virginia. His daughter Jill had married and settled there with her family, and she loved horses as much as he did. She introduced her father, now a world-famous writer, to the Farmington Hunt Club of which she was Mistress of the Hounds. He ordered a formal outfit from Abercrombie and Fitch to look the part of a foxhunter when he hunted with them and was photographed in it on a visit home, by his Oxford friend "Colonel" Jim Cofield, who said it was Faulkner's favorite portrait.

There were many reports that Faulkner never opened the fan mail he received, but when a literary friend asked him questions about one of his stories, he said "Write your questions down and send them to me." The friend was surprised at the invitation, since he had heard that Faulkner never opened his mail, but Faulkner explained with a twinkle "I know what to open." When anyone tried to ask a question about his books, he generally fell silent, though he proved in his later informal lectures at the University of Virginia that he was quite capable of talking engagingly about them if he chose to do so. Soon after the Nobel Prize had made him world famous, he accepted the role he was offered by President Eisenhower to be a cultural ambassador to the world. In this official capacity, he traveled to Japan, the Philippines, Thailand, India, Egypt, Italy, Germany, England, Ireland, Venezuela, France, and Greece for the Department of State, and in each place he talked amiably about his works, pleasing his foreign listeners and furthering the reputation of American culture abroad. For his *Paris Review* interview, in its "Writers at Work" series in 1955, he gave Jean Stein frank and honest answers about his work, and in 1957–58, while he was serving as Writer in Residence at the University of Virginia, he freely discussed his work with an audience of students and faculty. These sessions were recorded on tape, and his answers to questions were edited by Frederick Gwynn and Joseph Blotner, to be published to the world as *Faulkner in the University*, which quickly became an invaluable aid to understanding the complicated works of fiction he had produced. Though his fictional world was a microcosm of the American South, he knew it was a small part of the larger world, and he showed he was willing when the time came to play his part in that world. By then, Faulkner was near the end of a career that had lasted over thirty years, during which he had written a series of fictional masterpieces that transformed the real world where he lived into the mythical world of Yoknapatawpha County, Mississippi. Though he had written constantly about his native South, by the end of his life he had traveled far beyond its boundaries. He lived for a time as a screen writer in Hollywood, later as a writer in residence at the University of Virginia, often as a guest of his publisher in New York, as a visiting lecturer at Princeton and at West Point, on State Department visits to Paris, to Brazil, to Tokyo. Yet his true home, throughout his life, was the place where he had grown up, and to which he always returned, Oxford, Mississippi, the Southern college town which he personally added to the cultural map of the world.

Faulkner and Mississippi History

Singular though he was as an individual, William Faulkner was shaped by his place and time. He took great interest in the early history of his part of Mississippi, and generally accepted the viewpoint of his fellow citizens toward the rights and wrongs of human behavior, including the highly charged issue of race. His sense of Southern identity was so ingrained that as late as 1948, in *Intruder in the Dust*, he could re-enact in his imagination the disastrous charge of Pickett at the Battle of Gettysburg, from the point of view of a Confederate soldier who obeyed the command, long after the Union had won the battle and consequently the war. The words were so engraved in the mind of one reader, nationally syndicated columnist George Will, that sixty years later he would quote it from memory in a newspaper column he published on Oct. 16, 2008, one of many widely quoted proofs of the enduring power of Faulkner's words. Faulkner spoke again as a Southerner after the Supreme Court decided, in Brown vs. Board of Education in 1954, that segregated public schools were unequal and therefore illegal. He contended that being against racial integration in the United States would be like living in Alaska and being against snow. Nevertheless, he wrote a "Letter to the North" in *Life* magazine, in which he cautioned the rest of the nation against forcing too rapid a change in the long accepted Southern practice of racial segregation. Faulkner's article was published while the country was still sharply divided over the Supreme Court decision, and prompted one of his Oxford neighbors to say, when she saw Faulkner on the town square, "I liked what you said, Bill." Faulkner, it was reported, brightened at her remark, and was genuinely pleased by her comment, telling her in reply "I"m glad you did." He never rejected the Southern way of life, but portrayed it truthfully in his writing, remaining a faithful citizen of the town which had gradually learned to embrace the man it once kept at arm's length.

Mississippi was not famous for its writers when Faulkner appeared on the scene. Though Southerners value history more than most Americans, the history of Mississippi is comparatively short, and Faulkner made the most of what there was of it. Mississippi was not one of the original thirteen colonies that formed the United States in 1789, but was part of what was called the Old Southwest. It was admitted to statehood in 1819, three decades after America had declared its independence and established itself as a constitutional republic separate from England. It was only in 1836 that the town of Oxford became the seat of Lafayette County in Northern Mississippi. Faulkner was not born in the town which he made famous, but he learned many facts about it that were largely forgotten by the time he moved there He knew that the land had originally been occupied by tribes of roving Chickasaw Indians, who had made few attempts to civilize the region, which was still mostly wilderness when the white European settlers arrived. Faulkner would come to regret that the native population of Native American redskins had been forcibly displaced by the white settlers, though his own family was among them. In his lifetime there were few living inhabitants old enough to remember the scattered remnants of the Indian tribes that were still in the vicinity. I remember that as late as 1968, when I was visiting Oxford, I had a conversation with an elderly resident named Matthews who had grown up in the Tallahatchie River bottom, the site of Major de Spain's fictional hunting camp in Faulkner's greatest hunting story, *The Bear*. Mr. Matthews told me he had known a Negro man named Taylor Shaw, about 90 years old, who claimed he had seen Chickasaws in his boyhood, including the last of the Chickasaw chiefs, Tobatubby (also spelled Toby Tubby) whose burial mound, chosen by the chief himself, was on a knoll overlooking Tobatubby Creek at the spot where it joined the Tallahatchie River. Later, it had been flooded by the Sardis Reservoir, where Faulkner liked to keep a sailboat, the Indian burial mound now covered with a man-made lake surrounded by tall cedars. Mr. Matthews recalled that the remnant of the Chickasaw tribes had departed for Oklahoma after burying their chief, leaving no survivors to be seen in Mississippi. It was on Faulkner's conscience that the native Indians had been forcibly removed from his part of the South in 1833, sent westward on the Trail of Tears by President Andrew Jackson. He lamented the fact that there were no more native Americans to be seen in his part of the country. However, Faulkner's way of atoning for the guilt he felt was through his fiction, in which he created some notable survivors of the Native American tribes, making them the main characters in some of his best stories, "Red Leaves" in particular. Outstanding among these interracial characters is Sam Fathers, the veteran hunter who befriends young Ike McCaslin in *The Bear*. Sam Fathers, whose name means "Had Two Fathers," claims descent from all three of the original races, red, black and white, who were living in Mississippi at the time it officially became one of the United States. Sam Fathers is not only Faulkner's chief interracial hero, he is one of Faulkner's noblest characters, who guides the hunters in their pursuit of Old Ben, the fabulous black bear they eventually corner and kill. Their killing is justified by their wish to honor the massive bear, a symbol of the Lost Wilderness, in order to prevent it from being destroyed by much less sympathetic pursuers.

The Native American presence in the South was real, and is preserved in deeds found today in the Lafayette County Courthouse in Oxford, which show that Princess Hokah (or Ho Ka), daughter of Chief Toby Tubby (or Tobatubby) of the Chickasaw Nation, signed away the territory that would become Oxford to the first white settlers in 1836. Other former Indian owners of the land are mentioned in the courthouse records, including Ish mi ah tubby (like Issitibeha in Faulkner's fiction), Mah mah tubby (like Faulkner's Moketubbe), Pull um ma tubby, I yah wa, and Cum ho kah. The Chickasaw chief who signed the Treaty of Pontotoc in 1832 was called King Ishtehatopah. Though Faulkner never knew any American Indians personally, since none remained in northern Mississippi in his lifetime, he believed in their continuing presence, and invented fictional characters who bear names very much like those on record as original members of the Chickasaw tribe. Faulkner paid tribute to all the Indian names that remained on the land, starting with Mississippi, and going on to make fictional capital of the rivers north and south of Oxford in his stories. He accepted the Tallahatchie as the real name of the river north of Oxford, and elevated the Yoknapatawhpa south of Oxford to mythical status in his own preferred spelling. Faulkner's Indians were imaginary, but their origin was a historical reality, even if Faulkner could not have met a Native American in the region in his lifetime.

Faulkner immortalized the plantation South, antebellum and postbellum, with all its rapacity and slavery, much more realistically than Margaret Mitchell did in *Gone with the Wind*. In fact, his South is best compared fictionally with Hawthorne's New England, with its Puritanism and religious zeal. To relive New England history today you have only to read *The Scarlet Letter*, which dramatizes Puritan society more unforgettably than any written history could, making it a reality for later generations. To see the Old South as living history, you need only read *Absalom, Absalom!* a fictional account of the Civil War as convincing as any factual account. Aristotle held that literature is truer than history, since history must stick to the facts, telling us only what has been, while fiction gives us what might have been, the variety of human possibilities at a given place and time. Reading Faulkner, the Old South comes fully alive for his readers, although in fact it existed only for one generation in Mississippi. Mississippi became a state in 1819; Oxford did not become the seat of Lafayette (pronounced LaFAYette by natives) County until 1836. The Old South, the South as a separate nation, ended in 1865, with its defeat in the Civil War, so what Faulkner knew as the Old South lasted less than half a century. Hawthorne's Puritan New England lasted much longer in Massachusetts than the Old South lasted in Mississippi, but both of these rich and colorful American cultural regions, which have now disappeared, live again in the fictional accounts which Hawthorne and Faulkner bequeathed vividly and unforgettably to the history of the United States. They are more realistic than the many factual accounts that have been written about New England and Southern ways of life. Hawthorne and Faulkner wrote living history, displaying the full range of human behavior possible in a definite society at a given time.

Faulkner and Oxford History

There are maps of Lafayette County Roads in 1916 which show that in Faulkner's lifetime only three main roads led in and out of Oxford: Lamar Highway (named for Lucius Quintus Cincinnatus Lamar, Senator from

Mississippi, Secretary of the Interior, and Associate Justice of the Supreme Court), W.C. Falkner Highway (named for Faulkner's great-grandfather, the Old Colonel), and Jefferson Davis Highway (named for the President of the Confederacy). Of the three, only Lamar Street remains a principal thoroughfare through Oxford today.

Other old maps of Lafayette County show the names of regional districts around Oxford, which Faulkner adopted in his fictional Jefferson. Beat One was the central township, Beat Two was the northeast sector, Beat Three was the northwest sector, and Beat Four was the southern sector. There was also a Beat Five, but it does not survive in Faulkner's work. Beat Four is the district he mentioned most often, especially in *Intruder in the Dust*, where it signifies the backwoods territory around what he calls Frenchman's Bend, the lair of his fictional villains, the Snopeses and the Gowries. They are backwoods families who prey on the more civilized citizens of Jefferson. Beat Four acquired a darker symbolic meaning in Faulkner's fiction, one of the many subtle ways in which he made his fictional Yoknapatawpha County out of the real Lafayette County.

The Lafayette County courthouse has a written record of the first general election in Oxford, held in Craig's general store on April 2, 1836, when all the main officers of the town were chosen: Judge, Sheriff, Assessor, Clerk, Treasurer, Surveyor, Ranger, and Coroner. Oxford was designated as the county seat on June 20, 1836, located in Beat One of Lafayette County, consisting of "fifty acres donated by Chisolm, Martin & Craig...which site they do establish and declare it shall be known as the town of Oxford."

The first courthouse was made of logs at a total cost of $141.50. It took its place in the public square before the town of Oxford was officially founded. Roads were constructed in all directions, starting with a highway to Memphis that crossed the Tallahatchie River by means of Tobatubby's Ferry. Soon tavern licenses were issued, and as early as October of 1836 a contract for $23,000 was let to construct a brick courthouse to replace the original log house. It was to be two stories high, with a tin roof and a cupola adorned with a rod and a ball. In 1839, a log jail was constructed next to the courthouse, to be later replaced by a brick jail north of the town square. Many of Faulkner's stories and novels center around the county jail, where Lucas Beauchamp, a black man, was held as a prisoner accused of murder in *Intruder in the Dust*, until a young white boy and an aging spinster proved that it was the Gowries, rather than Lucas Beauchamp, who committed the murders, and Lucas was released from jail as an innocent man.

In 1891, an early history of Oxford was published in *The Oxford Eagle*, stating that the town lands were purchased by white settlers from the native Chickasaw tribe in 1836, the year Oxford was founded. The native Indians had been forcibly moved westward in 1833, on the infamous Trail of

Tears ordered by President Andrew Jackson, and by 1836 most of northern Mississippi had been taken over by white settlers. The *Oxford Eagle* account said candidly that "The Chickasaws were partly civilized, but had no towns. Some had small fields in cultivation, a few had fine large farms, some had none." Indian farms, such as they were, had been located in clearings, since "Most of the country was a continuous forest, with a dense growth of grass as high as a man's head." There was a trail that led through the forest until it crossed the Tallahatchie River by means of a ferry, which was named for the most widely known Chickasaw chief, Tobatubby, though the principal Chickasaw chief was Ishtehatopa. As soon as the white settlers arrived, they built a small store in the woods offering provisions for sale, and a bridge was built to the south, across what was then called the "Yocknapatalph" River. It was as early as 1837 that John Houston (like the builder of "Holston House" in Faulkner's fiction) was granted a license to sell liquor from his home. In the same year, the Cumberland Presbyterian Church was founded in a "bush arbor." Interestingly, there was a town south of Oxford called "Old Jeffersonville," long before Faulkner chose to name his fictional town Jefferson.

During his years in Oxford, Faulkner lived in a variety of homes. The first was the Old Baker Place, on "Second South" street, now 11th Street, where Murry Falkner first settled with his family from 1902–1905, when he owned a livery stable near the town square. The Falkners were considered an aristocratic family in Oxford, with a record of Civil War service, a law office, a bank, and a respectable position in the university administration. They were never wealthy, however, and their friendships included country people as well as townspeople. They were generally regarded as clannish and proud, with a fondness for large houses and extensive property in the old plantation style. None of their houses was especially notable while William Faulkner was growing up, neither the Old Baker Place on 11th Street, the Old Knight House on North Lamar, Oxford's main street, nor the Old Delta Psi House on the Ole Miss campus, where the family lived from 1920 to 1924, while Faulkner was taking a few college courses and serving as University Postmaster. After their marriage in 1927, Bill and Estelle Faulkner lived in an apartment in Miss Ella Meeks' house on University Avenue, between the town and the campus. It was in 1930 that Faulkner bought The Old Sheegog Place off Old Taylor Road, which had the white-columned appearance typical of a Southern mansion and became his permanent home. He gave it the more symbolic name of Rowan Oak.

The Old Sheegog house had been named for the early Oxford store-owner who built it, an Irish settler named Sheegog (sometimes spelled Shegog). The land was originally deeded to Robert Sheegog in 1844 by an Indian named E-Ah-Nah-Yea. It was bought in 1872 by John M. Bailey, and the woods around it came to be called Bailey's Woods. John Bailey's wife Julia willed it to her daughter, Sally Bailey Bryant, wife of Will Bryant, who sold it to Faulkner in 1930. Faulkner bought the house with four acres of Bailey's Woods in April but could not move in until the occupants vacated it in June of 1930. He did not own it outright until 1938, when he finished paying the mortgage, and a warranty deed for the property was issued in his name. Faulkner had agreed to pay $6000, with 6% annual interest on the house and land, in installments of $75 per month. The full sum was paid in 1938, with the addition of some 5-acre lots that brought Faulkner's total property to 45 acres including the house, a substantial estate. It was much neglected when he bought it, however, being equipped with a telephone but no electricity or indoor plumbing. The house was almost a hundred years old when he acquired it, and his first job of restoration involved jacking it up and replacing the supporting beams. When it was restored, he and Estelle moved in, and he hired three Negro servants to help in running it. Ned Barnett, who had worked for Faulkner's father, served as his butler and yard man; Josie May, who had worked for Faulkner's in-laws, the Oldhams, was his cook, and "Mammie Callie," Caroline Barr, who had been Faulkner's own mammy, was employed to look after Victoria ("Cho-cho") and Malcolm, Estelle's children by her first marriage. Caroline Barr was clearly the prototype of Dilsey Gibson, the devoted mammy of the Compson family in *The Sound and the Fury*. Ned Barnett, the Negro servant who stayed longest with the Faulkners after Mammy Callie, was probably the prototype of Lucas Beauchamp, the main character in *Intruder in the Dust*, who liked to wear a frock coat and always carried himself with dignity. When Faulkner sold "Red Leaves," the first of his Native Indian stories, to *The Saturday Evening Post* in 1930, he was paid $750, enough to enable him to install much-needed electricity throughout the house.

    Faulkner experienced some initial difficulty in supporting his wife and stepchildren in his early years. His first steady job after working in the university post office was working at night in the Ole Miss power plant. The university had offered him another sinecure, because while he kept the fire going in the furnace at night, he had time to do what he liked, which was to write. Faulkner would claim later that he wrote one of his best novels, *As I Lay Dying*, in only six weeks, using the back of a wheelbarrow as his writing table during long nights in the powerhouse. It was his fifth novel, after his third and fourth novels, *Sartoris* and *The Sound and the Fury*, had been published in rapid succession in 1929. To follow them with another masterpiece in 1930, *As I Lay Dying* was clear proof that Faulkner had discovered his true vocation in a sudden burst of inspiration. He had succeeded in inventing and populating his own imaginative world, the mythical kingdom of Yoknapatawpha County, Mississippi, by writing three successive masterpieces in two years. After many years of searching, Faulkner had by 1930 at last produced convincing evidence of his literary genius. It would take another two decades for his achievement to be fully recognized by the world at large.

Faulkner's Wife and Daughter

In January, 1931, a daughter was born to Bill and Estelle Faulkner, whom he had married in 1929, and they named her Alabama in honor of "Aunt 'Bama," the daughter of the Old Colonel, who lived in Memphis. Unfortunately, the baby lived only a week, and Faulkner became so desolate with grief that he cried out loud, and carried the casket on his lap to the cemetery to be buried in the Falkner plot. His grief lasted until June 23, 1933, when his only surviving daughter, Jill, was born. Dr. Bramlett, the physician who delivered her, gave her the name. When he saw it was a girl, he said to the proud father, "She's not a Bill; she's a Jill." The parents liked the name so much they kept it. By the time she was born, Faulkner had written and published his sixth and most sensational novel, *Sanctuary*. He had also bought his house in the woods, The Old Sheegog Place, and renamed it Rowan Oak. The name came straight from one of his favorite books, *The Golden Bough*, which mentioned a Scottish superstition that oaks were lucky trees and that rowan trees were especially charmed. He would live there with his wife and daughter for most of the rest of his life. He also lived in many other places, such as Hollywood and New York and at the end of his life in Virginia, but Oxford remained his home, and that was where he was buried after his sudden death on July 6, 1962, nearing the age of 65.

Faulkner doted on his daughter, Jill, his only surviving child. He was an attentive father who dutifully took her to school and went to her piano recitals, and most importantly let her talk him into going to Sweden to accept the Nobel Prize in 1950. He would consent to her wish to be the commencement speaker when she graduated from University High School in Oxford and later from Pine Manor College in Boston. As a teen-ager, Jill was permitted to read *Sanctuary*, his sensational story about a naïve college girl who is corrupted by men and becomes a prostitute. It affected her so deeply that she cried, and her reaction moved Faulkner to apologize and explain, entreatingly, "I'm sorry, honey, but I needed the money and that was why I wrote it." To a friend, Minnie Ruth Little, who complained that she had somehow lost her copy of *Sanctuary*, Faulkner would say "It's all right. You didn't want that one anyway." He seemed so genuinely ashamed of the book, which earned him more money than any of his earlier novels and made him an instant celebrity, that he begged his mother not to read it. To a friend who wondered why he had dared to write it, Faulkner said "If I hadn't written it, I might never have been known until the end of my life. Who knows?" His sentimental favorite among his novels was *The Unvanquished*, though he always regarded *The Sound and the Fury* as his best.

By 1940, Faulkner was the owner of a large house and the largest piece of land in Oxford township, and people began to think of him as rich and famous. Actually, he was relatively poor and unknown, for he had to ask his agent, Harold Ober, to lend him $100 to pay his debts, before his growing reputation enabled him to become a truly professional American writer who could earn his own living.

Faulkner's Family background

The Old Colonel William Clark Falkner

The family influences were strong as Faulkner grew up. The unique identity of Faulkner as a man and a writer derived from one definite source in his family. It was his great-grandfather, the first William Falkner, whose full name was William Clark Falkner, called "The Old Colonel," by his family, for whom William Faulkner was named, but whom he never knew except by reputation and family legend. William Clark Falkner began life as a poor boy from the hills of Knox County, Tennessee, who would one day walk barefoot from St. Genevieve, Missouri, to Ripley, Mississippi, to join and eventually take over his uncle John Wesley Thompson's law practice. The Falkners had moved west to Missouri from Tennessee about 1838, seeking greater opportunity, but William Clark Falkner, born in Knox County, Tennessee, on July 6, 1826, decided to strike out from Missouri in 1842 at the age of 16, reportedly after an argument in which his brother Joseph struck him with a hoe. (A full account of the Old Colonel's colorful life and violent death can be found in a 1962 dissertation at the University of Michigan, by Donald P. Duclos, *Son of Sorrow: The Life, Works and Influence of Colonel William C. Falkner, 1825–1889).* The Old Colonel fought in two wars--the Mexican War (1847) and the Civil War (1861–3)--and afterwards wrote three novels, built a railroad, and was elected to the Mississippi legislature. (He had earlier run for the legislature before the Civil War but had lost to his uncle, John Wesley Thompson). He was a poor boy who had worked hard as a military officer, a railroad builder, and a writer, until he had enough money to build a large Italianate house that became the showplace in the town of Ripley, Tippah County, Mississippi.

Faulkner's great-grandfather had killed two men in Ripley before the breakout of the Civil War: Robert Hindman, who had been in his company in the Mexican War, whom he stabbed in self-defense, and Erasmus Morris, a Hindman follower who attacked him after he was acquitted of the murder of Hindman in 1849. In 1861, at the start of the Civil War, he became Colonel by raising a troop of volunteers, the Magnolia Rifles, and being elected its colonel, taking them to the First Battle of Bull Run in Virginia, where he was described by Gen.P.T. Beauregard as "the Knight of the Black Plume" for his leadership in the battle won by the South. Col. Falkner led his troops to fight beside the victorious Confederate generals Stonewall Jackson and J. E. B Stuart in that successful battle, but was disappointed when his troops did not re-elect him colonel in 1862. Instead, they chose a man named Stone, who won by a single vote. Col. Falkner was further disappointed when he failed to gain promotion to Brigadier General (though he had been commended by Gen. Joseph E. Johnston for his valor).

The Old Colonel returned embittered to Mississippi in April, raising the First Mississippi Partisan Rangers in July and leading them into battle, but less successfully. He now belonged to the Army of Northern Mississippi, commanded by General Nathan Bedford Forrest, and his family would perpetuate the legend, possibly true, that Falkner had fought beside Forrest. He kept applying for promotion to Brigadier General, even writing a letter of request to Jefferson Davis, but never succeeded, and eventually lost battles at the head of his Partisan Rangers that caused him to become discouraged and stop taking an active part in the Civil War. That was in late 1863, well before the war was over. He later accepted the fact that the Civil War had been "a family quarrel and the family has settled it." When the war was over and the South had been defeated, he turned to other pursuits.

He first built the Ripley, Ship Island, and Gulf Railroad, a connector between two main railroad lines in Tennessee and Alabama, allowing rail travel to go all the way from Memphis to Mobile by way of a narrow-gauge railroad called the "doodlebug" railroad. After the War, he helped found Stonewall College for women and wrote a melodrama about the Civil War for its opening ceremonies called *The Lost Diamond*, of which no copy survives. In 1871, he assisted in building a further railroad connection to Middleton, Tennessee, with Richard Thurmond as one of his partners. In 1880 he wrote a novel titled *The White Rose of Memphis*, which was first serialized in *The Ripley Advertizer*, and soon became a bestselling novel in the aftermath of the Civil War. He proved to be a prolific writer, publishing an account of a murderer named McCannon who was in jail when he arrived in Ripley, as well as *The Siege of Monterey*, a long poem in imitation of Byron's *Don Juan*, about a battle of the Mexican War, and a short novel called *The Spanish Heroine*. His writing career continued with *The Little Brick Church* (1882) and *Rapid Ramblings in Europe* (1884), which was a series of letters following an extended trip abroad. His work was of the moonlight and magnolia school of fiction, in tune with the generally sentimental defense of the South after its defeat in the Civil War. Though he joined the Knights of Temperance, he was known as a heavy drinker, like his future namesake and great-grandson, the second William Faulkner. His success as a writer enabled him to build in 1884 a large house with a square tower, called the Italian villa, a centerpiece of the town of Ripley. Falkner traveled to Jackson to speak to the Mississippi legislature about extending his railroad further south, and in 1886, with aid of convict labor, he did build an extension of the Ship Island, Ripley, and Gulf railroad 38 miles south to Pontotoc, through the town he named Falkner, and New Albany, where the second William Faulkner was born. In time he acquired his partner Thurmond's interest in the railroad, since the two men could not get along with each other, and thus became owner and president of the railroad he had built.

Old Colonel's Statue in Riply MS cemetery

He did not stop there. In 1889, he ran for the Mississippi legislature, won the primary in August and was elected to a seat in November. But on the very day of his election, Nov. 5, 1889, he was fatally wounded, shot down in cold blood on the streets of Ripley by his now wealthy and jealous former partner and rival, Richard Thurmond. Thurmond and Falkner had long had a public feud in Ripley, and both men had prospered before the fatal encounter occurred. The newspaper account of the sensational murder called it cold-blooded and unprovoked, with Thurmond emerging from his office on the square, pistol in hand, to shoot an unarmed, totally astounded Falkner. Falkner and Thurmond were described in the local paper as "two of our wealthiest and most prominent citizens." After a funeral service in the Presbyterian Church, The Old Colonel was buried in the Ripley cemetery, beneath his larger than life effigy, which he had personally commissioned to be carved of Carrara marble from Italy. Eight feet tall and mounted on a fourteen foot pedestal, with a stack of marble books supporting his marble effigy, it dominated the graveyard. The assassin Thurmond was tried and acquitted in 1891, long after the murder, following a sensational trial, on a lesser charge of manslaughter. The jury had been stacked with Thurmond sympathizers. William Clark Falkner remained a controversial figure in Ripley even after his death, supported vigorously by those who elected him to the legislature, condemned by opponents who thought he deserved his fate. His son, John Wesley Thompson Falkner, who came to be known as the "Young Colonel," was so embittered by the trial and its outcome that he moved the family permanently to Oxford, while Thurmond moved to North Carolina hoping to leave his murderous reputation behind. The Young Colonel, John Wesley Thompson Falkner, graduated from Ole Miss in 1869, and on Jan. 20, 1887, there was an announcement in *The Oxford Falcon* that a law office was being opened in Oxford by Chas. B. Howry and J. W. T. Falkner "late of Ripley, Miss." Thus the Falkner family was well established in Oxford before Murry Falkner moved his family there in 1902, five years after the birth of the second William Falkner.

The Old Colonel's meteoric rise and fall endured in family memory, and his reincarnations figure notably in Faulkner's fiction. Yoknapatawpha County and its county seat of Jefferson are partly based on Tippah County and Ripley, as well as on Lafayette County and Oxford. The railroad that Faulkner's fictional Colonel Sartoris built in Jefferson, and the marble effigy overlooking it, belong to Ripley rather than to Oxford. The rumor persisted that the Old Colonel had fathered a "shadow family" of black Falkners, since many of that name are buried in the Ripley cemetery, and some even claimed to be his descendants. His namesake, the second William Faulkner, inherited his great-grandfather's pipe, the one he was smoking at the time he was murdered.

The chief connection of Faulkner's own ancestral family with his fictional characters is Col. John Sartoris, hero of *Sartoris* and head of the main aristocratic family Faulkner created. As Faulkner portrays him in both *Sartoris* and *The Unvanquished*, he fought on the Confederate side in the Civil War and survived to become the leading citizen of Jefferson, until he too died at the hands of a rival after the war. The main points of resemblance between the mythical Col. John Sartoris and the real Col. William Falkner were his distinguished Civil War record, his killing of two men, his dream of building a railroad, his partnership with Thurmond, and his brutal death. Faulkner did not identify Col. Sartoris as a writer, despite his great-grandfather's success as a novelist, probably because he thought the Old Colonel's most popular novel, *The White Rose of Memphis*, was pure escapism, portraying all the men as brave and all the women as pure, without any hint of humor. That his great-grandfather had been a successful writer mattered to his namesake, but not his sentimental treatment of the antebellum South. William Cuthbert Faulkner's realistic and often humorous depictions of the South before, during, and after the Civil War owed little to his illustrious ancestor, though he did in fact become a writer "like my great-granpappy," just as he had said he hoped to be. Unlike the first William Falkner, the second William Faulkner wrote as a realist and ironist whose work was original in substance as well as style. His fictional Col. Sartoris was a heroic figure and a natural leader, brave, honorable, and strong, but he could also be violent and overbearing, especially when facing the carpetbaggers who invaded the South after the Civil War. The real Col. Falkner had also been heroic, successfully building a railroad after the Civil War, the first of his many ventures. Col. Falkner originally had two partners in the railroad enterprise, but one dropped out, leaving Falkner and Thurmond to be the partners who finished the project. Col. Falkner was the main force in building it, but as soon as the railroad was running smoothly and making money, he seemed to lose interest in it. He decided to go into politics, and won election to the legislature before being gunned down at his moment of victory. *The White Rose of Memphis* became a bestselling novel and showed that his taste in literature was decidedly romantic. The writer he most admired was Sir Walter Scott, and he named some of the stations on his railway after characters in Scott's novels. His namesake, the second William Faulkner, admired the first William Falkner for his successes, for his many talents, and for the self-confidence he displayed in all his endeavors. He recognized, however, that his great-grandfather's arrogance probably led his jealous partner to bring his life to such a sudden and violent end. The stories the family told Faulkner may well have led him to think the Old Colonel had driven his rival and partner Thurmond to desperation, causing him to react impulsively to the Old Colonel's brief but ill-fated political victory.

Faulkner's fictional Col. Sartoris, like the Old Colonel, was overbearing, and his intemperate behavior caused him to be killed by his jealous partner. But the end result was quite different, because the violent death of John Sartoris at the hand of his rival drives his son Bayard, in "An Odor of Verbena," the last chapter of *The Unvanquished*, to renounce vengeance and declare publicly that he is tired of killing people. The family had always believed that the real Col. Falkner was not armed the day Thurmond shot him, though he habitually carried a pistol. Faulkner was well aware that hard feelings about Col. Falkner in Ripley did not die with him, nor with the departure of his murderer from town. Faulkner could remember family visits to Ripley in his boyhood, when people in town would pass on the other side of the street to avoid speaking to him, knowing that he was a descendant of Col. Falkner. He also remembered that people in Ripley talked about Col. Falkner as if he were still alive, as though they feared he might come back at any time for vengeance. He especially remembered how the Old Colonel's monumental effigy dominated the Ripley cemetery, towering over all the other graves. His fictional Col. Sartoris orders just such an imposing statue for himself, insuring that even in death he will occupy a commanding place in the Jefferson graveyard.

There is no doubt that Faulkner's great-grandfather is embodied in his fictional Col. Sartoris. He was also the prototype for another heroic character, Thomas Sutpen of *Absalom, Absalom!*, Faulkner's greatest Civil War novel. Thomas Sutpen, like the Old Colonel, came down from the hills to marvel at the plantations which had been built in the flat lands of the Mississippi Delta, and resolved that someday he would become a planter himself, building a mansion and founding a family dynasty. The story of Thomas Sutpen is more tragic however than that of John Sartoris. He fathers two families, one by a mulatto mistress on a French Caribbean island, and another on Sutpen's Hundred, his vast plantation outside Jefferson, by means of a highly respectable Methodist wife. Thomas Sutpen leads a troop of soldiers to Virginia in the Civil War, just as the Old Colonel had, but encounters a major obstacle to the fulfilment of his dream. He is betrayed by the two sons he has fathered by different wives. Charles Bon, the son of his mulatto mistress, goes from New Orleans, where he is living with his mother in an elegant brothel, to the University of Mississippi, thirty miles distant from Jefferson, and there befriends Henry Sutpen, the son of Ellen Coldfield, Sutpen's Methodist wife. The two men become friends at first, but turn into enemies and rival heirs to the family fortune, finally driving Henry Sutpen to kill Charles Bon at the front gate of Sutpen's Hundred. Thomas Sutpen himself later dies from the blow of an outraged helper whose daughter he has recklessly violated. The plots of *Sartoris* and *The Unvanquished* differ greatly from the plot of *Absalom, Absalom!* but both have to do with the defeat of the South in the Civil War, the main cause of suffering and death in both the Sartoris and Sutpen households. Col. Sartoris survives the war only to be killed by a jealous rival, while Thomas Sutpen survives the war only to be murdered by his outraged servant. Both are tragedies stemming from the Civil War, and both of his tragic heroes were modeled on Faulkner's own great-grandfather, the Old Colonel, the redoubtable entrepreneur for whom Faulkner was named, but whom he knew only through family legend. A third reincarnation of the Old Colonel can also be seen at a distance in Faulkner's fiction, in the person of General Compson, who is not a major character but is mentioned with a measure of awe in three Faulkner masterpieces, *The Sound and the Fury, Absalom, Absalom!*, and *The Bear*.

Though in real life Col. Falkner was elected but never able to serve in the state assembly of Mississippi, he was officially commended by the Mississippi legislature after his death. The commendation was printed in *The Oxford Eagle* in its issue of Jan. 16, 1890, as a "Resolution of Respect,":

> "Whereas, Col. W.C. Falkner was elected on Nov. 5, 1889, a member of the Mississippi legislature from the County of Tippah, and
>
> Whereas, on Nov. 6, 1889, the hand of death...was laid upon him and his services are thereby lost to his County and State...
>
> Resolved, that, in recognition of his pre-eminent services to his county, in war and peace, as soldier, statesman, writer and citizen, in every walk of life, this preamble and resolution shall be spread upon the minutes of the House...as a feeble tribute to his memory."

No wonder Faulkner's paternal family regarded the Old Colonel as the family patriarch and repeated stories about him to the younger generation of Falkners. Faulkner's maternal family, the Butlers, were also distinguished, but in a different way. The Butlers were from North Carolina like the fictional Sartoris family. They were regarded as Oxford pioneers, since Faulkner's maternal great-grandfather, Charles George Butler, had come to Lafayette County in 1836 and was responsible for laying out the town square and becoming the first sheriff. A man named Jacob Thompson (alias Jason Compson of *The Sound and the Fury*) was another prominent citizen of Oxford who would be appointed Secretary of the Interior. Northern Mississippi had been ceded to the U.S. in 1832 by the Chickasaw tribe, who were forcibly moved west to Oklahoma Territory on the Trail of Tears. The "Beats" or districts of Oxford were established by law, probably as a relic of slavery, since it was necessary to patrol the country roads at night to keep the Negro slaves at home. In 1839, the University of Mississippi was created south of Oxford. Faulkner's maternal great-grandfather owned the Butler Hotel on the town square, and married into the Bowen family, which had come from South Carolina as a plantation family friendly to the Falkners and the Butlers. The Bowens married into the Howry and Neilson families, and so became entrenched in Oxford society. Oxford prospered during the 1840's and 1850's as part of the Cotton Kingdom prior to the Civil War, but all Southern families suffered greatly during the War. The town of Oxford was burned in 1862 by General A.J. "Whiskey" Smith, partly in retaliation for the earlier Confederate burning of Chambersburg, Pennsylvania. Maud Butler as a child played with the daughters of Lucius Quintus Cincinnatus Lamar, Oxford's most famous citizen before William Faulkner, who rose to become Secretary of the Interior after the Civil War in President Andrew Johnson's administration. Maud's father, however, scandalized the family and the town in 1887 when he ran away with town funds, accompanied by an octaroon mistress who had been one of Jacob Thompson's slaves.

Faulkner birthplace in New Albany MS

Murry Falkner was the grandson of William Clark Falkner, the Old Colonel, and eldest son of John Wesley Thompson Falkner, the Young Colonel. He was serving as agent of the "doodlebug railroad" in New Albany at the time his eldest son, William Cuthbert Falkner, was born in 1897. The railroad was sold by the grandfather, J.W.T. Falkner, in 1902, and Murry then moved his family to Oxford, which had been his home at the time he and Maud Butler married. The Falkners and Butlers were both prominent in the town, despite the scandals attaching to them, and William Faulkner remembered that when they lived briefly in Ripley, there was ill feeling against the Old Colonel a decade after his death. His grandfather, J.W.T. Falkner, like his fictional Old Bayard Sartoris, was an eccentric individual like his grandson, and he drank so heavily that he sometimes had to be taken to a sanitorium to recover.

New Albany MS Train Station

Murry and Maud Butler, whose father was Sheriff of Lafayette County, married secretly on Nov. 1, 1896, and their first son, William Cuthbert Faulkner, was born in New Albany, Mississippi, on Sept. 25, 1897, where his father was general passenger agent of the railroad his grandfather, the first William Falkner, had built after the Civil War. The father, Murry C. Falkner, moved the family to the nearby college town of Oxford when William was 5 years old, and it was there that he grew up and attended school. Faulkner's grandfather, John Wesley Thompson Falkner, the "Young Colonel," had moved to Oxford much earlier. He was well established as a lawyer in Oxford by the time the younger generation of Falkners arrived. Murry Falkner's first occupation was as the owner and operator of a livery stable, which rented horses and buggies to townspeople and students, at a time when horses were the main means of transportation. He later became Secretary and Business Manager of the University of Mississippi and moved his family to the old Delta Psi fraternity house on campus. So Faulkner did live on a college campus for a time, though he was never a serious student and did not do well in school, early or late. He found the college atmosphere congenial, however, and would one day buy a house adjacent to the campus as his permanent residence.

Murry Faulkner's livery stable was located near the town square, and Faulkner's grandfather, the "Young Colonel," would often borrow a horse to go riding about town, usually in the direction of the Negro cabins, where he was rumored to have a sweetheart. The livery stable had a black hearse for funerals, to which a black horse would be hitched. The custom was that when one of the citizens died, a Negro man would be sent from house to house bearing a silver tray, on which there would be fern leaves, and a card announcing the death and the place and time of the funeral. This custom persisted even when the motor car replaced horse-drawn carriages, because it was believed to be a more dignified way of paying respect to the dead. Old customs lasted long in Oxford, a conservative town which housed a liberal university.

The town news and gossip in Faulkner's boyhood was carried daily through Oxford by a man who drove a fresh vegetable cart, bringing the news along with his vegetables. Laundry was done by hand by Negro washerwomen who carried bundles of laundry on their heads, exactly as described by Faulkner in his moving story, "That Evening Sun." Almost every family in town could afford to have a Negro servant who lived in a cabin behind the house and who did all the menial tasks such as cooking and washing for the family.

Faulkner's future father-in-law, Lemuel Oldham, was called "Major" Oldham and was known as the only Republican in Oxford. Faulkner's father, Murry, was a heavy drinker like the Young Colonel, and like Faulkner himself, and so the destructive behavior of the Falkner males was not limited to a single generation but passed down through four generations in the family. Faulkner's grandmother, Sallie Murry Falkner, who died in 1906, was called "Damuddy" (as in *The Sound and the Fury*) by the four Faulkner brothers, William, John, Jack, and Dean. There was a prominent Hightower in town, a successful businessman quite unlike the failed minister whom Faulkner named Rev. Hightower in *Light in August*.

Caroline Barr, the Falkner family Mammy, had been born into slavery in 1855, but she moved into the Falkner house in 1902 and became the beloved "Mammy Callie" who helped raise the Falkner boys. In 1900, 45% of Lafayette County had been black, and though the Negroes were emancipated by President Lincoln at the end of the Civil War, some young black males committed violent crimes like rape and murder and were feared by the white population. The result was a catastrophic number of lynchings throughout the South after the War. Some took place in Oxford, the most celebrated of which was that of Nelse Patton, who in 1908 murdered a white woman by cutting her throat. He was summarily lynched and castrated by a mob. Faulkner used the Nelse Patton lynching as the basis for the horrific lynching and castrating of Joe Christmas in *Light in August*. Southern white families were capable of lynching Negroes for committing violent crimes, while at the same time taking Negroes of both sexes into their homes as servants, treating them as members of the family, much as they had once treated them when they had been slaves. The intimacy of white and black families in the South was a fact of life, with or without slavery, and Faulkner's fiction shows that if there was racial hostility there was also racial harmony, a reality in his fiction as it was in his personal life.

William Faulkner was in some ways more like a Butler than a Falkner, since he was small in stature, only 5'5" tall, like his mother, and unlike his father, grandfather, and great-grandfather, all of whom were tall men, each of them around 6'. As a boy of 12, Bill fell in love with Estelle Oldham, whom he would later marry. The Oldhams were much more socially engaged than the Falkners, known as Presbyterians though they seldom went to church. Faulkner fell in love with Estelle Oldham when they were schoolmates, but he could not propose marriage to her because her family did not approve of him. She first married Cornell Franklin in 1921 because he came from a wealthy family and had the approval of her parents.

Faulkner and flying

Faulkner went his own way, enlisting in the Royal Flying Corps in Canada in 1918, (when he first added the "u" to his name, perhaps as a British flourish) and returning to Oxford in a few months, when World War One ended, wearing an officer's uniform with wings, though he had been promoted to lieutenant before learning to fly solo in a plane. He affected a British officer's accent and manner for some time after his discharge, fictionalizing himself as a pilot wounded in aerial combat. His cousin Sallie Murry said the time came when she realized Billy was beginning to tell so many lies she could never be sure when he was telling the truth. He was fascinated with flying, and paid for flying lessons in the 1920's, earning a pilot's license long after his service in the Royal Air Force.

The Memphis Commercial Appeal once published an article on "The Flying Faulkners" which credited the Faulkner brothers with building the first airplane in Oxford when William was only 12, Jack was 10, and Johnsy was 8. It didn't fly far, and ended up in a gulch, but when Faulkner profited enough from his books, he bought a Waco plane with a propeller that had to be spun by hand to start. He would sometimes land at the Memphis airport with cornstalks draped over the wings from having taken off in a cornfield. He wrote a novel about flying circuses called *Pylon* as well as many stories and parts of novels about flying. His youngest brother, Dean, learned to fly the Waco in 1934, but a year later he crashed in it and was killed. The crash was caused by a student pilot he was instructing, who froze on the controls.

The airport was later named the Dean Swift Falkner Airport in his honor. Faulkner was stricken with grief and stopped flying, but Johnsy became a pilot and joined several of the flying circuses that were popular in the 1930s. Johnsy's experiences were the basis of *Pylon*, since he got to know some of the daredevil pilots who risked their lives racing above automobiles down on the ground, or dropping flour sack "bombs." Johnsy became a charter pilot at the Memphis airport for a time, transporting photographers and emergency personnel. He even ran a small feeder airline from Clarksdale, Mississippi, to Helena, Arkansas. Johnsy claimed he had a sure cure for hiccups. It was flying his plane upside down.

Faulkner's stories of aerial combat in the First World War were imagined rather than observed, but they were among his first publications. It was "Turnabout" that attracted the attention of Howard Hawks and led to his first screenwriting in Hollywood. Flying figured in "All the Dead Pilots," and in two of his novels, *Soldier's Pay* (1926) and *Sartoris* (1929). He wrote an entire novel about flying circuses, *Pylon (*1935) In "William Faulkner: Author-Aviator" which appeared in T*he Cross and Cockade Journal* published by the Society of World War I Aero Historians (Vol. 9, No. 2, Summer, 1968, 159–62), Phil Stone's son, William E. ("Jack") Stone, told in detail the story of Faulkner's experiences with flying. He had tried to enlist in the US Army Signal Corps in April of 1917 when he was 20, just as the US entered the war on the side of the Allies, but was turned down because he was too short. After that effort failed, he went to New Haven and stayed with Phil Stone, who was in Yale Law School, sharing living quarters, working for a bookstore in New Haven, and even taking a job in an ammunition factory to make ends meet. When Phil Stone went back home to Oxford in June, Faulkner went to Toronto to enlist in the Royal Flying Corps. He had heard stories of aerial combat from returning veterans and wanted to be part of the action. He succeeded in enlisting in the Royal Air Force-Canada, as it was then called, on July 10, 1918. He was sent to the School of Aeronautics and took the regular program of flight training, where he learned wireless communication, artillery observation, and aerial navigation. He was then sent to the School of Military Aeronautics for advanced training, which may have included flight training in Curtiss "Jennys," though there is no proof that he ever flew a plane by himself. From there he was sent to the School of Artillery Cooperation and Aerial Fighting. But by then the First World War had ended and he was discharged on Jan. 4, 1919, with an honorary commission as Second Lieutenant in the RAF-Canada. When he returned to Oxford, he wrote a story about military flying called "Landing in Luck" which was published in the student newspaper, *The Mississippian*. He did no more flying until the 1930s, when he purchased a Waco plane and went on barnstorming tours with his brothers, all of whom learned to fly his plane.

When his brother Dean crashed and was killed in the plane Bill owned, Faulkner felt responsible for having taught him to fly and stopped flying, but continued however to keep his Canadian commission framed above his mantel in the study where he wrote, and shortly before his death in 1962 he bought a blue blazer and sewed an RAF emblem on the pocket. Scant though it was, he was proud of his military flight training all the rest of his life.

Faulkner and education

From 1903–1914, ages 6 to 17, Faulkner attended public school in Oxford, regularly at first, showing enough promise to be allowed to skip an early grade. But he became less and less interested in school as he got older, and was by his own admission "the world's oldest living sixth grader," never graduating but educating himself in his own way, mostly by prodigious reading. As a young schoolboy, he was quiet and reserved, usually better dressed and more mannerly than the other boys, but not distinguishing himself in any subject. He showed no conspicuous talent for the literary profession until he was an adult. None of his schoolmates thought him unusually bright, nor did they think him very different from themselves. His youthful playmates were his younger brothers and the Linder brothers, Dewey and Felix, who remained friends the rest of their lives. They played marbles and baseball like the other boys, rode horses borrowed from Murry Falkner's livery stable, and took long walks through the woods, often sleeping at each other's houses. They liked to plant seeds and watch them grow, but never harvested them for the dinner table. Esther Sneed, sister of Felix and Dewey Linder, told me that "No one thought we had a genius among us. William was just one of the boys."

Calvin S. Brown, who knew Faulkner in Oxford and later became a Professor of Comparative Literature at the University of Georgia, remembered games he used to play with Faulkner as the ringleader. Faulkner was a few years older than the other boys, and he liked to organize a game of hares and hounds, which involved laying a trail of paper slips through the woods, then calling on the boys to follow the trail, some playing hares and some playing hounds. The object of the game was for the hounds to catch the hares by following the paper trail, observing rules which Faulkner concocted to govern the chase. Calvin Brown thought the chase scenes that appear in some of Faulkner's stories and novels were based on the hares and hounds game he had engineered as a boy. Faulkner, he thought, turned the games he played as a boy into serious fictional episodes. Faulkner later organized his famous Hunt Breakfast at Rowan Oak with the hares and hounds game in mind, requiring his guests to follow a paper trail he had laid through Bailey Woods in the "hunt" he staged before they had breakfast.

Though Faulkner did not distinguish himself in school, he was rewarded for good behavior at least once, when he made the Honor Roll, along with his childhood sweetheart, Estelle Oldham, who would one day become his wife. This Honor Roll was announced in *The Oxford Eagle* on May 7, 1908, when Faulkner was ten years old: "Wayne Holcomb, Willie Lewis, William Falkner, Estelle Oldham, Esther Linder, Ethel McCharen, and Marjorie Owens are all members of the honor roll of the Oxford graded school, for their class standing and deportment did not fall below 90, they were not absent as much as three days and were not tardy." This evidence of good behavior early in his life was not to be repeated in his later years. But as a schoolboy in Oxford, three generations after his great-grandfather, the Old Colonel, had lived and died in Ripley, Faulkner would reply, when a teacher asked him what he wanted to be when he grew up, "I want to be a writer like my great-grandpappy." Faulkner eventually made good on that promise, far surpassing his great-grandfather's literary achievement, but it was the first William Falkner who had at least inspired his namesake to embark on a literary career.

Faulkner and Phil Stone were friends when Faulkner visited him at Yale in 1918, before he enrolled in the Canadian air corps. In later years he went on drinking expeditions with Phil Stone to Memphis, where he heard about a gangster named "Popeye" Pumphrey, prototype of Faulkner's villainous Popeye, who ruthlessly makes a prostitute of Temple Drake in *Sanctuary*. That was after he had returned to Oxford in 1921 to accept appointment as University postmaster, which had been sponsored by Phil Stone and his future father-in-law, Major Oldham. It was his first respectable position, at a time when to many in town, he was Count No 'Count, the black sheep of the Falkner family. Phil Stone was a loyal friend who always believed Faulkner had it in him to redeem himself someday by his writing.

In the early 1920's, Faulkner drove his Uncle John (younger brother of his father Murry) around the county to run for judge. He asked his friend Mac Reed, the druggist, to accompany him and make speeches promoting Uncle John's candidacy. Uncle John confided to Mac Reed that in his opinion, his nephew William was a lost cause who would "never amount to a hill of beans." Phil Stone staunchly defended Faulkner, telling friends that someday people would come to Oxford just to see where the writer William Faulkner lived. Phil Stone was one of the friends who helped Faulkner publish his first book, *The Marble Faun*, in 1924, the only book he would publish until he went to New Orleans and met Sherwood Anderson. Anderson took over the role of patron when he and Faulkner became friends, and Faulkner began to write regularly for Anderson's little magazine, *The Double-Dealer*. He would in time write his first novel, *Soldiers' Pay*, with Anderson's encouragement. Anderson recommended the book to his publisher, Horace Liveright in New York, with the assurance that "I think he is going to be a real writer." Phil Stone and Sherwood Anderson were his first champions, when Faulkner launched his writing career. Few people in Oxford shared their opinion, other than his family, and Stark Young, an Ole Miss professor who later became a noted novelist and critic in New York, and who believed Faulkner had enough literary talent to become a professional writer.

Faulkner was conscious that he had grown up with little formal schooling, and had learned to write on his own. To an inquisitive Japanese audience in 1955, while on a good will mission for the State Department, he tried to explain why his fiction was so complicated and hard to understand by confessing that "I have had no education. I never did like school and I have had to teach myself my trade." Of course, as he matured, Faulkner made up for his lack of formal schooling by becoming an autodidact, who read most of the classics of American, English and French literature on his own, going so far as to claim that he had read all of Balzac's *Comédie Humaine* in a week.

When Ole Miss was founded in the nineteenth century, the standard Classical Curriculum, centered on the study of Greek and Latin, still ruled higher education, based on the original model of the university that arose in the late Middle Ages in Europe. But increasingly, it was criticized as an ornamental education of no practical use, and in most American universities, the study of Greek and Latin was soon replaced by the study of English Literature and Modern Languages, together with Mathematics and Natural Sciences. As late as June 28, 1884, however, *The Oxford Falcon* (rival to *The Oxford Eagle*) published an editorial defending the Classics as the best course of study for a truly higher education, arguing that "the classical scholar" had advantages over the scholar of "merely modern languages" or of "scientific specialties" because "He has the breadth of the social and intellectual order behind him. He is on a level with what is hereditarily the best the world has known." Southern society was conservative and classically oriented from its beginning, and a fondness for the Classics persevered despite the popular outcry against it. Reluctant to change any established tradition, Southern schools and colleges clung to the earlier educational ideal longer than other regions of the country. Faulkner was never a diligent student at school or university, but he was a voracious reader, and instinctively educated himself by reading literary classics as the proper preparation for becoming the kind of writer he wanted to be. He read the epics of Homer and Virgil in modern translations, the Bible in its King James translation, as well as contemporary poets and novelists such as James Joyce, and in his writings he often quoted a variety of literary classics from Shakespeare to Keats. Thus, though he often admitted his lack of formal education, he educated himself by reading the standard classics, as he might have done if he had enrolled in the classes required for a college degree.

Faulkner's overall view of education tended to be fatalistic. He thought learning essential, but disliked the kind of formal education required in schools and colleges, preferring to educate himself by his own choice and according to his own tastes. He spoke frankly of his educational views in his earliest interview, written by Marshall Smith and published in *The Bookman* in December 1931. "Now about education," he said. "Man cannot be educated into happiness. The best education can do for him is to enable him to learn something about the history of mankind—that is, the printed word—and the printed word that lasts over centuries has for its skeleton tragedy and despair." Faulkner made up his mind early in life that reading was the best means of acquiring an education, and he concluded from his reading that literary classics are essential, but that they teach a bitter lesson about mankind. He said to his first interviewer, "So when a man learns to read, he learns of the tragedy and despair of his own kind which he himself may suffer."

Faulkner served for a time just before and after the First World War as Boy Scoutmaster in Oxford. He had been asked to do so by the minister of the Presbyterian Church, Dr. J.A. Christian, and he took the job seriously. He appointed a friend, J. D. Roach, as his assistant scoutmaster, and the two of them took troops of boys out hiking and camping, often to Wall Doxey State Park north of Oxford. Bill was already intent on a career as a writer, and would stay up late at night in his tent, writing in longhand while the Boy Scouts were asleep. The boys liked for Faulkner to tell them war stories around the campfire before they went to bed, but they disliked taking a bath every night as he required them to do. Their meetings were held in a room above Shine Morgan's appliance store on the town square. J.D. Roach, his assistant scoutmaster, said that Faulkner conducted the Boy Scout meetings with dignity, and was never seen drinking on any occasion. J.D. Roach became an electrician and worked for Faulkner at Rowan Oak, rewiring the house and installing an electric stove, although Faulkner insisted on keeping the old cast iron wood stove in the kitchen for sentimental reasons. Roach said that though Faulkner had a reputation as a heavy drinker, he never saw Faulkner drinking. He often went walking with Faulkner, and it was his impression that Faulkner knew every Negro in Lafayette County, stopping to talk with them at length when they met. One member of his old scout troop, Wayne Sands of Newton, Mississippi, remembered Faulkner as a dedicated scoutmaster, who said a formal goodbye to the troop in 1924 when he left Oxford for New Orleans and later sailed to Europe. The young scouts admired his outdoorsmanship, especially during a camping trip that he once led to Thacker's Mountain, five miles south of Oxford. J.D. Roach thought Faulkner abrupt and outspoken but never deliberately rude to anyone. He remembered the time when a candidate for sheriff named Melvin Hollowell, well known to Faulkner, came to him on campaign and solicited his vote. "Hell, Melvin," Faulkner told him, "you've got no more business being sheriff than I have." Faulkner's judgment was vindicated because Melvin lost the election. J. D. Roach said he liked working for Bill Faulkner and was always paid for his labor, though it might be months before the bill was settled. He said Faulkner did all his improvements on the grand scale, and he could remember that when he installed a heating plant for him at Rowan Oak, it was twice the size that was needed.

In 1919–20, Faulkner was allowed to enroll as a special student at Ole Miss, because though he had no high school diploma he had the recommendation of Stark Young, who was already a respected writer and teacher. He did not fare much better in his college studies than he had in public school, making a failing grade of D in his only English class, which he dropped the next term, but earning a top grade of A for two terms of French and a B for two terms of Spanish. During his brief, abortive career as a college student, he joined the Sigma Alpha Epsilon fraternity, a family legacy since his grandfather, father, and uncle had been members of the fraternity. He was beginning to write poems, short essays, and plays which were published in the college magazine. The editor of the magazine was George Healey, who later became the Editor of The *New Orleans Times Picayune*. Healey remembered that as a college editor he welcomed Faulkner's satirical cartoons. in the popular cosmopolitan style of John Held, Jr., and accepted some of his writing for publication, but seriously advised Faulkner at the start of his career to make cartoons his specialty and to give up trying to make a name for himself as a writer. Stark Young, who had backed Faulkner as a special student, moved from Oxford to New York, where he would soon gain fame as a novelist and theater critic. Faulkner followed him to New York and stayed with him while working as a clerk in Lord & Taylor's bookstore. That was a stroke of good luck, because there he met Elizabeth Prall, who would marry the up-and-coming writer Sherwood Anderson and move with him to New Orleans, providing the vital link between Faulkner and Anderson that proved indispensable in launching his literary career.

Faulkner and Ole Miss

Murry C. Falkner had become Secretary and Business Manager of the university in 1920, and moved his family to the former Delta Psi fraternity house, which was vacant because fraternities had been outlawed. Faulkner participated fairly actively in college life, enrolling as a special non-degree student from the fall of 1919 to the fall of 1920. Even while serving from 1921–24 as university postmaster, Faulkner frequently contributed stories and cartoons to the college magazine. He was rumored to belong to the "MOAKS," a club whose name had been abbreviated from the initials of the "Mystical Order of Ass-Kissing Sons of Bitches," though their activities were a mystery. He was definitely pledged to the Sigma Alpha Epsilon fraternity on Dec. 10, 1919, and was photographed as a member of its Mississippi Gamma chapter in 1920. Some of his fraternity brothers thought Faulkner rather peculiar, but since his father and uncle had been members of the fraternity, they were glad to offer him an invitation to join, which he accepted willingly. He had to be pledged *sub rosa*, in his Uncle John's house rather than in the fraternity house. The Governor of Mississippi in 1920 was Lee M. Russell, who as an Ole Miss student had not been invited to join any fraternity. After graduating, he had been elected to the state legislature, and in revenge, he had authored an anti-fraternity law that was enacted in 1912. It was still in force when he became Governor in 1920, and after his election, some students burned him in effigy on campus, following which outrage he made it mandatory that all Ole Miss students must sign an oath, swearing that they did not belong to a fraternity. The Board of Trustees of the university, who were appointed by the Governor, bore down hard on fraternities in 1920, prompting many of Faulkner's fraternity brothers to withdraw from the university in protest. Since he was not a regular student, he was not directly involved, but the entire Falkner family was indignant over the treatment of fraternities, because not only his uncle, but his father and grandfather, had been SAEs when fraternities were legal in the university. Bill Faulkner and his brothers Jack and John were legacies who considered fraternity membership an honor, even if clandestine. Bill Faulkner was never an active fraternity member, but he had the honor of being initiated by the National Secretary of SAE, William Levere. The list of Active Members of Mississippi Gamma of SAE for March 15, 1920, preserved at the fraternity's national headquarters in Evanston, Illinois, includes William Falkner (without the "u") as "S.S." meaning "Special Student." His brother Murry C.("Jack") Falkner is also listed. Jack Falkner later wrote his own book about *The Falkners of Mississippi*, in which he said that the SAE fraternity was the only club of any kind to which a Falkner ever wanted to belong. Every fraternity at Ole Miss was *sub rosa* from 1912 until the anti-fraternity law was repealed in April of 1926, but in 1920, when Lee Russell was Governor and Faulkner was enrolled as a special student, fraternities were still *sub rosa* and the social pressure against them was heavy.

As a special student, not working toward a degree, Faulkner was frequently seen on campus in 1919–20 and took an active part in the college life. Later on, when he came back from his European trip in 1925, he gave talks about his travels to students at the chapel vesper services on the Ole Miss campus. He took pleasure in telling them about how he rode a bicycle through Europe, shared the thrill of a tour of the countries he had seen—Italy, France, and England—and offered to answer their questions afterward. The students saw him as a man of the world, and listened eagerly to his accounts. None of them had ventured abroad, and they were impressed by his eyewitness accounts of his extensive travels in Europe. They did not think of him as a writer in 1920. By the 1930s, however, he had published books that were favorably reviewed, surprising students and faculty that someone with so little formal education was capable of becoming a reputable author. Few in Oxford read his books, however, because they were considered "dirty," unfit for respectable readers, and so most of the town and university were unimpressed by his growing reputation. His mother, "Miss Maud," later expressed the opinion that "Billy" Faulkner would never have been known to the world if his reputation had depended on the people of his home town. He would have to earn his fame in the larger world before the university and the town started to take pride in him as a favorite son.

The poems and plays he published in the college annuals at Ole Miss were a first entry into the literary world. His sketches appeared in public before his writings. In the 1918 *Ole Miss* annual, William Falkner (without the "u") signed a checkerboard sketch as an introduction to the "Social Activities" section, while his father, M.C. Faulkner (with the "u") was listed as Assistant Secretary of the University. In the 1920 *Ole Miss* yearbook, William Faulkner (with the "u") signed several pen-and-ink sketches in a style that resembled those of the English *fin de siècle* artist Aubrey Beardsley in *The Yellow Book*, as well as those of John Held, Jr., a popular illustrator in fashionable American magazines. Faulkner's cartoons were line drawings, then in vogue, highly stylized, pencil-slim figures of both sexes, with only the barest distinctions between them. In the same 1920 *Ole Miss* yearbook, William Falkner (without the "u") published a poem called "To a Co-Ed," while his brother, Murry C. "Jack" Falkner, Jr. (without the "u") was listed as a freshman student, and William Faulkner (with the "u") was listed as a Special Student. In that same year Faulkner produced his hand-lettered, hand-illustrated play, *Marionettes*.

In the 1921 yearbook he was listed again as William Falkner (without the "u"), "Property Man" of a dramatic club called the "Marionettes." His friend and fraternity brother, Ben Wasson, later to be his editor and literary agent, was president of the club. Faulkner appeared as both an artist and a writer, with some pen-and-ink sketches of college life and a poem called "Nocturne," hand-printed and illustrated, which was an English translation of an original French poem.

Self-Portrait by William Faulkner: "If I had not existed, someone else would have written me. . . ."

Self-portrait sketch in college

Faulkner had a peculiar genius for words. He could not however find a way to make good poems out of them, instead writing mostly weak imitations of good poems, but as soon as he began writing prose, he was quickly in command of the distinct style which became his trademark. Even before he wrote his first novel, he had written a short descriptive piece for the Ole Miss student newspaper, *The Mississippian*, that was a clear indication of his exceptional gifts as a writer. It was called "The Hill," and it appeared in 1922, when he was 24, no longer a student (he had been briefly enrolled in 1919–20) but was serving as an unlikely Postmaster of the university. "The Hill" began with a paragraph that was a foretaste of Faulkner's unmistakable style, which in his maturity would be both realistic and poetic, with a sureness of diction that was concrete in detail yet sonorous in sound and compelling in rhythm, carrying the reader along hypnotically, the words continuing without pause:

> Before him and slightly above his head, the hill crest was clearly laid on the sky. Over it slid a sibilant invisibility of wind like a sheet of water, and it seemed to him that he might lift his feet from the road and swim upward and over the hill on this wind which filled his clothing, tightening his shirt across his chest, flapping his loose jacket and trousers about him, and which stirred the thick uncombed hair above his stubby quiet face. His long shadow legs rose perpendicularly and fell, ludicrously, as though without power of progression, as though his body had been mesmerized by a whimsical God to a futile puppet-like activity upon one spot, while time and life terrifically passed him and left him behind. At last his shadow reached the crest and fell headlong over it.

The narrative is simply that of a man walking up and over a hill, but the description is so well worded that it seems to take on its own life and move with its own force, as inevitable as a force of nature. It would take years for Faulkner to learn how to put this gift to effective use in a full-scale piece of fiction, but he was already showing that such mastery was only a matter of time.

His father had moved upward in 1920 from keeping a livery stable to a position as Secretary and Business Manager of the University, where he kept a close eye on the accounts. Murry Falkner was a good manager, and soon developed a reputation as a trustworthy billpayer, one who took notice of all expenditures and would object to any negligent treatment of public funds. Mac Reed remembered that Murry Falkner once discovered the university had paid twice for the same purchasing order at Gathright-Reed drugstore and had firmly demanded repayment, though he was customarily a mild-mannered man. Murry was able to support his family comfortably while living on campus and kept his position for ten years, until 1930, when he was the victim of a political sweep by Gov. Bilbo. He was anxious, however, for his eldest son to have a steady job, so that he would no longer be dependent on the family breadwinner, and was instrumental in getting Faulkner appointed Postmaster of the University Post Office in early 1921. To qualify for the job, Faulkner needed a character reference, and he called on Dr. D.H. Bishop, the English professor who had given him a "D" in Shakespeare, to validate his application. The professor's willingness to back him for the job was probably an indication that his failing grade was not due to any lack of proficiency in English, but of his failure to attend class regularly or to take the final examination.

Ole Miss Post Office Faulkner managed 1921–24

Faulkner was appointed University Postmaster in 1921, thanks mainly to Phil Stone, the first to recognize Faulkner's budding talent as a writer, who wanted him to take the job of Ole Miss postmaster so that he would stay in Oxford rather than seek his fortune elsewhere. Faulkner was unprepared for the job, and initially reluctant to accept it, since it did not lead in a direction he wanted to go, but he saw that it would give him the leisure to continue writing while earning a regular salary. He managed to hold the unlikely position of University Postmaster for three years. The Ole Miss post office was housed in a little red brick building on campus, and Faulkner officiated there from 1921–24. He quickly became bored with receiving and filing mail, and spent most of his time behind the postboxes, typing poems with two fingers while letting the mail accumulate. His service was minimal, to the point of negligence, and even his friend Phil Stone admitted he was "the damnedest postmaster ever." Thus it was no surprise when eventually he was fired by the Postal Inspector, who had received numerous complaints from citizens that he was not posting the mail or delivering packages on time. One of the most irate complainants was Judge Heminway, who traveled to Europe and asked Bill Faulkner to forward his mail to an address abroad. Receiving nothing, he wrote an indignant letter to Faulkner asking what had happened to his mail. Faulkner wrote back "Please inform your correspondents of your correct address." Judge Heminway was so enraged by this reply that he would have had Faulkner fired on the spot if he hadn't been a loyal friend of the Falkner family.

There is no doubt that Faulkner took his duties as postmaster lightly, and those who observed him at work could see that he spent more time reading and writing or drinking and playing cards than sorting the mail. Sometimes a boxholder would ask to see his mail and Faulkner would calmly tell him, "Come on back here and look for it yourself." One who regularly saw him behind the scenes was Branham Hume, son of the Chancellor of the University and later Mayor of Oxford. He confirmed the fact that Faulkner spent most of his time doing what he liked best, which was writing. Faulkner kept his manuscripts in an L & A Underwear Box which he secreted behind the post office boxes, and added verses to it until his first book, a long poem titled *A Marble Faun*, was ready for publication. Faulkner appointed several assistant postmasters who enjoyed loafing with him, among them his brother "Johnsy," Branham Hume, and "Sonny" Bell, his drinking buddy. These three conspirators had a secret entry to the inner sanctum through the large package bins beneath the post boxes. Sonny Bell liked to play baseball outside the post office and then go inside to join Faulkner, where he would drink heavily, and then stretch out on the floor to sleep. The other two "assistant postmasters" would then have to remove him bodily and carry him home to finish sleeping it off.

While he was postmaster, Faulkner was contributing prose sketches and ink drawings to the college magazine. One of them was titled "Post Office Blues," dated 1923, which showed a caricature of himself that was quite recognizable, with small hawklike nose and slim moustache, dancing with a coed named Lottie Vernon. She became the wife of Guy Turnbow and the mother of Guy Turnbow, Jr., who later had Faulkner's pen and ink self-portrait framed, and placed it on his wall. It was a good example of Faulkner's skill in the visual arts, which he used to advantage in his early literary endeavors. Besides writing and illustrating a play called "Marionettes," he provided delicate pen and ink illustrations for his first book, *The Marble Faun*, published at his expense with the financial support of friends, by Four Seas Company in Boston in 1924.

It was in 1924, his final year as Postmaster, that he met the Fugitive poet Ridley Wills, who had come to Oxford from Nashville and wanted to meet him. They talked about writing as a profession, but Faulkner confessed to his fellow writer that he would rather be "a lay reader in the Episcopal Church" than pursue a more serious career as a professional writer.

Considering his behavior, it is remarkable that Faulkner's job as university postmaster lasted as long as three years, but at the end of that period he was summarily fired by the US postal inspector in Corinth for neglect of duties. The letter charging him with negligence and threatening him with prompt dismissal was sent to Faulkner in the fall of 1924, leaving him with no legitimate excuse for keeping a job he never sought. The document makes it clear that Faulkner fully deserved to be fired for a number of good causes:

Post Office Department

Office of Inspector

Corinth, Mississippi

Mark Webster, Inspector

Case No. 133733-C   September 2, 1924

SUBJECT: WILLIAM FAULKNER, UNIVERSITY OF MISSISSIPPI POST OFFICE

DEAR SIR:

The following charges have been made against you as postmaster of University, Mississippi:

1. That you are neglectful of your duties, in that you are a habitual reader of books and magazines, and seem reluctant to cease reading long enough to wait on the patrons; that you have a book being printed at the present time, the greater part of which was written while on duty at the postoffice; that some patrons will not trust you to forward their mail because of your past carelessness and these patrons have their neighbors forward same for them while away on their vacations; that you have failed to forward and properly handle mail for various patrons of the office, some of whom follows: M.G. Paseur, Rev. W.I. Hargis, Miss M.W. Means, W.A. Scarbrough, Jimmy Jones, Judge Heminway and many others; that you have closed up the box of John Savage and others after they had paid their box rent and you receipted them; that you returned C.O.D. parcel No. W 22705, from John Ward, Mens Shoes, New York City, addressed to H.E. Ray, Jr., after he had given you an order in person and left ten cents in money to forward to him at 924 Filmore St., Corinth, Miss., and you had notified him for postage and he sent you postage from Corinth as per your order, yet the parcel was returned to senders marked "unclaimed."
2. That in addition to the above careless handling of mail you failed to deliver a letter to Jimmy Jones until after he had gone to your father (who is Secretary of University of Mississippi) and got a note regarding the delivery of same (Jones being a well-known patron of your office); that on another occasion a contractor working at the University was compelled to get your father to help him get a

package out of the office, which you had held for two or three days; that you placed two or three letters in the box of Mr. R.L. Sullivan (the box next to Chancellor Hume's box) which had been written to Mrs. Hume by Dr. Hume while away from home, and since Mr. Sullivan was away on his vacation these letters remained in the box of Sullivan until placed in the box of Chancellor Hume by Assistant Postmaster Bell some three or four days after Dr. Hume had returned home and had made considerable inquiry about same.
3. That you are indifferent to interest of patrons, unsocial, and rarely ever speak to patrons of the office unless absolutely necessary; that you do not give the office the proper attention, opening and closing same at your convenience; that you can be found playing golf during office hours.
4. That you mistreat mail of all classes, including registered mail; that you have thrown mail with return postage guaranteed and all other classes in the garbage can by the side entrance, near the rear door, which was addressed to the following patrons: F.E. Farquer, Howard B. Wallace, Wm. Ross Kennedy, University Store, Dean J.H. Dorrah, University of Miss. Hospital, Gordon Hall Boarding House, Alex L. Bondurant, Mississippian, William R. Raley, Ricks Hall, Mrs. J. W. Harris, W.G. Kirkpatrick, Ike Edwards, Mrs. R.J. Shlrhan, Forrest Woods, J.W. Bergman, C.O. Harris, Traber Dobbins, T.H. Sandrelette, Mrs. P.E. Irley, Chas. C. Evans, Taswel P. Haney, Robt. Cannon, Walter Dement, R.E. Wilson and others; that this has gotten to be such a common occurrence that some patrons have gone to this garbage can to get their magazines, should they not be in their boxes when they looked for them.
5. That you do not prepare return receipts when requested by senders of registered mail; that you have two letters of foreign origin on hand that have been held since December 1921, and February 1922, that you have lost registered letter No. 104, from Arena, Miss., addressed to Mr. E.S. Roberts, and that you have carelessly handled several other registered letters.
6. That you do not give postage due mail proper attention, one instance being when a letter addressed to Rev. W. L. Hargis by Bank of Oxford, was held several days without notice being placed in addressees box, later being called for and delivered to senders.
7. That you have permitted the following unauthorized persons to have access to the workroom of the office: Dick Bell, D.B. Holmes, Jimmy Jones, M.A. Pigford and others, and have permitted card playing in the office.

You will please advise me in writing, within five days from this date, stating whether the charges are true, in part or wholly so, and show cause, if any, why you should not be removed. Failure to receive a reply in this prescribed time will be deemed as evidence that you have no defense to offer, and action will be taken accordingly.

Respectfully yours,
MARK WEBSTER
Postoffice Inspector
Corinth, Mississippi

The many complaints were certainly justified, and Faulkner's job with the government was abruptly terminated. Faulkner told a friend that the Postal Inspector forced him to resign because he wasn't handling the outgoing mail properly. "I'm damn glad he didn't ask about the incoming mail," he said. He sent a letter of resignation to the Postal Inspector in which he said "As long as I live under the capitalistic system, I expect to have my life influenced by moneyed people. But I will be damned if I propose to be at the beck and call of every itinerant scoundrel who has two cents to invest in a postage stamp. This, sir, is my resignation." He kept a slip labeled "W.C. Falkner, Outgoing Postmaster," which showed that he had received a total of $1300 for his work, paid in stamps and cash. It gave him great satisfaction, shortly after he was relieved of his duties, to send a copy of his first book, *The Marble Faun*, written while he was supposed to be sorting the mail, to the postal inspector who fired him. Faulkner did not take another job with the government until the 1950s, after he had won the Nobel Prize, when President Eisenhower asked him to be a roving goodwill ambassador for the U.S. State Department. This time he took the job seriously and traveled widely, commanding respect for the United States everywhere he went, and redeeming himself for his early negligence of public duty.

When Faulkner started writing seriously, his first publications were short poems, published in 1919 in *The New Republic* in New York, and in 1920 in *The Double-Dealer*, Sherwood Anderson's little magazine in New Orleans. He had not begun earning money as a writer, but received encouragement from his lawyer friend, Phil Stone, who when he returned to Oxford from Yale Law School opened an office just off the town square. Faulkner spent his time doing odd jobs, principally working for his grandfather's bank and painting houses. His grandfather, the "Young Colonel," J.W.T. Falkner, was president of the bank on the town square, and liked to sit outside the bank with an ear trumpet clenched in his teeth, since he was nearly stone deaf, so that he could hear what passersby might say. On the other side of the square was the Gathright-Reed drugstore, where Faulkner would go to see Mac Reed, his other loyal hometown friend, a graduate of the University of Mississippi and a partner in the drugstore, who knew and was liked by everyone in town. Though Faulkner was a native of Oxford, his main contacts with his home town were through his friendships with a lawyer and a druggist, both of whom offered encouragement and financial support for his literary efforts, which were becoming the main focus of his life and would be the eventual source of his livelihood.

Lafayette Co. Courthouse & Mr. Ike Roberts, hunting companion

Gathright-Reed Drugstore on town square of Oxford MS

Mac Reed & Bill Faulkner in Drugstore

Faulkner and New Orleans

Faulkner's fictional career—his real literary career--began two years after his first book was published, following his decision to leave Oxford and go to New Orleans in 1925. At that time, he was planning to go to Europe and perhaps make a name for himself as a writer, since he knew that many American writers were gaining recognition abroad. But in New Orleans he became a protégé of

Sherwood Anderson, who was enjoying a national reputation after the success of his 1919 novel *Winesburg, Ohio*. Faulkner admired Anderson's writing, and wrote a piece on Anderson which was published in *The Dallas Morning News* on April 26, 1925, which said that "Men grow from the soil, like corn and trees. I prefer to think of Mr. Anderson as a lusty corn field in his native Ohio." Of Anderson's most celebrated book, *Winesburg, Ohio*, Faulkner said "These people live and breathe: they are beautiful." He praised Anderson for not trying to write a continuous novel but presenting a series of short sketches set in the same locale, with "sharp episodic phases of people" described in a "halting questioning manner." He thought "I'm A Fool" a prize American short story, because it had "a personal emotion that does strike an elemental chord in mankind," and also because it was about horses, whose history "and the history of man are intermingled beyond any unraveling." Overall, he praised Anderson as "a field of corn with a story and a tongue to tell it with."

Anderson, who was born in Camden, Ohio, had owned a paint factory in Elyria, Ohio, before abandoning his business career and going to Chicago to make his name as an original storyteller and a fictional artist. He had gone south to become the literary lion of New Orleans at the time Faulkner met him, founding and editing a little magazine called *The Double-Dealer*, in which one of Faulkner's first poems was published. Through Faulkner's earlier friendship in New York with Elizabeth Prall, who was now Anderson's wife, Faulkner joined the circle of artists and writers who surrounded Anderson. It was at Anderson's house that Faulkner discovered Sir James Fraser's *A Golden Bough*, a cultural and anthropological study which greatly influenced him. Anderson suggested that he might move in with a young architect named William Spratling, who was living in a spartan upstairs apartment overlooking Pirates Alley in the French Quarter of New Orleans, and Faulkner found that he and Spratling hit it off immediately. They enjoyed drinking and talking together, and for recreation, they practiced shooting an airgun at people passing by in the alley below. They made a game of it, keeping a tab of their hits, mostly in the buttocks, and awarded extra points for certain targets, such as nuns and elderly Negroes. Their friendship produced a spoof of the cultural life of the city which amused many of their artist friends. They published it in 1926 under the satirical title of *Sherwood Anderson and Other Famous Creoles*. It was a thin volume featuring caricatures by Spratling of Anderson and other notable personalities in the New Orleans literary and artistic fraternity, with witty captions by Faulkner, and it gained instant notoriety among readers in the New Orleans artistic colony. Faulkner admired Anderson, not only for his writing, but also for his comfortable way of life. He observed that Anderson made a practice of writing during the day, then going out in the evening to join his friends in drinking parties, sometimes renting a houseboat on Lake Pontchartrain for short cruises, a practice Faulkner would fictionalize in his second novel, *Mosquitoes*. Faulkner had begun writing occasional sketches for the *New Orleans Times-Picayune*, but he had more serious ambitions, and it was under Anderson's patronage that he began writing his first novel, *Soldier's Pay*, a postwar tale of a veteran returning home to Georgia, blinded by a battle wound, which owed as much to Ernest Hemingway as to Sherwood Anderson. Hemingway like Faulkner was another of Anderson's protégés. Faulkner's first novel was indeed Hemingwayesque, a Lost Generation tale set in the aftermath of World War I, but it was original enough to attract critical attention, especially in its convincing portrayal of the wounded veteran Donald Mahon and his devoted female companion, Mrs. Powers, who were counterparts of Jake Barnes and Lady Brett in Hemingway's first novel, *The Sun Also Rises*. Faulkner's treatment of his characters was more sympathetic than Hemingway's, even if his novel lacked the authenticity of Hemingway's personal experiences on the Italian front in the First World War. When Faulkner had finished writing a draft of the novel, he asked Elizabeth Prall if she would show it to her husband. She did, and, according to Faulkner's own account, Anderson said he was too busy to read it, but if he didn't have to read it, he would send it with his recommendation to his New York publisher, Horace Liveright.

Plaque in Pirate's Alley New Orleans

Anderson kept his word, and thereby earned credit for launching Faulkner's literary career, which would in time surpass his own. Faulkner stayed long enough in New Orleans to write his first novel, but not long enough for it to be accepted and published, because the opportunity to travel to Europe came first.

Faulkner and Europe

In late 1925, he joined Spratling aboard the freighter, *West Ivis*, for a passage that had been reserved so that Spratling could write articles for *Architectural Digest*. Theirs was a leisurely ocean crossing that took 27 days to take them from New Orleans to Savannah to Mallorca to Genoa. Faulkner took a sheaf of his poems aboard with him, so that he could have the pleasure of tossing them in the ocean on the way, an act that he said "made him feel clean." He probably sensed that it was time to say goodbye to his poetic ambitions, now that he was anticipating the publication of his first novel, which marked a turning point in his career. He and Spratling landed in Genoa and made their way by train and on foot through Italy, Switzerland, France, and England, satisfying their wanderlust during six months of cheap, carefree travel. Faulkner had gone there knowing that some American writers had become successful expatriates. He admired Ezra Pound and T.S. Eliot, but was too shy to call on them in Rapallo or London where he knew they were living. When, after he won the Nobel Prize, Faulkner was asked by Pres. Eisenhower to head a Writers Group in a People-to-People initiative, Faulkner found to his surprise that his fellow writers had only one principal task in mind: to free Ezra Pound from imprisonment at St. Elizabeths. William Carlos Williams went so far as to write Faulkner a letter on behalf of his friend Pound, urging: "Quote to him [Pres. Eisenhower] the [NY] Time's excellent editorial of the literary section, quoting in turn Ernest Hemingway on Ezra Pound. And say if the President wants to advance the cause of cultural advancement in the U.S. to see to it that Ezra Pound is released. The government of Sweden gives the chairman of this committee [Faulkner] its greatest award and the government of the United States keeps its best poet in jail." Faulkner passed this advice on without any effect in freeing Pound. Though Faulkner especially admired the Irish poet and novelist James Joyce, he never met him, seeing him only once at a distance in a Paris cafe.

Faulkner's European trip had little immediate literary value, but it provided settings for scenes in Europe that he would later introduce in novels from *Sanctuary* to *A Fable*. He spent most of his time in Paris, and did some experimental writing there, including some "poetry in prose form" that he said was "so modern that I don't know myself what it means." (He probably meant the unpublished story "Elmer," in which he experimented with Joyce's stream-of-consciousness technique.) But his main interest in Europe in 1925 was viewing First World War battlefields, over which he had once dreamed of flying in combat, touring some of them while he was in France. He returned from his expedition to Europe by way of New York, in time to read a copy of his first novel, just published by Boni & Liveright. Then he went back to New Orleans, and settled down at Pascagoula, where he wrote and published a second novel, *Mosquitoes*, also from Boni & Liveright, in 1927. If his first novel was a Lost Generation narrative in the style of Hemingway, his second was social satire in the style of Scott Fitzgerald, Hemingway's chief rival as a young American novelist in the 1920s.

Faulkner and Helen Baird

Faulkner wrote *Mosquitoes* with a real-life counterpart in mind, following a brief but intense love affair with Helen Baird, a vivacious young woman from a fashionable Nashville family, who spent summers in Pascagoula with her mother. She was even shorter in height than he was, barely five feet tall (he was five feet five), and had made her debut with other young girls of good families in Nashville. One of the girls who debuted with her was Anne Bransford "Mimi" Wallace, who left a memoir of the occasion. It occurred in the winter of 1922 at the Belle Meade Country Club, where the debutantes formed a "gypsy cotillion" that emerged from a large kettle at one end of the ballroom. Mimi Wallace's recollection of the debut, as recorded by her daughter-in-law, Lallie Hudgings Wallace, was colorful: "I do remember the girl in front of me was Helen Baird and she was a cute girl but very theatrical. She came out of that kettle and did practically a dance on the stage. I thought I couldn't do anything like that, so I didn't try to copy Helen, but it was a fun party."

Helen Baird was 19 at the time Faulkner met her, the daughter of a prominent Nashville businessman, James H. Baird, who owned a sawmill and edited a magazine called *The Southern Lumberman*, which was nationally known for its entertaining and outspoken editorials. The family lived in Glenstrae, an antebellum mansion south of Nashville, which had once been used as a fortress to defend the city from early Indian uprisings, and later as a Confederate officers' lodging during the Civil War. Her father had died in a railroad accident in 1915, while still in his 40s, and the death of such a prominent citizen was widely lamented as a local tragedy. After his sudden death, Helen and her mother went on living in Glenstrae south of Nashville, while spending summers at a beach cottage they owned in Pascagoula. It was there she met William Faulkner, in the summer of 1925, while he was once more living in New Orleans in the apartment of William Spratling, and writing sketches and reviews for the newspaper. They met at a party in the apartment overlooking what was then Orleans Alley, later named Pirates Alley. From a letter he wrote to her, it is clear that Faulkner had been smitten at his first sight of Helen Baird: "I remember a sullen-jawed, yellow-eyed belligerent gal in a linen dress and sunburnt legs sitting on Spratling's balcony and not thinking even a hell of a little bit of me that afternoon."

He saw her afterward in Pascagoula, since he had the use of a vacation home next door to her aunt's, owned by Phil Stone's brother, Jack, a retreat where he liked to go to write. Faulkner was also writing sketches for the *New Orleans Time-Picayune* at the time, and knew Helen's brother, James Russell "Pete" Baird, a sports columnist who became a regular columnist with a well-known byline. Baird had invented "Picayunes," a series of one-line wisecracks which everyone in New Orleans enjoyed reading. Bill Faulkner and Helen Baird began dating in the summer of 1925, going back and forth from Pascagoula to New Orleans. It was a mutual attraction, although Helen's friends wondered why she would let herself be seen with a bohemian beachcomber who wore duck pants fastened with a rope belt, and liked to go barefoot. She called him "one of her screwballs." She was artistically inclined herself, and some friends thought an evening at her beach cottage in Pascagoula was like attending a French salon. For his part Faulkner fell madly in love with her, wrote love sonnets to her and proposed marriage to her, but though she enjoyed his company and thought him fascinating, she turned down his proposal. She doubtless sensed that Faulkner had real literary and artistic talent, but her mother did not approve of him, and that was decisive for Helen. Her mother once asked her, "How can you stand going around with someone who looks like that wild man?" So Helen declined the proposal and told Bill that she preferred to remain just friends. Her mother took her away to Europe in the late summer of 1925, partly to distance her from Faulkner. Faulkner was philosophical about the affair, and in his novel, *Mosquitoes,* gave a remark to one of his characters that no doubt reflected his feelings about Helen Baird: "You don't commit suicide when you're disappointed in love. You write a book."

Though he was still in love with her, he had to give up hope of marrying her, and so as a wedding present (in lieu of being invited to her wedding) he gave her two books, on the eve of her marriage in 1927 to Guy Campbell Lyman, of a prominent New Orleans family, a suitor whom her mother approved. Besides his hand-lettered and illustrated set of sonnets, *To Helen: A Courtship,* Faulkner also gave her a hand-lettered and illustrated short fictional fantasy piece, a mock medieval legend about a knight named Sir

Galwyn, which he called *Mayday*. More importantly, when he published his second novel, *Mosquitoes*, in 1927, he dedicated it "To Helen," though by then Helen Baird was married to another man. He had wooed and lost her, but his friendship with Helen Baird continued, and out of it he made fictional capital, first drawing on her as a model for Patricia Robyn, one of the principal characters in *Mosquitoes*, an intriguing young girl who flirts with men quite openly. *Mosquitoes* was his second novel, a social satire and a *roman* à *clef* about the New Orleans artistic set. One of the characters was named Pete, like Helen's brother, and the character who did most of the talking was a writer named Dawson Fairchild, modeled on Sherwood Anderson. Faulkner himself made a brief appearance in the novel as William Faulkner.

Faulkner never forgot Helen Baird. Twelve years later he would draw on her again when he created the character of Charlotte Rittenhouse, an even more free-spirited young woman than Patricia Robyn, in his 1939 novel, *The Wild Palms*, which he also dedicated "To Helen." Faulkner's friendship with Helen and her husband lasted long after their marriage. He wrote letters to her, autographed his books for her, and on one of several visits to New Orleans went hunting with her husband. She lived most of her later years in Pascagoula, dying there in 1972. Before her death, she met Faulkner by chance in 1955 while walking on the beach at Pascagoula, and afterwards painted a portrait of a grey-haired, grey-moustached Faulkner which, though not a flattering likeness, now hangs in the Wisdom Collection at Tulane University. In 1981 the Tulane University Press and the Yoknapatawpha Press in Oxford jointly published *Helen: A Courtship and Mississippi Poems*, containing the sonnets Faulkner wrote during his brief love affair with Helen Baird much earlier in his life. The poems are serious tributes, intentionally obscure in wording yet tantalizingly erotic, couched in extravagant metaphors and often archaic words, obviously meant to be a series of love sonnets in the Elizabethan fashion that never quite lived up to their intention. He would say dismissively of his poetry later on that he wrote it all "for the purpose of furthering various philanderings in which I was engaged." As a suitor he was unsuccessful, as a poet he failed, but by 1927 he had published his first two books of fiction and had finally found himself as the novelist he was meant to be.

Faulkner and his Wife

Faulkner's first love was not Helen Baird, but Estelle Oldham, an Oxford schoolmate who came from a respectable family in town. Her father, "Major" Oldham, was a lawyer who dabbled in politics, and who helped Faulkner get his job at the university post office, but he did not think

Faulkner would ever be a fit husband for his daughter. So though Bill Faulkner and Estelle Oldham were high school sweethearts, and both never graduated from high school, she didn't marry him until much later. Her first husband was Cornell Franklin, who was considered a much more promising bachelor than Faulkner, and whose family the Oldhams did consider fit for her. He was a promising young lawyer, whom she married before graduating from high school in 1918, and he took her to China with him where he prospered in the American community, but he proved unfaithful, after having fathered her two children, Victoria ("Cho-Cho") and Malcolm. Estelle divorced him in 1927 and returned to Oxford with her children, taking up her earlier romance with William Faulkner and agreeing to marry him at last, with or without her parents' approval. Neither family wanted them to marry and his friend Phil Stone advised him against it, but Faulkner defied them all and on June 19, 1929, he married Estelle in the Presbyterian Church at College Hill, a village near Oxford, because the Episcopal Church in Oxford, to which her family belonged, refused to let a divorced woman marry again. They asked Rev. D. W. Heddleston to marry them, since he was a part-time minister as well as a Professor of Philosophy at Ole Miss. They honeymooned at Pascagoula, taking along her son Malcolm Franklin and a black maid that had been with Estelle for a long time. She dressed in filmy gowns to walk on the beach and once became so drunk that she tried to drown herself, so the signs of instability were evident in her from the beginning of their marriage and persisted throughout their lives. Since their families were on opposite sides politically, the Oldhams being Republicans, rare in the South at that time, and the Falkners were Democrats, they agreed that they would never discuss politics.

Estelle was a worse spendthrift than Bill, running up credit accounts all over Oxford and Memphis, until Faulkner felt obliged, in June 1936, to publish an ad in the *Memphis Commercial-Appeal* stating that he would not be responsible for debts incurred by his wife. Her father, "Major" Oldham, was so enraged by this public denunciation of his daughter that he called Bill into his office to curse him out. Their marriage was not much affected, however, because they gave a birthday party for their daughter Jill that year as if nothing important had happened. Faulkner's marriage to Estelle also estranged him from his mother, who had never approved of Bill's wife, but he remained a faithful son who called on "Miss Maud" almost every day when he was in town and was always polite and respectful towards her.

Faulkner outside window of Drugstore

Marriage to Estelle also brought about a breach in his long friendship with Phil Stone, and from 1929 on they became more distant and eventually broke off relations altogether. Faulkner helped Phil in financial difficulties later, but Phil did not repay the debt, causing the two men to became further estranged. When Faulkner was buried in 1962, Phil Stone shared the position of Honorary Pallbearer with Faulkner's other oldest friend, Mac Reed, but by then the friendship with Phil Stone was a thing of the past, leaving only the friendship with Mac Reed intact and uninterrupted. Phil Stone openly expressed the view in his later years that Faulkner's work, which he had supported loyally in the crucial early period when Faulkner had few admirers, was overrated at the end of his life, and that Faulkner himself had grown conceited, but he was no doubt voicing his own sense of resentment at being excluded from the inner circle of friends to which he once belonged. Mac Reed, on the other hand, was loyal to the end, never questioning Faulkner's right to go his own way, do as he liked, and write whatever he pleased. He was not a literary confidant as Phil Stone had once been, but he was the man Bill Faulkner relied on for moral and sometimes financial support, and was glad to be Faulkner's main link with the Oxford community, which tended to look on William Faulkner as a familiar but eccentric figure whose writing had puzzled, embarrassed, and shocked the town, even if he became in time their principal man of the world.

Kathryn Andrews, the widow of a lawyer in Oxford, was related to two of the prominent early families, Jacob Thompson (very nearly Jason Compson) and Robert Sheegog, who built Rowan Oak. She was a schoolmate of Bill Faulkner and Estelle Oldham, and remembered them as high school sweethearts who wanted to get married but were prevented by Estelle's family, who insisted she marry a much more promising bachelor, Cornell Franklin. Cornell was an ambitious young lawyer from a prominent family in Columbus, Mississippi, with prospects of a successful career, while Faulkner, who came from a respectable enough family, had never graduated from high school. That Estelle never graduated either didn't matter because she married young.

Estelle had married Cornell Franklin in 1918, in a formal church wedding, she in a wedding dress and he in a white military uniform with a sword at his side. They went on a honeymoon to the Far East, first to the Philippines, then a U.S. territory, and on to Shanghai, where he rose to be a judge in the American community in China. They had two children, but in a few years Estelle left him, charging infidelity and obtaining a divorce. She returned to Oxford with her children, telling friends "I didn't marry the man I wanted the first time, but I sure mean to marry him now." Cornell returned for visits to see his children, and was friendly with Bill and Estelle, but his mother was the only member of the Franklin family who remained loyal to Estelle. She gave Estelle the furniture and table service which Faulkner could not afford to buy.

Faulkner emerging from Drugstore

After his divorce, Cornell Franklin married again, and when he came back to Oxford with his second wife, Dallas, they stayed at Rowan Oak with Estelle and Bill, an arrangement which many in town thought unseemly, but the two couples seemed to have no ill feelings towards each other. Estelle was accustomed to luxury as Cornell Franklin's wife, but had to give it up when she married Faulkner, making drapes for the house and even making her own dresses. Franklin sometimes came on visits to see his children, and it was through his family that Estelle acquired the dining table and fine silver, china, and crystal which she used for family meals, whether or not there were guests in the house.

Though Estelle was faithful to Faulkner (accepting his infidelity as she hadn't Cornell Franklin's), she was often embarrassed by his appearance and behavior in the town where they were both well known. Faulkner was impervious to the town's low opinion of him, but Estelle was sensitive to the social ostracism they suffered because of his unconventional ways. She knew he was gaining a wider reputation with his books, and when his most sensational novel, *Sanctuary*, was about to appear, she told a friend, "Billy has written a book that's going to shock people, but I think this one will sell." It was the book that helped him pay for Rowan Oak, because it led to his contracts in Hollywood to write screenplays. From 1931 on, Faulkner was able to make a living as a writer and did not have to take odd jobs in Oxford to support his family.

In their later years, relations between the Faulkners were often strained, because Estelle was jealous of the attention that was increasingly shown to Bill and felt she was being treated as an appendage to her famous husband. She like Bill was a problem drinker, and her bouts of drinking often had serious consequences as did his. Their friends were concerned about her, because they could see that she was acting as if she were merely a wallflower while Bill was the cynosure. They pitied her but could do little to relieve her loneliness, which set her apart from her husband, a man who relished solitude. Bill would go off on hunting trips that lasted for a week or two, leaving her to be unhappy all by herself. She liked to entertain but seldom could do so, since he preferred to write by himself, or sought the company of other men to go out hunting. She knew he was susceptible to the attractions of ladies, and there were many women who wanted to be near him as he became famous. Though he tried to keep his love affairs confidential, she knew that he had more than one affair, usually with younger women who eagerly sought him for advice about their writing. With few close friends in Oxford she could call on, it was difficult for Estelle to escape from her loneliness, and she frequently drank for consolation.

Faulkner and Hollywood

After Faulkner published *Sanctuary* in 1931, he was hired by MGM to write screenplays, and he went to Hollywood off and on for many years. He worked on nine different scripts in his first year as a screenwriter, from May of 1932 to May of 1933. Two of these scripts became movies, though they were not box office hits. They were *Lazy River* and *Today We Live*. He earned $6000 of easy money that year, a handsome sum during the Great Depression, but it did not make him unhappy when the contract was not renewed and he could go back home to Oxford. What mattered most was that he had met Howard Hawks that first year, they had become fast friends, and he left with the promise of more significant contracts for screenwriting later.

Howard Hawks was one of the best known movie directors in Hollywood, with a string of box office hits that eventually included Academy Award films. Hawks let it be known that when he met Faulkner in 1932 or 1933, he had already read and admired his books, and had thought of asking him to write a screenplay based on one of them. Hawks invited Faulkner to come to his office and discuss the possibility of collaborating on a film. Faulkner responded by coming to his office quietly, saying he had noticed Hawks' signature on one of his checks, and waiting in silence for him to speak. Hawks reported their conversation later: "I talked to him for forty minutes, outlining the screen play to him. He said it was all right, and he would be back in five days. I said, 'Do you need five days to think about it?' Faulkner said, 'No, five days to write it.'" Faulkner was good as his word, and returned in five days with a screenplay of *Today We Live* based on his story, "Turnabout." He had even written an acting part for Joan Crawford, who had been added to the cast after he began working on the screenplay. The film was produced, and Faulkner received his first screen credit for writing the script.

"Turnabout," the Faulkner story on which the film was based, had attracted the interest of Howard Hawks because it was action-packed, and Hawks was noted for his fast action movies. The story was a concentrated series of battle scenes by air and by sea during the First World War, told mainly by dialogue and brief descriptions. Faulkner had mastered the modern fictional technique, strongly masculine and tight-lipped, that Hemingway had perfected in his Post World War I stories and novels in the early 1920s. "Turnabout" unfolded elliptically and ironically in Faulkner's telling, forcing the reader to guess what action was really going on, offering glimpses of combat action with guns firing and bombs exploding. He contrasted the action of fighting a war in the air with fighting a war on the sea. The main characters were an American pilot and a British sailor, one of whom engaged in dogfights with airplanes in the sky over France, while the other one was battling by ship on the English Channel between England and France. The Allies were warring against Germany, whose planes and ships were shown in the movie, under the command of German airmen and seamen. As Faulkner presented it, the American pilot successfully bombed a German headquarters in France and returned alive, while the English sailor, who does most of his fighting in a drunken stupor, commands a patrol boat but is killed in action as he torpedoes a German destroyer. The story ends with terse bulletins citing the American pilot, Captain Bogard, for his heroism, and announcing that the British patrol boat is missing in action. It was early Faulkner, when he was still in the process of perfecting his fictional technique, but he was already challenging readers to understand what is really going on. The story had been published in *The Saturday Evening Post*, a popular vehicle for short fiction in the 1920s and 1930s, where Hawks read it and thought Faulkner could help him make it into a successful movie.

Today We Live, the movie Hawks derived from Faulkner's story, is long on action and short on mystery. In converting the short story into a movie, the screenwriters, only one of whom was Faulkner, changed the title from the rather ambiguous "Turnabout" to *Today We Live*, implying a case of heroic survival. The combat episodes were enveloped in the graphic realism only a camera can show. A romantic plot was added to bring a woman into the story, and only fragments of Faulkner's original dialogue were left intact. Hollywood film stars had of course to be hired as the main actors: Gary Cooper plays Captain Bogard, the dashing American pilot, and Robert Young is the drunken English sailor, engaged to Joan Crawford, an English heiress of a large estate, who lives in a richly furnished mansion featured as the film begins. In typical Hollywood fashion, the film transformed a war story into a Hollywood romance, with a happy ending photographed in the luxurious setting with which the movie began. We learn that Joan Crawford grew up as a playmate of Robert Young in the lush English countryside before the war began, and that he was a fast friend of her brother, a part played by Franchot Tone. When Gary Cooper enters as the prospective buyer of the English estate (the stock fictional tale of a rich American buying out an impoverished English landlord), she falls in love with him and he with her. They are separated by the war, but miraculously converge at the same British port, where the brave pilot, Gary Cooper, takes off on his heroic mission to fight and defeat what looks like the entire German air force. The unfortunate sailor, Robert Young, guides his torpedo boat on a suicidal mission to destroy a German ship, and dies heroically in action (beside Franchot Tone, his brother in arms). Gary Cooper and Joan Crawford are united in the happy ending, which shows them strolling arm in arm in the bucolic setting with which the movie began. It is pure Hollywood, converting a slight but original story by one of the masters of modern fiction into a romantic soap opera, against the backdrop of World War One. No wonder Faulkner regarded Hollywood as a money-making enterprise that occasionally produced popular art to entertain millions of people around the world. Faulkner had the ability to profit from the entertainment industry while having little respect for it, thus getting much more from Hollywood than Hollywood got from him.

Howard Hawks himself later gave an account of how the story became the movie and how he and Faulkner became friends. He had read "Turnabout" in the *Saturday Evening Post*, liked it, and bought the screen rights, then got in touch with Faulkner to ask if he would do a screenplay of it. The account of Howard Hawks, in his own voice, was recorded by a younger Hollywood director, Peter Bogdanovich, as a commentary on Faulkner's last screenplay, *The Land of the Pharaohs*, a Hollywood epic that was released in 1955, five years after Faulkner received the Nobel Prize for Literature. Hawks worked with Faulkner on a number of pictures, which started with *Today We Live* in the early 1930s and ended with *The Land of the Pharaohs* in the mid-1950s. Among the best movies made under Hawks' direction and Faulkner's screenwriting were *To Have and Have Not* (1944) based on a Hemingway novel, marking the first and only time Faulkner and Hemingway ever collaborated (distantly) as novelist and screenwriter, and *The Big Sleep* (1946) based on a popular Raymond Chandler whodunit. Both films featured Humphrey Bogart and Lauren Bacall as the romantic leads, and both were hugely popular. It was Hawks who told the famous story about Faulkner asking permission to work on a screenplay at home. Hawks consented, knowing that Faulkner was living at the time in a hotel called The Garden of Allah in Beverly Hills. But when he asked his secretary to call the hotel and ask for Faulkner, he learned to his surprise that Faulkner had truly gone home, checking out of the hotel and leaving California to go back to Mississippi, since "home" meant Oxford to him. Hawks was amused by the incident but not upset, since he was the director who had first discovered Faulkner's peculiar talents as a screenwriter.

Their first collaboration started with a screenplay by Faulkner based on his war story, which was later converted by other screenwriters—not by Faulkner himself--into a Hollywood romance. "I thought it might be a good idea to ask him to do it," Hawks later said, recalling that Faulkner came to his office and quietly smoked a pipe, while he listened to Hawks outline what he had in mind. "Faulkner didn't say one word, and I talked to him for about an hour and a half. Finally, he got up to go and I said 'Where are you going?' and he said 'You wanted me to write it, didn't you? I'm going to write it.' I said 'Well, couldn't you wait and have a drink and let us get acquainted?' and he said 'Sure,' and went off, and in six days he wrote a script that was one of the finest scripts I've ever read. I remember taking it to producer Irving Thalberg and saying 'I want you to read this and tell me what you think we ought to do with it.' And he read it and came back and said we'd just be making great big muddy tracks on it if we tried to fool with it. It was that good. Faulkner and I became friends and we did five or six stories together. Bill understood the technique of writing. He wrote well. He made contributions to anything he touched, because as I say he was a good writer, and people who are that good write like angels. They have a method of expression that is so good. When we were stymied on *The Land of the Pharaohs*, because none of us knew how a Pharaoh talked, Bill asked if there was any reason he couldn't talk like the owner of a Southern plantation. The Southern accent didn't quite fit in." (Hawks' account is part of the "Commentary by Peter Bogdanovich with Howard Hawks" which accompanies a Netflix DVD of *The Land of the Pharaohs*.)

Howard Hawks thought Faulkner a master of the screenwriting profession, because he had "the great ability to characterize and the visual imagination" necessary to put it into words. Hawks praised Faulkner for being "intelligent and obliging—a master of his work who does it without fuss." Nunnally Johnson, another Hollywood director, had a different opinion, saying that Faulkner "couldn't write dramatic material" and "didn't contribute anything to screenwriting." On the evidence of the films Faulkner helped to write, it is clear that Hawks was a better judge of Faulkner's screenwriting talent than Johnson.

Faulkner received screen credit for six of the films he worked on with Hawks: *Today We Live (1933), Road to Glory (1935), Slave Ship (1937), To Have and Have Not (1944), The Big Sleep (1946),* and *Land of the Pharaohs (1955).* Each time, Faulkner returned home from his stints of screenwriting with more easy money in his pocket.

Hawks, knowing that Faulkner liked to hunt, once arranged a hunting trip with Clark Gable. Gable was a major Hollywood star, while Faulkner was only an obscure screenwriter at the time. They talked about books, and Gable asked, "Mr. Faulkner, who in your opinion are the greatest living writers?" Faulkner answered seriously, "Thomas Mann, Dos Passos, Hemingway, and me." Gable looked at him with surprise, "Oh, do you write, Mr. Faulkner?" Faulkner replied without blinking an eye, "Yes, and what do you do for a living, Mr. Gable?"

In November of 1935 he was hired by Twentieth Century Fox to work on screenplays, and the result was financially, if not artistically, satisfying, since he wrote seven "properties," of which five were made into films, before returning home in August of 1937. Howard Hawks directed only one of them, *Road to Glory*, having persuaded the producer, Daryl Zanuck, to hire Faulkner to write the screenplay. The other films he worked on were *Slave Ship, Splinter Fleet, Drums Along the Mohawk,* and *Banjo on My Knee*. Faulkner got screen credits for both *Road to Glory* and *Slave Ship* which were relatively successful at the box office.

In addition to Daryl Zanuck, Faulkner worked with the producer Nunnally Johnson, who had doubts about Faulkner's ability as a screenwriter, but who was from Georgia and became a good friend of Faulkner. He wrote a valuable account of Faulkner's behavior while in Hollywood. He said that Faulkner came to his office first in 1935, a few days after burying his brother Dean, who had died in a crash of Faulkner's own plane. Faulkner was still in mourning and overwrought. He entered Johnson's office carrying a paper sack, slumped into a chair, and asked if Johnson minded his taking a drink. Johnson offered to pour him one, but Faulkner said no, he had his own supply. He pulled a pint of bourbon out of his sack and twisted the cap, cutting his finger in the process, and with his finger dripping blood he took a swig from it and offered the pint bottle to Johnson. The two men passed the bottle back and forth until it was empty, and as they drank, Faulkner told the gruesome story of his brother's death. The crash had occurred in Faulkner's Waco airplane, and he felt so guilty about it that he spent all night in the funeral parlor, helping the mortician shape his brother's mangled face into recognition. "And I did a pretty good job," he claimed, "because Dean's wife didn't scream when she saw him in the casket the next day—she just cried." However, it was decided that no one else should see him and they closed the casket for his funeral.

Faulkner was living in style at the Beverly Hills Hilton during his later screenwriting days, but once when he went out hunting to Catalina Island, he returned ragged and unshaven, causing everyone to flee in horror when he entered the hotel lobby, because there had been a robbery that day and they assumed he was the thief returning to the scene of the crime. Faulkner looked around, shrugged his shoulders, knocked out his pipe, and went nonchalantly to his room.

In 1935 Faulkner was working with Nunnally Johnson on the script of *Road to Glory* at Twentieth Century Fox. During his off-hours, he was putting the finishing touches on one of his fictional masterpieces, published in 1936 as *Absalom, Absalom!* One evening in November he left the galley proof of the novel on Johnson's desk, accompanied by a note saying it was his new novel on the theme of miscegenation, and he thought it would make a fine movie if Johnson cared to produce it. Faulkner added that he would be willing to sell the screen rights for $100,000. Johnson found the note amusing, but was not tempted to risk that much money on a new novel even if Faulkner was the author. It was never made into a film, though some critics have called it Faulkner's best novel. The irony is that Faulkner wrote it while he was in Hollywood working on screenplays.

At least one of Faulkner's fellow screenwriters, David Hempstead, marveled at how much Faulkner could drink while he was writing. He once asked Faulkner how he managed to survive on so much drink and so little food. Faulkner replied coolly "There's a damn lot of nutrition in an acre of corn."

In February 1936 Faulkner went to Hollywood to work on a script with Nunnally Johnson that became a film called *Banjo on my Knee*, set in the South. During that time he was invited to parties which he sometimes attended, but he was easily bored by the conversation, and escaped from one party by climbing out an upstairs window and scrambling down a trellis to the ground. At a party given by Claudette Colbert, he was invited to play tennis with the comedy star Zazu Pitts. With his writer friend Nathaniel West he hunted for wild boar on Catalina and Santa Cruz islands. He also worked briefly on the script of *Gunga Din*, a box office hit which starred Douglas Fairbanks, Jr., Joan Fontaine, and Victor McLaglen.

In July, 1936, Faulkner returned to Hollywood with his family and two colored servants, driving all the way from Oxford in their new Ford. They rented a large house six miles from the studio which had servants' quarters. He began working with Nunnally Johnson on the script for *Slave Ship*, starring the veteran comic actor, Wallace Beery, and the new child star, Mickey Rooney. The Faulkners gave parties occasionally; among their guests were Clark Gable and Ronald Colman. He sometimes rented a plane to go flying, for the first time since Dean was killed in his plane. He went on working into November on another film called *Submarine Patrol*, but with little enthusiasm, and in December his contract was terminated because he had not been submitting any screenwork. However, he earned the princely sum of $20,000 in 1936 in Hollywood. The following year, in the depths of the Great Depression, he published the novel he had written on his own in Hollywood, *Absalom, Absalom!* for which he dared to ask $100,000 for the screen rights, but the whole year he earned very little from royalties. He told his brother Jack, who came to see him, that "No one would work in Hollywood except to get what money they could out of it."

He went back to Hollywood nevertheless, and in March 1937, he was hired to work on the screenplay of *Drums Along the Mohawk*, a popular novel by Philip Van Doren Stern, but this time his drinking got out of hand and he had to stop for one of his periodic "illnesses." In June 1937, while still in Hollywood, he read a self-parody he had written to the guests at a dinner party. It was called "Afternoon of a Cow" and was about his own home and family, all tongue-in-cheek, which drew little praise from anyone except Maurice Coindreau, his French translator, to whom he gave a copy. Coindreau was able to have it published, first in French translation, later in the original English. It was during his time in Hollywood in 1937 that he wrote a story called "An Odor Of Verbena" which would become the last chapter of his novel, *The Unvanquished*, published in 1938. Clearly, he had not lost his touch as an original novelist while writing screenplays for money. It was also in 1937 that Saxe Commins replaced Ben Wasson as his principal editor for Random House.

Five years later, in July of 1942, Faulkner was hired by Warner Brothers to write screenplays for what turned out to be his greatest successes. He had tried to get a commission in the Air Force or the Navy during the Second World War but was turned down because of his age (he was 44). His salary as a screenwriter was only $300 a week, at a time when the top screenwriters were being paid $2500 a week, but he needed the money and was grateful for a steady job. He first worked on *The De Gaulle Story*, about the man who was the hero of the French Resistance and later was elected First President of France. His cowriter was the popular Western novelist, Max Brand (whose real name was Frederick Faust). Faust and Faulkner quickly became friends, aided by the fact that Faust drank as heavily as Faulkner, but Max Brand was soon sent to Italy as a war correspondent and was killed in action. Faulkner struck up an acquaintance with the British Imagist poet Richard Aldington, also in Hollywood writing screenplays. When Howard Hawks recruited Faulkner to help him make a Second World War film called *Air Force*, he conceived of a project of his own. Knowing how much Hemingway needed money, he decided to take what he called Hemingway's "worst novel," *To Have and Have Not*, and make it into a good movie. Hemingway was glad to sell him the screen rights, and Faulkner did just what he promised, making *To Have and Have Not* into a movie superior to the novel on which it was based. Faulkner benefited as much as Hemingway did from this collaboration, because in 1943 Faulkner earned $18,000 by working in Hollywood, while in the same year his total royalties from Random House amounted to a mere $300.

While Faulkner was working for Warner Brothers, he would drive to work every morning with the director Jerry Wald. On the way to the studio, he would ask Wald to stop at a liquor store so that he could buy a bottle of whiskey to take with him. During the day he would consume a fifth of bourbon while writing the screenplay, carefully placing the empty bottle in a drawer of his desk. The practice went on regularly, day after day, until a janitor noticed that the desk was full of empty whiskey bottles and reported the fact to Jack Warner, head of the studio. Warner immediately called Faulkner in to his office and asked him if he was drinking on the job. Faulkner said he was, and Warner told him to stop it at once. Faulkner coolly responded, "Well, Mr. Warner, if you prefer that I drink on my own time and sober up on your time, it's all right with me." No more words were spoken on that subject, and Faulkner continued his habit of drinking while he was writing. Clearly, Warner thought him too good at screenwriting to dream of firing him.

Faulkner was employed in Hollywood off and on from the summer of 1942 until September of 1945, almost the entire period of the Second World War, though he went home three times and stayed several months each time. During his fairly steady three-year stay in Hollywood, he worked on seventeen "properties," eleven of which were made into films, and two of which bore his name in the screen credits. These two proved to be classics, with Howard Hawks directing them both, one from Hemingway's novel, *To Have and Have Not*, and one from a novel by Raymond Chandler, *The*

Big Sleep, both starring the newly discovered romantic team of Humphrey Bogart and Lauren Bacall. Some of the other films Faulkner worked on were box office successes, such as *The De Gaulle Story, Country Lawyer, Battle Cry, and Stallion Road* (from a novel by Faulkner's friend and admirer, Stephen Longstreet). He also worked briefly but not decisively on other popular movies made at the time: *God Is My Co-Pilot, The Adventures of Don Juan, Mildred Pierce,* and *Petrified Forest.*

Howard Hawks shared Faulkner's liking for detective novels, and it was he who suggested that they make a movie of *The Big Sleep* by Raymond Chandler, a novel both admired. This film allowed Humphrey Bogart and Lauren Bacall to capitalize on their popularity in *To Have and Have Not.* Faulkner would say later that he had particularly enjoyed working on the script for this film.

Though Faulkner was a reliable enough screenwriter, he never really enjoyed the work and always said he did it strictly for the money. He admitted to Nunnally Johnson that he was willing to "do an honest day's work according to what the man said," but nothing more. However, he was very productive in this line of work. With a bottle of bourbon at his side, he could turn out as much as 25 pages of screen dialogue in a day, in his miniscule handwriting, a nightmare to Hollywood secretaries.

When Faulkner was asked about his work as a screenwriter, he was always self-deprecating. He called himself a "motion picture doctor" and confessed "I don't write scripts. I don't know enough about it." He liked Howard Hawks as a director and Humphrey Bogart as an actor, but he made few friends in Hollywood who were not writers like himself. His opinion of the movie industry was unrelenting: "Some good movies come from out there—God knows how, but they do." When he sold the film rights to one of his books, as he often did in his later years, his only restriction was that he would not be required to read the screenplay or see the movie. He once summarized his feeling about Hollywood definitively: "They don't worship money; they worship death."

Faulkner had many writer friends in Hollywood, including Nathaniel West, author of *Miss Lonelyhearts,* and of *The Day of the Locust,* a novel which drew on *Sanctuary.* Other friends and drinking companions were John O'Hara, William Saroyan, James M. Cain, Lillian Hellman, Dashiell Hammett, Budd Schulberg, and Scott Fitzgerald. They all frequented the Stanley Rose Bookshop on Hollywood Boulevard. He was invited by one Hollywood star, Tallulah Bankhead, to write a screenplay for her, but he declined with the excuse that anything he would write for her would ruin her reputation. Budd Schulberg wrote that "His body might wander off to Hollywood in search of financial intravenous feeding, but his soul continued to reside in Oxford, Mississippi." Schulberg liked to repeat the story Howard

Hawks first told that was most revealing about Faulkner's homing instinct, though he named another studio boss. Schulberg said that "The stories of Faulkner in Hollywood are as numerous as the Sam Goldwyn connection. An old favorite describes Faulkner working for Irving Thalberg at MGM, and asking his boss if he had any objections to Bill's working at home. Thalberg preferred to keep his writers safely pigeonholed in the Writers' Building, but in Faulkner's case he was willing to make an exception. A few days later Thalberg asked his secretary to summon Faulkner to a story conference. She phoned the Garden of Allah, where Faulkner was supposed to be staying, only to find that Faulkner had gone home with a vengeance—all the way to Oxford." The story was still a good one, even if Schulberg named the wrong director.

Clearly, Faulkner never liked living in California, and a neighbor in Oxford remembered that he would be so happy when he got back home he would roll in the grass outside his house, even if it was raining, because he said he hadn't felt rain in California for months. One of Faulkner's Hollywood friends was Buzz Bezzerides, who knew his weakness for drink and refused him a drink on request, whereupon Faulkner autographed all of his books on Bezzerides' shelf, but still didn't get a drink and had to go to another writer's house to indulge in his next binge.

One writer friend was Stephen Longstreet, for whose novel *Stallion Road* Faulkner did a screenplay in 1944. It was rejected by Warner Brothers as "impossible." Longstreet thought it "magnificent" but "utterly impossible to be made into the trite movie of the period." It was during one of Faulkner's best periods in Hollywood, when he helped write the screenplays for his two most highly acclaimed films, *To Have and Have Not*, from a novel by Ernest Hemingway, and *The Big Sleep*, from a novel by Raymond Chandler.

When Longstreet complimented Faulkner on his work, Faulkner was so pleased that he did what he had done for Buzz Besserides, autographing all his novels in Longstreet's library without being asked. Faulkner often refused to autograph his books, even if asked by friends or family, but he was capable of doing so impulsively for a friend.

Faulkner was a demon for work when he was writing screenplays, sometimes writing all night and breaking his own record, producing up to 50 pages of script the next day. He was so prolific that a member of the Writers Guild criticized him for his productivity, saying he was making it hard for his fellow writers to compete.

One idea for a novel came to him while he was in Hollywood, from a film producer he knew. The fellow spoke enthusiastically about having Christ and his apostles come to earth during the First World War and bring about a period of peace. Faulkner fell for it, and wrote a screenplay first, then when it was rejected, wrote *A Fable*, published in 1954. By then Faulkner's fame guaranteed that it would be successful, and it won him his first Pulitzer Prize for Fiction in 1954, though critical opinion held it to be one of his least successful novels. The outline for the novel can still be read where Faulkner wrote it, on the walls of his office at Rowan Oak, preserved for visitors to see. He acknowledged in publishing the novel that the idea was not his originally but came from a movie producer he knew.

Faulkner always expressed a low opinion of Hollywood screenwriting, though he benefited from it many times over. He told Stephen Longstreet, "The way I see it, the studio work is like chopping cotton or picking potato bugs off plants; you know damn well it is not painting the Sistine Chapel or winning the Kentucky Derby, but a man likes the feel of some money in his pocket." He had made up his mind that his books would never sell, and finally admitted to himself in 1945 that "I ought to know now I don't sell and never will earn enough outside of pictures to stay out of debt." That was when he was deeply discouraged about his achievement, and it took Malcolm Cowley's edition of *The Portable Faulkner*, for which Faulkner drew a new map of Yoknapatawpha County, to restore his faith in himself as a writer of merit. It was published in 1945 and Faulkner's reputation began to improve at last. His self-assessment at this low point in his career was that: "All my writing life I have been a poet without education, who possessed only instinct and a fierce conviction and belief in the worth and truth of what he was doing, and an illimitable courage for rhetoric (personal pleasure in it too: I admit it) and who knew or cared for little else." He read the black novelist Richard Wright's two novels, preferring *Native Son* to *Black Boy*, and sent Wright a letter saying "I think you will agree that the good lasting stuff comes out of an individual's imagination and sensitivity to and comprehension of Everyman, Anyman, not out of the memory of his own grief."

When he left California after one stint of screenwriting, he was in a hurry to take a pregnant mare back to Mississippi in a horse-trailer, because as he told Longstreet, "Gotta get her to Mississippi. No mare of mine is going to throw a foal in California." His parting words when he left Longstreet behind in Hollywood were: "We really live in the world of our mind, we only move about in the visible one."

Faulkner went back to Hollywood for a month in 1951, after he had received the Nobel Prize, to do a script for Howard Hawks at $2000 a week, on a book called *The Left Hand of God*. He did the script so quickly that he received a bonus, and for a month's work he earned $14,000. In 1954 he learned that his young mistress Joan Williams had married, and that his daughter Jill was engaged, leaving him more alone than he had been for some time. In 1955 he was invited by Jerry Wald, a Hollywood producer and friend, to come to Hollywood for some screenwriting, but he said bluntly,

"I have never learned how to write movies, nor even to take them very seriously." Nevertheless, when Howard Hawks invited him in 1955 to work on *The Land of the Pharaohs*, starring the English actors Jack Hawkins and Joan Collins, he took his last job as a screenwriter, traveling first to Europe and then to Egypt to write dialogue on location. Together, he and Howard Hawks tried to re-invent Egyptian dynastic history and the building of the Pyramids, but it was not a great success. On the way, he arrived in Paris drunk with a gash in his skull, and again in Cairo he had to be carried off the plane on a stretcher—still unable to control his drinking. He had proved during his long career as a screenwriter to be better at writing scripts from other stories and novels than from his own work. *Intruder in The Dust* was the only film made from a Faulkner novel which had a successful run at the box office, the only one filmed on location in Oxford and vicinity, but Faulkner did not write the screenplay for it; he served only as a consultant to the Director, Clarence Brown.

In the 1930s Faulkner had earned enough leisure to invite his brothers and friends to Rowan Oak for evenings at the poker table. Jack and Dean Faulkner were the most frequent winners at poker and many friends lost money to them. A friend who played poker with Faulkner recalled that he once showed them a towel which he said he had brought back as a prize from one of the girls he visited in Memphis, while he was doing "research" for *Sanctuary*. His wicked sense of humor led him to say that if a movie were made from the novel he would play the part of the corncob. He once treated a Faulkner scholar, Carvell Collins, to his mocking definition of a Southern gentleman: "A Southern gentleman is a man who will help a little old lady across the street, and then, when he gets her safely to the other side, rape her." He would sometimes make joking remarks about his books, but if anyone tried to bring them up as a topic of conversation, he would quickly shut up like a clam and refuse to talk about them at all. He liked being coy about his books, enticing people with a few brief glimpses into his fictional world.

With the proceeds of his novel, *The Unvanquished*, published in 1938, Faulkner bought a farm outside town near Puskus Creek. His brother John, known as "Johnsy," told his photographer friend, "Col." J. R. Cofield the story about it. Johnsy was running a flying service at the local airport, and one day Bill drove up in a red roadster and waved piece of paper in the air triumphantly. It was a check for the movie rights to *The Unvanquished*. Johnsy was astonished to see the sum of $25,000 written on it, a princely sum in those days when the Great Depression still lingered. Bill showed his brother the check and told him "Now I can buy that farm I've always wanted." He had found a farm for sale east of town and bought it mainly to grow hay for his horses, not to raise food for his family. Becoming a gentleman farmer late in life allowed him to make good on his frequent claim that "I'm a farmer, not a writer."

He sold the screen rights to *The Unvanquished*, but it never became a movie. Faulkner learned later that MGM had purchased the screen rights with no intention of producing a film. The studio wanted to use it as a bargaining chip with David Selznick, who owned the movie rights to the much more popular Civil War novel, Margaret Mitchell's *Gone with the Wind*. MGM had contracts with the stars Selznick wanted to feature in the movie, Clark Gable, Leslie Howard and Olivia de Haviland, while Selznick had the movie rights, so the two film companies reached a compromise. Thus the more popular Civil War novel would become a film that won the Academy Award and set records at the box office. Faulkner had written a better Civil War novel than Margaret Mitchell, but his Hollywood profit came from the competition between two major movie studios.

Faulkner and finances

Bill Faulkner was notorious for not paying his debts. One business man in Oxford, Will Lewis, owner of the Neilson department store on the town square, received a check from Bill that bounced when he tried to cash it. When he confronted Bill about it, Bill said coolly, "Keep that check—some day it'll amount to something." Will Lewis framed the uncashable check and put it on his wall as a Faulkner autograph.

Faulkner was often in debt because he was a spendthrift who had expensive tastes, and though *Sanctuary* was his breakthrough into fame and fortune, he flirted with bankruptcy for many years, earning a reputation as a credit risk who never paid his bills on time. Nevertheless, he lived as he liked to live, in his antebellum house in Oxford, at the Algonquin Hotel in New York and the Beverly Hills Hilton in Hollywood, in the style he preferred, whether or not he could afford it. As soon as he got a little ahead of his creditors, he would go on a spending spree: flying lessons for the first time in 1933 after a stint of screenwriting, the purchase of a private plane, spirited horses to ride, a farm to grow hay for them, and sometimes lavish entertainments at Rowan Oak, such as the famous Hunt Breakfast.

Faulkner as host

The Hunt Breakfast was one affair Faulkner organized that would make national news. After his death an account of it was published in *The Saturday Evening Post*, in its issue of October 9, 1965. It was Faulkner's most elaborate party. He staged it at Rowan Oak on a Sunday, offending some Oxford citizens who were as usual attending church and sharing quiet family time at home. Faulkner was indifferent to public opinion, always doing things his own way. He asked "Uncle Ned" Barnett, who served as butler in the Faulkner household, to dress in formal clothes and welcome the guests with a drink as they came to the party. The party was entirely Bill Faulkner's idea, conceived after a deer hunt in the Mississippi Delta provided venison for his table. The table was set with silver knives and forks and porcelain plates, and guests were directed to their seats by means of place cards engraved with foxes for the women and hounds for the men. He sent out formal invitations requesting that his guests come on horseback if they owned horses, and if they did not, they could borrow horses and dress appropriately for the occasion. Bill met the guests at the entry gate, accompanied by his hounds, and escorted each guest in person to the house. There they were welcomed by Uncle Ned dressed in livery, who offered each one a shot glass of bourbon as a starter. They were then taken on a "hunt" through Bailey Woods, following a trail of paper strips which Bill Faulkner himself had planted as a guide. When they came back to the house for breakfast, they were served an elaborate meal which featured quail as well as venison. The party began on Sunday morning and lasted until late afternoon. It would be the talk of the town for weeks afterwards, with some local preachers denouncing it from the pulpit, but for all the stir it caused, it was a highly successful event. The guests felt honored to be invited, and many thought it was the most carefully planned party they had ever attended. Since it was known that Faulkner seldom gave parties at his house, the whole event was exceptional, and it demonstrated that if Faulkner chose to hold a social event in style, he could play the role of perfect host. The lucky guests carried fond memories away with them, and would describe all that happened in detail to those unlucky enough to miss the festivities. Among the guests were his neighbors, Dr. and Mrs. Ashford Little, who were not surprised by the display of Faulkner's fine manners. He had once helped them entertain a young man who came to Oxford especially to meet Faulkner. He was writing a thesis on Faulkner's fiction, and Faulkner invited them over and served them a bowl of hot rum punch as a favor to their guest.

The Faulkner name

There were many stories about how William Falkner without the "u" became William Faulkner with the "u." They vary from the intentional to the accidental, and involve other family members who also changed the spelling of their name. His first public use of Faulkner with the "u" was on his RAF-Canada enlistment in 1918, but he did not use it consistently. The Last Will and Testament he wrote in June 1960, when he was living most of the time in Charlottesville, Virginia, begins: "I, William Faulkner, being the same person as William Falkner, of Charlottesville, Virginia." Those two spellings in his final legal document are proof that he had never legally changed the spelling of his name, though all his published books are by William Faulkner, not Falkner, and when he signed his name to anything, it was usually with the "u" rather than without it.

At least one woman who knew him well believed that his name was symbolic. She saw in his features a "falconer," the face of a man who trained hunting hawks. He did have a beak-like nose, and his small stature and high voice were suggestive of a hawk. He loved hunting, and would probably have been pleased with the name-symbolism if he had thought of it, but it wasn't a matter of choice, as were the names of his characters. "Sartoris," he once wrote, had "the dying sound of horns at Roncevaux," invoking the hero of a medieval French epic about Roland, one of Charlemagne's knights, who lost his battle against the Moors in Spain. Perhaps William Faulkner really was William the Falconer, even if he never knew it. The names Faulkner used in his fiction were often taken from people he knew in Oxford, both white and black. For instance, the name of Luster, the young black man who looked after Benjy Compson in *The Sound and the Fury*, was very close to the name of a young black woman who worked for the family at Rowan Oak, Luda Belle <u>Lester</u>.

Faulkner and the Cemetery

Faulkner's grave in St. Peter's Cemetery

In St. Peter's Cemetery, outside Oxford, the graves of William and Estelle Faulkner are side by side in a plot set apart from the rest of the Falkner and Oldham families, though the town cemetery is full of graves with connections to both families. Notably, near Faulkner's grave in St. Peter's Cemetery is that of Robert Sheegog (Aug. 31, 1801–Aug. 29, 1860) one of the original settlers in Oxford and builder of what became Faulkner's principal home, the Old Sheegog Place, which he renamed Rowan Oak. Nearby is the grave of Dr. Thomas Dudley Isom (1816–1902) another pioneer Oxford settler. In the main Falkner plot are the graves of Faulkner's nearest relatives: John W.T. Falkner (Sept. 2, 1848–Mar. 3, 1922) Faulkner's grandfather, known as "The Young Colonel," Sallie Murry Falkner (Oct. 14, 1850–Dec. 21, 1906), his grandmother (Faulkner called her "Damuddy"), Murry C. Falkner (Aug. 17, 1870–Aug. 7, 1932), his father, and Maud Butler Falkner (Nov. 27, 1871–Oct. 16, 1960) his mother, whom he called "Miss Maud." Dean Swift Falkner (Aug. 15, 1907–Nov. 10, 1935) his youngest brother, crashed and died in Faulkner's plane, when he was only 28, and Faulkner wrote the epitaph on his gravestone: "I bare him on Eagle wings and brought him unto me" (paraphrasing Deuteronomy 32, 11–12, "As an eagle stirreth up her nest, fluttereth over her young, spreadeth abroad her wings, taketh them, beareth them on her wings, so the Lord above did lead him.") The grave of Faulkner (Sept. 25, 1897–July 6, 1962) has a simple religious epitaph: "Beloved Go With God," no doubt written by Estelle, who survived him by a few years. The most elaborate grave in St. Peters Cemetery is not Faulkner's but that of Augustus Baldwin Longstreet, author of *Georgia Scenes*, and Chancellor of the University of Mississippi from 1849–56. An obelisk above the grave bears the elaborate message that he "was born in Augusta, Georgia, on the day the sun crossed the line, A.D. 1790. He sleeps by the side of his wife, of whom he never thought himself worthy, and who never thought herself worthy of her husband. In every innocent movement of his life, she went hand in hand, and heart in heart with him for over fifty-one years. Death was a kind visitor to them both." Longstreet himself wrote a shorter epitaph by his own hand, just before his death on July 10th, 1870. "He leaves behind him a memory as beloved as it was honored." The graves of Lucius Q. C. Lamar (1825–1893), for whom the main street of Oxford is named, and his wife, Virginia Longstreet Lamar (1826–1884), daughter of Augustus B. and Frances F. Longstreet, are also in St. Peter's Cemetery, as is the grave of Faulkner's "Mammy," Caroline Barr, "Mammie Callie" with the farewell tribute, "Her white children bless her." After Faulkner held the funeral for her in his own house, he dedicated his next novel to her, *Go Down, Moses*, published in 1942: "To Mammy Callie, Caroline Barr, who was born in slavery and who gave to my family a fidelity without stint or calculation of recompense, and to my childhood an immeasurable devotion and love."

Faulkner and race

There were three distinct races in the South, and all three were carefully chronicled by Faulkner in his stories and novels: 1. White Europeans 2. Black Africans and 3. Native American Indians. They were known by the conspicuous color of their skin, but Faulkner understood the subtler differences between them in appearance and behavior, and in the way they spoke English. Faulkner was a master of dialogue, distinguishing accents in his work more credibly than other American writers have, even including Mark Twain. He saw that the three races differed as much in their speech as their manners, and he dramatized the difference in ways that make his fiction unique, and that most readers find fascinating The South was racially mixed, but the races were never fully integrated. White Europeans were the civilizers who cultivated the land, formed the towns, and instituted the laws governing them, and they were dominant by virtue of numbers, importing black Africans as slaves to work the land, serve the whites, and adopt many of the habits of the dominant race. Most profoundly, the blacks were converted to Christianity by the white race, becoming worshipping Christians who learned to read the Bible and to sing the hymns of a religious faith that was foreign to them. It had a strong appeal to them, because they saw their fate mirrored in the Old Testament wanderings of the Jewish race who were enslaved by the Egyptians. They expressed their longing to be free in Negro spirituals like "Go Down, Moses" which Faulkner used as the title of one of his finest novels. Dedicated to his own Negro Mammy, Caroline Barr, it was published just after her death at the age of one hundred. The native American red people, who occupied much of the country when the white settlers arrived, were never assimilated into the plantation families as the black people had been. They were either bought out or driven out as the new territory was settled, kept apart from both the white and black races, regarded as too proud to become slaves and incapable of finding a place in the plantation system developing rapidly across the South.

Faulkner portrays Native Americans realistically yet sympathetically. He was never a reformer of the social system into which he was born, but a truthful observer of real differences that allowed the three races to live in proximity, the black race working the plantations as slaves of the white settlers, the red race playing the role of hunters in the wilderness. The plantation society of the antebellum South was a modified feudal hierarchy like the medieval fiefdoms of Europe, but it was racially divided and not destined to last. Faulkner's Mythical Kingdom was rooted in the plantation society which had expanded westward from the Virginia Colony to the Old Southwest. It was an extension of the earlier social pattern European settlers brought to the New World, slavery replacing what had been serfdom. The plantation system managed to flourish for a couple of centuries in the South, until the South made the fatal mistake of trying to secede from the United States and become a separate country with its own social system. The feudal plantation society was soundly defeated in the Civil War by the industrialized democratic society that had developed in the North. The postbellum South would, as Faulkner saw, inevitably grow decadent, unable to survive as an Agrarian society based on slavery. It continued to exist on its memory of the past, but slowly accommodated itself to the industrialized society which had defeated it, retaining only the manners and speech that still distinguished it from other regions of the United States.

In the post-Civil War South, white families were still the shapers of the community. They varied widely, from the once aristocratic plantation owners like the Sartoris, Compson, and McCaslin families, brought up to honor the old chivalric customs, to the backwoods denizens of rural villages, the enterprising, self-aggrandizing Varner, Bundren and Snopes families. Faulkner's stories and novels center on these families. Faulkner's South was essentially a feudal system that had to end with the Civil War, but that stubbornly retained the memory of what it once had been, a civilized but stratified society, which yielded reluctantly and gradually to enterprising families like the Snopeses, who came from the backwoods and flourished in a more competitive society, progressing from the Hamlet to the Town to the Mansion, just as Faulkner portrayed them in his later fiction.

After the Civil War, Negroes continued to be dependent on the white families who had once owned them as slaves, becoming house servants and field hands following Emancipation. Faulkner clearly shows, however, that in their subordinate position, they are often more reliable than the whites they serve, more compassionate in their treatment of other human beings, the strong sustaining members of a white society visibly degenerating around them. Many of Faulkner's black characters are worthier individuals than the whites on whom they depend. It is to Faulkner's lasting credit that he created black characters who are credible and sympathetic human beings, strongly appealing despite their generally inferior social status. It was Faulkner's gift, as one French critic, Marcel Brion, wrote at the time of his death, to be "the white spiritualist of the Negro race."

Faulkner did change his views about the relations between the races after the Supreme Court desegregated the public schools in 1954, saying in his remarks on "American Segregation and the World Crisis" to the Southern Historical Society in Memphis on Nov. 10, 1955, that "as a white Southerner, and maybe even any white American, I too curse the day when the first Negro was brought against his will to this country and sold into slavery." But to recognize the historical fact of slavery, he said, is not to condone the unequal status of black vs. white Americans, for "To live anywhere in the world of A.D. 1955 and be against equality because of race or color, is like living in Alaska and being against snow." Faulkner made many statements about race in view of the rising Civil Rights movement, even going so far as to say that if a shooting war ever arose between black and white Americans, he would be prepared to shoot down Negroes in the streets. He later repudiated such a desperate claim, saying it was "one that no sober man would make nor any sane man believe" denouncing his remark as both "foolish and dangerous." More rationally, he argued that Negroes should stand up for their own "immortal individual dignity," and affirm to the world that "if violence and unreason come, it must not come from us." Faulkner agreed with Martin Luther King that non-violent resistance to racial segregation was the best policy, a position which has largely prevailed in the country at large since Faulkner's death. Soon after the Supreme Court ruled that segregation was illegal in public schools, and before many Southerners were ready to embrace racial equality, Faulkner wrote a courageous statement for *Ebony* magazine in September, 1956, titled "If I Were a Negro," appealing to American blacks to endorse the doctrines Jefferson voiced in the Declaration of Independence, addressing a plea to the black race at that historic period:

"We must learn that our inalienable right to equality, to freedom and liberty and the pursuit of happiness, means exactly what our founding fathers meant by it: the right and opportunity to be free and equal provided one is worthy of it, will work to gain it and then work to keep it."

In a letter to the Editor of *The Memphis Commercial Appeal* in 1957, he further clarified his racial views, writing that he thought an American Negro did not necessarily want to force his way into American churches and schools, but that "He simply wants the same right the white man has: to <u>choose</u> himself not to enter them." When a former black servant of the Faulkners asked him to finance a lifetime membership in the NAACP, Faulkner declined, saying he did not agree with the NAACP policy of forced integration of Negroes into white society, but believed that "Since they are a minority, they must behave better than white people. They must be <u>more</u> responsible, more honest, more moral, more industrious, more literate and educated. They, not the law, have got to compel the white people to say, Please come and be equal with us."

But Faulkner's most eloquent tribute to the black race was given, not in a public statement, but as a brief eulogy for his "Mammy," Caroline Barr, who died in 1940 at the age of 100. Faulkner conducted the funeral for her himself, in the drawing room of Rowan Oak, where his own body would lie in state one day. It was a personal and heartfelt tribute to her:

"As oldest of my father's family, I might be called her master. That situation never existed between Mammy and me. She reared all of us from childhood. She stood as a fount not only of authority and information but of affection, respect, and security. She was one of my first associates. I have known her all my life and have been privileged to see her out of hers.

"She was a character of devotion and fidelity. Mammy made no demands on anyone. She had the handicap to be born without money and with a black skin at a bad time in this country. She asked no odds and accepted the handicap of her lot, making the best of her few advantages. She surrendered her destiny to a family. That family made some appreciation of it. She was paid for the devotion she gave but still that was only money. As surely as there is a heaven, Mammy will be in it."

After his eulogy, a group of Negroes sang spirituals. Then her casket was taken to the Negro Baptist Church for a public funeral service, after which it was taken to St. Peter's Cemetery and buried, with a stone marking her grave: "Caroline Barr "Mammie Callie" Her white children bless her." Both William and Estelle Faulkner attended the public funeral service as well as the burial service for Caroline Barr.

The Memphis Commercial Appeal published the text of Faulkner's remarks and a brief personal history in its issue of February 5, 1940: "Callie had been born on the Barr Plantation in Pontotoc County in 1840, and named Caroline Barr—using the white owner's surname, as was the custom in slavery days. She stayed on the plantation until after the Civil War, then went to Oxford with her former owner, Colonel Barr. Later she went to work for Murry Falkner, father of William, and stayed with the Falkners until her death. She died of a stroke in her cabin behind Faulkner's mansion."

Faulkner said in Japan in 1955 that "I grew up with Negro children, my foster mother was a Negro woman. I slept in her bed and the Negro children and I slept in the same bed together. To me they were no different than anyone else. I noticed that with my own children. It's only when the child becomes a middle-aged man and becomes a part of the economy that that latent quality [of racial discrimination] appears."

In 1955, on his visit to Japan for the State Department, Faulkner made a prediction about the future of racial relations in America. He said "I think that in a few hundred years the Negro in my country will vanish anyway. He will be assimilated into the white race simply because there are more white people. He has a force, a power of his own, that will enable him to survive.

He won't vanish as the Indian did, because he is stronger and tougher than the Indians."

There were no longer any Indians left in Lafayette County in the early part of the twentieth century when Faulkner grew up there. The native Choctaws and Chickasaws had all been forcibly relocated to Oklahoma Territory in the 1830s on the Trail of Tears which President Andrew Jackson initiated to prevent further wars between white settlers and the indigenous tribes who occupied the lands. But there were Indian names and legends remaining in Mississippi which Faulkner adopted for his fiction. Yoknapatawpha appears in various forms on early maps: "Yokanapatawpha" was the nearest to Faulkner's spelling, but the name of the river south of Oxford might be spelled on some maps "Yockany Patawfa" and it was in time shortened to Yocona, pronounced "Yockony," the familiar local name in Faulkner's time and later. The spelling which Faulkner used is the same as that on the "Yoknapatawpha Drainage Bonds" which were sold to finance a water control project in Lafayette County. The real Indian chief named Tobatubby (close to Faulkner's fictional Ikkemotubbe) was remembered with a mound in the forest that local people knew about, like that which Faulkner fictionalized as Sam Fathers' grave in *The Bear*. Faulkner made believable characters of the Indians, and in the commanding personality of Sam Fathers he showed that a mixture of all three races could produce noble human beings. The fictional Sam Fathers was descended from an Indian chief, from whom he inherited an aristocratic bearing, as the hunter who knew how to conquer Old Ben, the last great bear of the wilderness.

Faulkner's early friendships and marriage

Phil Stone was the first friend to recognize Bill Faulkner's writing talent and encourage him to develop it, starting from the early years of their friendship. He thought Faulkner was better at fiction than at poetry, and tried to steer him in the direction of writing stories instead of poems. In 1924, he urged Faulkner to read Joyce's *Ulysses*, which had a profound effect on his narrative technique. Faulkner would later voice his debt to the Irish writer, saying "You should approach Joyce's *Ulysses* as the illiterate Baptist preacher approaches the Old Testament: with faith."

Phil Stone & Bill Faulkner

Mrs. Sallie Elliott was secretary to Phil Stone from 1925–30, when he was just getting his start as a professional writer, and she often typed his manuscripts to send off for publication. They would usually be written in pencil in Bill's miniscule hand, and punctuated by Phil Stone in a more legible form. Phil Stone insisted on having a perfect final copy despite the difficulties of deciphering Bill Faulkner's handwriting. Phil was committed to helping Bill get his start, even though it was discouraging at first. Mrs. Elliott said she was glad to do Phil Stone's legal work but hated trying to read Bill Faulkner's manuscripts and put them into readable type. He would come into the office in shirt and trousers, barefoot, and she would work hard to decipher whatever he brought her, sometimes calling on Phil Stone for help. During the period she worked for Phil, she remembered typing a number of stories and several novels, since Bill Faulkner was in one of his most productive writing periods though he had published very little. It is probable she typed his first four novels, though she could not remember the names of them, only that they were in her opinion "filthy." They would have been *Soldier's Pay, Mosquitoes, Sartoris,* and *The Sound and The Fury*. She had time to do extra work for Bill Faulkner because Phil Stone's legal practice was faltering at the time and there were few legal documents to handle.

Mrs. Elliott expressed astonishment that someone with as little formal education as Bill Faulkner should have such a wide vocabulary. He was regarded by most of the town as a bohemian who dressed and acted like a farmhand, and whose behavior was so eccentric he was derided by most of the town as totally lacking in ambition or talent. Much later on, when Bill Faulkner was famous and gave the commencement address at Jill Faulkner's high school graduation, taking exactly 4 ½ minutes to deliver, she asked him how he felt about speaking in a school from which he had not graduated. He said, "This is the first time I knew that a high school graduation could be so enjoyable." Sallie Elliott had come to know him well and marveled that someone capable of being such a gentleman would write about such grotesque and vicious characters. She said everyone in town regarded him as a hopeless drunkard much of the time. Once at a party at his house, she said, his daughter Jill told her friends, "If you see Pappy, just don't pay any attention to him: he's drunk."

Mrs. Elliott owned only one autographed Faulkner book, *Intruder in the Dust*, which she asked him to sign one day when he was passing by her house on his morning walk to the town square. He had never offered to sign a book for her, including those she had typed for him. Her relation with Faulkner was through Phil Stone, who was her employer, and the manuscripts passed from Bill to Phil to her and back to Phil and then Bill. It was strictly a business arrangement in which she always worked for Phil, not for Bill, so he felt no obligation to her. He would be courteous to her when they met, but that was all. She said there was no sense of a special friendship between them, ever.

When Bill first courted Estelle, in the early 1920s, she was considered the most eligible belle in town, while Bill was the least eligible bachelor. Later in their marriage, Bill became more prominent and Estelle less prominent, but the town regarded them as a couple who went their own way and did not expect social approval for anything they did. People were curious about them but respected their privacy. Their daughter Jill would become a more familiar person in town than her parents were.

Faulkner could be sociable when he chose to be. As a young man he belonged to a group his age who would meet after work. They called themselves simply "The Bunch." Peggy Whitehead was a member of "The Bunch," who liked to socialize with Phil Stone. Phil was an eligible bachelor who enjoyed the company of women as well as men. Bill Faulkner was a younger friend who was nearer the age of "The Bunch" and who renamed them "The Safety Pin Club." Bill and Phil were the only male members; the rest were young women, including Dorothy Oldham, who was Estelle Oldham's sister. Dorothy said that Phil Stone always wore a hat to cover his bald head, and went as far away as Charleston, Mississippi, for his haircuts, because he didn't want anyone in Oxford to see him getting a haircut. The only time he took off his hat was in court, when a judge told him he would be held in contempt of court if he didn't remove it.

The Bunch met on Sunday afternoons, a practice which was considered wicked by many townspeople, who thought them a racy crowd of young people. They met in Phil Stone's law office or in a restaurant called The Tea Hound. Bill Faulkner was the leader of the Bunch, entertaining them with stories they enjoyed hearing. They knew he had a fertile imagination but didn't think of him as a writer. His behavior could be unpredictable and moody. Sometimes he could be the life of the party, at other times morose and silent, at still other times drunk and distant. The Bunch engaged in intelligent conversation on a variety of subjects, but they were never a literary society, and Bill Faulkner, who was taciturn most of the time, talked easily at length if he felt like it.

Peggy Whitehead remembered an incident which happened long after The Bunch dissolved because it stuck in her mind. Andrew Price, the Negro man who looked after Bill Faulkner's horses, fell helplessly off a horse in front of her house and she tried to help him up but couldn't move him. She quickly called Rowan Oak and asked to speak to her friend Bill. A Negro houseboy answered the phone and said "Mr. Faulkner not at home." She insisted on speaking to him, saying "I know he's there. Go and tell him to answer me this minute." Bill did come to the phone finally, and she told him he needed to claim his "nigger" or she would have to call the ambulance. That alarmed him, and he told her "Don't let the law get hold of him, or they'll charge me $300 to bail him out. I know that nigger's as drunk as can be but please hold off calling the ambulance until I get there." He soon appeared in front of her house, helped the Negro man up off the street, propped him up, and supported him back to Rowan Oak. Later, whenever she saw Andrew, he would say "I haven't been drunk any more since you saw me fall down."

When The Bunch were younger and together more often, Bill Faulkner usually came barefoot to meet them, since he had formed the habit of going barefoot into town, knowing that everyone would notice it. Peggy Whitehead thought he really liked to shock the townspeople with his ragged dress and rude manners, and deliberately went around looking like a tramp to attract attention. He always did as he pleased, being elaborately courteous on occasion, or defiantly cold and arrogant if he chose to be. She thought he was never simply negligent but always conscious of the figure he cut with his friends and neighbors in Oxford. Phil Stone was also a loner who went his own way without caring what people thought about him, but except for wearing a hat all the time he was not nearly as eccentric as his friend Bill.

Phil Stone kept a small roulette wheel in his office and during off-hours presided over little games of chance with his friends. He took a strong interest in politics, and sometimes participated as a supporter of one candidate or another, but never as a candidate himself. He helped Branham Hume in his effort to become Mayor of Oxford. Bill Faulkner took little interest in politics, except once when his Uncle John ran for judge, and he went on the campaign tour but asked his friend Mac Reed to do all the talking.

After Faulkner's marriage to Estelle, Faulkner and Phil Stone drew apart, but in 1939 he called on Faulkner to help him out of a debt contracted by his father, General Stone, and Faulkner willingly agreed. He made up the sum of $6000 which Phil Stone owed by taking an advance of $1200 from Random House for his next book, and borrowing $4800 on his life insurance. Thus he repaid his personal debt to Phil Stone for his patronage in the early years when he was struggling to become a writer. That Phil Stone did not choose to repay Faulkner for his generosity would estrange them in subsequent years.

Peggy Whitehead, like many people who knew Faulkner in his home town, read some of his books and thought him a good writer, but not a great one, and in her view he began to believe too much in his own greatness, causing a breach in his friendship with Phil Stone as well as with other old friends. The Oldham family had disapproved of Estelle's romance with Faulkner, and had forced her to marry Cornell Franklin against her will. She regretted it, since Franklin proved unfaithful, and she divorced him, coming back to Oxford with the intention of taking up where she and Bill Faulkner had left off. He was willing, and she married him despite her family's continued disapproval, and despite having two children to raise They were married at College Hill Presbyterian Church rather than in Oxford, because her family still wouldn't countenance her marriage to Faulkner, though it was clear she still loved him. Bill and Estelle asked an old friend, Dr. Heddleston, a Professor of Philosophy at Ole Miss who served as supply pastor for the church, to officiate at their wedding.

The man Bill Faulkner sought out more than any other in Oxford was Mac Reed, co-owner of Gathright-Reed Drugstore on the town square. Theirs was a personal friendship that began in the early 1920s and continued until Faulkner's death in 1962, forty years later. It was cemented in 1922 when Bill asked Mac to accompany him on a campaign trip for his Uncle John Falkner, who was running for County Judge. His uncle lost the election, but Bill Faulkner and Mac Reed visited a number of towns and villages in Lafayette County to campaign for him. Bill asked Mac to speak on his behalf, since Bill hated public speaking as much as he hated politics. At each campaign stop, Bill would stand quietly by and Mac would dutifully praise his uncle as a lawyer who deserved to be a judge. Though his uncle did not become a judge, Bill was grateful to Mac Reed forever afterwards. Dr. Ashford Little, who knew them both well, was sure that Bill Faulkner went into the Gathright-Reed drugstore every day he was in town just to visit with his friend. Mac

Reed was unfailingly hospitable to everyone in town, making the drugstore Oxford's mecca. He not only dispensed non-prescription medicines to those who asked for them (he was not a pharmacist like his partner, Byron Gathright) but was ready to offer advice on all the various patent medicines, lotions, and nostrums which the drugstore stocked for its customers. The drugstore provided a magazine rack for browsers, and a rental library for anyone looking for a book to read, and offered a selection of new books for sale, including those by William Faulkner. Faulkner would come in regularly to talk with Mac, often staying to browse through the magazines and rental books, sometimes borrowing a book to take home, frequently buying tobacco for the pipe he perennially held in his mouth. He asked Mac to save any stale cigars for him because they made excellent pipe tobacco. Since their friendship was known to everyone in town, Mac Reed was often asked by customers as well as visitors if Faulkner would autograph the books they bought. Faulkner was notorious for refusing to give autographs, even to old friends or relatives, no matter how well he knew them, but he never refused a request from Mac Reed. Mac's daughter, Kitty, once took it upon herself to ask Faulkner to autograph one of his new books for her, and he obliged willingly, saying, "I can never refuse a favor to Mac Reed."

Faulkner was a regular customer at Gathright-Reed. He charged his purchases frequently and Mac accepted them, as other merchants in town were reluctant to do. Mac would patiently send bills to Faulkner's home every month without response, and then one day, Faulkner would come in after many months in debt, and write one check for the whole amount. Mac swore that Bill Faulkner always paid his bills in full, if not always on time, but not all Oxford merchants would have agreed. Mac remembered that only once, in all the time he knew Faulkner, did he refuse to let Faulkner charge a drug on credit, because Bill had come in visibly and fragrantly drunk. Mac had to tell him in his firmest but gentlest voice, "We just have to have our payments in cash these days, Bill." Faulkner was taken aback, but quickly recovered his composure. "I don't blame you a bit for saying that, Mac," he said as he left the drug on the counter, went away, and returned in a few minutes with the cash to pay for it.

On another occasion, about 1924, Mac recalled that Faulkner came into the drugstore and asked for a loan. Mac said he didn't have cash to spare, but could borrow on his life insurance if Bill really needed the money. He offered to advance as much as $50 if Bill would promise to pay it back in time for Mac to meet his annual premium on the insurance. Bill saw that it was a serious offer and asked for paper to write out a promissory note for $50. Mac said that wouldn't be necessary, that he would take Bill's word for it, but Bill insisted on giving him written proof of the loan. About a month later, before the premium was due, Bill Faulkner came back with the full $50 in cash. Mac offered to return the promissory note but Faulkner demurred, saying "Just tear it up," which was exactly what he did.

Mac Reed knew all the Faulkner family well, and they in turn knew and appreciated what a good friend he was to Bill, unlike many people in Oxford who had been snubbed by him or who had been unable to collect on his debts to them. Faulkner was forgetful by nature, and it was from "Miss Maud," Faulkner's mother, that Mac learned that Bill's forgetfulness went back to his boyhood. She said that once when he was playing in the house with his youngest brother, Dean, Bill locked him in a closet and then went downstairs to hunt and peck on his typewriter, already in the process of becoming an author. When Miss Maud, who had been out of the house, came back from an errand, she heard a noise upstairs. When she investigated the cause of it, she found Dean still locked in the closet, exhausted from crying for Bill to come and let him out. When she confronted Bill, demanding to know what had happened in her absence, Bill said offhandedly, "Oh, I guess I forgot him."

Bill Faulkner once told Mac Reed a humorous story about a Negro man who worked on his farm. The man had engaged in trading mules while he was drunk, and he later realized he had traded away a better mule than he received. He came to Faulkner and asked, "Mr. William, can't I sue for the return of my mule, on the ground that I was too drunk to know what I was doing?" Faulkner was unmoved, and told the man bluntly, "If you were fool enough to trade that mule when you were drunk, and you thought it was a fair trade, you've got no right to claim it was unfair when you're sober." Faulkner was usually sympathetic with black people, but in this case, he could see no legal remedy for the man's self-inflicted misfortune.

Faulkner held barbecues occasionally at Rowan Oak, and when he did, he would give his guests explicit directions for getting there: "You leave the square and come down South Street (now South Lamar) to Old Taylor Road. Turn right. Go on Old Taylor Road uphill a piece and go west till the road starts to bend left. Look to the right and you will see my place back in the cedars." Faulkner always referred to the Oxford streets by their earlier names: "North Street" for North Lamar and "South Street" for South Lamar, "Second South" for 11th Street, "Depot Street" for Jackson Avenue, and "Mill Street" for South 2nd Street.

When Faulkner became famous, a group of Ole Miss students got together and sent him a $10 check, saying they had heard he got ten dollars a word for his writing and asking him to send them one of his words. He answered, "Thanks."

When Faulkner won the Nobel Prize in 1950, he received $30,000, a handsome sum, and he wanted it to be spent wisely. So he asked his friend Mac Reed to keep the money in the drugstore safe, and dispense it as

Faulkner himself would indicate. Mac readily agreed, and for a number of years he waited for Faulkner to come and request funds, which he did on more than one occasion. The money went to young people Faulkner knew, who could not afford a college education but were qualified to earn one. On Faulkner's personal direction, Mac Reed issued checks to two black students in the Oxford area, and to a Japanese girl Faulkner met on his tour of Japan for the State Department. Faulkner had personally created a Faulkner Foundation with Mac Reed and his brothers Jack and Johnsy as Trustees, to administer the Nobel Prize money in case of his death, but the informal arrangement lasted only a few years, because in 1957 the remaining funds were turned over to an official William Faulkner Foundation at the University of Virginia, after Faulkner had accepted a position as Writer in Residence there. The funds were duly invested and earned interest to provide an ongoing Faulkner Prize for promising young novelists.

In 1961, the last full year of his life, Faulkner had become affluent enough to pay an income tax of $30,000, the full amount of his Nobel Prize award.

Byron Gathright, Mac Reed's partner in the drugstore, told an amusing anecdote about Faulkner from his personal experience. In 1931, Byron had been given the responsibility of recruiting Bill Faulkner to take part in an Oxford Junior Chamber of Commerce benefit show. Everyone knew that Faulkner came to the store every day to see Mac Reed, and so Byron buttonholed him one day to ask if he would consider playing a role in the Jaycee production of a popular comedy called "Corporal Egan." Bill told Byron he had just bought the Old Sheegog Place and was trying to make it a home fit to live in, but promised to think about the invitation. He thought about it and later surprised Byron, saying he'd like to take a part in the play. When the time came for the performance, Faulkner secretly arranged for a jug of moonshine whiskey to be provided to the members of the cast between scenes that would be accessible in the basement of the Oxford Grammar School Auditorium where the play was being staged. A colored boy was stationed to pour drinks between acts, and the crowd was treated to a performance such as they'd never seen before. It got funnier and funnier as the cast, including Bill Faulkner, got drunker and drunker. Bill had learned his lines for the play, but he started ad-libbing with his wry sense of humor, and the audience, knowing how normally reserved and unapproachable Faulkner was, could hardly believe what a talented comedian he was on stage that night. They all agreed it was the most successful show the Oxford Junior Chamber of Commerce had ever put on.

There was a Baptist minister in town whose first wife committed suicide (just like Rev. Hightower's wife in *Light in August*) and he married again. His second wife lived in the Wright-Purser mansion on University Avenue, leading from the town square to the Old Miss campus. She had been a classmate of

Estelle Oldham, and recalled that Estelle, like Bill Faulkner, never graduated from high school. Jill Faulkner would say of her father that "Pappy and I think formal education isn't really important," though she was herself a graduate of University High School in Oxford and Pine Manor College in Boston, and Faulkner was the speaker at both of her commencements.

Professor A. Wigfall Green, who admired him, thought Faulkner liked to change his costume at will, according to his humor, and noted that "Faulkner shocked the staid natives of Oxford by walking about the streets barefoot and by sitting on the floor of the local drugstore reading magazines. His favorite costume consisted of an olive drab Army shirt, a pair of wellworn Army trousers, and yellow shoes."

Mrs. Will Lewis knew Bill Faulkner from childhood on and was particularly close to his cousin, Sally Murry. She thought Bill cool but courteous in his manner, but she adored his father, who was "Uncle Murry" to Sally Murry. She felt that Faulkner's mother, "Miss Maud," received an undue amount of attention from Faulkner's admirers, while his father was really the more amiable personality. She showed me a picture of her school class in 1911 with Bill Faulkner standing next to her. She could remember when the Yoknapatawpha Drainage Company was formed, in order to keep the Yocana River within its banks, since it frequently overflowed in the spring floods (just as the Bundren family discover to their dismay in *As I Lay Dying*). In school, she said Bill Faulkner would line up, with the boys and girls in separate lines, to go out for recess, and then would disappear. He was never seen at school after recess. Mrs. Lewis said that his cousin Sally Murry often followed his example, playing hooky after recess.

Mrs. Lewis testified that no one who knew Bill as a boy thought he had unusual talent. They were all surprised when he turned out to be a professional writer. He had been befriended by Stark Young first, and later by Phil Stone, both of whom believed in his talent, but people who had grown up with him thought he was lazy and unambitious, a drifter rather than an achiever. "He could be completely alone in a crowd if he wanted to be," she said, and sometimes he deliberately snubbed her, although they had grown up together. He never liked to talk about books but did like to talk about horses, so people learned to ask him about horses if they wanted him to speak to them. He preferred the company of people who had not read his books, and once he told the wife of a friend not to read anything he had written, though she had been urged to do so by a Faulkner fan, because he wanted them to remain friends.

After Bill and Estelle were married in 1929, they lived in the apartment of Miss Ella Meek, who was credited with giving the university its nickname of "Ole Miss," a term of affection used by black slaves for the mistress of a plantation in the antebellum South. The name was well known, and long after its origin was forgotten, everyone referred to the University of Mississippi as Ole Miss.

Faulkner and his immediate family

Col. Cofield thought Bill Faulkner had stronger character traits than anyone he knew except for "Miss Maud," Faulkner's mother. He believed Faulkner's own character derived more from his mother than from his father, though his grandfather, John Wesley Thompson Falkner, was a powerful influence in the family as Faulkner grew up. It was he who insisted that the Falkner boys memorize a Bible verse every day and repeat it before they were allowed to have breakfast. Faulkner's writing demonstrates his thorough knowledge of the Bible, which he often quoted in his fiction. Cofield said Faulkner's mother could reason with her son when he would listen to no one else. She was a small woman like her son, weighing no more than 100 pounds, and spoke in a soft voice, yet she could dominate the family as no other member did. Her pupils were dark, almost black, and according to Col. Cofield, who photographed them both, "Miss Maud's black eyes could outflash Bill's."

One of Maud Butler Falkner's tricks to stop her son's drinking binges was to move from her little house on Lamar Street out to Rowan Oak, and coax him back to his senses by a combination of strong tea and whiskey, gradually reducing the amount of whiskey in the tea until it was nothing but tea, never telling Bill that she was weaning him off the bottle a little at a time. When she had accomplished her mission, she would move back home. Bill would plead with her to stay, telling her he was still too weak to get out of bed without a shot of whiskey, but she would say indignantly, "Huh! You've been drinking nothing stronger than tea for three days. Get up and put your clothes on and get to work!" He had no choice but to obey her.

It was "Miss Maud" who told Col. Cofield that Bill Faulkner began sporting a mustache as soon as he was old enough to grow whiskers, because he had the "Faulkner mouth," so slim that his father Murry nicknamed him "Snakelips." From about the age of 12, Faulkner began to cultivate the mustache to accentuate his upper lip, going through several color phases from blonde to brunette to grey to white, but it was always a prominent facial feature, starting in his later boyhood.

Miss Maud was an artist in her own right. Her hobby of painting flowers blossomed into a career at the age of 69, and she sold hundreds of paintings, not only of flowers, which were her favorite subject, but of birds, of people, and of cabin scenes with Negroes. Her son respected her work, and once suggested she put more Negro children in her cabin scenes, "You know how crowded those cabins always are, Mother." She painted so many flowers that she said she hoped she never had to paint another moss rose. She was proud of being an old-fashioned painter but resented comparisons with the consciously primitive works of Grandma Moses, which were popular in the country. When asked why she had become a professional painter so late in life, she said "It's nice to be independent at my age."

In the younger generation of the Faulkner family, his nephew Jimmy Faulkner, elder son of Johnsy, was his favorite. He had served as a Marine Air Force pilot in the Second World War, fulfilling a lifelong ambition of his uncle, which strengthened the bond between them. Jimmy was a playmate of Malcolm Franklin, Estelle's son and Bill's stepson, and Faulkner featured him in the only story Faulkner ever wrote about his own family, a self-parody called "Afternoon of a Cow" in which Faulkner and his nephew were the principal characters. Jimmy was often called on to look after Bill when he was too "sick," (meaning too drunk), to look after himself. He took Faulkner to the nearby sanitorium at Byhalia many times, including the last time, in 1962, where Bill Faulkner died suddenly of a heart attack. Faulkner left his nephew a bequest of $5000 in his will, a reward for many personal services which had brought Jimmy Faulkner in closer touch with his uncle than anyone in the younger generation of the family except his daughter Jill.

Jimmy Falkner called his uncle "Brother Bill" and said his sense of humor was what he remembered best. "When he was laughing, you only saw it in his eyes; they would sparkle, and crinkles would come at the corners." Faulkner was happiest with children, content just to watch them play. He once told Jimmy that he enjoyed watching a television cartoon series called "Huckleberry Hound" with Jimmy's children. "You mean you like to watch them watch it?" "That's right," Faulkner laughed.

Jimmy said his uncle was capable of playing games with people who badgered him for interviews. To a reporter who once rode with him from Memphis to Oxford, he pointed out places along the way, telling him that "Some of my kinfolks live up there." Jimmy knew he had no kin in the vicinity, but he was sending the reporter on a wild goose chase in search of information about him. He would sometimes answer the phone at Rowan Oak saying it was "Mr. Faulkner's residence," and then, if they asked to talk to him, he would say, "Mr. Faulkner's not at home."

Jimmy said the Faulkners perpetuated the same first names in every generation. Each male member would be given the familiar John, William, or James, as a first name, varying the middle name, as in the case of William Clark Faulkner (The Old Colonel) and William Cuthbert Faulkner (the writer). He himself had been named James Murry Falkner because his father, nicknamed Johncy, didn't want to have another John Wesley Thompson Falkner (The Young Colonel) in the family. The name of J.W.T. Faulkner had already passed down through four generations of Falkners.

Like most Americans, Jimmy said, Faulkner hated paying taxes to the government. When he sold the movie rights to a new novel, he told Jimmy that his agent had warned him, if he earned any more money that year, he would have to pay it all to the government. Jimmy heard him swear, "I'm not going to write another word, damn it." On another occasion, when Jimmy met his uncle at the Memphis airport, he forgot to pay the landing fee. Faulkner insisted on paying it for him, saying he would take the deduction off his income tax. "But Brother Will," Jimmy objected, "$1.50 isn't going to take much off your taxes." Faulkner explained that the amount didn't matter. What mattered was that "As an American citizen, it's my constitutional right to cheat the government out of every cent I can."

Jimmy agreed that his grandmother, "Miss Maud," had the strongest will in the family. She stood about 4'11" tall and weighed about 85 pounds, but she could bend any male member of the family to her will, including "Brother Bill." When the statue of a Confederate soldier was placed in the town square, with his rifle resting on the pedestal below him, she commented "If I'd made that statue, its rifle wouldn't be at rest." The Confederate statue had been placed in its position at the dictate of another member of the Faulkner family, "Aun-tee," the sister of Murry Falkner, who wanted to be able to see it clearly from her front porch on Lamar Street. When Jimmy was in training as a Marine pilot in South Carolina, Miss Maud came to visit him, and he introduced her to some of his Northern friends. She shocked them by asking him "Are these the god-damned Yankees you have to live with?" The Northern boys laughed to hear a woman use such profanity. Though his father and his uncle were painters as well as writers, Jimmy thought his grandmother was the best painter in the family.

He confirmed that Miss Maud was the only one who could control Faulkner's drinking by serving him strong tea with whiskey and gradually reducing the liquor until he was only drinking tea. Faulkner would fall for the trick while she was with him, but would go back on the bottle afterwards. Jimmy had his own way of dealing with his uncle's drinking bouts, fooling him after several days of steady drinking by making him promise to quit drinking next Tuesday. On Sunday Jimmy would tell him it was Tuesday, and Faulkner would start sobering up. But as soon as he was sober enough, he saw he had been tricked, and accused Jimmy of lying to make him stop drinking. Jimmy confessed, "Yes, I did, Brother Will, but aren't you glad you sobered up?" "No, sir," he said, and started drinking again.

Faulkner's story, "Afternoon of a Cow" was a hilarious self-parody. In it, Jimmy Faulkner was one of the real-life characters, along with Malcolm Franklin, Faulkner's stepson. Jimmy said the story was largely based on fact, since he could remember that he and Malcolm were given a .22 pistol to shoot, and they fired it in the pasture next to Rowan Oak, starting a grass fire that was the main incident in Faulkner's spoof. Some cows were frightened by the fire and ran into a deep ditch, from which they were unable to extricate themselves. The cows didn't think it was funny, he said, but Faulkner did. Jimmy said that when he read the story later, he saw what an outrageous sense of humor his uncle possessed. What was painful to the boys and the cows was hilarious to Faulkner. The name "Afternoon of a Cow" was Faulkner's witty parody of a well-known poem by the French poet Arthur Rimbaud: "L'Après Midi d'Une Faune" ("Afternoon of a Faun.")

Faulkner doted on his daughter, Jill, and was an attentive father who dutifully took her to school and went to her piano recitals when she was a girl. Jill Faulkner was always honest in speaking about her father, and would say of him quite openly, "Pappy liked the ladies." He not only liked them, he treated them with extravagant kindness. He paid a visit to his mother every day when he was in Oxford. He gave a hand-lettered and illustrated book of sonnets to Helen Baird in 1927, after proposing marriage to her and being refused, and then after she was married to another man he dedicated two of his novels to her. Two of his mistresses wrote books about their affairs with him. Meta Carpenter Wilde wrote in her memoir, *A Loving Gentleman*, that Faulkner made a bed of jasmine petals for her in Hollywood in the 1930s, and most telling of all, in the 1950s he gave the manuscript of *The Sound and The Fury*, which he personally regarded as the "best failure" of all his books, to Joan Williams, a mistress half his age, who first came to see him because she wanted to be a writer. Joan Williams would later write a novel fictionalizing their romance as *A Winter Love*. Jill knew that it was to please her that her father had traveled to Stockholm to receive the Nobel Prize for Literature in person, and later to deliver the commencement address when she graduated from University High School in Oxford, and again when she graduated from Pine Manor in Boston. His wife, Estelle, was his first sweetheart, and though he could not marry her when they were younger because her family didn't approve of him, he married her later, after she had divorced her first husband and brought two children home from China to live with them. Faulkner would do anything for the ladies he loved, and he loved a number of ladies, young and old.

The ladies in their turn did much for him. Jill and her mother knew about his philandering in Hollywood and elsewhere, but they accepted it as further evidence of his eccentricity. Meta Carpenter Wilde Rebner (she married again after her affair with Faulkner) wrote *A Loving Gentleman* in gratitude to Faulkner, and Joan Williams (who also married after her affair with Faulkner) wrote *A Winter Love* as a tribute to him. Jill always called her father "Pappy," a term of endearment which he fancied. Her influence was crucial in bringing him to Virginia, where he joined the Farmington Hunt Club with her, and became for the first time a serious commentator on his own works. It was because Jill had married a young lawyer, Paul Summers, Jr., and settled in Charlottesville, that Faulkner was persuaded to accept a position he had refused many times before, of being a Writer in Residence at the University of Virginia. As Faulkner's literary executrix, Jill Faulkner Summers was knowledgable and generous to everyone interested in her father and his work, never becoming a jealous guardian of his reputation.

Jill's loyalty to her father was tested many times, yet she remained devoted to him despite his philandering. He had love affairs with many younger women, and did not conceal his affairs from his wife and daughter. Jill told me that he often embarrassed her by his drunkenness, and more than once she had begged her father to stop drinking. When she heard him singing "When pansies fair and violets blue," as he always did as he began a drinking binge, she knew he was about to indulge himself in one of his bouts and would try to dissuade him. She pled with him to listen to his own daughter and give up drinking for her sake, but he would only look at her coldly and say "No one remembers Shakespeare's children."

Jill had grown up at Rowan Oak and continued to keep and ride horses in Virginia as he had taught her to do as a girl in Mississippi. Jill kept Faulkner's favorite jumper, Powerhouse, on her farm after his death, and she became a breeder of fine hunters as her father had been. "Pappy used to ride every day at Charlottesville," she said, "as he did at home, and he enjoyed going on fox hunts with other gentleman farmers in the Virginia countryside. He had more privacy here than at home, and he liked that." She admitted that "Pappy felt hounded at home and he never felt that way here." He had admitted, when asked, that Virginians were snobs, but said it was all right with him, because "he liked snobs."

Jill explained why her father gave the house in Oxford the name of Rowan Oak. "Pappy told me he had read *The Golden Bough* and learned of a Scottish superstition about the magical powers of the rowan tree, also called the mountain ash or mountain oak, often associated with the mistletoe, which was Fraser's 'golden bough.' Pappy kept a copy of *The Golden Bough* in his library and I remember it as one of the first adult books I ever read." She said her father did not have a particular oak tree in mind but liked the good luck implied by the name of Rowan Oak. She said her father often read her stories from books of mythology with lots of supernatural creatures in them, stories full of ghosts and superstitions of all kinds: "He liked that sort of thing," she admitted, "and so did I."

As for his writing, Jill said "Pappy wrote whenever the mood struck him." She said he was unpredictable in everything he did, but she had learned how to predict his behavior better than most people. He was always kind toward her, but he could be "bearish," she said, when a writing mood came over him. In her early childhood he wrote in the library at the front of the house, but in 1952, after he had won the Nobel Prize, he converted a back porch into an office where he could write with greater privacy. She said he would write any time, day or night, but preferred to write in the morning. When he wasn't writing, he was reading: "He kept a book in every room of the house, so that he wouldn't have to look far for one if he wanted to read. Pappy read books the way some people eat popcorn, by the handful." Jill said she had learned to follow her father's practice of reading more than one book at a time, alternating between them until she had finished.

Sometimes, she said, her father would read aloud to her passages he had written. "I think he wanted to see how they sounded." As she got older, he would sometimes ask her to transcribe some of his writing from his miniscule script to a typed copy, since he was never good at typing and his typescripts could be as hard to read as his manuscripts. She got to be good at deciphering his miniature script but sometimes had to ask him help her with his words. When she typed the pages of his handwriting, she would unconsciously correct the text for spelling, punctuation, and grammar, because "I believed in good grammar, even if Pappy didn't." Once his trusted editor at Random House, Saxe Commins, wrote to Bill to stop letting his daughter type for him, because she was changing his natural style too much.

Jill admitted that she was her father's favorite, and that she had persuaded him to go to Sweden to receive the Nobel Prize, "But once he decided to go, I think he really enjoyed it. He'd never liked to make public speeches before, but this time he knew he had an opportunity to say something that needed saying. I think he was surprised by the worldwide response to his acceptance speech in Stockholm, and so he went on speaking almost every time he was asked. At first, he would write out the speech carefully beforehand, but later he spoke impromptu, with just a few notes. I heard him speak in French, in Spanish, and once even in Greek! He liked to hear and use other languages, and had a natural ear for them."

Jill felt that her father had mellowed greatly in his later years, and was more at ease in meeting strangers and going to public ceremonies, but he still didn't like large gatherings, and if he had the choice he would always prefer the intimacy of his family and a few old friends. If a public occasion seemed inevitable, he would accept it with as much good humor as possible, and he did enjoy his job as Writer in Residence at the University of Virginia, as well as the goodwill tours he made as roving ambassador for the Department of State. He continued writing to the end of his life, whenever the mood struck him, alternating between longhand and two-finger typing: "When he got tired of one, he'd try the other." Sometimes she thought he wrote so fast that it seemed the words were being dictated to him rather than composed by him. He worked from memory, not from books, and he had such a storehouse of experience that he didn't have to think it through; it seemed to be already there, waiting to be set down in writing. He would have periods when he seemed to be charging his batteries, so to speak, not doing any writing, and then he would write continuously for long spells, day after day, and well through the nights.

I asked Jill if she thought her father had deliberately built a wall of silence around him, to keep the world at bay, if necessary, by ignoring it. She said, "No, I think his manner developed naturally; he wasn't one to pry into other people's business, and he didn't like to have them pry into his business." She said he never went out of his way to be rude to people, but if they insisted too much on intruding on his privacy, he felt he had the right to snub them. She thought he was the kind of person who minded his own business and expected others to do the same—or to suffer the consequences.

I asked her if she had any favorites among her father's books, and she said she liked them all, but some better than others. "I can't read *Pylon*, and some other stories like it. It's not that I'm prudish, but that kind of writing just bores me." She wasn't bored by *Sanctuary*, and thought it was a better novel than her father was willing to admit, even if it had made her cry the first time she read it. She thought she had read everything her father had written, at one time or another, but found some of the later stories and novels too wordy and therefore boring.

Jill said her father was most himself with children, and he came to Virginia as much to be with his grandchildren as with her. When his first grandson, William Cuthbert Faulkner Sommers, was born on April 15, 1956, he came to Charlottesville from Oxford to see him. That visit led to his appointment as Writer and Residence at the University of Virginia the following year. She said he was proud that one of his grandsons was named for him, and he enjoyed telling stories to them as he had once told them to her and her friends.

I asked her if she thought it strange that her father, who was so taciturn himself, should have invented characters who were tireless talkers, like Ratliff and Gavin Stevens. She agreed, and said she thought her father just couldn't get some of his characters to shut up. "I think he got tired of hearing Gavin himself," she said, and she felt he was also less sympathetic to the prolific Snopes clan than to the Sartorises and the Compsons and the Bundrens and the McCaslins. In other words, he looked on his created people in the same critical way he looked at real people.

Louis Cochran, who was the Editor of *The Mississippian*, the Ole Miss magazine, and later wrote books himself, said that he learned from some of his friends that Bill Faulkner was a poet. He invited him to contribute something, and Faulkner promptly produced one of his earliest published works, a sonnet "To a Co-Ed." Cochran said that no one really knew Faulkner, because he kept things to himself, but if he said he would write something for the magazine, he could be counted on to do so. Cochran thought Faulkner's talent for drawing was greater than his talent for writing, and acknowledged that Faulkner had surprised him later on by becoming an outstanding writer. He admitted his own books had brought him little fame, but Faulkner's fame was established so widely throughout the world that he was known simply as "Faulkner," the mark of universal success. Of the many funny stories he heard about Faulkner, he believed what he was told, that Faulkner had gone to brothels in Memphis to get material for *Sanctuary*, but if one of the ladies solicited his favors, he would say, "I'm here to do research." As an FBI specialist in the white slave trade, Louis Cochran testified that there was no doubt *Sanctuary* was authentic. Faulkner understood the degradation women suffered in "the world's oldest profession" but was interested in their condition morally, not pornographically. He said that *Sanctuary*, Faulkner's most shocking novel, was a masterpiece, because of its deep insight into human evil.

In 1920, when Louis Cochran and Bill Faulkner knew each other at Ole Miss, there were only about 600 students on campus, most of whom knew each other. Faulkner had come back from service in Canada at the end of the First World War, wearing a uniform and swaggering around town, filling the students with envy. "If you saw him on campus, he acted as if he didn't see you, but if you spoke to him, he would stop and talk very agreeably and politely with you. I liked him, but he was a Faulkner, and everyone looked on him as part of a special breed, according him the sort of distant admiration he seemed to expect." He said he knew that Faulkner had talent much greater than his own, but could remember paying 75 cents for Faulkner's first book, *A Marble Faun*, which the bookseller said she couldn't sell. Cochran said "I think Faulkner was wise to abandon poetry; it was not his strength." Faulkner's novels were much better, he thought, but the only place in Oxford where you could buy them was the Gathright-Reed drugstore. Cochran wrote a short article about Faulkner for *The Memphis Commercial Appeal* in which he said that he had been Faulkner's first editor, and believed he had real talent, which would eventually result in fame and fortune. But he also knew the Ole Miss librarian in his day would never allow a book by William Faulkner to be placed on her shelves.

"Colonel" J. R. Cofield. was the professional photographer in Oxford who took many pictures of Faulkner, often on request. Cofield confirmed that Faulkner was unusually photogenic, which gave him the satisfaction of making handsome portraits of him. Faulkner's face was highly expressive, the features sharply delineated. The renowned French photographer, Henri Cartier-Bresson, made a number of notable photographic studies of Faulkner, at home and at West Point. J. R. Cofield of Oxford knew Faulkner well, and induced him to have his picture taken more often than he might have wished. The results were some of the most distinguished of all the

Faulkner portraits. Cofield had admired Faulkner from the time he first met him, because "he was even more fascinating as a man than as a writer." Most Faulkner portraits are serious, whether formal or informal, since Faulkner seldom smiled, though Col. Cofield said he once caught a smiling image of Bill Faulkner at the wedding of his niece, Dean Faulkner, when he was standing in the reception line greeting guests. He asked Faulkner to autograph the books of photographs he published, and Faulkner usually agreed, but the only voluntary autograph Faulkner ever gave him was on the back of a picture Cofield had taken of a mule, meant for an illustration of a passage in *Sartoris* which eulogizes the mule. Faulkner had written that the mule was a beast of burden worthy to be immortalized by "some Homer of the cotton field." Col. Cofield showed his picture of the mule to Bill Faulkner, and praised Faulkner's description of the mule in his novel. Faulkner agreed, "It sounds pretty good by itself, don't it?" Then on an impulse he asked, "Would you like me to autograph this for you?" and proceeded to write his name on the back of Cofield's photograph of the mule.

Faulkner looked quite handsome in most of the portraits Col. Cofield made of him, but on one occasion he demanded and got a grim picture of himself to use in applying for a commission in the Army Air Force as World War II was beginning. In 1941, when the Japanese attacked Pearl Harbor, Faulkner was 44 years old, and the Army refused to commission him on the grounds of age. He thus missed combat in both World Wars, and it may have been in compensation that he wrote his second "war novel," *A Fable*, which fictionalized the battlefront in the First World War even more fully and directly than he had in his first war novel, *Soldier's Pay*. These two novels were among his weakest, perhaps because they memorialized a conflict he had never witnessed personally, though he had wished for the experience when he was younger. His novels about the Civil War, *Absalom, Absalom!* and *The Unvanquished*, were much more realistic and convincing than his novels about the First World War. The conflict within his country, between the North and the South, fought mainly on Southern soil, was more real to him than any conflict on foreign soil.

Bramlett Roberts, a lawyer in Oxford and son of "Mr. Ike" Roberts was one of Faulkner's hunting companions. He regarded Faulkner as a "real man" who was loyal to his friends, and who came to see Mr. Ike often during his final illness. Bramlett said Faulkner spoke very little, but "Bill was one of the best listeners I ever knew." He became more voluble when he drank, a fact that may have been one reason for drinking so often. His eyes were so expressive, sometimes seeming to dance, and at other times to squint, that he could communicate without saying a word. Once he came to dinner at the Roberts house. He said nothing until he got up from the table, but as he left he told them "I've enjoyed the evening very much, gentlemen." He could be very friendly when he met you, or he could ignore you completely. His companions sometimes made fools of themselves, trying hard to get Faulkner to talk, but he would remain silent. Bramlett said that when you were with him, you knew you were in the presence of a great man, though he was typically shy, modest, and taciturn, but according to Bramlett, Faulkner never made you feel uncomfortable with him. Mr. Ike, Bramlett's father, told him that Faulkner was a tireless hunter who could walk all day in the woods and sleep outdoors in a sleeping bag. He was capable of stalking deer by standing motionless for hours, waiting for a single shot, then firing and sometimes hitting his prey, but not always, because he wasn't a deadeye with a rifle. He was an enthusiastic hunter who enjoyed killing game and was never squeamish about it. He liked to talk about outdoor sports, hunting first of all, but also flying and sailing. He did not like to talk about politics and he hated dirty jokes and loose talk about women. He would tell jokes on himself about his drinking, but "if he had drunk as much as people thought he did, he could never have written all those books." He was sober most of the time but occasionally went on sprees and drank to excess. He did not like to talk about his books, but once, when Bramlett Roberts asked him why he wrote *Sanctuary*, he said he had grown tired of writing stories and books that couldn't be published and didn't sell if they were published. "You might say I wrote *Sanctuary* on a dare. I wanted to break into print, and make money on a book of mine, and I did. If I hadn't written *Sanctuary*, my name might never have been well-known until after I was dead. Who knows?" Bramlett had read much of what Faulkner had written, and he believed that there was the full range of humanity in his work, because he portrayed some characters who were much better than he was and some that were much worse, but if you read all he had written, you knew that on the whole he had a balanced view of human beings.

Bramlett Roberts thought Faulkner respected human dignity wherever he found it, regardless of race, sex, or age. Faulkner recognized that the South had much to answer for, and thought it had brought most of its troubles on itself, but he felt that everyone deserved the freedom to be what he wanted to be, to be given the opportunity to earn what he could, without being hindered or favored by others. Bramlett believed that Faulkner was a critic of the South because he was a critic of humanity, with all its strengths and weaknesses. Bramlett said that Faulkner liked to read Charles Dickens for his social criticism, and sometimes brought a Dickens novel along to read on the hunt. He also liked to read Sherwood Anderson, an early influence on his own writing. Faulkner once expressed the view that Anderson withheld some of the honest truth about human beings, for fear of being judged a monster. Faulkner had no such fear, Bramlett said; he wrote realistically about men as he saw them and tried to be as honest in judging them as it was possible to be.

Faulkner, Bramlett Roberts said, was a natural writer, who wrote more easily than he talked. He was never at a loss for words when he had a pen in his hand or a typewriter handy. He died before he was written out, and had more books in his head than he could ever complete, because he was a constant observer of human beings and never lacked for subject matter. He wrote directly from life, mixing fact and fiction so that you could never be sure what he had actually witnessed and what he had made up. Bramlett thought that knowing Faulkner as a man was a great privilege, because his character was as solid as his work, and he understood the full capacity of human beings for good or evil.

Christine Drake, who had been an English major at Vanderbilt, came to live with Faulkner's mother for two years from 1951-53. She said Miss Maud was a bundle of energy, pursuing her own vocation of painting with determination every day. She liked to copy Old Masters for sale, especially favoring Vermeer, and did many paintings of flowers that were marketable. She once said, in an aside to Christine Drake, "I think I can't bear to paint another primrose." She also did portraits on occasion, and painted both Bill Faulkner, her son, and Mammy Callie, the Faulkner family governess, in likenesses that Faulkner kept in his library where he did much of his writing. Miss Maud was determined to be financially independent after her husband's death, and was independent in other ways as well, saying once of a dish that was offered her for dinner, "I don't like that. Those Falkners are the ones who like it." She might well have been a model for Aunt Jenny in *The Unvanquished*, as well as for Rosa Coldfield in *Absalom, Absalom!* or for Miss Habersham in *Intruder in the Dust*, all doughty women who could be as stubbornly individual as the men. But she was an artist in her own way, and she appreciated the artistic talents of her sons, William and John, who were always "Billy" and "Johnsy" to her. She said "I never lost my faith in Billy" though he tried her patience many times over. She seemed confident that "Billy" would make it as a professional writer despite the town's low opinion of him, and she seemed to know that "Johnsy" would not do well as a writer or a painter, even with the indulgence of the town. There were times when she seemed almost incredulous about William Faulkner's success, as if she wondered whether he could really be her son.

For his part, Faulkner was customarily loyal and polite to his mother, calling on her just to say hello, especially on Sunday mornings. He would be quite formal in his behavior toward his mother, and deferential to her companion. Once he complained of a headache, and arriving earlier than usual, before Christine Drake was out of bed, he whispered to his mother, "I hope we don't wake the young lady." His mother retorted in a loud voice, "I hope we do. She ought to be out of bed by now anyway." That woke her up. She dressed and joined them, but Faulkner said nothing more to either of them, sitting silently while the two women tried to make polite conversation. After perhaps an hour of sitting and saying nothing, aware that the two women were conversing without him, he got up from his chair and bowed to them, saying, "I feel better now. Thank you, ladies, for an interesting visit. I must be going."

Christine Drake remembered an amusing anecdote a friend of Faulkner's had told her about him. He came to the town square as usual one day, and was surprised when a Negro woman who had once worked for him said: "Mr. Bill you been havin' some of your books come out and I been readin' 'em all." He thanked her and said he hoped she would continue to do so. A few years later she saw him again and apologized for not having read his two latest novels because 'I ain't been able to focus so well since my husband cut my throat." Miss Drake asked Faulkner, on one of his visits to his mother, "Did she really say that?" All Bill Faulkner answered was, "Yep, that's what she said, all right."

Miss Maud showed Miss Drake her collection of Faulkner books which he had inscribed for her, and offered to let her read them, but she couldn't bear to borrow books that were personal gifts, fearing she might sully them. She thought Miss Maud read some of the books but not all of them, and liked certain characters Faulkner had created, even if she did not find the harsh realism of his treatment of human beings to her taste. She was offended when *Life* magazine did a pictorial essay on Faulkner, and immediately wired the editor to cancel her subscription, though it had been given to her by her son Jack.

She painted some folksy scenes of Southern landscapes with Negro cabins and black children playing in the fields, attracting a New York art dealer who offered to take them to a gallery for sale. She was elated to think that her paintings might reach a sophisticated public outside the South, and hoped that "At last someone might buy my paintings for some reason other than the Faulkner signature." But when the art dealer brought them back unsold, after the Supreme Court's desegregation ruling in 1954, she was bitterly disappointed by the explanation he gave: "People up here don't want to look at this kind of picture any more."

Another neighbor, Mrs. Marjorie Fox, wife of a law professor at Ole Miss, who lived in "Linfield," one of the Oxford Pilgrimage Homes built in 1837, used to watch Faulkner walk into town every morning along Old Taylor Road. He was aloof and distant and seldom spoke to anyone or even looked their way. But on one occasion, when her mother was visiting her from England, the two women were walking back from town on a very hot day and were surprised to see Faulkner stop his battered station wagon near them and offer them a ride. They were relieved to accept his offer, and got in the car for the ride home, a short distance away. Her mother carried on a lively but one-sided conversation with Bill Faulkner, since whatever she said to him, all he would answer was "Yes'm." When he stopped in front of their house and got out, her mother said "Mr. Faulkner, I've enjoyed talking with you and I hope to see you again. I don't see very well at my age, but if you see me, just yell out 'Hello, Mrs. Gibbons!'" To her surprise, from then on, whenever Faulkner walked by their house, he would tip his hat, bow, and call out loudly, "Hello, Mrs. Gibbons. How are you today?"

Faulkner was well known in Oxford despite his reticence and aloofness, and many people felt free to offer their opinions of his eccentric behavior to strangers who inquired about him, as they often did. A newspaper reporter came to town and asked if anyone could give him a few facts about the writer William Faulkner. One man, dressed in rough work clothes, proceeded to fill the reporter's ear with stories of the peculiar habits and undoubted achievements of Bill Faulkner. When he walked away, the reporter asked "Do all the farmers around these parts go to the university?" A listener said to him, "That was no farmer. That was the dean of the law school." Dean Robert Farley knew Faulkner well, and he happened to be dressed for yard work when the reporter plied him with questions.

One of Faulkner's early admirers was an English professor at Ole Miss, Harry Campbell, who published one of the first books about his work, and who once held the Oxford Rotary Club spellbound with a reading of one of his earliest stories, "Two Soldiers."

In general, the town's opinion of Faulkner was as "some kind of oddball" who was never seen to be working as most men did to make a living, who was delinquent in paying his bills, and had the reputation of a deadbeat who chalked up debts all over town. Oxford businessmen were indulgent up to a point, but often became exasperated by his refusal to pay on time. What they didn't know was that Faulkner was capable of prodigious writing feats which the town never saw. The most famous was his claim that he had written one of his best novels, *As I Lay Dying*, in six weeks on the back of a wheelbarrow which was used to carry coal to the furnace in the university powerhouse. It was believable, however, since Faulkner was the supervisor while other men did the shoveling, so he had the leisure to write while others worked.

His habit as a grown man was to stroll down Second South Street (now S. 11th Street) to the town square, and then plant himself in front of the Gathright-Reed drugstore, leaning against the window and watching the citizens come and go, usually without speaking to them even when they spoke to him, and then going into the store to browse the magazine rack or the rental bookrack, exchange a few words with his old friend Mac Reed, and walk back home again in the same leisurely way. One of his younger friends remembered saying "Hello, Mr. Bill" to him and getting no recognition from Faulkner, but on another occasion Faulkner spoke directly to him without being asked, saying "Come here, Aston, I want to talk to you a minute." He was unpredictable in his manner towards others, sometimes very polite, sometimes rudely aloof, and people accepted it as his odd way of behaving. He might well have been living in his imagination rather than in the real world much of the time.

Faulkner bought a 1937 Ford phaeton new and drove it till it fell apart in the 1950s. Sometimes Faulkner could be very practical in helping his neighbors, contrary to his usual distant manner. The wife of a Methodist missionary remembered that he once offered her a piece of advice to prevent her pipes from freezing in the winter; "Just put a piece of wood in the tank, Mrs. Bourland. The water will freeze around it and it will keep the pipes from bursting."

Mildred Murry Douglas Hopkins, wife of a doctor in Oxford, was a girlhood friend of Jill Faulkner and often played with her at Rowan Oak. They were inseparable friends and her father was very kind to them. He was naturally reserved but enjoyed entertaining them with stories, and she came to be treated like a member of the family. She knew the Faulkners were peculiar but she got used to their habits, and they seemed to be happy for her to be friends with Jill and come to the house as often as she liked. One of their playmates was a little black girl, the daughter of Lula Belle Lester who worked for the Faulkners, who was called "Little Estelle" by the adults but "Boojack" by Jill and Mildred Murry. They had no consciousness of racial differences in their play, whether with dolls in the house, or outside wading in the creek or fishing. Once the three girls were taken on a trip together to Jackson, Tennessee, as if it were a perfectly natural friendship. As they grew up, however, the white girls began to ride their ponies together, while the black girl took little part in their activities because the racial divide between them had become too obvious.

Jill's father never rode with the two girls, because he didn't acquire a horse until later, when they changed from ponies to horses for their rides in Bailey Woods. Jill owned a horse called "Lady" which had been bought in California while Faulkner was writing screenplays in Hollywood in the early 1940s. What Mildred Murry remembered most vividly were the annual Halloween parties at Rowan Oak. Faulkner delighted in telling ghost stories to children and invented a ghost for Rowan Oak, which he called "the ghost of Judith Sheegog." It was said that she had died falling from a ladder when trying to elope. The family claimed to hear her playing the piano downstairs when they were in bed, and Cho-cho claimed she saw her one night. Once when Mildred Murry Douglas was having dinner with the Faulkners, in the dining room with silver and crystal on the table according to their custom, they heard a noise upstairs and she was told it was the ghost of Judith Sheegog. They said her grave was in the woods below Rowan Oak, and that her spirit rose up every Halloween and walked to the house. This ghost was visibly "resurrected" by a figure in a white sheet slowly walking towards the little girls who were frightened to death. She could remember that she was once shown a letter addressed to Judith Sheegog from Victoria Franklin, "Cho Cho," who was visiting her father Cornell Franklin in China. Bill, Estelle, Jill, and Mildred Murry took the letter down to the "grave of Judith Sheegog" and buried it. Faulkner solemnly read a ghost passage from a Shakespeare play to commemorate the ceremony. No one was allowed to smile or laugh until they had returned to the house, but she recalled nervous laughter when they were safely indoors again. Other children Jill's age were often invited to the Halloween parties and eagerly listened to the ghost stories Faulkner liked to tell, since he had acquired a reputation for scaring them silly and they loved it.

Mildred Murry went over to Rowan Oak so often to see Jill that Faulkner seldom interrupted his work to greet her, whether he was chopping wood with his shirt off or planting flowers in the yard. He would pause briefly and motion to her, "Go on in, Mildred Murry, you're at home." The house seemed shabby to her compared to her own home, with a broken down front porch and a back porch that was used for picnics and parties. Sometimes she would see him reading or writing in the library, using pen and ink or a portable typewriter to set down his thoughts. He had not yet added the office to his house, and did his writing in the clutter of a room full of books and lawn chairs and even saddles. Sometimes he would give the little girls a few of the pages he was writing, and tell them to punctuate it as they saw fit, making it read more clearly if they could. She said it always seemed to her that his writing needed punctuation and they would do their best to improve it and hand it back to him. Whether he accepted their punctuation she never knew. Sometimes Faulkner would take Jill and her friends on picnics, when he would be at his merriest, tossing them up in a blanket for fun, watching them wade in a pond while he sang "Water Boy," telling them stories which the children loved to hear.

Hodding Carter, Editor of the *Delta Democrat-Times* in Greenville, Mississippi, was a frequent visitor to Oxford and knew Faulkner well. He said Faulkner could be quite inhospitable to strangers who tried to intrude on his privacy, and he objected especially to hunters coming into Bailey Woods in search of small game, such as quail and squirrels. He put up a "No Trespassing" sign at his gate and expected it to ward off unwelcome visitors, though it was sometimes ignored by people seeking to get a glimpse of the famous author. He was known to dig holes in the gravel driveway leading to Rowan Oak to impede uninvited guests, and on at least one occasion he embarrassed one of his friends who was seated on the porch with him. Hodding Carter was on such good terms with Faulkner that he was allowed to publish on his own press an episode of the novel, *A Fable*, called *Notes on a Horse Thief*, in a special limited, autographed edition. Hodding Carter said of Faulkner that "his ways of discouraging the uninvited and unwanted tourist could be indescribably Rabelaisian." It was Carter who liked to tell the story about the time when he was sitting in friendly conversation with Bill Faulkner on his porch, when he became so indignant to see an intruder walk right through the gate and up the gravel drive toward the house that he stood up, said "Well, he's come to have a look at me and I'll give him an eyeful," opened his fly, and urinated into the bushes. His behavior shocked Carter, but successfully repelled the stranger.

Carter, a Southern journalist and editor who greatly admired Faulkner as a writer, called him a "renegade in his homeland" because he supported the Supreme Court desegregation order in 1954. However, he affirmed that "By every standard, Faulkner is Southern, as much so today as ever. The town in which he lives by choice is an epitome of Southernness. So is the faded majesty of the ante-bellum home in which he dwells there. He is Southern in his pride in the past, in his chumminess, in his love of the land; and in the ambivalent love and outrage with which he confronts the South." Faulkner publicly expressed his support for the Supreme Court desegregation order in November of 1955, when he addressed the Southern Historical Association convention in Memphis. He said that racial segregation had been declared illegal, but he felt that racial integration might not be acceptable, even to American Negroes. He warned that if public school integration were forced too quickly on the South, a new Civil War might be the unintended result. Faulkner died in 1962, before more radical Civil Rights legislation was enacted by Congress and Martin Luther King led a non-violent resistance movement in the country, but he foresaw a troubled period of racial relations coming, in which the South would have to learn to live with school desegregation. He was speaking as a Southerner, anticipating that forbearance on the part of both the white and the black races was needed to maintain civil order. Faulkner was neither conservative nor liberal in his social views. He was a moderate who hoped that a balanced view of racial integration would prevail over any possible violent reaction. Certainly his fictional treatment of the black race was realistic but compassionate, sympathetic with their aspiration to rise from slavery to full equality with the white race they had long served. His black characters can be heroes as well as villains, but each of them is as believably human as any white character. The ultimate test of Faulkner's racial views is to be found in his fiction, where he is neither an advocate nor an opponent of the existing relations between blacks and whites, but an honest recorder of the behavior of both races towards each other. He took the historical view of Southern society, dealing with antebellum slavery as well as postbellum emancipation, always recognizing the dignity and worth of every individual, black or white. Joe Christmas, the main character in *Light in August*, is a tragic figure of mixed race, while Lucas Beauchamp, the main character of *Intruder in the Dust*, is a heroic figure of mixed race. Faulkner saw as many possibilities of good and evil in the black race as in the white race. Dilsey Gibson, a black servant in the Compson family but a major character in *The Sound and The Fury*, is one of his finest creations. "Dilsey is one of my own favorite characters," he said to his audience in Virginia, "because she is brave, courageous, generous, gentle and honest. She's much more brave and generous and honest than me." Dilsey is the best proof that his black characters could be more virtuous than his white characters. She stands for the ultimate evenhandedness of Faulkner's views on race.

There are many real counterparts of Faulkner's fictional landmarks, such as Dutchman's Bend on the Yocony River—which is Frenchman's Bend in Yoknapatawpha County—and the Old Shipp Place, one of many weather-beaten mansions slowly decaying in the countryside, which could be the Old Frenchman Place, and the village of Taylor near Oxford with a general store like the Varner store, and Tobatubby's gravemound in the woods, like Sam Father's grave in *The Bear*, venerated by Ike McCaslin. There are also personal names that are very close to the fictional names Faulkner made famous, such as Jacob Thompson for Jason Compson and Boatright for Bookright, and Suratt for a character whose name Faulkner changed to Ratliff because he didn't want the real and fictional names to be the same, and Ike Roberts for Ike McCaslin. There was also a legendary bear in the Delta called "Old Reel Foot" which the hunters talked about but never saw, corresponding to Faulkner's fictional "Old Ben," the huge symbol of the Wilderness in *The Bear*. "Popeye" was the real name of a Memphis gangster, Popeye Pumphrey, and "Mr Binford" was the name of a Memphis vice crusader, which Faulkner slily gave to one of Miss Reba's dogs. Faulkner picked up some of his names from buildings on the Ole Miss campus, such as Vardaman, Peabody, and Isom. From the Old Sheegog Place where he lived, he took the name of Rev. Shegog, the black preacher from St. Louis, who delivers the Easter sermon on "the ricklickshun and blood o' de lamb" to Dilsey and her family in *The Sound and The Fury*. Faulkner and his brothers called their maternal grandmother "Damuddy," just as the Compson children do in *The Sound and the Fury*. Phil Stone had twin great-uncles, Theophilus and Amodeus Potts, nicknamed "Uncle Buck" and "Uncle Buddy," like the fictional brothers in *Go Down, Moses*.

Since Faulkner started his literary career in New Orleans with the help of Sherwood Anderson, it is probable that he went to some French Quarter brothels with Anderson, but not likely that he was ever involved in "rum running" as he later claimed, though he certainly would have been familiar with bootleggers in that Prohibition era.

Faulkner preferred writing at home to writing anywhere else, but if the opportunity presented itself he could write wherever he happened to be, which might be Hollywood or New York instead of Oxford. Random House provided him office space on occasion and once when he was in New York early in his writing career, he stayed in the apartment of a friend, Corey Ford, who wrote for *The New Yorker*. Ford reported in *A Time of Laughter* (1967) that Faulkner wrote with his shoes and socks off, pounding his portable typewriter in the middle of the living room, under the watchful eye of a Scottish housekeeper, who would pounce on the sheets he sometimes ripped out of the typewriter and threw on the floor and promptly burned them in the fireplace. Faulkner seemed to pay little attention to anything except what he was writing and wasn't bothered by her fastidiousness.

Sometimes when Faulkner was in New York alone, Faulkner liked to go to Woolworth's and buy cheap notebooks, return to his apartment, take off his shoes and socks, sit on the floor, and with a bag of peanuts and a bottle of gin, fill the notebooks with handwriting, and when he had no more blank notebooks, take them to Ben Wasson's office to be transcribed on the typewriter by a secretary.

When Robert Coughlan did a piece for *Life* magazine in 1954 on "The Private World of William Faulkner," it enraged Faulkner's mother and enraged Faulkner himself even more. Faulkner wrote a rebuttal of it called "The American Dream: What Happened to It," contending that the invasion of privacy was destroying the individual freedom of Americans.

By the early 1940s, when the Second World War was about to erupt, Faulkner was well enough known to attract the attention of the New York publishing world, and Brooks Atkinson, the theatre critic of the *New York Times*, was sent by his editors to Oxford to see how Faulkner's home town was faring after the Pearl Harbor attack had plummeted the nation into war. He noted that "On Saturday, which is 'country day,' the people from the farms throughout the county, both black and white, flock to the square to trade and talk with their friends. Oxford changes its habits slowly, if at all." He concluded that "nothing has changed the square much since Union soldiers burned it during the Civil War." He made a point of meeting Bill Faulkner, its most famous living citizen, who was serving as Home Defense chief, and his friend Mac Reed, who was serving as chairman of the Selective Service Board. He was amazed to see that "Mack Reed, druggist and civic leader, is on the jump in his store and out." Mac Reed would be especially active if a band of Oxford boys was about to depart for Army training camp, and would give them a rousing send-off:

"When the boys clamber aboard the bus, Mack Reed, chairman of the [draft] board, says good-bye to each boy in turn, shaking hands and calling him by his first name, but his bus-side manner has been criticized. One of Oxford's selectees recently sent him a word of advice from camp: 'Don't tell the boys good-bye in such a final tone of voice,' he said."

Brooks Atkinson was taken out to Rowan Oak by Branham Hume, then Mayor of Oxford and son of the Chancellor of the University of Mississippi, as well as one of Faulkner's oldest friends. As they approached the house, Faulkner's daughter Jill saw them and called out "Pappy, Branham Hume and another gentleman are here to see you." Faulkner emerged in tennis shorts and shoes, and proceeded to hold the interview quite informally on his porch. The Atkinson piece was published in the Sunday, July 26, 1942, issue of *The New York Times*, VII, 11 & 27, headed "Oxford, Miss., In This Year of War."

Faulkner's compassion for others

Although Faulkner could be aloof to the point of rudeness at times, he could also be quite considerate if he chose. He was particularly kind to a mentally handicapped daughter of the Calvin Browns, reading to her many afternoons and even writing a poem especially for her which was greatly appreciated by her parents. Once at a dinner party at the home of friends, Dr. and Mrs. Ashford Little, a guest pulled out a chair for one of the ladies, who missed the seat and slipped under the table. Bill Faulkner was seated opposite her, and quickly got up out of his chair and pulled it out, then slipped under the table himself. All the guests were surprised at this unexpected gentlemanly gesture, but they laughed together when Faulkner and the lady stood up again. The dinner proceeded convivially, after Faulkner had saved a guest from public embarrassment by his quick reaction to her plight.

Mrs. Duncan, an Oxford woman who knew Faulkner well, remembered instances of his kindness to her. Once when she was walking along the town square she slipped on a banana peel and fell sprawling on the sidewalk, unable to get up again. Several people saw her distress but did not offer to help her. Faulkner drove by in his pick-up truck and stopped, got out, helped her to her feet, then offered to take her to a doctor. She told him she was all right and could go back home without any help. The next day he called at her door with his hounds beside him and asked if she were feeling better. He said "I bin worried about you since yestiddy" and was ready to help her see a doctor until she assured him she was fine. On another occasion, when she was babysitting for a neighbor, a little boy she was supposed to be watching wandered away and didn't return. She saw Bill Faulkner walking nearby and asked if he had seen the little boy. "No, ma'am," he said, but when she said she was going to ask the police to help her find him, Faulkner said, "Mrs.

Duncan, that ain't necessary. You go on back in the house and look after the other children and I'll find him for you." He went to Bailey Woods and found the little boy playing happily, unaware that he was missed, and Faulkner walked him back to the house where Mrs. Duncan was babysitting. She was greatly relieved.

Mac Reed remembered a similar incident, when he saw Bill Faulkner walking along the town square with a little boy, who was calmly eating an ice cream cone. Seeing Mac, Faulkner asked him "Do you know whose little boy this is?" Mac said he didn't recognize him, and wondered how Bill came to befriend him. Faulkner said he saw the little boy looking lost outside the movie theatre and took him to the drug store for an ice cream cone to quiet him down. The two men waited together until the frantic mother came out of the theatre and claimed her little boy gratefully, saying he had left his seat while she was watching the movie and had not come back.

Faulkner's writing habits

In his early years, Faulkner liked to write in longhand at an old-fashioned standup desk with a footrest. His neat but miniscule handwriting was hard to read, and later he would write at a desk with a portable typewriter, making his manuscripts more legible, but he never learned touch typing and so laboriously hunted and pecked his way through his stories and novels.

His mature practice was to write a story first in longhand and then revise it with interlineated passages and longer passages pasted in. Then he would do a typescript on his portable typewriter, using his patented hunt-and-peck technique. He would revise as he went along. Finally he would do a complete typescript with a carbon copy, keeping the carbon copy when he sent off the original for publication.

Faulkner usually did all the revising himself, but in his early days he let Phil Stone make suggestions, and in a famous case turned over what he called *Flags in the Dust* to his friend and fraternity brother Ben Wasson, who changed it into *Sartoris* and made it publishable--as it hadn't been before his revision. Then there was the even more celebrated case of *Sanctuary*, which reached the galley proof stage before Faulkner himself decided it had to be revised for publication even if it cost him money, and he handled that revision entirely on his own. There were later editors he respected, especially Saxe Commins at Random House, whose suggestions he would take, and an agent named Lemuel Ayers who helped him extensively with *Requiem for a Nun*. The book was an experiment in combining a novel with a play, and Ayers first made some recommendations orally as they shared a drink of "tall corn," and then by means of a long memorandum he wrote to Faulkner which Faulkner kept with his manuscripts. Ayers suggested strengthening the dramatic intensity of the play-scenes by improving the dialogue, making it more dramatic, less philosophical, especially in the final scene with Temple Drake. Mainly Ayers was trying to persuade Faulkner to be less preachy than he tended to be in his later novels, less didactic and more dramatic. It was good advice, which Faulkner heeded to some degree, but not enough to change the discursiveness of his later work. No doubt the worldwide interest in his Nobel Prize acceptance speech had convinced Faulkner that he could be an essayist as well as a novelist, and the mixture of argument with story made the later novels more topical and less universal than the early novels had been. In one earlier novel, *Go Down, Moses*, Faulkner composed a genealogical chart of the McCaslin-Edmonds-Beauchamp family just to help him keep his characters straight—a problem familiar to many readers of his fiction.

Faulkner was capable of extreme concentration when he was writing and didn't like to be interrupted. Children who came to the house were told not to disturb "Mr. Bill" when he was writing, which he often did in the family library just off the front door. It was only later in life that he added an "office" to his house and cultivated privacy when he needed it. Sometimes he would be seen writing outside the house, as a friend of Jill's once observed. Faulkner with his shirt off was seated on a blanket in the yard, writing in longhand on a sheet of paper with a book beside him. The friend, Aston Holley, asked with boyish curiosity, "What you doin', Mr. Bill?" Faulkner looked at him quietly and patiently and said "Lemme read it to you, Aston." Aston stood in silence for a few minutes while Faulkner read out what he had just written, reading rhythmically as though in a trance. Aston understood none of it but listened politely, and when Faulkner finished, he said "Thank you, Mr. Bill" and ran out to play with Jill and Jimmy. He never again asked Faulkner what he was doing.

When he was at home and in a writing mood, he would write anywhere inside or outside the house. Estelle told an interviewer early in his career that "There are times when Billy will go into his workroom and stay for hours. He hasn't any key, so he takes the door knob off and carries it inside with him. No one can get in and he is quite secure." He started out writing in the clutter of his library, then in the office he built for himself for greater privacy, but he could write in his backyard on a blanket, or in the hayloft above his horses, and even sometimes in his bathtub. He said once "My own experience has been that the tools I need for my trade are paper, tobacco, food and a little whisky." He was asked if the whisky had to be bourbon, and he answered, "No, I ain't that particular. Between scotch and nothing, I'll take scotch." According to one interviewer, "The most he has penned in one day…was when he climbed to the crib of the barn one morning with his papers, pencils and a quart of whisky and pulled the ladder up behind him. By the time daylight began to wane, he had ripped off 5,000 words." When he was writing anywhere, inside the house or outside, not even his wife or daughter dared to disturb him, and the servants were warned, "Don't bother Mr. Bill." They didn't.

Faulkner's most revealing account of his writing practices and principles was delivered to *The Paris Review* in 1956, when he was interviewed by Jean Stein. It was there that he said: "A writer needs three things, experience, observation, and imagination...With me, a story usually begins with a single idea or memory or mental picture." This interview was the beginning of some public soul-searching about his work which was extended further by his informal talks the next year at the University of Virginia, which were recorded verbatim and published as *Faulkner in the University*. These two sources provide the main insights into Faulkner's creative process as he himself analyzed it reflectively late in his life. They give what only he could give, an account of what he was trying to do in works that have baffled many readers ever since they were published. He did not pretend to be the definitive commentator on his fiction, but when he was asked serious questions about his work, he tried to give serious answers.

Faulkner's friend Phil Stone, who knew as well as anyone what was in his mind as he worked his way towards a literary career, contended that "one of the most important influences in Bill's whole literary career" was a book called *The Creative Will* by Willard Huntington Wright, the author of the Philo Vance detective novels. Phil Stone held an opinion about Faulkner few others did, "If people who read him would simply read Wright's book they would see what he is driving at from a literary standpoint." Faulkner himself never mentioned the book in print, so Stone must have been basing his opinion on conversations they had, but some justification for his view can be found in Wright's subtitle for his 1916 book, *Studies in the Philosophy and the Syntax of Aesthetics*. Wright, best known for his Philo Vance detective novels, wrote "A book may deal with the most squalid and tragic phases of life and still be a great work of art fraught with compelling artistic beauty." That statement is true in much of Faulkner's work, which has repelled many readers by its brutal realism. Wright regarded the French novelist Honoré de Balzac as "the colossal literary artist," a view Faulkner might well have seconded, speaking as he did in his *Paris Review* interview of how Balzac linked his novels into a continuous whole he called his Comédie Humaine. Phil Stone told a friend in 1931 that "Bill shares with me the opinion that Balzac is the greatest novelist who ever lived." One of Wright's opinions might have applied to Faulkner. It was that "True style—one which attests to mastery—is an ability to change one's manner at random so as to harmonise the expression with the thing expressed." Wright held that "The true test of an artist's genius is not his strength or fascination of personality, but his ability to organize. The greater he is as an organizer...the more exalted he is as an artist." Faulkner said in his *Paris Review* interview that after writing his first novel, he realized "that not only each work had to have a design but the whole output or sense of an artist's work had to have a design." Wright's opinions about fiction may or may not have influenced Faulkner, but he did seem to practice the art of the novel as Wright had envisioned it, linking all his novels and stories into his Mythical Kingdom of Yoknapatawpha County. No other American author has attempted such a monumental feat of the imagination as Faulkner accomplished, deliberately gathering all the novels and stories he wrote into what seems a continuous whole.

Faulkner sometimes acknowledged literary influences, but most of the time he avoided all literary connections and spoke contemptuously of what he called the "precious literary quarterlies." In 1931, he accepted an invitation to attend a Southern Writers' Conference at the University of Virginia, along with Sherwood Anderson, John Crowe Ransom, and Allen Tate, but he usually avoided all literary company. In 1946, when the Russian writer Ilya Ehrenberg visited the United States and expressed a wish to meet him, he declined, saying to Phil Stone "He wants to talk ideas. I'm not interested in ideas. I'm a writer, not a literary man."

He did agree to meet some classes of Professor A. Wigfall Green, an early Faulkner admirer in the Ole Miss English Department, and for a fee of $250 he delivered some pronouncements about modern literature, calling James Joyce "the father of the modern novel" and Sherwood Anderson "the father of the American novel," but disparaging Ernest Hemingway as a writer who "lacked courage." When Hemingway read Faulkner's remark, he said he thought he had shown courage when he drove an ambulance for the Italians in the First World War, and he called on Faulkner, who had never taken active part in any war, to apologize for his remark.

Faulkner's most famous public speech by far was his Nobel Prize Acceptance Speech in 1950, but after he realized how successful it was, he overcame his early shyness and gave some memorable talks in his later years. At the inducement of the principal of University High School, when Jill was a senior, she asked her father if he would give the commencement address to her graduating class. He agreed, and he gave the shortest such speech ever delivered on such a ceremonial occasion, less than five minutes long. It was a serious speech, rephrasing many of the sentiments expressed in his earlier Nobel Prize speech, praising freedom of expression and upholding the moral principles he had voiced on behalf of all writers in Stockholm. Faulkner affirmed in his later years that he was a dedicated American patriot, a believer in the right to enjoy "life, liberty and pursuit of happiness" articulated by Jefferson in the Declaration of Independence. He accepted President Eisenhower's invitation to serve as cultural ambassador for the Department of State, delivering talks to admiring audiences in such farflung places as Japan, France, and Venezuela, extolling the principle of individual freedom which to him was the bedrock American virtue. He agreed to speak at Jill Faulkner's graduation from Pine Manor in phrases that echoed his Nobel Prize address. And most significantly, he agreed to become Writer in Residence at the University of Virginia for a year, in 1957–58, because his daughter Jill had married and settled on a farm near Charlottesville. In that role, he would leave a permanent legacy of personal comments on his work, since his informal sessions were taped and later published as *Faulkner in the University*, forming a most valuable resource for readers of Faulkner who want to understand his frequently complex and difficult writings. He had often refused earlier invitations to speak, especially at Ole Miss, with the excuse that "I get all mixed up when I get on my feet." He had commandeered his friend Mac Reed to go along and speak for him in the 1920s, when he was trying to get his Uncle John elected judge, and when in the 1940s he was refused a commission in the US Air Force because of his age, he took a post as head of Home Defense for Lafayette County, and drove around the county to let the Principal of the University High School speak for him. He was driving a battered station wagon then, successor to a series of battered cars for which he was famous, and toured the villages near Oxford on behalf of Home Defense. He would introduce the high school principal and then sit down on the platform to listen quietly as another man exhorted his countrymen to be aware of the threats to safety in rural Mississippi, about as far from any possibility of a hostile invasion as was conceivable. The crowds were generally small, and once no one at all came to hear him talk about Home Defense, because they were listening to a championship fight on the radio.

Faulkner's advice to young writers

Young writers constantly asked Faulkner for advice about how they could break into print. Faulkner would usually tell them "Don't publish too soon. A man should take a lifetime to publish a single book of poems." He was not using himself as an example, having published dozens of books in his lifetime. One young aspiring writer in town named Charles Nelson came to him with a book of poems he had published at his own expense, just as Faulkner had done when he started his career. Faulkner looked the book over carefully, and without opening it, returned it, saying "They put a real nice cover on it, didn't they?" Nelson was disappointed by Faulkner's offhand treatment of his book, but his sister fared better. She chose to write a paper on Faulkner for her history class at Ole Miss, and had the nerve to walk into the private domain of Rowan Oak with her boy friend, hoping to get Faulkner's help in explaining his work. Faulkner was on his porch in a rocking chair, reading a recently popular historical novel, *Drums Along the*

Mohawk, by Philip Van Doren Stern. He invited the young pair to sit with him, put down his book and asked her what she wanted to know. It was in 1939, when he had just published *The Wild Palms*, and she asked him if he thought it was his best novel. "I always think my last novel is the best," he replied, "but I'm never satisfied with it, and so I have to go and write another one." She asked him how he started writing fiction. Faulkner answered that he started with a single character slowly coming to life in his mind, and describing that character led him to imagine other characters the first one might have known. He said he soon found he was writing a book. She asked if he had a plot in mind before he began, and Faulkner said it usually wasn't necessary, because there were really only three possible plots for any novel. He outlined these plots for her right there on his porch:

1. Love—a boy and girl meet, fall in love, and then either marry and try to make the best of a life together, or fail to marry and go off alone and unsatisfied.
2. Money—someone makes a pile of money and tries to do something good with it, or tries to make money and fails but keeps on trying.
3. Death—someone is dying or threatened with death, and either dies or somehow escapes death.

She asked him if he got his characters and plots from reading other novels and stories, and he said that when he was young he read purely for pleasure, but as he got older he began to recognize how the books he liked had been written, and so learned techniques of writing from other writers. He said writing couldn't be taught, and must come naturally to be worth any reader's time, and that only by trial and error could a writer be sure that what he wrote might be of value to others. He told her he wrote mostly with pen and ink, because it was an effort to hunt and peck on a typewriter.

Charles Nelson could remember a time when Faulkner rented a room overlooking the town square to use as his office, and put a sign on the window that read "Private—Stay Out!" The thought occurred to him that Faulkner wanted people in town to know he was writing, but he didn't want to be disturbed while he was doing it. Faulkner seemed to him to have a curious penchant for publicity and privacy at the same time. He agreed with what Phil Stone once said of Faulkner, that he had a Greta Garbo complex: he wanted to be world-famous and at the same time completely alone.

Faulkner and music

Faulkner seemed to dislike music of any kind in public, and would pay the manager of a downtown restaurant to turn off the background music when he was having dinner there. When an Italian reporter asked about his taste in music, he insisted that "Music makes me nervous. I don't listen to it at all." Privately, however, he enjoyed hearing classical music as well as Dixieland jazz, and in the early years of his marriage, when he would come home exhausted from a night in the university powerhouse, Estelle would play the piano to soothe his nerves. There is a scene in his early novel, *Sartoris*, where one of the main characters, Horace Benbow, goes calling on Belle Mitchell, who plays the piano while he listens. Faulkner showed his appreciation for Negro spirituals by naming one of his best novels *Go Down, Moses*, and his ear for the blues by titling one of his finest stories, "That Evening Sun," a phrase from William T. Handy's popular "St. Louis Blues."

There is no doubt that Faulkner had an instinctive appreciation for many of the fine arts, educating himself by reading literary classics of all kinds. Maurice Coindreau, his French translator, credited him with achieving "symphonic form" in his novels, suggesting that he agreed with the Symbolist poet Stéphane Mallarmé, who held that "All arts aspire to the condition of music." Faulkner had an intuitive grasp of artistic form and an ear for the inherent rhythm of words that gave his work both intellectual and auditory excellence, confirming that he had musical as well as literary talent.

Faulkner read most of the time when he wasn't writing, He made a practice of keeping a book in every room of his house, so that there would be something handy to read if the mood struck him. He would read several different books alternately until he had finished them. Though he seldom read his mail, he told his friend Roark Bradford to write him a letter, promising him "I know what to read." He once said to someone who asked him if he ever read his mail, "I read my mail every three months." He would occasionally take a stack of unopened mail to his mother and say, "You like to get letters—read these."

Faulkner and drinking

Excessive consumption of hard liquor was a constant worry in Oxford, from the time John Houston was licensed to sell it from his private home in 1837. It became a particular concern when the University of Mississippi was founded in Oxford in 1848, whereupon the state legislature passed a law prohibiting the sale of liquor within 5 miles of the university. Leading business men in town argued unsuccessfully that the law should be repealed, pointing to the sad fact that "while the prohibitory law damaged the town commercially, it did not, in fact, diminish the consumption of ardent spirits within the restricted territory."

Faulkner's friend and family physician, Dr. Felix Linder, said that Faulkner was not an alcoholic but a "periodic drinker," just like other male members of his family. Even his grandfather, the "Young Colonel," John Wesley Thompson Falkner, who was a lawyer and banker, was notorious for getting drunk, sometimes offering liquor to friends in his bank, and driving a goat cart recklessly about town. His father Murry was often taken away for the "Keely Cure" at a hospital near Memphis. Bill Faulkner could go for weeks and months without touching a drop of liquor—he abstained for a whole year after Jill was born--and then one day he would go on a binge and drink himself so sick he would have to be put to bed. Estelle drank with him, and so she could never control her husband's drinking, instead often drinking with him till they were both drunk. A hemorrhage frightened her into joining Alcholics Anonymous for a while, but not for long, and when she fell down drunk once and broke her collarbone, Felix Linder had to set it and nurse her back to health. Faulkner had many different doctors over the years but none of them could cure him of his addiction to alcohol. He said to one of them, "Never ask me why. I don't know the answer. If I did I wouldn't do it."

Faulkner had an average of two serious drinking bouts a year for thirty years. He called them "collapses." Sometimes they ended in a hospital, but he always seemed to recover completely from them, until the last one, and retained his sense of humor even in his cups, genially offering a policeman a drink during Prohibition, when he was driving through Washington. In spite of his heavy drinking while writing, he would always complete his scriptwriting on time, and might write novels as well, notably *Absalom, Absalom!* which he finished after returning from Hollywood to Oxford on Jan. 31, 1936. He had to be taken briefly to Byhalia for "drying out" before finishing it.

There were many people in Oxford who drank socially with Faulkner, and who thought his drinking problem was exaggerated, because he seemed able to hold his liquor as well as anyone. One party that moved from Oxford to Memphis and lasted from afternoon to night caused concern among his friends, because he had been consuming drink after drink and they knew his reputation for excessive drinking. But he stayed on his feet and the party returned home without incident. Next morning he seemed perfectly normal with no hint of a hangover. He usually drank lightly and preferred beer to hard liquor, remaining quite sociable at the party. They knew, however, that when he drank in the privacy of his home he sometimes went on binges and had to be taken to a doctor or to his mother to be brought to his senses again. His favorite drink for many years was Canadian Club, but his characteristic answer to anyone who asked his preference was, "I'm not particular about what I drink. Between scotch and nothing, I'll take scotch."

Felix Linder knew Faulkner's drinking habits better than most people in Oxford, and told anecdotes about it in private. He said that one rainy Sunday morning Bill Faulkner knocked at his back door, clad only in shorts, and asked for a bottle of whiskey. Dr. Linder was a friend and neighbor who knew that Bill Faulkner always came to the back door like a servant, not to the front door like a friend. Not wishing to offend him, Dr. Linder gave him just a small bottle, hoping to prevent his drinking more than was good for him, and Faulkner thanked him and walked away. But then he came back and knocked at the door again, asking if Dr. Linder would mind wrapping the bottle in a newspaper, because he didn't want to be seen in public with a bottle in his hand.

One admirer asked Faulkner if he always drank when he was writing. "Not every time," he replied. Felix Linder remembered once when Faulkner knocked on the door of his mother-in-law, Mrs. Oldham, complaining that he felt ill. She let him lie down but soon discovered that he refused to get up again, so she called the doctor for help. When Dr. Linder examined him, he said there was nothing wrong with him except that he needed to sober up. With that, Major Oldham, Faulkner's father-in-law, spoke up. "All he needs is to get up and have some exercise." When Bill Faulkner heard this, he suddenly got up, walked briskly down the stairs and out of the house, then came back and promptly went to bed again.

Faulkner hunting

His friend Dr. Felix Linder thought Faulkner "peculiar" in his dress, varying from fancy dress that was fit for a king, to rags a tramp might wear, without explanation, just to please himself. Though they were friends and neighbors, Bill Faulkner was capable of snubbing him as he did so many other townspeople. Felix Linder thought it was not rudeness or snobbishness on Faulkner's part but complete indifference to the opinions of others.

Felix Linder went on hunting trips with Faulkner, sometimes locally in Bailey Woods, but sometimes as far as the Sunflower River in the Delta, which was still wilderness, where they could hunt for deer. On a hunt, Faulkner would wear his oldest clothes and sleep outside, not in the shelter of a tent like the other hunters. He never bothered to wash and was generally unsanitary in his habits. The hunters did not hire a guide but hunted on their own, bringing along two or three colored men to do the cooking and cleaning up. It was every man for himself on a hunt, and Faulkner would shoot a rifle with any of them. "We would stay on the hunting ground for a couple of weeks during the winter season, hunting all day in the woods and camping out at night," Felix Linder remembered. Bill hunted with a 30–30 rifle, while other hunters carried shotguns. The oldest man on the hunt would usually be Mr. Ike Roberts, and he would be the leader. Faulkner once told a friend that the happiest hunting experience he ever had was stalking a huge buck for a day and a night, only to see the deer elude him without letting him fire a shot.

Faulkner started hunting in the woods of Panola County near Batesville, known as The Delta, although it was 50 miles east of the Mississippi River and 300 miles north of the actual Mississippi Delta below New Orleans. In the early twentieth century it was still bottom land, with virgin timber, located below the Tallahatchie River. Phil Stone had inherited a hunting camp there, but the area had been invaded by a railroad line and a sawmill, signs of civilization creeping into the wilderness exactly as Faulkner lamented in his hunting stories, "The Bear" and "Delta Autumn." The hunters would ride the train to Stone Stop and walk to the hunting camp, a simple wooden hut equipped with a camp kitchen and iron cots. Much earlier in Mississippi history, deer and bear had been seen in the woods, but the steady conversion of the forest into cotton fields drove big game west where the woods were wilder. The last black bear had been killed there in 1931. By the time Faulkner went out hunting, there were no bears left, just deer.

Faulkner's later hunting site was farther south and west in what was still the Delta region, a wilderness with stands of virgin timber, still a habitat for deer but no longer for bear. It had become a protected area called the Delta National Forest, lying between Greenville and Vicksburg on the east banks of the Mississippi. There, along the Big Sunflower River, about 150 miles south and west of Oxford, commercial hunting camps had been formed which could be joined for a fee. The deer season was late November and early December, but bear had not been seen after the flood of 1927, when most of the Delta was under water. There had been a Civil War engagement in the area known as the Battle of Rolling Fork, when Union boats came up a branch of the Mississippi and were fired on by Confederate cannons. The Confederates were driven back to Vicksburg, where a siege led by Gen. Ulysses Grant ended in victory for the Union troops. Faulkner s' great hunting story, *The Bear*, took place in the 1880s, long after the Civil War, when wild game was in abundance, not only deer but bear and even panthers. The Ivory-billed Woodpecker, now generally believed to be extinct, called according to Faulkner "Lord to God by the Negroes," could still be heard and seen in 1880, but between 1890 and 1935 deforestation steadily occurred and wildlife gradually disappeared. It was in 1935 that the Delta National Forest was set aside and the area was reforested, thus allowing deer and ducks to be hunted regularly in season.

Bill Faulkner on a hunt was typically taciturn, and so were most of the hunters, but he would sometimes carry silence to extremes. Once when his old friend Felix Linder was out walking near Bailey Woods where Faulkner lived, Faulkner quietly joined him, without a word of greeting. They walked together for some distance, until Faulkner left him as quietly as he had come, never even saying goodbye.

One of Faulkner's writer friends in Hollywood, Budd Schulberg, complained that when he later saw Faulkner in New York, he was unable to get him to talk. "From the late '40s through the middle '50s," Schulberg said, "I saw Faulkner frequently, not actually as friend to friend but as the mutual friends of Saxe Commins, an editor we both loved dearly. One morning I came to Saxe's New York office to work on the galleys of a novel of mine and found Faulkner already there, bent over the galleys of *Requiem for a Nun*. I called out, 'Hi, Bill. How've you been?' He ignored me. I sat down next to him and tried again. 'How are you, Bill?' Stony silence. I shrugged, and bent to my own galleys. At 12:30 I turned to my silent colleague again. 'I'm going across the street for lunch. Like to join me?' He never even looked up." In the late afternoon, still in the same office, Schulberg said he suddenly heard a voice: "Budd! Awfully good to see you. How've you been?" It was Bill Faulkner, seven hours after Schulberg had greeted him. Schulberg said he was surprised to see that Faulkner was aware of his presence for the first time that day.

Felix Linder's older brother Dewey, a dentist in Oxford who had been a schoolmate of Bill Faulkner, remembered that Faulkner did not go farther than the sixth grade before he "sort of dropped back." Dewey noticed later that Bill appeared with him in a sixth grade photograph, and then appeared in the same grade with his younger brother Felix. He said Bill really meant it when he called himself "the world's oldest living sixth grader."

Faulkner and politics

Faulkner's family had chosen to live in Oxford because it was a college town, and Faulkner loved living there. Though he left it for substantial periods from time to time, he remained loyal to it all his life. Having a university in town kept Oxford from being too provincial, and Faulkner benefited from its presence, even though he took little advantage of the system of formal education it offered. He lived with his family on the Ole Miss campus while his father was serving as Business Manager, and he respected the institution, though he was more a part of the town than of the university. The town was more conservative than the university, and politically, the Falkner family sided with the town in their politics. Faulkner knew that his great-grandfather, the Old Colonel, had been elected to the state legislature, but he personally took little interest in politics. It was politics that had led Col. Falkner to being killed in cold blood on the street of Ripley, and that had led his grandfather, the Young Colonel, to move the family from Ripley to Oxford, hoping to get away from the violence of a frontier town. The Falkners were Democrats, like most Southerners at that time, but they were conservative Democrats, who supported notoriously conservative Mississippi politicians like Senators Vardaman and Bilbo. Faulkner was aware of their views and used the Senators' names satirically in his fiction. He was independent in his politics, and his writing shows respect for both the liberal and conservative viewpoints, though he tended to be more conservative as a young man, more liberal as he grew older. Most of his life, he held the strongly religious and moral convictions of the majority of Southerners, showing sympathy for all the characters he invented, treating them with the liberal generosity he had acquired from living in a college town.

The political history of Oxford was much affected by the defeat of the Confederacy in the Civil War, as was reflected in the March 12, 1885, issue of *The Oxford Falcon*, which commended President Grover Cleveland for appointing L.Q.C. Lamar to his cabinet as Secretary of the Interior. It praised Lamar as the most respected postwar statesman of the South. Mississippi had suffered along with the rest of the South for rebelling against the country, which after the War had elected Ulysses S. Grant, the victorious Union general, as its President. Grant's successor, Grover Cleveland, however, appointed L.Q.C. Lamar to his Cabinet, signaling a welcome change of heart towards the South, which was now engaged in seeking a legitimate place within the American Union. Lamar, a native of Oxford, was the Southern politician looked to as a leader in the effort of reconciliation. In 1888, Lamar was appointed an Associate Justice of the U.S. Supreme Court, elevating him to a position of high honor which lasted until his death in Macon, Georgia, on Jan. 23, 1893. Faulkner knew about every event in the Civil War that affected the Oxford region, in particular the burning of Oxford by Gen. Smith in 1864, and often took visitors to see the "Dead House," as it was called, on the Ole Miss campus, where soldiers wounded in the Battle of Shiloh were taken, and where bullet holes could still be seen in the walls.

Dewey Linder remembered being with Faulkner when they listened to a radio broadcast of Harry Truman's inaugural speech after he was elected President in 1948. Bill didn't want to listen but the other men did, and so he consented to listen with them. When President Truman finished his oration, promising the American people he would lead them to better times ahead, in the honored fashion of a president-elect, Faulkner remarked somewhat wistfully, "It's a wonderful country, if only we could afford it." Faulkner took no part in politics and seemed not to have a preference for one political party over another, but he noted the characteristic American tendency to see the future as always an improvement on the past, and expected its political leaders to give the country a boost of optimism, regardless of their party.

Dewey Linder said that Faulkner was always regarded as "different" in school, but no one suspected him of having genius. He was quiet to the point of being unsociable, and rather than joining his classmates when they played at recess, he would usually stand aside and observe them, apparently lost in thought. Dewey knew from reading Faulkner's books that he had been concealing his talents as a writer, which included deep insights into human nature few men had. Faulkner had once confessed to Dewey that "I've never been sick in my life that wasn't from drinking." Like his brother Felix, who was Faulkner's family doctor, Dewey believed that Faulkner's early death was caused by drinking, more than by his fall from a horse. He thought that at Byhalia, where his nephew Jimmy Faulkner took him to "dry out," Faulkner was given a shot to kill the pain of his injury, which compounded his heavy drinking and caused the heart attack that killed him at the age of 65.

Children who were often in Rowan Oak never saw Faulkner drunk, though they heard stories about his excessive drinking. He was careful to keep his drinking private as far as possible, but when he was on a binge he depended on others to look after him, including his mother, doctors he knew, and his nephew Jimmy. Once Faulkner went with his friend Col. Evans to Batesville to buy liquor, Oxford having continued prohibition long after it had been repealed by much of the country. They were stopped by a highway patrolman on suspicion of transporting liquor, but when the trooper saw it was Bill Faulkner in his old Ford car, he waved them on, saying "Go on, you don't have a license to drive anyway."

Faulkner and religion

As for his religion, Faulkner was a Protestant Christian in the broadest sense. His mother's family, the Butlers, were Baptists, and his father's family on both sides, the Falkners and the Murrys, were Methodists. The boys were baptized in the Methodist Church. As long as his grandmother Murry played the organ in the Methodist church in Oxford, the younger Falkners attended church regularly and went to Sunday School as well, though Bill Faulkner sometimes went to sleep during Sunday School, lying down full length on the floor. According to his brother Jack, the Methodist Sunday School had convinced all four Faulkner brothers of the existence of God, something they never questioned. The Falkner brothers and Linder brothers often played baseball in Bailey Woods after church, but they were careful not to be seen, because any kind of entertainment was strictly forbidden on Sundays. It was their Murry grandfather, a staunch Methodist, who insisted that his four grandsons must memorize a Bible verse every morning, and repeat it before they could have breakfast. As a boy, Faulkner attended Sunday School alternately in the Baptist and the Methodist churches, to please both sides of his family. When he married, it was in the Presbyterian church, but he and Estelle were considered members of the Episcopal Church to which the Oldham family belonged, and it was the church from which he would be buried. Faulkner thus had connections with all four of the main Protestant denominations in Oxford. The wife of the Baptist minister confirmed that Bill Faulkner had been "a very broad Christian." The Falkner family was carried on the Methodist rolls for a long time after the Murry grandmother, who played the organ, was replaced by a younger organist. A Methodist delegation called on Faulkner at Rowan Oak to ask him why he had stopped attending church. He was courteous to them without offering any explanation or pledging a donation. In his later years he was seldom seen inside a church, but he liked to go with his family to the Christmas Eve service at the Episcopal Church.

Faulkner's published writing shows that he held strong religious as well as moral convictions throughout his life, shaped by the Protestant churches and Sunday Schools he had attended. His work shows a Puritan fascination with Original Sin, typical of the strict Calvinist faith that many devout Southerners shared. Faulkner once expressed his personal belief that by the age of eleven, every child had committed every possible immoral act in his imagination, proof that the doctrine of Original Sin was ingrained in him. Estelle's sister, Dorothy Oldham, said Bill Faulkner once asked her, "Do you know what's the trouble with me?" She said she didn't, and he said "I'm a puritan." He also astonished a woman in Virginia who asked him about his faith by saying: "Madam, I'm a Swedenborgian." He might joke about religion, but Faulkner's Christianity is evident in his works. It is expressed for instance by Quentin Compson's fixation on his sister's chastity in *The Sound and The Fury*. He wants to take Caddy with him into the "clean flame" of Hell, a just punishment for her promiscuity. It is also exemplified in the allegory of Good and Evil in *Sanctuary*, where Temple Drake, a fallen woman, thinks of the Fall of Man in the Garden of Eden, and believes that the Snake was there before Eve. There is the fierce morality of the MacEacherns in *Light in August*, who raise Joe Christmas with stern discipline as long as he is living with them. Faulkner spoke of the provincialism of Henry Sutpen in *Absalom, Absalom!* "with his puritan heritage—that heritage peculiarly Anglo-Saxon—of fierce proud mysticism" which he inherits from his Methodist grandfather, Mr. Coldfield (a fictional variation of Jim Cofield, Faulkner's photographer). What Faulkner admired in Christianity was not so much the Puritanism as the doctrine of Original Sin.

He spoke seriously about religion in Japan in 1955, when questioned by a non-Christian audience whether he believed in Christianity: "I believe in God. Sometimes Christianity gets pretty debased, but I believe in God, yes, I believe that man has a soul that aspires to what we call God…I think that the trouble with Christianity is that we've never tried it yet." In his *Paris Review* interview in 1956 he took a more definite view of religious faith: "No one is without Christianity, if we agree on what we mean by the word.

It is every individual's code of behavior by means of which he makes himself a better human being than his nature wants to be, if he followed his nature only… It shows him how to discover himself, evolve for himself a moral code and standard within his capacities and aspirations, by giving him a matchless example of suffering and sacrifice and the promise of hope."

Faulkner and farming

One of the myths Faulkner liked to purvey about himself was that "I'm a farmer, not a writer." He did buy a farm in Beat Two of Oxford Township, near Puskus Creek, but not until 1938, when he became a gentleman farmer by virtue of selling the movie rights to his novel, *The Unvanquished*. His brother John, "Johnsy," who later lived on the farm, told the story of its purchase to "Col." J. R. Cofield, the town photographer. Faulkner had received a check for $25,000 from Hollywood and he had always wanted to own a farm. He found a farm for sale east of town, near Puskus Creek, and he bought it to grow hay for his horses, not to raise food crops. He never made a living by farming, but he took pride in riding a horse or driving a tractor on his farm, leaving the real farm work to a Negro man named Rienzi. Once he took his nephew Jimmy Faulkner and a friend, Aston Holley, out to the farm to watch a jackass at stud, but the jackass failed to perform its duty on schedule, and the young lads returned disappointed by this intended lesson in natural reproduction. Faulkner did not apologize for the failure of the jackass to do his duty.

Faulkner named his place Greenfield Farm. It pleased him that it had once belonged to Joe Parks, a country man who had come to Oxford and worked his way up, becoming president of what had once been the Falkner bank. He no doubt recognized that in the previous owner of his farm he had the prototype of Flem Snopes, the backwoods entrepreneur he invented, who became the main character in three novels, *The Hamlet*, *The Town*, and *The Mansion*, which together would be known as the Snopes Trilogy. Like Flem Snopes, Joe Parks moved from the country to the town, prospered by ingenuity and hard work, and in time brought all the members of his numerous clan to Jefferson. Faulkner's fictional Snopes family proved that he had the imaginative power to transform common people like Joe Parks into memorable invented characters.

Faulkner's farm was near the Puskus Lake Recreation Center northeast of Oxford, which Faulkner marked on his hand-drawn map of Yoknapatawpha County as the place where the fictional MacCallum family lived, and where Bayard Sartoris often went hunting with his dogs. The farm never produced any food crops, but plenty of hay for the mules and horses Faulkner kept in his barn. Faulkner would sometimes supervise the work of his hired hands, and his brother John lived on the farm for a while and managed it for him. Toward the end of Faulkner's life, a Negro couple came to live on his farm, and after his death, the wife grieved for him, telling visitors "I just cain't believe Mr. Bill's gone."

John Cullen, one of the hunters who often accompanied Faulkner to the Delta to hunt deer, said that Faulkner was "reckless" in his preference for such demanding pursuits as hunting, flying, and horseback riding, and paid the price for it when his horse Stonewall tossed him to the ground and hastened his early death. Faulkner did like to dress as a farmhand, looking as ragged as any farmer when he went on a hunt.

John Cullen said Faulkner had few close friends, and was quite content to go hunting with strangers as well as familiar companions. He was typically reserved, keeping quietly to himself, but he would sometimes join conversations around the campfire and laugh out loud. Cullen testified that "he could be as merry as anyone I know when he was amused." Faulkner enjoyed the jokes but did not like to hear dirty stories. He would quietly disengage himself from the group when an off-color joke was beginning to be told. Mac Reed confirmed that Faulkner disliked obscenities. On his drugstore visits, if someone started a risqué story, he would excuse himself with "Pardon me, gentlemen, but I have some business to attend to."

John Cullen said that on a hunt Faulkner could stand perfectly still for hours to stalk a deer. He would drink with the men around the campfire in the evening, but John Cullen recalled only once when he let his drinking get out of control, and had to be rushed to a doctor for help in sobering him up.

Faulkner never liked to talk about his books, even with men who seldom read them. Mac Reed said he never asked Faulkner about his books, knowing he didn't like to talk about them. Ben Wasson, a long-time friend of Faulkner who had edited his books and acted as his agent, complained in later years that Bill had "cut him off." Mac Reed told him "Bill and I always remained on friendly terms because I never try to discuss his books with him. I know he doesn't like to talk about his work, and he knows I'll never ask him about it." John Cullen remembered that when Faulkner heard he had won the Nobel Prize, they were on a hunt. He took the news calmly and went on drying dishes. They had just enjoyed his favorite meal of coon and collards, and when the news about his Nobel Prize sank in, he started a drinking bout which almost made him miss the plane for Sweden.

John Cullen lived simply, in a rustic cabin in the woods near Oxford with few amenities. He wrote and published a few hunting stories himself, including one about a fabulous bear called "Old Crooked Foot." He greatly admired Faulkner as a writer, for converting his hunting experience into universally appreciated fiction. He said that Faulkner had an ear for Negro dialects, true to life yet perfectly adapted to his stories. He admired Faulkner less as a hunter, since he considered Faulkner just a "fair" woodsman, and saw him as a man for whom farming was not an occupation but a hobby. Hunting trips with Faulkner and their boon companions, Mr. Ike Roberts, Big Red Bright, and Bud Miller were the happiest days of his life. When the deer season opened in late November, they would go to Cypress Lake in the Delta, and stay for a week or two, hunting, camping, drinking, and telling stories. Sometimes the hunting trips degenerated into gambling and bringing "wild women" to the camp for entertainment, in which case Bill Faulkner would quickly leave for home. He did not like it when the hunt turned into an outdoor casino and floor show.

Faulkner and sports

A friend who knew Faulkner growing up said that all the Faulkner brothers were athletic as well as artistic. Faulkner led a sportsman's life from boyhood on, participating in games with his three brothers as they grew up, learning to ride horseback, to hunt in the woods, to play an expert game of golf, to sail a small boat, and to pilot a plane, first with the Canadian Royal Flying Corps in 1917–18, and then in an airplane which he bought for himself in the 1930s. He kept horses in the barn at Rowan Oak, and in the 1940s he hired a colored man named Andrew Price to look after his horses. Andrew's wife, Christine, was the family cook, and the couple lived in a small wooden house behind Rowan Oak, which was weathered but comfortable, and tended a vegetable garden to provide food for their table. Andrew liked "a mess of collards" for dinner, he said, and he testified that "Mr. William," as he always called Faulkner, "sho was a good man." Faulkner gave him a cabin to live in, and paid him $5 wages every Friday for his work. When he said he wanted to buy a truck to help him work, Faulkner wrote a check for $750 as an advance on his wages, so that he could buy it outright. Andrew worked hard to repay him, in $50 installments over a period of years.

Faulkner customarily kept three horses: a saddle mare, a jumper named Tempe which Jill learned to ride, and a big grey horse named Stonewall, on which Faulkner liked to take an early morning ride when he was at home, following a trail through the woods that led to the Ole Miss campus. According to Andrew Price, it was when Faulkner came back from one of those morning rides in the summer of 1962 that Stonewall suddenly balked and threw Faulkner down hard, so that he "went over his head and hurt himself real bad." Faulkner returned home on foot, in great pain, and never fully recovered from the fractured ribs he suffered, which led to his early death. To Andrew, who tended the horses, Stonewall was a "crazy" horse, and he warned Faulkner not to ride him, but Faulkner stubbornly insisted on riding alone through the woods in his early sixties. "When Mr. William make up his mind, ain't nobody can change him," Andrew said. Faulkner treated the accident stoically, never complaining about his serious injury, until it became necessary to go to a doctor for treatment.

Faulkner sometimes hunted squirrels or rabbits in Bailey's Woods surrounding Rowan Oak, but was glad to go on extended hunting trips with friends in the Mississippi Delta. He raised and trained bird dogs for hunting, and kept a small fyce (fox terrier) as a pet, but did not try to raise larger hunting hounds (like Lion in *The Bear*).

Faulkner sometimes took Andrew with him to his farm near Puskus Creek to help him bring in the hay crop. They would carry the hay home to feed the horses. That was the only crop Faulkner raised on his farm, hiring helpers to do the work. His claim of being "a farmer, not a writer" was a persistent lie, though he did like to play the role of gentleman farmer or Southern planter. He trained Andrew to look after his horses with care, and he enjoyed riding them for exercise.

Andrew continued living in his cabin after Faulkner died, being allowed by the family to stay as long as he liked. He said he had no plans to move, though "I bin studyin' 'bout dat a long time." At 77, he had chronic "ahteritis" and "high blood," but didn't think seriously about returning to Pontotoc, his home until Faulkner hired him to work for him in Oxford. He still kept a house in Pontotoc, but someone had stolen the "bob wah" that he used to fence it in. "Ah know some good folks theah, white and black, but look lahk them black folks wouldn't treat me that way." He didn't trust the sheriff of Pontotoc to recover his stolen barbed wire, but thought he just might go over there himself some day and see if he could find it.

When I asked Andrew Price if Faulkner was a hard man to work for, he said "No suh, he never raised his voice with me. Mr. William always spoke soft, but he could sho let you know what he wanted you to do. Sometimes he would get mad enough to shout "Hell!" but nothing stronger ever came from his lips. If he asked you to do something for him he would say 'Yas' just once, but if he didn't want you to do something he would say 'No, No, No!' three times. He loved Jill more than anyone on earth, and he loved the three grandsons she gave him, too. Mr. William sho was a good man, best Ah evah knew."

Andrew Price said that after horseback riding, what Faulkner liked to do most was flying., but when his brother Dean was killed in a plane crash, taking a passenger up in the plane Faulkner owned, he "got shet of it" but continued to enjoy flying in rented planes. Faulkner once said to Andrew, "I might take you on a plane ride to Virginia," after he had become Writer in Residence at the University of Virginia, but Andrew told him, "No suh, Mr. William. An airplane might fall *on* me some day, but it won't fall *with* me." Andrew chuckled, remembering "Dat wuz one-a de few times Ah evah heard Mr. William laugh out loud."

Faulkner loved all sorts of games, playing tennis or badminton outside with friends, or ping pong inside. One of his tennis partners was Branham Hume, who regarded Faulkner as "pretty fair" at the game but added "his form was better than his game."

He especially liked sailing on Sardis Lake in the home-made sailboat he bought from Dr. Arthur Guyton. He named it the *Ring Dove*, the name of the boat in Joseph Conrad's story, "The End of the Tether." Sometimes he would sail it next to the *Min-ma-gary*, the houseboat which he and Col. Evans had built, so that if the wind dropped, he could hitch a ride back to the dock. Once he was out sailing with Estelle and Jill until 3 a.m. because there was no wind and the temperature was over 100 degrees. When he sailed by himself, as he often did, he would carry a few hard-boiled eggs and a couple of bottles of beer for his lunch, and happily stayed on the lake for hours, sailing by himself.

On Sunday afternoons, which were very quiet in Oxford, Faulkner and the Ashford Littles would take their children picnicking and fishing, and Faulkner joked that these pastimes were "The Sunday Afternoon Bible and Athletic Society."

In his younger days Faulkner played golf on the local course and became so expert at it that he once shot a lower score than the visiting professional golfer. He would practice his strokes by shooting balls through a rubber tire. He was once lucky enough to score a hole-in-one, earning the prize of a new pipe to smoke.

Faulkner enjoyed frog-gigging with Col. Hugh Evans at night in ponds around town. The two men wore hats with torches to see the frogs. One night Col. Evans heard a sizzling sound and realized he was singeing Bill Faulkner's hair with his torch. When he asked Bill why he didn't "holler" Bill said "I thought you could smell me, Hugh." On another night, they were driving out to Sardis Lake for frog-gigging, and Hugh mistakenly drove right into the water, since there was no sign to indicate they should stop. Hugh asked Bill why he hadn't warned him in time, and Bill replied unconcernedly, "I was thinking that if you didn't stop pretty soon, we'd be in the water."

Andrew said he never saw Mr. William writing, but he heard him many times. "Evah time Ah heah dat ol' tahpwrahtah goin', Ah know'd Mr. William was writin'." He liked to write in the "front study" (library) or in the "back study," the office he added to Rowan Oak about the time Andrew Price began working for him in the 1940s.

Faulkner greatly enjoyed sailing on Sardis Lake in his later years, in the sailboat he named *Ring Dove*. But his favorite water sport was serving as captain of a houseboat he built with Col. Hugh Evans, a retired Army officer who had been head of the ROTC unit at Ole Miss. He named it the *Min-*

ma-gary in honor of Minnie Ruth Little, Dr. Ashford Little's wife, and when it was finished he held an elaborate launching ceremony. For it, he drew up a charter entitled "Provisional Navy of the Confederate States of America." The houseboat was constructed in Faulkner's yard and took a year to complete with the help of Negro labor. Bill had purchased an Admiral's uniform for the launching on June 2, 1948, and wore pop-bottle-cap medals. Passengers were piped aboard with a genuine bo'sun's pipe, and he served them lamb raised on his farm, which he had barbecued himself the night before the launching. Faulkner entertained friends on the *Min-ma-gary* many times after the launching, happy to serve as captain of the ship.

Faulkner and the Nobel Prize

The Nobel Prize established Faulkner as a world writer for the first time and led to his becoming a bestselling author at last. It started with a phone call to his home on Nov. 10, 1950 from a Swedish journalist in New York, who told him he had just been awarded the 1949 Nobel Prize for Literature and asked him for his reaction to the news. (The prize had been delayed for a year because the Swedish Academy could not agree on a unanimous vote the previous year.) Faulkner at first replied that he was greatly honored but that he could not go to Sweden to receive it because he was too busy being a farmer. He had already refused to go to New York to receive the Gold Medal of the National Institute of Arts & Letters, using the same excuse. He did not tell his wife and daughter about the Nobel Prize until they had heard it from relatives who read about it in the newspaper. He agreed to be interviewed by Phil "Moon" Mullen, Editor of *The Oxford Eagle*, about it because Mullen insisted and came to his house personally. Faulkner did not tell the Swedish reporter that he was less than flattered by the honor, knowing it had been given previously to Pearl Buck and Sinclair Lewis when he thought Theodore Dreiser and Sherwood Anderson were more deserving of the honor. But when his old friend Mac Reed drove out to Rowan Oak to congratulate him personally, he seemed dazed by it, and said "Mac, I still can't believe it." A reporter from *The Memphis Commercial Appeal* came to his door and Faulkner told him "You know I'm a hard bloke to get along with. I feel quite grateful for the news, but no statement until I send one to Sweden." He sent a letter to the Swedish correspondent who had called him, containing some of the sentiments he would eventually express more fully in his Nobel Prize Acceptance Speech, and the next day he left on a hunting trip he had planned with friends in the Delta National Forest on the Sunflower River near Rolling Fork, Mississippi. His hunting friends had heard about the prize, but all Faulkner would say to them when he joined them was that he would gladly give a dish towel to the Swedish Ambassador if he appeared at the hunting camp. The hunters dined that night on coon and collards, their customary fare on hunting trips.

Only a conspiracy by his wife and daughter convinced Faulkner that he should go to Sweden to accept the award in person. Jill did most of the persuading, since she was editor of the high school newspaper and saw it as an event of international significance she could report on personally. When Faulkner agreed to go to Sweden to accept the Nobel Prize, his wife Estelle called his regular Random House editor, Saxe Commins, at his home in Princeton, and asked if he would mind to rent a tux for Bill and bring it to the airport. Saxe Commins was surprised, but agreed to do it, and asked for Faulkner's measurements to be sure he ordered the right size. Estelle said "Wait a minute and I'll see." She left the phone off the hook, found a tape measure, and took the measurements straight from her husband, then picked up the phone and relayed them to Commins, who rented the tux and met Bill at the airport in New York to give it to him. The pictures of Bill at the Nobel Prize award ceremonies in Stockholm show him handsomely dressed in black tie, because his wife and his editor saw that he had the proper formal attire. He neglected to shave for the occasion, however, and wore an old trench coat over his tux on the way to the ceremony in the Stockholm Town Hall. He was presented to King Gustaf by a sponsor from the Swedish Academy who praised him as a "deep psychologist" and "experimentalist" and called him "the epic writer of the American South." His fellow recipients of the Nobel Prize for peace were the British pacifist philosopher Bertrand Russell and the American Negro Senator Ralph Bunche. Faulkner later said the ceremony "was as long as a Mississippi funeral." He gave his famous address at a banquet following the award ceremony, but few could make sense of it, because he read it softly and rapidly in a Southern drawl that was hard to follow. When it was printed its impact was felt throughout the world, quoted approvingly in newspapers everywhere.

Faulkner returned home to acclaim, but told a friend "The tramp has become famous," adding in all honesty "I was unhappy when you first met me and I'm more so now than ever." To his young mistress, Joan Williams, he wrote about the ordeal of writing: "You have to have something in your very entrails to be said; you don't have that yet but don't worry about it; it is not important whether you write or not; writing is only important when you want to do it, and nothing nothing nothing else but writing will suffice, give you peace."

Faulkner's last days

In September, 1956, Faulkner was invited to Washington to discuss the new "People to People" program of President Eisenhower. For the first time since his days as Postmaster of University, Mississippi, Faulkner accepted a government job as head of the Writers' division of the new program, which was intended to personalize international relations worldwide. He agreed to send out a public letter to a list of American writers, inviting them to participate. He convened a meeting of the writers in New York to discuss what could be done, but it ended, he said later, in a conflict over whether, and how, to free Ezra Pound from St. Elizabeths. Faulkner was willing to go as far as issuing a joint statement that the American government was "keeping its best poet in jail," but he found that the willingness of writers to dissent over every issue they discussed was too great to make a consensus possible, and he quickly gave up the task of coordinator, calling it impractical.

He took the position of Writer in Residence at the University of Virginia for the Winter term of 1957, from January to March. He willingly agreed to let his informal talks—they were never lectures--be tape recorded for later publication. He also agreed to keep office hours when students could come in and ask him questions. Some of his remarks were reported in the newspapers and created a stir in the local community. When he said that all Virginians were snobs and that he liked snobs because they left you alone, he provoked a flurry of letters which he was amused to read. He found he had more respect in Charlottesville than he had ever enjoyed in Oxford, and he liked that change. When not involved in his official duties in the classroom or the office, he refused as usual to discuss his books, preferring to talk about hunting. He was invited to join the local hunt club, for which he ordered a set of "pinks," a formal hunting costume, from Abercrombie & Fitch in New York, and had his picture taken in them next time he was in Oxford by his favorite photographer, "Col." J. R. Cofield. The formal seated portrait became his favorite of many portraits.

In March, 1957, he accepted an invitation to go to Athens for the State Department and sailed on a yacht through the Greek islands while he was there. He made a talk in which he said that Athens was the "cradle of civilization," that the Greek gods were still potent amid the ruins of Classical Greece, "near and still powerful, not inimical, just powerful...free of man's folly and trouble...[with] time to watch what man did without having to be involved in it." When the Greek government awarded him a Silver Medal, he accepted it with further praise: "When the sun of Pericles cast the shadow of civilized man around the earth, that shadow curved till it touched America. When someone like me comes to Greece he is walking the shadow back to the source of light which cast the shadow." When he returned to Virginia, he told students that he had seen "the Hellenic light" and the "Homeric wine-dark sea," and had found the Greek past benevolent, unlike the past in other European countries, which seemed Gothic and forbidding and "a little terrifying."

Faulkner returned to Oxford in the summer of 1957, but agreed to serve again as Writer in Residence at the University of Virginia in the spring of 1958. Faulkner lectured informally in 1960, and in the spring of 1962 he served his last term as Emily Balch Lecturer at the University of Virginia. In May, 1962, he went to West Point on the invitation of the Superintendent, Gen. William Westmoreland, where he read the horse race scene from his latest novel, *The Reivers,* and was photographed by Henri Cartier-Bresson in his costume of pepper-and-salt tweed suit and bowler hat. Jill and Paul Summers accompanied him, since Paul had graduated from West Point in 1951.

Back in Virginia, he turned down an invitation to have dinner at the White House with President Kennedy, because, he said, "I'm too old at my age to travel that far to eat with strangers." The "strangers" would have been other winners of the Nobel Prize. He enjoyed the European style of fox hunting on horseback, and at the age of sixty he joined the Farmington Hunt in Charlottesville and learned for the first time how to jump a horse. It proved to be a fatal lesson, since falling from a horse led to his early death five years later. Faulkner was never a skilled horseman, but he was a brave and stubborn one. "I'm scared to death of horses," he once admitted, "and that's why I can't leave them alone." He suffered fractured ribs, collarbone, and vertebrae over the years, and yet none of his injuries deterred him from riding horseback regularly and even from learning to jump horses at the end of his life, at the age of 62, against his doctor's orders. One such jump on his favorite horse Stonewall led to a fall and hospitalization from which he never recovered. He died of a heart attack at Byhalia, Mississippi, a sanitarium where he had often gone to recover from bouts of heavy drinking.

It was from Dr. Felix Linder that Jim Cofield got a detailed account of Faulkner's final days. He said Faulkner was trying to train his horse Stonewall to be a jumper, but was still working on him when he took what proved to be his fatal ride in the summer of 1962. While crossing Old Taylor Road on his way back to Rowan Oak, Stonewall suddenly reared up and threw him on the pavement. Horse and rider returned separately, but when Faulkner got back and saw Stonewall in the paddock, he grabbed the reins and mounted him again, determined to show him who was master. Badly bruised though he was, he rode the horse for another hour, dismounting only when he was sure the horse had been tamed. He went inside and collapsed on the bed, and his wife called Dr. Linder to come at once and examine her husband. Bill was conscious but in acute pain when the doctor arrived, and all he would say was "Stonewall gave me a spill." The doctor examined him and found he was black and blue all over. He offered to put him completely to sleep, but Faulkner insisted that he wanted an anesthetic that would staunch the pain but would not drug him into unconsciousness. Dr. Linder gave him a prescription for a painkiller, to be filled at Gathright-Reed drugstore, and Faulkner bought and took several doses of it, but found it only partly effective, and began drinking for further relief. In spite of his injuries, he was able to make a successful visit to West Point in the company of his daughter Jill and her husband, Paul Summers, a West Point graduate, but when he returned he continued drinking and taking the painkillers until he had to be taken by his nephew Jimmy to Byhalia for recuperation. That was where he died of a heart attack, brought on by the injuries he suffered when he fell from the horse.

At the end of his life Faulkner was living in Charlottesville much of the time and still riding recklessly on horseback, resulting in a fall in the snow in January of 1962, which caused him to be hospitalized with broken teeth and a brain concussion—at the age of 64! When he was well enough, he went back to Oxford and went hunting with his nephew, Jimmy Faulkner, in the course of which he confided to Jimmy that he had a premonition of death. He had himself photographed by "Col." Cofield in preparation for having his portrait painted by Murray Goldsborough. Murray Goldsborough did a preliminary sketch of Faulkner a few months before his death, which he enlarged into two full-length oil paintings, one seated and one standing, for the libraries at the University of Virginia and the University of Mississippi. They hang there today in honor of a writer who gave both universities the literary reputation they have today, which both are proud to claim, just as Oxford is proud to claim that it was once "The Home of William Faulkner." The preliminary sketch Murray Goldsborough made of Faulkner was acquired by Miami University in Oxford, Ohio, and now is framed on the wall of the Twentieth Century Reading Area of the Miami library, beside a case holding the books Faulkner gave to Mac Reed, which Miami acquired from his daughter, Kitty Reed Costikyan.

Faulkner had planned to move to a farm outside Charlottesville near his daughter Jill, and had asked Linton Massey, head of the Faulkner Foundation, to guarantee a loan of $50,000 for the purchase of Red Acres Farm, near The Knole, where Jill was living with her husband and his three grandsons. He didn't live to make the move he planned.

Faulkner took his last morning ride on horseback on June 17, 1962, when he was thrown down hard on Old Taylor Road by Stonewall, a temperamental jumper he had bought in Oklahoma. He picked himself up and limped home on foot, and then insisted on getting back on Stonewall and taking him through some jumps to prove he was still the master. He tried to ease the pain of his injuries with drugs prescribed by the doctor and with heavy drinking, but neither sufficed, and on July 5, 1962, Jimmy helped Estelle take him to Byhalia, the sanitorium where he died of a sudden heart attack on July 6, 1962, a few months short of his 65th birthday. The end was unexpected, though he had told Andrew Price, who looked after his horses, after his horse had thrown him to the pavement two weeks earlier, "I want to go home." His body was placed in a plain cypress casket for the funeral in the Episcopal Church, and with Phil Stone and Mac Reed, his oldest Oxford friends, as Honorary Pallbearers, he was taken to St. Peter's Cemetery, and buried in a new plot below the Falkner family plot which was already full.

Faulkner died on July 6, 1962. Uncle Mac wrote me that day:

Dear Bill:

Bill Faulkner died at two-thirty this morning.
Dorothy Oldham, sister-in-law, called at five to say, "We lost Bill this morning. Heart attack."
He had, apparently, recovered from injury sustained when a favorite horse spilled him. He had been urged to stop trying to bring his "Jumpers" along for perfect performance.
My last visit with him: A few moments in the store four or five days ago as he borrowed my pen, autographed a book, The Reivers, and asked if I would fill in the necessary information for mailing to a lady in Sweden. "I los' my glasses somewhere this mawnin'," He said.
Mabel and I had read in July Vogue the article covering Bill's visit to West Point...on page 70. The writer was careful to explain that *heart* was pronounced "Hot" but let him speak of *horse* as "Horse." It was always "Hoss" as I look back 39 years.
He was a friend. The most unusual I ever had.

Yours,
Mac (signed)

Part II: Faulkner the writer

CHAPTER 1

In the Beginning was *Sartoris*

The first thing to understand about William Faulkner is that he was both a Southerner and a Modernist. As a writer, he was both a traditionalist and an experimentalist, a doubly complex writer whose work is a challenge to any reader. As a Southerner, his roots went deep. He belonged to the fourth generation of his family in Mississippi, born in 1897 in New Albany, a small town in northeastern Mississippi, not far from the Alabama and Tennessee borders, the heart of the Deep South. At the time he was born, his father was managing a railroad station on a line that had been built by his great-grandfather, the first William Falkner (who spelled his name without the "u"). Today, the birthplace of the second and more famous William Faulkner (who added the "u" to his name) is marked by a plaque in front of a modest bungalow in the middle of town, not far from a railroad stop named Falkner (without the "u"). A little farther north on the rail line is the town of Ripley, the county seat of Tippah, where the first William Falkner lived until he met a violent death. His marble effigy still towers over the Ripley cemetery, supported by a column of stone books that mark his grave. The man who is buried there made sure he would not be forgotten. He had ordered the effigy to be carved from Carrara marble in Italy, specifying that it should be taller than any other statue in the cemetery. Naturally, he became a hero to his family, especially to his great-grandson and namesake, the second and more famous William Faulkner, whose simple grave is marked by a flat stone slab in St. Peters Cemetery outside Oxford, identified only by his name.

The full name of the great-grandfather was William Clark Falkner, but he was better known in the family as "The Old Colonel," because he had fought in two wars, being wounded in the Mexican War, and leading his cavalry troop, the Magnolia Rifles, to the first Battle of Bull Run in Virginia, a Confederate victory in which he fought so bravely that General Beauregard called him "The Knight of the Black Plume." His beginnings had been much humbler. Born in the mountains of East Tennessee, he went west to Missouri with his family, then walked east and south all the way to Mississippi on his own, to settle in Ripley, the seat of Tippah County, before the Civil War. His uncle, John Wesley Thompson Falkner, was practicing law there, and so he started his career as a country lawyer, only becoming a Colonel later in the Civil War. After the South's defeat in that war, he returned to Ripley to manage a plantation of over a thousand acres, and to build a narrow-gauge "doodlebug" railroad, the Ripley, Ship Island, and Kentucky, a vital connection between the cities of Memphis, Tennessee, and Mobile, Alabama. That was not the last or least of his accomplishments. He became a writer and authored two novels about the Civil War, one of which, *The White Rose of Memphis*, went through thirty-five editions after its publication in 1881. He had one more ambition to fulfill. He became a politician, ran for a seat in the state legislature, and was elected from Tippah County. The victory brought his highly successful career to a sudden end. On the day of his election in 1889, at the age of 64, he was shot dead, point blank, on a corner of the main street of Ripley, by a jealous rival who pled guilty to the deed and was tried in court, but was acquitted of the murder on the grounds of self-defense.

William Cuthbert Faulkner knew about his great-grandfather, but never knew him in person. However, he was weaned on family stories about the Old Colonel, and as a schoolboy, when a teacher asked him what he wanted to be when he grew up, he boldly declared "I want to be a writer like my great-grandpappy." William Cuthbert Faulkner, who was the namesake of William Clark Falkner, more than fulfilled his ambition. He would become not just *a* writer but *the* writer who gave Southern Literature a world reputation, and would call the principal hero of his fiction Colonel John Sartoris, clearly modeled on "The Old Colonel." *Sartoris* was the name he would give to the first major novel of his career, beginning what would become his lifework, a series of novels and stories that together make up his Mythical Kingdom of Yoknapatawpha County, Mississippi. *Sartoris* was published in 1929, twenty-seven years after the Falkner family had moved to Oxford, a college town that was his home the rest of his life and the chief inspiration for his fictional world. William Faulkner was the eldest of four brothers, children of Murry Cuthbert Falkner and Maud Butler Falkner, and was only five years old in 1902, when the family moved from New Albany to Oxford. He would grow up and go to school there, and in time would live up to his hope of becoming a writer like his great-granpappy. He went far beyond the Old Colonel's deeds, becoming nationally and internationally known, winner of the prestigious 1950 Nobel Prize for Literature.

Faulkner's love of the South was grounded on a thorough knowledge of Mississippi, which he acquired through birth and residency, and through consciously seeking, with little formal education, an intimate acquaintance with its past as well as its present. It helped that his family had lived in Mississippi for four generations, and that Oxford, settled a few decades before the Civil War, was a well-established college town when the Falkner family moved there. Mississippi had been Chickasaw territory when the first settlers came to occupy it in the late eighteenth century, after the American Revolution had succeeded in founding a new nation, from earlier colonies in Virginia and the Carolinas and Georgia. They brought with them, to what was then called the Old Southwest, a pattern of life that had originated in the Jamestown Colony of Tidewater Virginia a century before. Most of the settlers were white Protestants who bought land from the Indians, and following the customary pattern of Southern society, proceeded to clear the wilderness to establish their plantations, using the labor of black slaves imported from Africa to build their houses and cultivate the land, raising crops of tobacco and rice, and increasingly cotton, to prosper in the period before the Civil War.

Faulkner himself was a townsman, not a farmer, but he knew that the South had been largely an Agrarian settlement, with small and large plantations sustaining three fixed classes of rich whites, poor whites, and black slaves. Faulkner liked to claim later on that he was a farmer, not a writer, and he did own a plot of land in the country near Oxford, but writing was his chosen vocation and farming was only an avocation. The dominant plantation society, which flourished and prospered throughout the South until its defeat in the Civil War, still prevailed in Faulkner's lifetime, though the institution of slavery on which it depended had been ended by the war, impoverishing the region for a long time afterward. Faulkner grew up in a family that had fought for the Confederacy and lost, yet Southern identity was still based primarily on the plantation economy, former black slaves being incorporated into white families, not merely as workers but as family members. Blacks who had once been slaves continued to live with their owners, waiting on them, cooking their meals, and helping to raise their children. Southerners valued their past. Even after losing the war, they were reluctant to give up their way of life, blacks and whites living together in the same household, with an intimacy familiar to any reader of Faulkner's stories and novels. He and his brothers had a black "Mammy" whom they loved and who loved them, who is commemorated in his fiction most endearingly in the character he called Dilsey Gibson, the black servant who was the strongest member of the white Compson family in his most famous novel, *The Sound and the Fury*. Faulkner came to think of her as the finest character he had ever created. "She's much better than I am," he told the students at the University of Virginia in 1957, when they attended his classes as Writer in Residence at the university that had been founded by Thomas Jefferson, one of the founding fathers of the United States.

Faulkner was born long after the Civil War, but though as a writer he was a singular American genius, he was in many ways a traditional Southerner, who viewed the Civil War as a tragedy for his region. That tragic sense is evident everywhere in his work, and when asked, as Writer in Residence at the University of Virginia, what had first inspired him to become a writer, he said it was "the instinctive desire to tell the outlander just what we were, just what we might have had that we felt was great, excepting four years of war in which we knew we had no chance to win it." (*Faulkner in the University*, p. 136) Faulkner was well aware that most Americans thought of Mississippi, his native state, as backward, still clinging to its Agrarian identity and culture. Some would joke that Mississippi had more writers than readers, but Faulkner insisted, in an essay on his native state in *Holiday* magazine, that he loved Mississippi "not for its virtues but despite its faults." It was the virtues, in his view, that drove the South to fight the Civil War, to defend its honor and protect its freedom to live as it chose, but he recognized that its faults had outweighed its virtues and doomed it to lose that war.

Faulkner's tragic view of life was not exclusively Southern or American; he shared it with writers as great as Shakespeare and Sophocles. But it was undoubtedly his tragic view that led him to become the South's greatest writer, as well as its most severe critic, for unlike many traditional Southerners who could not accept their defeat in the Civil War, Faulkner believed the South deserved to lose the Civil War. He admired the bravery and loyalty of Confederates like his great-grandfather, those who had elected to secede from the Union that threatened their way of life, and who tried vainly to defend their homeland from the forces arrayed against them, but his conscience pained him too much to overlook their guilt. They had, in his opinion, spoiled the pristine wilderness and made nature into a commodity for human use, dispossessing the native red men and enslaving black men from Africa to work their plantations. To Faulkner, the history of the South was both heroic and tragic, its excess of pride leading as in Greek or Elizabethan tragedy to an inevitable fall from grace. He was a Southerner who was willing to criticize the South, and many readers outside the South found it hard to understand his kind of Southern traditionalism.

Other readers were put off not so much by his Southernness as by his Modernism, as much a part of his work as his tragic view of the South. Faulkner was one of the new generation of American writers who revolutionized the way literature was written. Modernism in English and American in literature started in the second decade of the century, before the First World War, and flourished during the Twenties and Thirties, even into the Forties, but lost its momentum after the Second World War. It produced along the way what has been called the Southern Literary Renaissance, with Faulkner as a major contributor, part of a larger American Literary Renaissance that had started before he began writing. It had started in poetry, not fiction, under the leadership of Ezra Pound and T.S. Eliot, two American writers of genius, whom Faulkner never met, but whom he greatly respected. Their experiments with free verse as a medium for poetry generated a movement called Imagism which Pound led and which culminated in Eliot's brooding masterpiece, *The Waste Land*. Faulkner read the poetry of Pound and Eliot when he first began writing in the Twenties, and he tried hard to become like them a poet himself, but he soon saw that poetry was not his métier, and he turned to prose, a medium which suited him much better, and in doing so responded to another writer of genius, James Joyce, whose experiments with stream-of-consciousness narration in *Ulysses* was as revolutionary as Pound's Imagism and Eliot's *The Waste Land*. The novel as Joyce conceived it had a shape and style it never had before. Faulkner was not the first Modernist to experiment with new ways of writing, but he was among the most original and gifted of those who embraced it. As Pound and Eliot revolutionized poetic style, Joyce and Faulkner revolutionized fictional style, and Faulkner became as much a Modernist as they were. He probed deep into human consciousness, writing sentences that never seemed to end, exploring subconscious as well as conscious thoughts, treating taboo subjects like race and sex with brutal frankness, mercilessly plumbing the depths of human depravity, all with the aim of making every novel and story he wrote unique and unprecedented. Like Pound and Eliot and Joyce, Faulkner pushed his imagination beyond rational understanding. Another Southern novelist, Katherine Anne Porter, called him a "Dionysian" writer who wrote "of the world of illogic and human feeling and complete giving over to emotion rather than reason." She said she was quite willing to read a Faulkner novel five times if necessary to understand it, and many readers have agreed with her. They have found Faulkner difficult to comprehend at first reading, but they could plainly see that his audience has grown worldwide, despite what often seems his deliberate cultivation of obscurity. Anyone who wants to understand Faulkner fully knows he must be taken for all he was, both a Southerner and a Modernist, both a traditionalist and an experimentalist. Faulkner clearly meant to make his work a challenge to his readers, but he offered them a considerable reward. The reward is a profounder understanding of human nature, by treating the South as a distinct American region which had suffered bitter defeat trying to defend its way of life, and by taking his idiosyncratic Faulknerian style as a legitimate innovation in fictional technique. To appreciate Faulkner in the deepest sense means to take him at his word, especially in his Nobel Prize Address of 1950, when he spoke of "the human heart in conflict with itself which alone can make good writing because only that is worth writing about, worth the agony and the sweat."

Faulkner was a Southern writer, but as a writer he was never merely provincial. He set out to be a world writer from the beginning, to create out of the materials closest to him a world of his own making, the Mythical

Kingdom of Yoknapatawpha County, Mississippi, which did not exist before he wrote about it and which was his crowning achievement as a writer. The Swedish Academy, in awarding him the Nobel Prize for Literature in 1950, called him "the epic writer of the American South." It was an honor he earned in just over three decades, from *Sartoris* in 1929 to *The Reivers* in 1962, the time it took him to stake out a new territory of the mind. It had taken him the first thirty years of his life to discover what he could do with words, and another thirty years to fulfill his vision. When he published the last of his Snopes novels, *The Mansion*, in 1958, he called it "the final chapter of, and the summation of, a work conceived and begun in 1925." At the end of his epic achievement as a writer, he knew that the opportunistic Snopes family was as important to Yoknapatawpha County as its opposite, the aristocratic Sartoris family, and he knew he had started the Snopes family with "Father Abraham," the first episode of the Snopes saga which he wrote in 1925, which was never published in his lifetime. Even as late as 1962, the year of his death, he was adding one more fictional chapter to his saga of the South. His final novel, *The Reivers*, was comic, not tragic, and it completes the story of Yoknapatawpha County, Mississippi, adding a few more colorful names and hilarious episodes to the list of its inexhaustibly colorful inhabitants.

Faulkner's Mythical Kingdom is divided, like Caesar's Gaul, into three main parts, or rather, three historical periods: 1. the Antebellum South, prior to the Civil War 2. the Postbellum South, after the Civil War, and 3. the Post World War South. In his total achievement Faulkner converted history into myth, mixing fact and fiction so freely that he could go backward and forward in time with the generations of any given family. In chronicling the lives of the Sartorises and their kin, the Compsons and the McCaslins, he might go backward in time, while with the Snopeses and their kin, like the Bundrens and Varners, he might go forward in time. *Sartoris* is set in the Post World War South, while *The Unvanquished*, published a decade later, goes back to the Antebellum, Bellum, and Postbellum South in earlier generations of the Sartoris family. *The Hamlet*, the first of his Snopes novels, is set in the Postbellum South, while his second Snopes novel, *The Town*, is set in the Post World War South, and the third Snopes novel, *The Mansion*, which rounded out what is called his Snopes Trilogy, goes still further into the Post Second World War South. Faulkner's fluid treatment of time in his work gives it a dimension which is really beyond time, *sub specie aeternitatis*, in which the human pageant seems almost to emerge from before time began and to vanish after time ends, giving the full range of his work a sense of eternity, a timelessness that derives ultimately from the Bible, which he often called simply The Book. As a young boy, his Methodist grandfather had made him recite a different Bible verse every morning before he could eat breakfast, and so early in life he came to know the Bible as thoroughly as a good Protestant was expected to know it. He quoted and paraphrased the Bible throughout his fiction. When Dilsey says, at the end of *The Sound and the Fury*, "I've seed de first en de last," she is thinking of the Compson family which she has served so faithfully, but she is also looking beyond life, for her simple faith assures her that her name will be written in The Heavenly Book. She won't be able to read it, because she is illiterate, but she is certain that when her name is called at the end of her life, "All I got to do is say Ise here."

Though Faulkner was born to be a writer, it took him a long time to learn what kind of writer he was born to be. He was not a child prodigy. In fact, those who knew him well as he grew up in Oxford, Mississippi, wondered if he would ever amount to anything. He was not sure of it himself. It took Faulkner the first thirty years of his life to discover how to be the kind of writer he wanted to be, and the last thirty years to be that kind of writer, to discover for himself how he could become a great writer in the most provincial circumstances. The process of self-discovery took twenty years of growing up and another ten years of learning what to write about, as well as how to write about it. He tried first to write poetry, and even published a few poems, the first in 1919 when he was only 22, but he soon realized that he did not have a gift for poetry and he wisely abandoned it for fiction. He called himself a "failed poet" because in his view poetry was the highest form of literature. He had tried hard to write it: his first book was a long verse fantasy called *A Marble Faun*, which he published in 1924, at his own expense, with the financial help of a few old friends in Oxford. It was not a success, and is seldom read today, though it is a rare book in any library because it was his first. It is late Romantic poetry couched in quite conventional tetrameter couplets, not a daring Modernist experiment in free verse, and its subject is equally conventional, no more than the passage of seasons from spring through summer to fall and winter, as observed by an imaginary living statue, a Marble Faun capable of hearing the pipes of Pan and following him through the woods. Faulkner's first book can be called nature poetry in the broadest sense, but it is not the South as he would later come to portray it; rather, it is a vague wooded landscape where exotic European birds like the rook and the nightingale are heard by a fanciful listener, the Marble Faun, who has to be Faulkner himself in disguise. Wisely, he abandoned poetry after his first experiment, and turned decisively to prose. He would say later "I wrote poetry when I was a young man till I found that it was bad poetry, would never be first-rate poetry." He said he had learned that every word had to be exactly right in a poem, whereas in a short story you could use more words for what you wanted to say, and in a novel still more, and these forms of literature gave him the freedom to express whatever subject he chose in whatever way he saw fit. So having failed in his first experiment to write poetry, he developed his own form of poetic prose, which is at its best so compelling it can carry the reader through passages that seem to be a flowing river of words. One of his greatest admirers was the Russian poet and novelist, Boris Pasternak, who thought Faulkner's style was the new model of verbal expression. "I believe that prose is today's medium, elaborate rich prose like Faulkner's," said Pasternak, whose poetic novel *Dr. Zhivago* ends with a set of poems.

It was Sherwood Anderson, more than any older writer, who convinced Faulkner that the American small town offered new possibilities for artistic treatment, and that colloquial American English offered a new medium of expression. As a young man who wanted to be a writer, Faulkner left Oxford for a time and went down to New Orleans just to meet Anderson. The two writers became fast friends. Anderson had attracted a number of talented young American writers like Ernest Hemingway and Hart Crane to become contributors to the little magazine he was editing, which he called *The Double-Dealer*. Faulkner not only admired Anderson as a writer; he also admired Anderson's way of life. He observed that Anderson had a regular routine, staying by himself and writing assiduously every morning, then going out in the afternoon and evening to party with his friends. Faulkner adopted a similar pattern of behavior and began to publish a few prose sketches in the *New Orleans Times-Picayune*, going on later to write his first novel. When he told Anderson's second wife, Elizabeth Prall—whom he had known earlier when he worked in a bookstore in New York--that he had finished writing a novel, she took the news to her husband. The message she brought back to Faulkner was "Sherwood says if he doesn't have to read your novel he'll recommend it to his publisher." That's what he did, and that's how Faulkner got his first novel, *Soldier's Pay*, published in New York in 1926. Of course Sherwood Anderson did read it before recommending it to Boni & Liveright.

Soldier's Pay is well worth reading. It was Faulkner's first experiment with fictional form and it is not a bad novel. It is original in its way, narrated with the episodic technique which Faulkner used in many of his novels, consisting of short, self-contained scenes with little transition between them. The central figure is a wounded veteran who is virtually speechless all the way through the novel, who does not initiate the action but waits for those who look after him to do so. Its main setting is the South, but not the South as he would come to see it. The passive hero around whom the action revolves is Donald Mahon, returning by train after the First World War to his home town of Charlestown, Georgia. He is a sympathetic but doomed character, willing to be ushered by others toward the inevitable death that is clearly his fate, a fate which he appears to accept without protest. He had been a hero in the war, flying a British plane over France in support of Allied forces, until he was shot down, mortally wounded and blinded by a German gun, reduced to no more than an empty shell of a man, now on his way home to die. He is blind and nearly mute, more dead than alive, but Faulkner places him at the center of the action, and he carries the weight of a fairly uneventful plot, which opens with his railroad journey from New York to Charlestown, Georgia, and ends with his death and funeral in his home town. Faulkner gives him a brief passage of interior monologue, just before he dies, as he remembers his fatal flight over the front lines, when he was hit in the head and blinded by German gunfire. The memory is narrated as though it were happening in his mind, though it is not yet the stream-of-consciousness technique Faulkner would later develop. Donald Mahon speaks very few words in the course of the novel, but he is the object of everyone else's concern, and Faulkner succeeds in making him a hero, not in his own eyes but in the eyes of others. The others are: Joe Gilligan, the friendly soldier who stays with him all the way home; Margaret Powers, the widow of an American officer who has been killed in the war, who nurses him all the way home on the train, and after he returns home, finally marries him out of sympathy just before he dies; his father, Rev. Mahon, the Episcopal rector who hardly knows the proper way to treat his dying son; his fiancée, Cecily Saunders, who is so shocked by his scarred appearance that she runs off with a rival suitor, one who has taken his place in the town when he went off to war, and a strange character with the peculiar name of Januarius Jones, a classical scholar who likes to quote Latin but flirts openly with the women, Mrs. Powers and Cecily, who look on him as a ridiculous figure, and finally, various townspeople who call on him at the rector's house, in a show of formal sympathy with little real feeling. The tone of the novel is fatalistic throughout, a tone frequent in Faulkner's fiction, and it approaches the threshold of tragedy when Donald Mahon dies. There is a particularly moving scene at the end when his father, Rev. Mahon, walks with Joe Gilligan through the town at night and they pass a Negro church, where, from outside, they listen to the congregation singing. Faulkner speaks for the two men as they listen to the voices of sincere Christians in their worship of God, knowing how much meaning it gives to their otherwise desolate lives. By implication, worship in the black church casts a harsh light on the nominal Christianity of the majority of white people in this small, very conventional, Southern town.

> The singing drew nearer and nearer; at last, crouching among a clump of trees beside the road, they saw the church with its canting travesty of a spire. Within it was a soft glow of kerosene serving only to make the darkness and the heat thicker, making thicker the imminence of sex after harsh labor along the mooned land; and from it welled the crooning submerged passion of the dark race. It was nothing, it was everything; then it swelled to an ecstasy, taking the white man's words as readily as it took his remote God and made a personal Father of him…

> They stood together in the dusk, the rector in his shapeless black, and Gilligan in his new hard serge, listening, seeing the shabby church become beautiful with mellow longing, passionate and sad. Then the singing died, fading away along the mooned land inevitable with tomorrow and sweat, with sex and death and damnation; and they turned townward under the moon, feeling dust in their shoes.

Soldier's Pay has such moments of powerful expression, especially at the end, but in it Faulkner is clearly trying to find himself as a writer, aware that he is capable of rising to momentary heights of eloquence but not yet knowing how to control them, and aware that the rural and small-town South is his chosen setting, though he has not yet mastered it. As a Lost Generation novel of the period after the First World War, it proves he can tell a story and create believable individual characters, but hasn't yet found the territory and the people that are closest to home.

He wrote a very different second novel, *Mosquitoes*, which was published in 1927 by the same New York publisher whom Sherwood Anderson had recommended for his first novel. It is about the fashionable literary-artistic set in New Orleans, which included a memorable fictional portrait of Sherwood Anderson in the character of Dawson Fairchild. It was a more successful experiment in fictional form than the first, more controlled and consistent in style, but though it was also about the South, it was not yet centered on the place and people he knew best. This time he chose New Orleans as his setting, a Southern city with a vaguely exotic French charm, and he wrote about it more satirically than tragically. His style in this novel was nearer Fitzgerald than Hemingway, more like *The Beautiful and Damned* than *The Sun Also Rises*, a style suited to the sophisticated people of the city which he had chosen to write about. His atmosphere was not fatalistic this time but witty and leisurely, an atmosphere favorable to the writers and artists who liked to attend bohemian parties in artists' studios or on a houseboat on Lake Pontchartrain. What Faulkner showed in his second novel was his versatility. He followed his postwar novel about a wounded veteran from a small Southern town, with a novel about people of the urban South who had nothing more serious to do than to amuse themselves by talking endlessly about art and literature and music. His first novel had been sombre and brooding, with a plot that centered on a life no longer worth living, lightened by moments of darkly poetic descriptions, mirroring the mood of weariness that had set in after the First World War. His second novel was much lighter in tone, much wittier in dialogue, on the whole a social satire about urban life during the Roaring Twenties in America.

Mosquitoes also departed from his first novel in being what the French call a *roman à clef*, "a novel with a key," drawing on thinly disguised portraits from real life. Two of the main characters were modeled on people Faulkner knew well, fictionalized but recognizable as members of the circle of literary and artistic friends Faulkner had cultivated in the city. Dawson Fairchild, writer and raconteur, is the strongest character in the novel, and he is quite clearly modeled on Sherwood Anderson, whose novel *Winesburg, Ohio*, was one of Faulkner's favorites, and whose presence had drawn him to New Orleans in the first place. The other character based on someone he knew was Patricia Robyn, a sprightly young lady with a wicked sense of humor, an apt variation on the flapper, or what today might be called a liberated woman. Her real-life counterpart was Helen Baird, a Nashville girl Faulkner had met in New Orleans and had fallen in love with. She came from a prominent Nashville family, and in 1925 she shared a summer cottage on the beach at Pascagoula with her mother, not far from the borrowed beach cottage belonging to Faulkner's Oxford friend Phil Stone, where Faulkner was living and writing at the time. She proved to be the most interesting woman in Faulkner's life other than his wife, though he had clandestine affairs with many other women. By his own admission he fell in love with Helen Baird at first sight and courted her as long as she encouraged him. He even proposed marriage to her, though he had little chance of success, since her mother disapproved of him as a disreputable beach bum unworthy of her daughter's attention. Faulkner did indeed walk about barefoot in tattered clothes, but Helen Baird found him amusing as a companion. Her mother however was worried enough to take her daughter off to Europe at the end of the summer to make sure she didn't accept his proposal. Her refusal disappointed Faulkner, who was serious about marrying her, but who managed to swallow his pride and make her a major character in *Mosquitoes*, a novel he was just then writing, which when he finished it he dedicated "To Helen." Faulkner himself appeared in the novel as a minor character under his own name, so it obviously pleased him in his second novel to play around imaginatively with people he knew. It added interest to the novel, though he never tried it again.

Helen Baird was a Nashville girl of a prominent family, and Faulkner was certainly enamored with her; about that there is no doubt. He made her the model for a character in his second novel and dedicated the novel to her. He went even farther, writing an elaborate series of love sonnets addressed to her, which he presented to her in a hand-written booklet on the eve of her marriage to another man. The sonnets were no better than his other poems, but he wrote them for the woman he was destined to love and lose, something her husband, Guy Lyman, who came from a prominent New Orleans family, could never do. Faulkner gave her his tribute in writing, and after her marriage he remained friends with her, visiting her and her husband in later years. Helen Baird was the daughter of a lumberman turned publisher, who was half of the Baird-Ward publishing company in Nashville, and she lived with her parents in an antebellum home named Glenstrae, south of Nashville. She had many young lady friends, one of whom, Anne Bransford (later Wallace). dictated a memoir to her daughter-in-law, Lallie Hudgings Wallace, which mentions Helen Baird prominently. Anne Bransford and Helen Baird made their debut together at the Belle Meade Country Club in 1922, when Helen Baird was only nineteen. That was three years before she met Faulkner in New Orleans. The Bairds were an active part of Nashville society, and it was expected that their daughter would have the customary debut with other young ladies her age.

Here is a full account of how Anne Bransford Wallace remembered Helen Baird in her unpublished memoir:

> I made my debut in the winter of '22 and '23. My grandmother and grandfather...had a big party for me at the Belle Meade Club. It was a black and white ball in the winter. And then we had the Cotillion Club. It was a gypsy cotillion and I remember we had to come out of a kettle at the end of the ballroom... My dress was a gypsy costume. I don't remember exactly all about it but I do remember the girl in front of me was Helen Baird and she was a cute girl but very theatrical. She came out of that kettle and did practically a dance on the stage. I thought, if I have to do that I will just die and I can't do anything like that. So I didn't try to copy Helen, but it was a fun party.

This sketch of Helen Baird in real life matches Faulkner's description of his character, Patricia Robyn in *Mosquitoes*, quite well. She had the same devil-may-care, fun-loving personality, and she loved going to parties in New Orleans and flirting with the men. Helen Baird (later Lyman) is known today because of her brief romance with Faulkner, but Anne Bransford Wallace's memory of her as in her younger years matches Faulkner's own first impression of her in 1925, as reflected nostalgically in a letter he wrote to her much later in his life. In New Orleans, Faulkner had shared an apartment with a young architect named William Spratling, overlooking what was then called Orleans Alley, later named Pirates Alley, behind St. Andrews Cathedral in Jackson Square (now the site of Faulkner House Books). They invited their friends to a party in their apartment in 1925. Helen Baird was invited to come with her brother, Pete, a columnist for the *New Orleans Times-Picayune* whom Faulkner knew. He was clearly smitten by her at first sight, as he would later write in a letter to her: "I remember a sullen-jawed, yellow-eyed belligerent gal in a linen dress and sunburnt legs sitting on Spratling's balcony and not thinking even a hell of a little bit of me that afternoon." Patricia Robyn, his character in *Mosquitoes*, is a flirtatious tomboy who carries on with most of the men around her but never becomes really serious with any of them, exactly as Helen Baird appears to have behaved with Faulkner. He contrasts Patricia Robyn, a bold and breezy socialite in *Mosquitoes*, with the wise-cracking talespinner, Dawson Fairchild. They are the most memorable characters in Faulkner's second novel, and both were based on people he knew, who tend to give the narrative its most lively and intriguing moments when they are present.

Faulkner experimented more consciously with form in his second novel than he had in his first. *Soldier's Pay* is episodic, but it is a straight chronological account of Donald Mahon's final journey home, which takes place in nine chapters with multiple scenes. *Mosquitoes* is even more episodic; it might be called staccato in its arrangement, because it is divided, not into chapters, but into days and hours. The main characters are introduced in the Prologue as they plan their party aboard a yacht, and the novel consists of their four separate days on the yacht, finishing with an Epilogue when they return to their normal lives in New Orleans. There is a sculptor named Gordon as well as the novelist Dawson Fairchild, whom he describes as "a benevolent walrus." The other characters are younger and older friends who admire the artists and seek their company as often as possible. One is a man named Talliaferro (pronounced "Tarver"), who is a widower aged 38, a successful business man in the city who likes to think of himself as an art patron, mimicking Maecenas in ancient Rome. There is Mrs. Maurier, a wealthy socialite eager to invite the artists and their acolytes to an extended party on her yacht. By far the most interesting female character in the novel is Patricia Robyn, identified as the niece of Mrs. Maurier. "Pat" makes catty remarks about the other characters, as she throws herself wildly about, much to the distress of her aunt, Mrs. Maurier. After the novel's Prologue, they all board the yacht which Faulkner names *Nausikaa*, after a Greek princess in Homer's *Odyssey*, to begin their four days of adventure.

Each day on the boat is divided into hours, starting early in the morning and ending at midnight. The guests aboard include not only those introduced in the Prologue, but the brother of Patricia Robyn, who is called "Josh" or "Gus" though his name is Theodore, and a young couple Patricia has invited on the spur of the moment, Pete and Jenny, who are inseparable and banter amiably with each other, and a Major Ayers, who is British and doesn't want anyone to forget it, and two ladies, Mrs. Wiseman, sister of Julius, "the Semitic man," and Dorothy Jameson, a painter, and a young fellow named Mark Frost, who describes himself as "the best poet in New Orleans," but whom Faulkner describes as a "ghostly young man," a writer "who produced an occasional cerebral and obscure poem in four or seven lines." Thus Faulkner placed a small artist's colony on board Mrs. Maurier's yacht: a sculptor, a painter, a novelist, and a poet. The dominant figure among them is clearly that of Dawson Fairchild, the older novelist who obviously feels at home in the company of fellow-artists and admirers. He frequently offers his friends a drink from a bottle of whiskey he keeps hidden below deck (the novel was written during Prohibition), and likes to regale them with stories about Andrew Jackson, the hero of the Battle of New Orleans, and his supposed descendant, Al Jackson, who is the proprietor of a fish ranch in Louisiana, where he has crossbred sheep and fish and styles himself a "fishherd." When the guests aren't listening to Fairchild spin a tale, they amuse themselves in various ways, playing cards, swimming, or dancing to the music of a Victrola. Nothing the least significant happens during their four-day party, but everyone finds the cruise a pleasant way of passing the time.

There are a number of romantic intrigues on the boat, mostly involving the young girls, Patricia Robyn and Jenny, both of whom are quite susceptible to male attention. Jenny is usually paired with Pete as the couple Patricia invited to come aboard the yacht, but sometimes she is the object of attention of older men like Mr. Talliaferro, who sees her sleeping on the deck one morning and tries clumsily to stroke her body. He is having a fantasy about her which echoes the final words of Joyce's *Ulysses*, in the stream of consciousness style which Faulkner was consciously imitating.

> Hard this floor his old knees yes yes Jenny her breath Yes yes her red soft mouth where little teeth but showed parted blondness a golden pink swirl kaleidoscopic a single blue eye not come fully awake her breath yes yes He felt eyes again, knew they were there, but he cast all things away and sprawled nuzzling for Jenny's mouth as she came awake.

Jenny wakes up and quickly repels him with disgust, then goes back to sleep. Patricia Robyn is a flirt like Jenny, and she engages in chatter with many of the men on the boat, including David, a young steward she meets one morning and invites to go swimming with her that night. They go out in the dark in the yacht's tender, and he rows while she takes a dip in the water in her swimsuit. She teases him to take off his clothes and join her in the water, which he does, and they pretend to practice lifesaving, until they climb back in the boat after their romantic interlude, which she has relished to the frank bewilderment of her casually met companion. Patricia is the brazen female, David the shy male, and their encounter at night alone in the water is titillating but inconclusive.

Patricia and Jenny share a cabin on the boat, and on the second night they have a conversation about men. Jenny offhandedly tells Patricia that she has met a shabbily dressed man in New Orleans who claims that he is "a liar by profession and he made good money at it." Patricia is intrigued and wants to know his name, but Jenny has trouble remembering it, trying Walker and Foster before she remembers it was Faulkner. This conversation leads to an inside joke, since Patricia Robyn, who is really the fictional counterpart of Faulkner's sweetheart Helen Baird, retorts: "Faulkner? Never heard of him." Since Faulkner dedicated the novel to Helen, she must have found the exchange amusing. As Patricia and Jenny go on talking between their bunks, Patricia suddenly asks Jenny if she is a virgin; they barely know each other, but Jenny turns the question back, and Patricia swears she is a virgin; so does Jenny. For two young girls to talk freely about virginity adds to the erotic flavor of the novel, which Faulkner carefully cultivates throughout, but seldom pushes beyond the talking stage. The eroticism which is discreet in his second novel will become much more explicit in his later novels.

On the Third Day, Patricia Robyn decides on a whim to elope with David, the steward, and they go off together in the tender. They wander for most of the day in the woods and swamps, getting bedraggled and weary from walking, and being tormented by the mosquitoes which raise painful red welts on Patricia's bare legs and cause her to cry out: "They hurt me." David has to carry her most of the way back to the yacht. When they finally get back, Mrs. Maurier asks her niece, "Patricia, where have you been?" "Walking," the niece snaps back—and that is all the explanation she offers for her escapade with a young boy she barely knows. Fairchild talks freely about "words," which he says have a life of their own when they are written down and published, and his friend Julius, the Semitic man, agrees, saying "Lucky he who believes that his heart is broken: he can immediately write a book and so take revenge." He follows with a remark which sums up Faulkner's abortive love affair with Helen Baird: "No, you don't commit suicide when you are disappointed in love. You write a book." *Mosquitoes* has more words than actions, consisting mostly of conversations about life and art, uttered by the artists and writers and their entourage, with some quotable lines, but few emotional conflicts of the sort that will dominate his later fiction.

The Fourth Day aboard the *Nausikaa* consists mostly of discussions of art and literature, salted with Fairchild's generally cynical comments. He is from "a lower middle class family" in Ohio, just like Sherwood Anderson, and defers to anyone better educated than himself, "a man of undoubted talent despite his fumbling bewilderment in the presence of sophisticated emotions." Faulkner had similar things to say about the real Anderson, whose style he characterized in a review as "fumbling for exactitude." But on that last day aboard the yacht, Fairchild tells his tallest tale. It is about his fictional Al Jackson, who "claims to be a lineal descendant of Old Hickory," and who has been raising sheep in the swamps of Louisiana so long that they have gradually evolved into a new animal species which he calls "sheepfish," replacing their wool with scales and learning to swim underwater. They are herded not only by the master breeder Al Jackson but by his brother Claude, who is so attentive to his sheepfish that he turns into an alligatorman himself, and frightens every living thing in the swamp. Fairchild claims that "there was a sort of shark scare at the bathing beaches along the Gulf coast. It seemed to be a lone shark that kept annoying women bathers, especially blondes, and they knew it was Claude Jackson. He was always hell after blondes."

Soon afterward, they dock in New Orleans, and the Epilogue follows the members of the boating party to Fairchild's apartment in the French Quarter where he talks further about art and literature, and becomes quite eloquent, defining artistic genius as "a Passion Week of the heart, that instant of timeless beatitude which some never know, which some, I suppose, gain at will, which others gain through an outside agency like alcohol, like tonight—that passive state of the heart with which the mind, the brain, has nothing to do at all, in which the hackneyed accidents which make up this world—love and life and death and sex and sorrow—brought together by chance in perfect proportions take on a kind of splendid and timeless beauty." Thus Faulkner, at the end of his second novel, begins to show the sort of mastery of words which will come to full fruition in his later novels, starting with *Sartoris*.

Mosquitoes was a new experiment in the form of fiction, but not the best Faulkner had in him, and Sherwood Anderson knew it. He told Faulkner to go back to Oxford and write about his home town. Faulkner followed his advice and produced the first of his Yoknapatawpha novels, *Sartoris*, in 1929. It was the beginning of his Mythical Kingdom, though he never mentioned the name of Yoknapatawpha in it. This book, his third novel and much the best he had written so far, was rejected by his first publisher and by twelve others, until drastic revision and condensation by his friend Ben Wasson (whom he had known as an SAE fraternity brother at Ole Miss) made it publishable. Somewhere along the way the title was changed from *Flags in the Dust*, suggesting a Civil War theme, to *Sartoris*, a family name that Faulkner had invented to suit the principal landholders of his fictional town. *Sartoris*, the third novel Faulkner published, was the beginning of the whole Yoknapatawpha cycle, and thus it is no exaggeration to say that in the beginning was *Sartoris*, and the rest of his fictional career followed as if by some inevitable and miraculous imaginative process.

Sartoris launched what could be called his third career, the major phase of his life work, in 1929. He had tried first to be a poet, then to be a novelist, and had proved to his satisfaction that he had genuine literary talent. The first novel was better than his poetry, the second novel was better than the first, but it was not until he left New Orleans and went back home to Oxford to write that he discovered himself to be not merely a talented writer but a writer of genius. Here is how he would put it to himself honestly: "I'm a failed poet. Maybe every novelist wants to write poetry first, finds he can't, and then tries the short story, which is the most demanding form after poetry. And, failing at that, only then does he take up novel writing." *Sartoris* showed that at last he had mastered the art of fictional narrative, the form of literature that suited him best.

He dedicated *Sartoris* to Sherwood Anderson, who had given Faulkner his start as a novelist in 1926. Its success had led to the publication of his second novel, *Mosquitoes*, in 1927, still with Horace Liveright, Anderson's publisher. But to his great disappointment, Liveright turned down his third novel, and even told him he shouldn't try to get it published. He did try, despite the discouragement, but when twelve other publishers rejected it, he had to turn to his college friend Ben Wasson, who was also writing novels, to condense it into publishable form. Faulkner hadn't forgotten what Sherwood Anderson had done for him, and in 1929 when the novel was finally published, he dedicated it "To Sherwood Anderson, through whose kindness I was first published, with the belief that this book will give him no reason to regret that fact." Anderson had the good judgment to know that Faulkner's first two novels were not the best he could do, and it was Anderson, a Midwesterner from Ohio, who told Faulkner to go back home to Mississippi and write about what he knew best, which Faulkner had the good sense to do. He left New Orleans and returned to Oxford, Mississippi, where he finally found the freedom he needed to write exactly as he wished. With *Sartoris* he stood for the first time squarely on his home ground, the place he would finally make into Yoknapatawpha County, his Mythical Kingdom.

Faulkner crossed a huge divide when he moved from *Mosquitoes* to *Sartoris*. He was no longer imitating Lost Generation writers like Hemingway and Dos Passos, nor writing satirical escapades of the Roaring Twenties like Scott Fitzgerald and James Branch Cabell. In his third career, Faulkner was creating a world of his own, which did not exist before. It was the South in the broadest sense, which Faulkner regarded as having the most homogeneous American culture, despite its mixture of races. It had survived defeat in the Civil War without losing its old chivalric Christian code, derived from the older feudal European culture, supercharged with the evangelical zeal of American Frontier Protestantism. In an interview in 1952 Faulkner spoke of his love of the South as "the only really authentic region in the United States, because a deep indestructible bond still exists between man and his environment. In the South, above all, there is still a common acceptance of the world, a common view of life, and a common morality." (*Lion in the Garden*, p. 72) Faulkner thought of his family as descendants of the Scottish clansmen who had fought and lost to the English in the Battle of Culloden in 1745, and who, after their decisive defeat, crossed the Atlantic and relocated themselves in the Southern mountains and the Tidewater plantations, until they fought and lost another war in 1865. He told a Japanese audience, on a State Department tour in 1955, that "the people in my country were mostly of Scottish origin," and that "We have to be clannish just like the people in the Scottish highlands, each springing to defend his own blood whether it be right or wrong." Besides the homogeneity of its people, Faulkner was taken with the natural beauty of the Southern landscape, writing as early as 1925, in a piece for Sherwood Anderson's *The Double Dealer*, that "The beauty—spiritual and physical—of the South lies in the fact that God has done so much for it and man so little." Faulkner composed his Mythical Kingdom from a combination of character and setting, based on the place he knew best, his hometown of Oxford, Mississippi, which he had come to view as a microcosm of the entire South.

Not only had he found an original setting for *Sartoris* but an original style. It was the colloquial American idiom, about which he had written as early as 1922, in a short piece for the Ole Miss student newspaper: "Nowhere, today, saving in parts of Ireland, is the English language spoken with the same earthy strength as it is in the United States; though we are, as a nation, still inarticulate." Like Hemingway, he thought that a truly national literature had begun with Mark Twain, whose *Huckleberry Finn* used the language of the American frontier artistically for the first time. Mark Twain, Faulkner said, was the grandfather of his generation of American writers; Sherwood Anderson was the father. He eventually succeeded in expanding and diversifying the native idiom which Twain and Anderson had already used so effectively. But he had learned from international writers as well, especially from novelists like Joseph Conrad and James Joyce, and in his best work he was able to unite the American colloquialism of Twain and Anderson with the techniques of psychological narrative practiced by Conrad and Joyce. *Sartoris* was the first novel in which Faulkner's style and setting coalesced into an artistic whole.

Faulkner's own account of what had happened to him between his first and third novels was expressed in a 1956 interview:

> With *Soldier's Pay* I found out writing was fun. But I found out afterward that not only each book had to have a design but the whole output or sum of an artist's work had to have a design. With *Soldier's Pay* and *Mosquitoes* I wrote for the sake of writing because it was fun. Beginning with *Sartoris* I discovered that my own postage stamp of native soil was worth writing about and that I would never live long enough to exhaust it, and that by sublimating the actual into the apocryphal I would have complete liberty to use whatever talent I might have to its absolute top. It

opened up a gold mine of other people, so I created a cosmos of my own. I can move these people around like God, not only in space but in time too. The fact that I have moved my characters around in time successfully, at least to my own estimation, proves to me my own theory that time is a fluid condition which has no existence except in the momentary avatars of individual people. There is no such thing as *was*—only *is*. If *was* existed, there would be no grief or sorrow. I like to think of the world I created as being a kind of keystone in the universe, that small as that keystone is, if it were ever taken away the universe itself would collapse. My last book will be the Doomsday Book, the Golden Book of Yoknapatawpha County. Then I shall break the pencil and I'll have to stop. (*Lion in the Garden: Interviews with William Faulkner*, p. 255)

Sartoris begins with the ghost of Colonel John Sartoris, a hero of the Confederacy, appearing in the consciousness of his son, Old Bayard Sartoris, and it ends with the death of his grandson, Young Bayard Sartoris. All the male members of the Sartoris family seem to be governed by a self-destructive urge that impels them toward death. It is this irrational, suicidal force which is "pure Sartoris" in the eyes of the redoubtable aunt of Old Bayard, Virginia Sartoris Du Pre, Aunt Jenny, who has come from South Carolina to live with them, carrying a sprig of her symbolic flower, the sweet-smelling jasmine. She knows what she is talking about, because she has lost her husband in the Civil War, and we learn that her brother, Colonel John Sartoris, was shot to death shortly after the defeat and surrender of the South, while his brother, the first Bayard Sartoris, had died during the war because of a foolhardy raid on a Yankee camp. As if a violent death were inevitable in the Sartoris family, Col. Sartoris's son, Old Bayard Sartoris, dies of a heart attack brought on by a wild ride in a motor car which his grandson, Young Bayard Sartoris, races recklessly about the countryside, terrifying everyone in sight, and Young Bayard Sartoris himself dies while testing a private plane near Dayton, Ohio, after the First World War, during which his twin brother, a later John Sartoris, had been killed in aerial combat with a German pilot. Aunt Jenny is a Sartoris herself. "I inherited them," she admits, but that doesn't keep her from blaming the Sartoris men, calling them fools who are determined to die: "Sartoris," she says, "It's in the blood. Savages every one of 'em." The suicidal behavior of all the Sartoris men is brought on by their strong will to live recklessly and die violently, a death wish that is the besetting sin of the Southern aristocratic families throughout Faulkner's fiction. As a Sartoris friend, the young lawyer Horace Benbow, says of them, "Funny family. Always going to wars and always getting killed." It seems to be a kind of willing self-sacrifice which they do not understand but which dooms them from birth. It is as inevitable as the defeat of the South in the Civil War, which Faulkner attributes ultimately to Original Sin, the Puritan conscience at work in the New World.

Faulkner was doing something he hadn't done before in his third novel: he was incorporating his own family history into his fiction. He had based two of the characters in *Mosquitoes* on people he knew well, Sherwood Anderson and Helen Baird. Now he was basing the figure of his principal hero, Colonel John Sartoris, on his own great-grandfather, the Old Colonel William Falkner. Colonel Falkner had fought in the war and then had come home to build a railroad first, and when he profited from it, to build the largest house in town. Faulkner's fictional Col. Sartoris is a reincarnation of his own great-grandfather. Col. Falkner had ordered a life-size statue from Italy to be erected in the town cemetery in his honor, as a permanent reminder of his heroism to the townspeople. So does Col. Sartoris in the fictional town which will eventually be named Jefferson. The only change Faulkner made was to have the railroad come straight through the town, modeled on Oxford rather than Ripley, and to place the statue of Col. Sartoris in the town cemetery, where it could be seen and admired by his great-grandson, the Young Bayard Sartoris. Faulkner's ingenuity in using family history to enliven his fiction gave *Sartoris* a more personal touch than his first two novels. The name of Colonel Sartoris is mentioned over and over in his stories and novels, and every time he mentions it, his own family's past is being invoked as an integral part of his visionary South, weaving family history and legend into his Mythical Kingdom of Yoknapatawpha County.

Though the novel focuses on the Sartoris dynasty, there are some interesting minor characters who contribute to its richness. Aunt Jenny is one of Faulkner's sturdiest and most sympathetic female characters, a Sartoris herself but not of the male line and therefore much more durable. She is there at the end when all the male Sartorises have met violent deaths, trying to comfort Narcissa Benbow, the heroine of the novel, who was engaged to marry the Young John Sartoris before he went off to the First World War and got himself killed in an aerial dogfight. She has transferred her affection to his twin brother, Young Bayard Sartoris, finally marries him and has his son, whom she names Benbow Sartoris. Aunt Jenny sniffs at her, "Do you think that'll do any good?" "Do you think you can change one of 'em with a name?" Narcissa is very sympathetic herself, another female victim of the hellbent Sartoris patriarchy, and at the end of the novel, Narcissa softly plays the piano in the Sartoris mansion, offering the beguiling picture of a young widow who will have to live the rest of her life with memories of the two brothers she loved. The name Sartoris, Faulkner suggests, may be "the game itself," that is, life, "For there is death in the sound of it, and a glamorous fatality, like silver pennons downrushing at sunset, or a dying fall of horns at Roncevaux." Faulkner in this final passage extends the meaning of the name Sartoris to a medieval epic, *Le Chanson de Roland*, "The Song of Roland," which depicts the heroic battle of the French knights and soldiers of Charlemagne's army against the Moors—a battle they lost, as immortalized in the poem. So Faulkner finished his third novel with a flourish, placing it squarely on the world stage--not simply about the South, not simply about the American Civil War, but about tragic heroism throughout history, in war after war, where the outcome never mattered as much as the nobility of those who fought and bled for their land and its people. *Sartoris* stands at the threshold of Faulkner's Mythical Kingdom because for the first time he knows he is dealing with human experience in one place and time that has its counterpart in other places and times.

The novel is also notable for its humor, which was not conspicuous in his first two novels but is an element in his third novel that he will cultivate brilliantly in his later fiction. It centers on the first of a long line of creditable Negro characters he will create. Simon Strother is the black retainer of the Sartoris family, a descendant of slaves and an obedient servant to Old Bayard, but a man who has a mind of his own. He is proud of working for the first family in town, as if it made him a Sartoris himself. Simon is a deacon in the black Baptist church, but he gets into trouble with them when as church treasurer he "borrows" money from the collection plate to support an illicit love affair. The minister is forced to lead a delegation to call on Old Bayard to demand repayment of the money Simon has taken from the church coffers. Old Bayard is furious with Simon, but writes a check for $67.40 to pacify the minister, who then pronounces Simon's reinstatement in the best dialect humor of the Old Southwest, "Deacon Strother, ez awdained minister of de late First Baptis' Church, en recalled minister of de pupposed Secon' Baptis' Church, en chairman of dis committee, I hereby reinfests you wid yo' fawmer capacities of deacon in de said pupposed Secon' Baptis' Church. Amen." Faulkner's dialect humor brings Mark Twain back to life. He liked practicing it so much he made use of it in his fiction from then on, with even greater versatility than Twain had shown. Constance Rourke, in her definitive study of *American Humor*, argues that ignorance is always funny, and ignorance is conveyed by the use of language in nonstandard forms, a fact that clowns and comedians have used to advantage for centuries in many different languages.

Faulkner also introduced in his third novel, in a minor way, the principal family other than the Sartorises who will populate his fiction. They are the Snopeses, the white trash contrasted with the aristocratic Sartorises. They will become his rustic clowns later on, the comic villains of his fiction, but in *Sartoris* they are represented by the sinister figure of Byron Snopes, who is a cashier in Old Bayard's bank, a disreputable peeping tom who is constantly stalking Narcissa Benbow and who even sneaks into her room at night to steal her underwear. The Snopeses are unscrupulous whenever they appear, but usually laughable, so Byron is not a typical Snopes. He is only a minor character with a limited role to play in Faulkner's third novel.

Faulkner has not yet named Jefferson as the county seat of what he will later call Yoknapatawpha County, but his description of the town which is the setting of the novel serves as a fictional counterpart of Oxford, Faulkner's home town:

> The courthouse was of brick, too, with stone arches rising amid elms, and among the trees the monument of the Confederate soldier stood, his musket at order arms, shading his carven eyes with his stone hand. Beneath the porticoes of the courthouse and on benches about the green, the city fathers sat and talked and drowsed, in uniform too, here and there.

Faulkner will elaborate this portrait in his later fiction and give the town a name, but he is already describing the small, somnolent Southern town that lives mainly on its past, which will be the setting of so many of his stories and novels.

As a narrative, *Sartoris* is more straightforward than most of Faulkner's novels, but it is still punctuated by ellipses or unexplained gaps in the action, which are trademarks of Faulkner's fictional technique. We learn about midway through the novel that Old Bayard has died of a heart attack brought on by Young Bayard's reckless speeding, but we don't see it happen, and at the end of the novel we do not see but know that Young Bayard has married his late brother's fiancée, Narcissa Benbow, because she has borne him a son that will survive him, after he has died in a plane crash, flying as recklessly as he drove. The dynastic fate of the male Sartoris line, generation after generation, gives this novel a historical depth lacking in his first two novels. The steady procession of male Sartorises to violent death suggests some kind of curse on the family, as in Greek tragedies where the tragic flaw is linked to ancestral crimes, as in *Oedipus* and *Agamemnon*. The curse is never stated, but is implicit in the action, since Faulkner connects the Sartoris doom with two wars, the Civil War in which the first Bayard Sartoris died, and which Col. John Sartoris survived only to die violently afterwards, repeated in the death of a later John Sartoris in the First World War, which his twin brother, the Young Bayard, survives only to die himself in a plane crash a few years later.

The tragic destiny of the Sartorises is parallel to that of the Compsons in the next novel he wrote, *The Sound and the Fury*, as it is again in the Sutpens of *Absalom, Absalom!* These novels are high among the masterpieces Faulkner wrote during his Tragic Phase, the first decade of his literary career. *Sartoris* is not as truly tragic as his later novels will be, but it does have an echo of Classical

Greek tragedy. It also has an echo of a writer much nearer to Faulkner in place and time, Edgar Allan Poe. "The Fall of the House of Usher" is probably the most famous story Poe wrote about his romantically Gothic South, and it is about a brother and sister who die together in an old mansion that crumbles with them. *Sartoris* has overtones of Southern Gothic, starting as it does with the ghost of Col. John Sartoris, which inhabits the Sartoris mansion where Old Bayard lives, where Young Bayard becomes another victim of the Sartoris curse. Faulkner might have called his first Yoknapatawpha novel *The Fall of the House of Sartoris*. But to say that the novel echoes Poe as much as it echoes Twain and Anderson is only to say that it belongs to a lofty tradition of American fiction, and that the Mythical Kingdom of Yoknapatawpha County, Mississippi, is not exotic but native to the United States of America, however unforeseen and unlikely it might have seemed when it first appeared.

CHAPTER 2

Jefferson and Yoknapatawpha

The Sound and the Fury is second only to Joyce's *Ulysses* among the masterpieces of the modern novel. It is justly famous, but few people read either of these pre-eminent modern novels all the way through because Joyce and Faulkner erected an imposing barrier to comprehension. They chose to tell their stories, not as straightforward narratives from a first-person or third-person point of view, but as thoughts inside the minds of individual characters, a technique which became known as stream-of-consciousness narration. It was a new technique when Joyce first perfected it in 1922; Faulkner brilliantly adapted it to his use in 1929. These two novels have been without a rival ever since, and they often top any list of modern fictional masterpieces.

Some gifted writers have tried to equal them, notably Virginia Woolf in *Mrs. Dalloway*, but though the technique has been used by other writers, Joyce and Faulkner are still the most influential practitioners of stream-of-consciousness narration. Their two novels exemplify modern fiction in the same way that the poetic technique of fragmentary internal monologues in free verse, invented by Ezra Pound and T.S Eliot, exemplify modern poetry. Both literary techniques were revolutionary when they were introduced, and they are still mystifying to many readers, but all modern art, according to the English philosopher-poet T.E.Hulme, "no longer deals with heroic action, it has become definitely and finally introspective and deals with expression and communication of momentary phases in the poet's mind." (Quoted in the Introduction to *The Imagist Poem: Modern Poetry in Miniature*, edited by William Pratt, p. 38)

Reading *Ulysses* or *The Sound and the Fury* means entering into the subconscious workings of the human mind, exploring thoughts before they issue as spoken or written words. Opening the mind by means of narrative technique is a process of self-discovery that is as fascinating as it is baffling when first encountered in print. It may even seem deliberately obscure, as if Joyce and Faulkner wanted to make their novels harder to understand. Of course they could have told their stories in the conventional way, by means of complete sentences and paragraphs and chapters, rather than by means of isolated words and partial phrases linked by association, not by logical reasoning. But they were Modernists, seeking a new form of expression, and instead of presenting speeches and actions already completed, they dared to imagine they were looking inside the minds of their characters, seeing words and images forming in the mind before they were shaped into coherent grammatical structures. Joyce and Faulkner were taking fictional character portrayal to a deeper level than had ever been tried before, offering a more intimate experience of the innermost human consciousness, exposing the secret self to view. It was a challenge only writers of genius like Joyce and Faulkner could have imagined, but they succeeded in proving that writers could depart so radically from traditional storytelling that many readers would be bewildered and other writers would be amazed by the ingenuity.

Though these two novels have been in print for nearly a century, they remain unmatched, because subconscious thought is simply harder to depict than conscious thought. Joyce and Faulkner for the first time made words mirror preconscious reality, as if the irrational were trying to become rational. To begin reading either novel is to see the human mind struggling to make sense of experience. The thoughts are not logical and consecutive; they are instinctive and associative. Reading *Ulysses* or *The Sound and the Fury* for the first time is likely to be shocking as well as exhilarating. They give the reader more than he expects, the thrill of exploring the thinking process itself, gaining insights into the human mind that cannot be had by any other means. If the novels were more intelligible, they would be less realistic. *Ulysses* and *The Sound and the Fury* remain the most original and daunting works of fiction, because they offer the illusion—it is only an illusion--of seeing the human mind unconsciously at work, as if we were thinking to ourselves, which is exactly what we are doing most of the time. It is true they are difficult to understand, but it is also true that no serious reader can ignore the illumination they provide, with storytelling unfolding through unspoken thoughts.

To understand why *The Sound and the Fury* stands apart from the rest of Faulkner's work, why it became Faulkner's own favorite novel, is to accommodate ourselves to its singular technique. That he wrote it early in his fictional career is a measure of his genius. It has remained ever since as much a mystery to be solved as a story to be read. The mystery is how Faulkner came to write it. He was still trying to get *Sartoris* published when he began working on what would be his fourth novel, and he finished it in six months, in time to publish it in 1929, the same year *Sartoris* appeared in print. He had clearly broken new ground with *Sartoris*, the first of his Yoknapatawpha novels, but he had not yet named his fictional county nor its fictional county seat. It was in *The Sound and the Fury* that he named the county seat Jefferson, and in his next novel, *As I Lay Dying*, which he published in 1930, he named his fictional county Yoknapatawpha. In two years he had achieved a double feat of imagination, adapting a new narrative technique to his use and introducing a new imaginative territory to explore.

The Sound and the Fury quickly become his favorite, the novel he said he worked hardest on, the one he regarded as his "best failure." Since it is also the most difficult for readers to understand, we have to believe what he later said, that he did not write it as much for an audience as for himself. Faulkner knew he was consciously adapting Joyce's revolutionary stream-of-consciousness technique to a totally different subject matter, which was a fictional triumph in itself. Joyce's novel was exclusively about his native Irish city of Dublin. Faulkner's was about the rural small-town American South, his native territory, a very different part of the earth. Though Joyce and Faulkner compare in psychological depth and complexity, their characters are totally different. Joyce explored the minds of three main characters, Stephen Dedalus, Leopold Bloom, and Molly Bloom, related not by blood but by choice and circumstance; Faulkner's four main characters are Benjy, Quentin, Caddy, and Jason Compson, three brothers and one sister who have grown up in the same family. The language in each novel is eloquent, poetic, and dramatically suited to the characters: they *are* what they think. Faulkner once marveled that Joyce had been "electrocuted by the divine fire." He went on to say that "you should approach *Ulysses* as the illiterate Baptist preacher approaches the Old Testament: with faith." He could have said the same about *The Sound and the Fury*.

It was an act of faith on Faulkner's part to tell a story through the minds of his characters; it is an act of faith for the reader to believe that it works. In *The Sound and the Fury*, the reader quickly learns that point of view is as important as plot. To start reading it is to place ourselves inside the mind of a character whom we do not yet know. As we get our bearings, we gradually perceive that the character himself does not know what is going on. The novel opens in the mind of Benjy, who cannot make sense of his experience because he is an idiot who lacks the power of reason. So we are forced to make sense of it ourselves. The reader has no choice but to become an active participant in the novel, casting about for clues, which can be found outside the novel as well as inside it. Outside the novel is the larger context of all the other novels Faulkner wrote, in particular *Absalom, Absalom!*, a later novel about the Compson family, in which Quentin Compson, a student at Harvard, is the main narrator, with his father and grandfather as co-narrators. Faulkner himself provided a further clue by drawing a sketch map of Yoknapatawpha County as an illustration for the later Compson novel. The larger context of *The Sound and the Fury* includes two of his finest short stories, "That Evening Sun" and "A Justice," which are also about the Compson family, with a much younger Quentin as the eldest child. The larger context even includes the "Appendix" Faulkner wrote for *The Portable Faulkner* in 1945, which carries the history of the Compsons back before the novel begins and forward after it ends. He had been asked to provide an aid to understanding the novel. Faulkner took it as an opportunity to expand his imaginary world in further directions, characterizing each member of the Compson family in the course of extending their stories backward and forward in time.

If Faulkner created a new territory of the mind with *Sartoris*, with *The Sound and The Fury* he opened up a new vista in that territory, within the interior world of individual human beings. *Sartoris* made his vision of the American South a fictional reality; *The Sound and the Fury* raised it to a universal plane of human experience. The individuals whose minds he chose to explore were members of a once-aristocratic family that was rapidly disintegrating. Benjy, Quentin, and Jason Compson were brothers, but as unlike each other in every other respect as it was possible to be, and each was obsessed with a fourth main character, Caddy, the sister they could never forget, whom we see through their eyes, never through her own. In his remarks at the University of Virginia in 1957, Faulkner explained that "Caddy was still to me too beautiful and too moving to reduce her to telling what was going on, that it would be more passionate to see her through somebody else's eyes, I thought." (*Faulkner in the University, ed. Frederick Gwynn and Joseph Blotner*, p. 1) Caddy has grown up with them, but she has been ostracized from the family by her reckless promiscuity. Faulkner himself shared the family obsession with Caddy, saying that "To me she was the beautiful one, she was my heart's darling." (*Faulkner in the University*, p. 6) and he gave a frank account of how he worked his way through his early novels to the sudden revelation he experienced in *The Sound and the Fury:*

> When I began it I had no plan at all. I wasn't even writing a book. I was thinking of books, publication, only in reverse, in saying to myself, I won't have to worry about publishers liking or not liking this at all. Four years before I had written *Soldier's Pay*. It didn't take long to write and it got published quickly and made me about five hundred dollars. I said, Writing novels is easy. You don't make much doing it, but it is easy. I wrote *Mosquitoes*. It wasn't quite so easy to write and it didn't get published quite as quickly and it

made me about four hundred dollars. I said, Apparently there is more to writing novels than I thought. I wrote *Sartoris*. It took much longer, and the publisher refused it at once. But I continued to shop it about for three years with a stubborn and fading hope, perhaps to justify the time I had spent writing it. This hope died slowly, though it didn't hurt at all. One day I seemed to shut a door between me and all publishers' addresses and book lists. I said to myself, Now I can write. Now I can make myself a vase like that which the old Roman kept at his bedside and wore the rim slowly away with kissing it. So I, who had never had a sister and was fated to lose my daughter in infancy, set out to make myself a beautiful and tragic little girl. (quoted from William Faulkner's own Introduction to *The Sound and the Fury*, written in 1933 but unpublished in his lifetime, which can be found in *The Sound and the Fury*, Norton Critical Edition, ed. by David Minter, p. 220)

When he finished the book, he gave it a title out of Shakespeare, a sure indication that this time he knew he was adding a volume to world literature. The words of his title come from the mouth of one of Shakespeare's principal tragic heroes, Macbeth, after he has usurped the throne of Scotland by murdering the king, and is nearing death himself:

> Tomorrow, and tomorrow, and tomorrow
> Creep in this petty pace from day to day
> To the last syllable of recorded time.
> And all our yesterdays have lighted fools
> The way to dusty death. Out, out brief candle!
> Life's but a walking shadow, a poor player
> That struts and frets his hour upon the stage
> And then is heard no more. It is a tale
> Told by an idiot, full of sound and fury,
> Signifying nothing.

Faulkner's novel is a tragedy, but it is Faulknerian, not Shakespearean. There is no tragic hero, as in Shakespeare's play; the minds of the three brothers are obsessed by tragic events that are overwhelming their family, and they respond to their common fate in very different ways The most intelligent of them is certainly Quentin, who at only nineteen, during his freshman year at Harvard, is already bent on committing suicide. It is not however the end of life as he sees it, for he imagines a life beyond death, in which he will take his doomed sister Caddy down with him into "the clean flames" of hell, to share eternal damnation with her. Macbeth's tragedy was final;

he saw no aftermath; but Quentin does not shrink from imagining Hell; he seems eager to sacrifice himself forever out of his love for Caddy and his shame at her promiscuity, and in his mind he envisions the two of them burning together in the flames of Hell as if it were purgative and cleansing, not punitive and painful.

Quentin's quest in this regard is closer to Dante than to Shakespeare, since he would willingly descend into the Inferno that awaits the damned souls in *The Divine Comedy*. It is also Biblical, since Quentin thinks of his sister Caddie as if he were Adam and she were Eve, hearing "the voice that breath'd over Eden" before the Fall of Man. She cannot seem to resist her promiscuity, which Quentin takes much more seriously than she does. At one point Caddy tells Quentin "there's a curse on us its not our fault," as if they were characters in a Greek tragedy, caught in a cycle of inherited fate like Orestes and Electra, the doomed children of Agamemnon in the tragedies of Aeschylus. Quentin is the one Compson who is most aware of the family tragedy, but he is unable to prevent it. He is as introspective and suicidal as if he were Shakespeare's Hamlet, as eager to descend into Hell as if he were Dante, as conscious of inherited family guilt as if he were one of the Greek tragic heroes.

One character stands apart from the family tragedy: Dilsey. She is the central figure in the final section of the novel. She does not narrate it. Faulkner himself is the narrator through a third-person viewpoint, but it is as if we are seeing the Compson tragedy through her eyes. Her vision goes beyond the downfall of the Compson family and reaches upward toward the Kingdom of Heaven, for Dilsey's kind of evangelical Protestant Christianity makes her believe that for all her suffering she will have her reward after death, when her name will be in the Great Book, and when her name is called, all she will have to say is "Ise here." *The Sound and The Fury* may be difficult to understand, but it invites comparisons with some of the greatest works in world literature, one more reason why it is his masterpiece, a world classic as well as a chapter in the saga of Yoknapatawpha County, Mississippi.

The Sound and the Fury presents us with four separate points of view, in four contrasting narrative styles, with a plot that emerges piecemeal from the narrative. Three parts happen in the same time frame, Easter weekend of 1928, but in a disjointed and interrupted sequence. The initial events take place on April 7, 1928, Easter Saturday, in the confused mind of Benjy, the idiot child in the Compson family. They are followed by the events of June 2, 1910, the last day in the life of Quentin Compson, whose mind is more rational than Benjy's but is concentrated on his own suicide; then in the third chapter we have the events of April 6, 1928, Good Friday, which happens entirely in the mind of Jason, the only "sane" brother, and ends on April 8, Easter Sunday, not inside any character's mind, but narrated impersonally and centered on Dilsey, who goes to church with Benjy Compson, her grandson Luster, and her daughter Frony to hear the Easter sermon preached by Rev. Sheegog from St. Louis in the Negro church. She comes out of church saying "I've seed de first en de last" of the Compson family, and then we watch Jason fail in his mad attempt to catch his niece Quentin, who has stolen the money he had systematically robbed from her mother Caddy and has run away from home with a carnival drummer, whom she is unlikely to marry.

Of all the four parts, it is the second section which is the longest and most poetic. The Quentin monologue is in fact the most beautiful piece of writing Faulkner ever did, and he followed it with Jason's monologue, which is the ugliest piece of writing he ever did. The contrast is stunning, as if he wanted to pose good and evil, beauty and ugliness, against each other in the same family. Quentin Compson, for all his weakness, is Faulkner's noblest character; Jason Compson is his meanest, and they are brothers. Faulkner dramatized so much of the potentiality for good and evil in human nature in *The Sound and the Fury* that it is no wonder it has long been considered his finest work, despite the formidable task of fully understanding it, however many times you read it.

The main barrier to understanding is that Faulkner concealed the main events of the plot, so that they have to be extricated piecemeal by every reader. Caddy grows up with three widely different brothers in a close-knit family, and she hastens its descent into ruin by her defiant immorality, in response to natural urges she cannot resist. She sees prophetically that there are forces impelling them to their own destruction. In 1898, when she is only seven, she is already defying her elders by climbing a tree next to the house to peek in on her grandmother's (Damuddy)'s funeral. She has been playing in the creek with her brothers and has soaked her dress, and when she climbs the tree they see her muddy drawers. Faulkner said that the germ of the whole novel was the image in his mind of Caddy's muddy drawers, a symbol of her character as a fallen woman. That's what she becomes as she grows older: she takes up with many different men, eventually marrying a man she scarcely knows in order to legalize her unborn child, whose real father she doesn't even know, and so she names her daughter Quentin for the brother she loves. In 1900, Benjy's name is changed from Maury to Benjamin, since his parents have had to recognize that he will never be normal, and they don't want him to live any longer with the name of his mother's brother, Uncle Maury, an idler who sponges off her family. Childhood episodes are reported between 1900 and 1910, when the four Compson children are still young and living at home, and then the major event occurs. It is Caddy's wedding on April 25, 1910, which breaks the family up for good. A little more than a month later, on June 2, 1910, her older brother Quentin, a freshman at Harvard, commits suicide by drowning himself in the Charles River. He is driven to death by his love for Caddy and his shame at her promiscuity, for Quentin is such an uncompromising idealist that he hopes he will go to Hell with her after death. Caddy does not share Quentin's Puritan conscience; she knows she is bad, but shows no remorse for her immorality. Quentin sees the flaw in her character but is willing to die for her just the same, failing to convince his father that he has committed incest with her in a misguided effort to deserve the everlasting damnation he seeks.

Caddy's marriage lasts less than a year. As soon as her husband discovers that she was pregnant when he married her, and the baby is not his, he divorces her, and in 1911, the year after her wedding, she takes her unwanted daughter, named Quentin after her dead brother, home to be raised by the rest of the Compson family, which has been reduced to her alcoholic father Jason, her sickly mother Caroline and her cruel brother Jason. But most of the responsibility of raising young Quentin is borne by Dilsey, the Negro "mammy" who has raised all the older Compson children.

By 1911, Caddy has exiled herself from the family and Quentin has drowned himself, and in 1912 Father Compson finally drinks himself to death. All that remains of the Compsons are the sickly Mother Caroline (proud she is a Bascomb, not a Compson), the mean and petty brother Jason, and the imbecile Benjy, who is unable to speak intelligible words or to look after himself. It is Benjy who "narrates" the first section of the novel, in such haphazard fashion that most of the events he remembers have to be deciphered from the later sections. His mind cannot distinguish past from present, and is constantly moving back and forth in time without being able to distinguish them.

There are only two events of consequence in the Compson family after Caddie marries and Quentin and Father die. First is Benjy's 33rd birthday on April 7, 1928, the event with which the novel begins, when Compson land has been sold for a golf course to pay for Quentin to go to Harvard; the second occurs when Caddy's daughter Quentin escapes from her sadistic Uncle Jason, on April 8, 1928, to elope with a carnival drummer she has recently met. She breaks into Jason's room and steals his hoard of money, intended for her by Caddy but confiscated by Jason, who pursues her desperately in the final action of the novel but never catches her.

The novel does not end there. It has started with Benjy and his young Negro keeper, Luster, watching golfers play on what had been the family pasture, and it ends with Benjy being driven to the cemetery by Luster to view the graves of his father and his brother. Quentin had escaped the night before with money she stole from her uncle Jason, which he stole from her mother and has been keeping in a secret box in his room. Quentin the daughter is much more "fallen" than her mother Caddy, but there is poetic justice in the act of taking from her scheming uncle the money her mother intended for her, as there is in the way she escapes the Compson household: she climbs down the drain pipe just as her mother as a little girl climbed up the pear tree. Faulkner's symbol of evil in Caddy's muddy drawers is mirrored in her daughter's escape with the stolen money. All that remains is for Benjy to be taken to Easter service in the Negro church by Dilsey, and then driven by Luster to the cemetery where his brother and father are buried. The novel begins with Benjy moaning at the sound of golfers shouting "Caddie," on the golf course that once was the Compson pasture, and ends with Benjy bellowing again, this time because Luster has deliberately taken the wrong turn around the town square of Jefferson.

Finally, after Jason returns from his fruitless chase and forces Luster to drive Queenie (their horse) on the right side of the Confederate monument that stands by the courthouse, Benjy contentedly rides along, sitting peacefully in the carriage on his way to the cemetery, his eyes "empty and blue and serene again," with a wilted flower in his hand. Thus the novel begins and ends as a tale told by an idiot, full of sound and fury.

To summarize the plot of Faulkner's novel is to recognize that though there is a unifying thread of action running through all four sections, it must be actively pursued by the reader because Faulkner only gives it indirectly. The main subject of the novel consists of four complementary styles and points of view directed toward the same family tragedy. Benjy cannot distinguish present from past, but he tells the central story of Caddy climbing the pear tree to peek in on Damuddy's wake. His thoughts pass back and forth from present to past a total of fifty times, each change of time indicated by italics, unaware of the difference between his childhood and adulthood because "he been three years old thirty years," as Luster says.

Quentin is much more rational in his monologue, though he is planning his own suicide that very day, and he dwells on the past because it matters more to him than the present. He knows and condemns what Caddy did as a little girl and as a woman, and he feels personally guilty for the wrongs she has committed, a vicarious consciousness of sin which is driving him to suicide. What happens to him in Cambridge, Massachusetts, connects in his mind with what happened earlier in Jefferson, Mississippi: He has a fight with the brother of a little Italian girl he meets in a bakery when he was only trying to look after her, and he is arrested for it, and he fights with Gerald Bland, his Harvard classmate, because of some insolent remarks about loose women, just as earlier at home he was bloodied in a fight with one of Caddy's boyfriends, Dalton Ames, who breaks his nose fighting over her. He remembers Caddy's wedding obsessively, tries vainly to convince his father that he has committed incest with her, but his father doesn't believe him. His section has begun in his Harvard dorm room, methodically preparing to drown himself in the Charles River. It ends in the same dorm room just before he goes out to drown himself. We do not see it happen but we know it will.

Jason is quite different from either Benjy or Quentin; he is the "sane" brother who is full of resentment for everything in his life, which to him is all present, not past; even Caddie's marriage and divorce and return with her illegitimate daughter Quentin are events he remembers with bitterness as if they were still happening to him. His mind is a battery of complaints against his brothers and his sister and his mother and his niece and even Dilsey, who has raised him as she has raised the others. Jason whines his way through life, and his self-induced afflictions mount to a crescendo when he realizes to his horror that his niece Quentin has eloped with his ill-gotten treasure stolen from her mother, his own sister Caddy. The three brothers together bear witness to the Compson tragedy of which they are a part.

Dilsey is a witness, too, but she is not a part of it, and therefore we do not have to see inside her mind, because she endures it all uncomplainingly. It is she who says at the end, "I've seed de first en de last." She has taken Benjy to the Easter service in her church, where she hears the sermon about "de Ricklickshun en de Blood of de Lamb." The Compson family tragedy has universal implications, and Dilsey understands it best because she has suffered through it with them. She knows them all and cares for them all, but is immune to their guilt, since she is outside the circle of blood relations, not being a Compson herself. Faulkner abandons the monologues in the last section of the novel and presents her objectively in stark realistic detail, but he gives her the last words as a witness to the downfall of the Compsons. Her ability to survive their downfall rests firmly on her strong belief that despite the tribulations of earthly existence she will have her reward in heaven, sustained as none of the Compsons are by a persistent faith in a loving God. Faulkner said late in life that Dilsey was the finest character he ever created. She is like a Greek chorus to the Compson tragedy: lamenting their ruin, sharing their suffering, but untouched by their fate.

Faulkner said he wrote the same story four times over, each from a different point of view, trying to get it right, and failing even though he tried a fifth time. Actually, the story is broken into multiple glimpses of the past and present of the Compson family. Benjy's section begins in the present, with his 33rd birthday on April 7th 1928, but his mind is full of memories of past events. He remembers the scene when Caddy climbed the pear tree in her muddy drawers in 1898 to peer in on Damuddy's wake. He remembers playing with Caddy as a little boy, being comforted by her, having his name changed from Maury to Benjamin in 1900. He remembers the drunken celebration of Caddy's wedding in April of 1910, and his castration at a later date for pawing a neighbor girl. Benjy remembers a time in the past when his brother Quentin told their father about a schoolyard fight with another boy, an event which happened in the distant past, before 1910, and immediately afterward he sees his niece Quentin in a heated argument with her uncle Jason in the present time of 1928—a twenty-year gap between two different Quentins, easily bridged in Benjy's mobile mind. Altogether, he recollects eight distinct moments in thirty-three years, from 1898 when his grandmother died and Caddy climbed the pear tree, to 1928, his 33rd birthday and the present time of his narrative. Since there is no pattern to his shifts backward and forward in time, his thoughts are especially hard for the reader to follow. Faulkner had originally thought of using four different colors of ink to distinguish times present from times past, but it wasn't practicable, and he chose to use italics to show shifts in time, which help a little but not always enough. The reader can only feel pity for Benjy, who can think but is unable to express his thoughts and feelings, which are principally of deep affection for his sister, whose presence gave him the only joy he has known in his life. His section comes first in the novel, as it lives up to its Shakespearean title, "a tale told by an idiot, full of sound and fury."

Quentin is much saner than Benjy, knows the difference between past and present, but associates the past with Caddy, and dwells on it much of the time while he is describing his actions in Harvard Yard and the town of Cambridge in June of 1910. The events he narrates have little connection with what happens in the Benjy section. He is anticipating his suicide by drowning which we never see, remembering Caddy and her lovers which Benjy barely noticed, having long conversations with his father about matters of life and death, innocence and guilt, which Benjy would have been incapable of understanding.

The principal plot of the second section is Quentin's fairly straightforward narrative of the mostly trivial happenings on his last day alive (June 2 1910). He wakes up and gets dressed to leave his college room, deliberately breaking his watch, which is a symbol of the end of time for him, and then taking it to a jeweler in Cambridge as if for repair, but declining to leave it, stopping at a hardware store to buy two flat irons that he will use to drown himself, wrapping them as if they were a parcel of shoes, then secreting them under a bridge over the Charles River for later use, seeing his classmate Gerald Bland rowing on the river, taking a trolley to the outskirts of Cambridge where he meets and talks first with little boys who are fishing in the river for a prize trout, and then encountering a little Italian girl in a bakery shop, befriending her, buying her a bun and ice cream, trying to help her find her way home, then being accused by her brother of kidnapping her, fighting the indignant brother and being arrested by the town marshall and taken to court, being rescued from the village court by his Canadian roommate Steve McCannon and two Southern classmates from Harvard, paying a fine for trying to help the little girl and then fighting again with his classmate Gerald Bland over some insulting remarks about women.

Interspersed in his objective account of the day's happenings are stream-of-consciousness passages about growing up in Mississippi, remembering his fight with Dalton Ames, one of the lovers who bullied Caddy, her marriage in April to Herbert Head, the crass banker from Indiana who was kicked out of Harvard for cheating, his obsessive shame over his sister's promiscuity, his heroic wish to die with her and descend into the "clean flame" of hell to be punished with her forever. He remembers when Caddy said the whole Compson family was under a curse and she herself felt dead while still alive. He recalls vividly his heated argument with his father, when he tried to claim responsibility for Caddy's pregnancy—a claim which his father dismisses as a foolish attempt at self-sacrifice for the sister who only did what came naturally to her. Life is all too "temporary" for Quentin, whose life ends with meticulous preparations to leave his college dorm room and go out to drown himself, as if his suicide were a rational act.

Jason's monologue has no stream-of-consciousness passages because he has no memories to cherish or regret. He lives mostly in the present, and when he thinks of the past it is in vindictive flashes about how his father drank himself to death, how Caddy came to Father's funeral on her last visit home, how Jason sadistically teased her with a passing glimpse of her baby daughter, which she had abandoned to her family when her husband divorced her for infidelity. Jason's thoughts are transparent and self-revealing, a series of angry dialogues with the women he is forced to live with and support, Dilsey and his mother and his niece Quentin, together with sarcastic comments about his idiot brother Benjy, "Jackson's star freshman" whom he has coldly ordered to be castrated for menacing young girls. He is antagonistic to everyone in the family, black and white, though in his mother's eyes he is not a Compson but a Bascomb, the only child she really cares about.

In contrast to his brothers Benjy and Quentin, Jason is totally unsympathetic, cruel and miserly, now the head of the Compson household but hating all those he is obliged to house. He steals the money Caddy sends for her daughter's room and board, and hoards it secretly, laughing to himself at those foolish enough to think they'll have a reward in heaven. Jason resents the fact that he has been left alone to provide for the survivors of the Compson tragedy, by a father who drank himself to death, by a sister who had a love-child and abandoned it to her family, and by a brother who drowned himself. As soon as Jason's monologue begins, we are inside Jason's vulgar and peevish mind: "Once a bitch always a bitch, what I say." He is speaking about his own niece, Caddy's daughter Quentin, who like her mother has disgraced the family by her wild behavior.

Whether he is thinking to himself or speaking his thoughts out loud, the tone is the same, a dreary monotonous diatribe against everyone, a stream of unrelieved vituperation directed at the world. Jason is the unhappiest man alive and he blames everyone but himself for his troubles. He was born unhappy and has stayed that way, unlike poor Benjy whose ignorance is his only escape from unrelieved misery, and idealistic Quentin who finds relief in imagining he will go to hell with Caddy. Jason thinks he is a victim of other people, including the broker who handles his cotton stocks, and the owner of the hardware store where he grudgingly works.

Jason's monologue is unrelievedly prosaic because of the narrowness of Jason's mind, but his thoughts reveal his character as clearly as those of his brothers Benjy and Quentin, whose monologues are highly poetic in their rambling flights of fancy and flashes of memory and warm affection for their sister. Jason takes sadistic pleasure in browbeating everyone around him, including his long-suffering mother, who thinks Jason is burning the checks Caddy sends for her daughter's upkeep, which he cashes and hoards in his room. He has a secret mistress in Memphis, whom he regards as a better woman than his sister Caddy and his niece Quentin because "I've always respected an honest whore." Dilsey, who tries to protect his mother and his niece from Jason's torments, tells him to his face, "You's a cold man, Jason, if man you is."

His bitterest venom is directed at Quentin, his niece, who defies him again and again with her casual love affairs, and tells him openly "I'm bad and I'm going to hell." He threatens her and pursues her and steals the money her mother sends her and generally persecutes her. But in the final section of the novel, on Easter Sunday, Quentin has her revenge, when she steals her mother's money concealed in a box in Jason's room and runs off with the carnival drummer, in the last main episode of the Compson family tragedy. Jason goes after her in vain, trying unsuccessfully to enlist the sheriff to help him, but the sheriff knows Jason too well to believe he has really been robbed by his niece, and so Jason finally has to give up the chase in frustration.

Faulkner was lucky that the editor who received the manuscript of *The Sound and The Fury* in the new publishing house of Cape & Smith in New York was Evelyn Scott, a Tennessee novelist, who read it with growing amazement and told Hal Smith that it was "an important contribution to the permanent literature of fiction." She thought Faulkner's idiot was even more convincing than Dostoevsky's idiot, because he was more innocent, and she expressed her high opinion of the novel in an essay which the publisher distributed along with it. Faulkner was sure of his own opinion: "I like the one which caused me the most trouble. That is *The Sound and the Fury*," and he added "I wouldn't say the best but the one I loved the most." He had worked hardest to make it right, writing it section by section and revising it heavily along the way. He remembered the rest of his life what he had gone through to produce it, writing it in six months, between April and October 1928, first in Oxford and then in New York, and finishing it in a Greenwich Village apartment, where he had to be revived by friends who found him drunk and asleep on the floor. He had been driven to write it by what he remembered as an all-consuming urge:

> I wrote it five separate times, trying to tell the story, to rid myself of the dream which would continue to anguish me until I did. It's a tragedy of two women; Caddy and her daughter. Dilsey is one of my own favorite characters, because she is brave, courageous, gentle and honest. She's much more brave and honest and generous than me. It began with a mental picture. I didn't realize at the time it was symbolical. The picture was of the muddy seat of a little girl's drawers in a pear tree, where she could see through a window where her grandmother's funeral was taking place and report what was happening to her brothers on the ground below. By the time I explained who they were and what they were doing and how her pants got muddy, I realized it would be impossible to get all of it into a short story and that it would have to be a book. And then I realized the symbolism of the soiled pants, and that image was replaced by the one of the fatherless and motherless girl climbing down the drainpipe to escape from the only home she had, where she had never been offered love or affection or understanding.
>
> I had already begun to tell the story through the eyes of the idiot child, since I felt that it would be more effective as told by someone capable only of knowing what happened, but not why. I saw that I had not told the story that time. I tried to tell it again, the same story through the eyes of another brother. That was still not it. I told it for the third time through the eyes of the third brother. That was still not it. I tried to gather the pieces together and fill in the gaps by making myself the spokesman. It was still not complete, not until fifteen years after the book was published, when I wrote as an appendix to another book [*The Portable Faulkner*] the final effort to get the story told and off my mind, so that I myself could have some peace from it. It's the book I feel tenderest towards...I never could get it right. (from "Lion in the Garden," *Paris Review* interview with Faulkner by Jean Stein, published in 1956, reprinted in *Lion in the Garden: Interviews with William Faulkner*, pp. 244–45).

Faulkner came to judge the characters he had created with detachment. He thought the evilest of them all was Jason Compson, who was no monster but a petty, mean human being who enjoyed making others suffer. The best of all in his eyes was Dilsey, the colored servant of the Compson family, who endured Jason's vile and petty ways in order to protect other members of the family from him, especially his hapless brother Benjy and his rebellious niece Quentin. Faulkner confessed he felt humbled by Dilsey, saying "she's much better than I am." Thus, looking back at it later, he saw that *The Sound and The Fury* contained his best and his worst characters, and was superior to anything he had ever written or ever expected to write:

> I learned only from the writing of *Sanctuary* that there was something missing, something which *The Sound and the Fury* gave me and *Sanctuary* did not. When I began *As I Lay Dying* I knew that it would be also missing in this case because this would be a deliberate book. I set out deliberately to write a tour-de-force. Before I ever put pen to paper and set down the first word, I knew what the last word would be and almost where the last period would fall. Before I began I said, I am going to write a book by which, at a pinch, I can stand or fall if I never touch ink again. So when I finished it the cold satisfaction was there, as I had expected, but as I had also expected that other quality which *The Sound and the Fury* had given me was absent: that emotion definite and physical yet nebulous to describe: that ecstasy, that eager and joyous faith and anticipation of surprise which the yet unmarred sheet beneath my hand held inviolate and unfailing, waiting for release. It did not return. The written pages grew in number. The story was going pretty well: I would sit down to it each morning without reluctance yet still without that anticipation and that joy which alone ever made writing a pleasure to me. The book was almost finished before I acquiesced to the fact that it would not recur, since I was now aware before each word was written down just what the people would do, since now I was deliberately choosing between possibilities and probabilities of behavior and weighing and measuring each choice by the scale of the Jameses and Conrads and Balzacs. I knew that I had reached that stage which all young writers must pass through, in which he believes that he has learned too much about his trade.
>
> I received a copy of the printed book and found that I didn't even want to see what kind of jacket it had on it. I seemed to have a vision of it and the other ones subsequent to *The Sound and The Fury* ranked in order upon a shelf while I looked at the titled backs

of them with flagging attention which was almost distaste and upon which each succeeding title registered less and less, until at last attention itself seemed to say, Thank God I shall never need to open any one of them again. I believed that I knew then why I had not recaptured that first ecstasy, and that I should never again recapture it; that whatever novels I should write in the future would be written without reluctance, but also without anticipation or joy: that in *The Sound and The Fury* I had put perhaps the only thing in literature which would ever move me very much: Caddy climbing the pear tree to look in the window at her grandmother's funeral while Quentin and Jason and Benjy and the negroes looked up at the muddy seat of her drawers. (from Faulkner's own Introduction to the novel, quoted on pages 218–19 of The Norton Critical Edition of *The Sound and the Fury*)

The Sound and The Fury became in Faulkner's eyes a singular masterpiece that he finished with a feeling of ecstasy he would never again experience. Most readers tend to agree that it his finest but not that it is his only masterpiece. Allen Tate thought that Faulkner had written five masterpieces, more masterpieces than any other American novelist: *The Sound and the Fury, As I Lay Dying, Sanctuary, Light in August,* and *The Hamlet. As I Lay Dying* would certainly be on any reader's list of his best novels and in some ways it outdoes them all, since the entire novel is made up of stream-of-consciousness narration, and there are fifteen separate points of view instead of just four. The characters contrast sharply with each other, and the action moves forward rapidly and continuously towards a satisfactory resolution, so it is apparent that Faulkner was learning how to make the form of the novel increasingly elastic, with growing confidence in his powers of execution.

He said he wrote *As I Lay Dying* in six weeks on the back of a wheelbarrow, when he was shoveling coal at night in the Ole Miss powerhouse, and he published it in 1930, just a year after *The Sound and the Fury*. In it he named his mythical county for the first time and expanded it to include a larger imaginative territory. The principal action moves from the Bundren farm south of the Yoknapatawpha River to the Jefferson cemetery where the family takes Addie Bundren to be buried in the Bundren family plot. Included in the sweeping panorama are the farm house where the Bundrens live, on a hill above the river, and the farms of the Tulls and Samsons and Armstids and Gillespies where they stop briefly or pass on the way to Jefferson. Central to the action is the river which gives the county its name, the Yoknapatawpha, normally a placid stream with bridges leading across to the Jefferson road, (Faulkner claimed Yoknapatawpha was a Chickasaw Indian word meaning "water flows slowly through flat land,") but after days of constant rain it has become a raging flood that washes the bridges away, forcing the Bundrens to go a long way around in their journey to the cemetery, making a twenty-mile journey twice as long. Action in *The Sound and the Fury* had centered on the town of Jefferson, with its courthouse square and Confederate monument, and the spacious Compson house on the edge of town, adjacent to the pasture that had been sold for a golf course. Jason's pursuit of his niece Quentin only goes as far as the neighboring town of Mottson west of Jefferson. The Bundrens cover more ground than Jason did, starting their journey by a dirt road from the south, riding a wagon pulled by mules with Addie's casket on top. The time setting is 1913, before the First World War, earlier than *The Sound and the Fury*, which was largely 1928, the year when Faulkner was writing the novel, and earlier even than *Sartoris*, set in the period just after the First World War, around 1919. So more of the historical past of Yoknapatawpha County is seen in *As I Lay Dying* than in previous novels, but the characters think in the present, as if the events were happening to them not then but now, their thoughts containing few memories of the past events which dominate the minds of Benjy and Quentin.

As I Lay Dying is a more diversified narrative than *The Sound and the Fury*, consisting of fifteen separate points of view separated into fifty-nine discreet episodes. Some of the monologues can be just as mystifying as in the earlier novel. When Darl says "we had reached the place where the motion of the wasted world accelerates just before the final precipice" and adds "It is as though the space between us were time: an irrevocable quality," he is projecting a vision of the entire universe prompted by the sight of the Yoknapatawpha River in flood. The family has to risk their lives trying to cross it, and the mules drawing the wagon are drowned, and Cash who has built his mother's coffin breaks his leg when a log crashes into it, but they do finally cross it with Addie's coffin. So what Darl is seeing is a scene of violent action which looks like the end of the world, an apocalyptic vision which raises the level of meaning far above the soggy rustic locale.

Darl is the most interesting character in the novel. He seems to be gifted with second sight, for he knows somehow that his mother Addie has committed adultery with the Rev. Whitfield, though it is a secret between them, and he is sure that Jewel is their son, though everyone thinks he is her husband Anse's son, and he knows further that his sister Dewey Dell is pregnant by Rafe though only she has secret knowledge of it. Darl's inner thoughts go so deep into the minds of others that his father Anse declares: "It's like he had got to the inside of you, some way." The most mystifying monologue is not that of Darl, however, but the one Addie Bundren utters after her death, a ghostly utterance which must be coming from the coffin in which they are carrying her body. She muses fatalistically, as the central character in this drama of a family of poor whites living close to the earth and barely able to make a living from it, "I could just remember how my father used to say that the reason for living was to stay dead a long time." All in all, the wide range of meditations by the Bundrens and their country neighbors in Yoknapatawpha County is quite remarkable, considering that these are not the once-proud Compsons who live in a big house in Jefferson with Negro servants and have a son at Harvard, but a dirt-scrabble farm family, who live in a small house on a hilltop in the country and cultivate a meager plot of land for sustenance. Faulkner's feat of imagination in *As I Lay Dying* compares in originality with *The Sound and the Fury*, since it fills the minds of narrowly provincial characters with thoughts that go far beyond the small world they inhabit.

The title, *As I Lay Dying*, sounds poetic and mysterious, but Faulkner had the source in his memory, remote though it was from him in time and place. They are the words spoken by the shade of Agamemnon to Odysseus in Book XI of Homer's *Odyssey*. Agamemnon was a king, the commander of the Greek forces that conquered Troy, but when he returned victorious to his palace at Argos, he was slain in his bath by his unfaithful queen, Clytemnestra. When Odysseus miraculously journeys to Hades to consult the dead spirits, the ghost of Agamemnon complains to him, "As I lay dying the woman with dog's eyes would not close my eyes as I descended into Hades." The parallel in Faulkner's novel is the figure of Addie Bundren, for she lay dying as the novel began, and it is her journey in a homemade casket to be buried in her family plot in the Jefferson cemetery that makes up the main plot of the novel. Her monologue shows that a farmer's wife can have thoughts as deep as those of a Greek hero.

It was Faulkner's boast that he wrote *As I Lay Dying* in six weeks on the back of a wheelbarrow, while working nights in the university powerhouse, and that he knew the last word of it as soon as he wrote the first word. A look at the original typescript shows that it took him 47 days--almost seven weeks—to write it, and that he spent some days later revising it. Faulkner was working hard at this time of his life to support his wife, before he could earn a decent living as a writer. He had taken a job as a "coal passer" who shoveled coal from the pile and wheeled it to the fireman, who then shoveled it into the furnace. It was a night job; if he worked fast early in the evening, he would have the leisure to write in the wee hours of the morning, when the demand for electric power tapered off. His claim that he "never changed a word" of it was not literally true, but he made fewer revisions than in his two earlier novels, *Sartoris* and *The Sound and The Fury*. *As I Lay Dying* is shorter than his earlier novels, and once it starts, it moves so steadily and chronologically from beginning to end that the bizarre plot acquires a sense of inevitability, justifying his claim that it was the easiest book he ever wrote, a *tour de force*. He was helped, he said, by the humming of the dynamo in the powerhouse, a soothing sound he grew to like so much he thought of installing a dynamo in his house, to make all his novels easier to write.

What is original about *As I Lay Dying* is not only the contrapuntal form of short stream-of-consciousness monologues but the surprising choice of characters. Faulkner himself had much more in common with the Sartorises and Compsons, the educated and landowning class of Southerners, than with the Bundrens, poor farmers eking out a precarious existence from the land and seldom going to town. Yet they are the thinking narrators of this novel, and they are as believable in their observations and meditations as the more civilized residents of Yoknapatawpha County. They express themselves in characteristic turns of phrase that distinguish them from each other. Darl is the most mature. He thinks philosophically and poetically in nineteen of fifty-nine monologues, a third of the book ("Life was created in the valleys," he muses typically, "It blew up into the hills on the old terrors, the old lusts, the old despairs.") while his youngest brother Vardaman is the most childlike and naive, thinking over and over "My mother is a fish," willfully identifying the huge dead fish he has caught with his mother who has died. The novel combines interior and exterior monologues, so that sometimes we are inside the mind of a character, seeing his thoughts, while at other times we see the actions of others which he describes. It is notable that Darl, the most intelligent and sensitive of the Bundrens, is committed to the asylum in Jackson for arson at the end of the novel, just as Quentin, the most observant and intelligent of the Compsons, seems consumed by a death wish that drives him to suicide. Faulkner gave special insight to his most perceptive characters, often those whom others think mad. "He smell hit," Roskus says of Benjy, as if he sensed the Compson tragedy first, long before Dilsey declares at the end, "I've seed de first en de last."

As I Lay Dying is even more of a jigsaw puzzle than *The Sound and the Fury*, but it has greater unity of tone and plot. Faulkner succeeds brilliantly in telling the story of a family's arduous journey through the eyes of fifteen different characters, young and old, male and female, who speak to themselves more than they speak to each other. The plot is simple but gripping. The wife and mother of a family of poor dirt farmers lies dying, having exacted from her husband Anse a solemn promise that she will be buried with her family in the Jefferson cemetery. Her son Cash is a carpenter, who methodically constructs her coffin just outside her window where she can watch him. She dies, early in the novel, and the rest of the action consists of the family's effort to carry her body in its casket from their hilltop farm all the way to the Jefferson cemetery, normally a distance of twenty miles. It would be an easy enough journey to make in good weather, even for the wagon and mules that are their sole means of transportation, but incessant rain at the time of Addie's death causes a flood on the Yoknapatawpha River, washing the bridges away and making the journey twice as far and much more hazardous. Not only is the flood on the river an almost insurmountable barrier, but the corpse of Addie begins to smell, attracting vultures to their wagon, prompting Darl to set fire to a neighbor's barn one night to rid the countryside of the nuisance which the family has created by promising to take Addie's body to Jefferson for burial. They do succeed at last in their epic quest, but only through difficulties they never could have anticipated, and the success of their expedition is so burdened with catastrophe that by the end there is little to congratulate themselves for, except that they have kept their promise despite all obstacles.

The plot is a succession of fairly shocking episodes—Cash building Addie's coffin while she watches from her bed, Jewel's secret farming at night to earn a wild mustang to ride, the whole family fording the flooded river with the wagon-laden casket, escaping the burning barn where the body is nearly cremated, traveling with a reeking corpse followed by menacing vultures, the pregnant Dewey Dell's seduction by an opportunistic druggist, the final burial of Addie in the Jefferson cemetery with borrowed shovels. Though the narrative is punctuated by shifts in the point of view, the action is continuous, except for Addie's startling central monologue within her casket. Like *The Sound and the Fury*, point of view is more important than plot, and interest centers on the minds of the characters, ranging from gruff but likable Old Doc Peabody, whose presence in the Bundren household gives it a semblance of sanity, to the fanciful little boy, Vardaman Bundren, who catches a fish and identifies it with his dying mother. Faulkner keeps the continuity of plot flowing through frequent passages of polyphonic prose, expressing the deepest thoughts and feelings of his characters. The individual dialects show less contrast than in *The Sound and the Fury*, because the characters are all of the same class of poor white country people, yet each monologue is dramatically effective. There are no Negro accents to be heard in *As I Lay Dying*, because the Bundrens and their neighbors cannot afford servants like the Sartorises and Compsons; they are poor farmers who have to work hard for their living, and Faulkner treats their poverty realistically, yet sympathetically, imparting wisdom as well as humor to their meditations.

For simple country people, they show at times surprising eloquence in their thoughts. Dewey Dell, as her name indicates, is the first of many earth-mother characters Faulkner created, and she is pregnant through much of the novel, but she can describe herself metaphorically, "I feel like a wet seed in the hot blind earth." Vardaman is a little boy of ten who catches a fish as big as he is, identifies it in his imagination with his dying mother, and when he sees her die, thinks wistfully, "It was not my mother. She went away when the other one laid down in her bed and drew the quilt up. She went away. 'Did she go as far as town?' She went further than town." Darl is the visionary who knows instinctively when his mother Addie is dead, though he and Jewel are not present at her deathbed, because they have gone to a neighbor's farm to work for money for the journey to Jefferson. Yet he visualizes it as it happens: "her eyes, the life in them, rushing suddenly upon them; the two flames flare up for a steady instant. Then they go out as though someone had leaned down and blown upon them." Cash, a carpenter who builds Addie's coffin beneath her eyes, reflects near the end of the novel, when she has been buried in Jefferson and Darl has been committed to the insane asylum in Jackson: "Sometimes I ain't so sho who's got ere a right to say when a man is crazy and when he aint. Sometimes I think it aint none of us is pure crazy and aint none of us pure sane until the balance of us talks him that-a-way. It's like it aint so much what a fellow does, but the way the majority of folks is looking at him when he does it." And Addie herself, the central character, says resignedly from her coffin after her death that "people to whom sin is just a matter of words, to them salvation is just words too." None of these speeches is dramatically plausible, since they are spoken by rural people with little formal education, yet they are authentic expressions of human nature, true even if improbable, and so Faulkner makes us believe that peasant farmers can be rustic philosophers. We are willing to suspend our disbelief throughout *As I Lay Dying*, as Coleridge said poetic symbolism induces us to do.

There is more humor to lighten the action in *As I Lay Dying* than in *The Sound and The Fury*, and it comes from a variety of sources. For instance, as they are passing through Mottson with their reeking coffin and the town marshal confronts them as a public nuisance, Anse offers up a brief account of their laborious progress with Addie's coffin to the Jefferson cemetery:

> "We're doing the best we can," the father said. Then he told a long tale about how they had to wait for the wagon to come back and how the bridge was washed away and how they went eight miles to another bridge and it was gone too so they came back and swum the ford and the mules got drowned and how they got another team and found that the road was washed out and they had to come clean around by Mottson, and then the one with the cement came back and told him to shut up.

The "one with the cement" is Darl, who is carrying a sack of concrete powder to set Cash's broken leg, and they proceed to do so, not anticipating that the cast would cause him much more torment than his broken leg. Cash doesn't complain when his foot turns black and they have to crack the cement case to free him. Dewey Dell, who is pregnant the whole time the family is traveling, and who believes she can abort her unborn child with a dose of patent medicine, goes to a drugstore to purchase it with the ten dollars her lover Rafe has given her, and is slily seduced by a drugstore clerk who pretends to be a doctor and takes her down to his cellar for "treatment." Then, when the Bundrens finally reach Jefferson, she takes off her rough clothes and puts on her best Sunday dress and shoes, to enter Jefferson in style. Before they can bury Addie in her family plot, after having miraculously survived flood and fire, they have to borrow shovels to dig the grave. Anse shrewdly goes to a widow's house to borrow the shovels, and when he returns them, he proposes to her and she accepts, quickly becoming the new Mrs. Bundren. Such is the comic ending of a mainly tragic story, about an epic journey that took ten hazardous days to complete. Anse is amazingly resilient at the end. He fulfills his promise to his wife and immediately buys a new set of false teeth before bringing the new Mrs. Bundren home with him. His last words provide the bizarrely happy ending to a devastatingly grim tale. "Meet Mrs. Bundren" he says cheerfully to Cash and Jewel and Dewey Dell and Vardaman when he comes back from delivering the shovels.

But it isn't a really happy ending after all because they have coldheartedly committed Darl to the state asylum in Jackson for arson, and have seen him off, handcuffed and laughing hysterically, with two deputies in a train. It is really Darl who has the last word about the Bundrens, long before the mission is completed. He muses to himself, after fording a flooded river, suffering Cash's broken leg, and watching the drowned mules floating swiftly downstream:

> How do our lives ravel out into the no-wind no-sound, the weary gestures wearily recapitulant: echoes of old compulsions with no-hand on no-strings; in sunset we fall into furious attitudes, dead gestures of dolls. Cash broke his leg and now the sawdust is running out. He is bleeding to death is Cash.

Darl's fatalistic thoughts are more fitting for what has happened to his family than the unexpectedly cheerful words of Anse, the man who calls himself the most "misfortunate" man alive. Anse's last words may make *As I Lay Dying* look like a tragicomedy, but it is more tragedy than comedy. Darl is a much more sympathetic character than Anse, and has more monologues than all the rest, and it is he who is separated from the family and sent off to the asylum at the end. There are many comic scenes in the novel, when Dewey Dell, who is pregnant and barefoot, dresses to go into town, when Vardaman catches and carries home a fish bigger than he is, when Cora Tull, an earnest Christian too proud of her faith clucks her tongue at the dying Addie, and when Doc Peabody comments wrily on the Bundren misfortunes, but there are tragic characters like Darl and Jewel and Addie and Cash whose monologues dominate the checkered story of *As I Lay Dying*. It is more humorous and readable than *The Sound and the Fury*, but it is nevertheless dark and brooding much of the way, for when the Bundren family has survived its harrowing ordeal by flood and fire, it has left Addie and Darl, their wisest members, behind, in the graveyard and the asylum. The total outlook in *As I Lay Dying* is tragic, as it is in *The Sound and the Fury*, but both novels are redeemed by Faulkner's deep insights into human nature.

Faulkner is telling us in these two masterpieces that though life in Yoknapatawpha County is hard, the people who live there, whether male or female, young or old, rich or poor, black or white, are strong individuals with minds that look steadily and think constantly about life, who have hearts capable of deep feeling, from compassion to rage, and souls that are unique, each one possessed of a peculiar destiny that is like that of no other person in the world.

CHAPTER 3

Popeye and Joe Christmas

It was in writing *Sartoris* that Faulkner discovered his Mythical Kingdom and introduced the first of his major fictional families, headed by the ancestral patriarch, Col. John Sartoris, who had built his Southern plantation and led the fight to defend it against the invading Yankees. But he lost the Civil War, and came home in defeat to restore whatever was left of the way of life the Confederacy had created and maintained in the brief century of its existence. His will had been broken, but his ghost still lingered in his house, causing his descendants to follow his destructive downward course, generation after generation. That novel set the pattern of behavior in Faulkner's world, and *The Sound and the Fury* was his first masterpiece about this new imaginative territory, Yoknapatawpha County, Mississippi, with its fictional county seat of Jefferson, where another of his main fictional families, the Compsons, lived and died, the degenerate descendants of a governor and a general, watched over by Dilsey, the long-suffering Negro servant descended from slaves. It was she who summed up their downfall in the final episode of *The Sound and the Fury*, "I've seed de first en de last." The tale told by an idiot son of the Compsons greatly enlarged the field of Faulkner's vision, penetrating deeply into the minds of his characters, in stream-of-consciousness narrations of their thoughts, not in spoken words or actions. *As I Lay Dying* used this same psychological method of storytelling to expand Faulkner's fictional territory further, naming it for the first time Yoknapatawpha County, a name Faulkner borrowed from the river that flowed near Jefferson. The Bundrens were not aristocrats like the Sartorises and Compsons. They were a family of hard-working farmers with no ancestral burdens of guilt but with obligations to the dead as well as the living, since they had to cross the river with the body of the family matriarch, Addie Bundren, in a coffin, to reach the Jefferson cemetery where she wanted to be buried. Each of these three early novels would have guaranteed Faulkner the reputation he would one day gather as a major American novelist, but they were as yet known to relatively few readers, and he had yet to earn a decent living by his writing. It is a fact that he wrote his third major novel while shoveling coal at night in the university powerhouse. Faulkner knew he could write; his books were proof of it, but he needed a much larger audience if he hoped to have a professional career as a writer. He set out to reach that larger audience with his next novel, *Sanctuary*. It was a scandal and a financial success that made him not only popular but notorious. He would later express some embarrassment that it had worked so well, but he had done exactly what he set out to do, which was to become a novelist people read and talked about. *Sanctuary* was his ticket to fame and fortune.

Faulkner sent the manuscript of *Sanctuary* to his publisher, Harrison Smith, before he had finished writing *As I Lay Dying*. Smith was so shocked when he read it that he held up publication, telling Faulkner that if he published it they would both be in jail. So Faulkner finished *As I Lay Dying* and sent it off, and Smith elected to publish it immediately, in 1930, a year after he had published *The Sound and the Fury*. However, he changed his mind about *Sanctuary*. He decided to publish it despite his misgivings, and sent Faulkner the galley proof to read and approve for publication. It surprised Faulkner, since he had accepted the publisher's earlier verdict that it was unpublishable. When he read the galleys, however, it was Faulkner who was shocked by what he had written. If the publisher was ready to take the risk, it was Faulkner who had misgivings. He read it over again and found it to be what he called a "bad book." He asked Smith to let him revise it, though it was at a late stage of publication, because he was dissatisfied with the structure of the narrative—not with the sensational story he had written about gangsters and prostitutes. Smith agreed to allow Faulkner to rewrite the book if he would pay half the additional cost, leaving Smith to pay the other half out of future royalties. Faulkner was willing to go that far to improve the novel, and so he undertook the arduous job of revising it, still hoping it would be the one to win him fame and fortune. When it was published, he had some regrets about writing a novel entirely to make money, which in his opinion was not a worthy aim for a writer, but the book succeeded in spite of his misgivings. *Sanctuary* not only attracted a much wider audience, but many readers came to regard it as one of his masterpieces.

The revision took him a month of steady work, but he was better satisfied with the novel when he sent it back to Smith in December of 1930, and he was pleased when it was published at last in 1931. His revision had tightened it considerably, making its susceptible heroine, Temple Drake, more central to the action, and adding a savage scene of lynching, when an angry mob attacks and kills a man accused of a murder he did not commit. Faulkner reordered the opening pages, starting the novel with a dramatic confrontation scene, at a spring in the woods of Yoknapatawpha County, between the ruthless gangster Popeye and the refined lawyer, Horace Benbow. He added a flashback to account for the sadistic behavior of Popeye, the villain of the novel, documenting his unhappy childhood as an illegitimate child orphaned by his mother. Faulkner's revisions condensed the action of the novel and made its beginning and ending more effective, without removing anything that was sensational. *Sanctuary* is still the most compelling and naturalistic detective novel Faulkner ever wrote, full of sordid and gruesome details, with broadly allegorical meaning. It is a tale of weak goodness, embodied in the college girl, Temple Drake, and the well-meaning lawyer, Horace Benbow, both victimized by powerful evil, embodied in the ruthless gangsters Popeye and Red. Faulkner told his friend Ben Wasson, who had helped him get *Sartoris* published, that what was most shocking to him as the author of *Sanctuary* was not the awful things that happened to his naïve young heroine, Temple Drake, but "how all this evil flowed off her like water off a duck's back." The name of Temple was meant to be ironic, as was the title *Sanctuary*.

Sanctuary has always been Faulkner's most controversial novel, shunned by some readers because of its horrifying details, but despite his own disclaimers, it really is one of his best. It is a story about the deflowering of an innocent young girl and her subsequent moral corruption. He said it was "the most horrific tale I could imagine," a study of good and evil in which evil appears to triumph. Katherine Anne Porter, a great admirer of Faulkner, thought he had gone too far, that in the figure of Popeye he had made evil too attractive. But Milton, after all, was accused of making Satan the hero of *Paradise Lost*, and some of the greatest characters in literature are personifications of evil: think of Iago in Shakespeare's *Othello*, or Claggart in Melville's *Billy Budd*. Popeye is certainly one of the prime villains in world literature, and clearly the most memorable character in *Sanctuary*, but Faulkner left no doubt in any reader's mind that Popeye is a villain, not a hero. He dies as scornfully as he lived. When he is given the death sentence for a murder he didn't commit, he asks the hangman to fix his hair. The hangman promptly drops the trap. It may not be perfect justice, but it is certainly a just end for Popeye. When Faulkner was asked once, by an Oxford friend, why he had written *Sanctuary*, he was honest about it. He said he had grown tired of writing stories and books that couldn't be published, or that didn't sell if they were published. "You might say I wrote *Sanctuary* on a dare. I wanted to break into print, and make money on a book of mine, and I did. If I hadn't written *Sanctuary*, my name might never have been well-known until after I was dead. Who knows?"

We don't know whether, without it, Faulkner would have become famous during his lifetime, but *Sanctuary* settled the question once and for all. It was published in January, 1931, and sold 7000 copies in two weeks, more by far than any novel he had written. In 1932, the year after it was published, it was the first of his novels to be translated into French, and was immediately hailed in a preface by André Malraux, a respected novelist and critic, as "marking the intrusion of Greek tragedy into the detective story." The French critic saw what American critics did not see, that *Sanctuary* belonged to the high tradition of Western literature, and his opinion began the French admiration of Faulkner which continues today. French readers recognized that his real purpose was art, not money, even though they were drawn, like the American audience, to what was clearly his most sensational novel. It was Faulkner's sixth novel in less than a decade, as original as anything he had written. With it, Faulkner took the conventions of popular detective fiction beyond the excitement of a thriller, into the perennial contest between good and evil, producing the sense that the events that happened were fated, as in Greek or Elizabethan tragedy. *Sanctuary* marked a turning point in Faulkner's career, making him famous and at the same time revolutionizing the popular genre of the murder mystery that Edgar Allan Poe had invented a century earlier.

True to form, it is a thriller, building an atmosphere of suspense that keeps the reader breathless, wondering what shocking event will happen next. Few classic novels have as much raw emotional power as *Sanctuary*. It opens in the dark forest of Yoknapatawpha County in rural Mississippi, and it ends in the equally dark woods of the Luxembourg Gardens in Paris. It combines the pace of a detective novel with the battle between good and evil, a potent combination for a moral tale. Popeye pursues Temple relentlessly, until he has transformed her completely from a frightened young girl into a hardened addict. Sordid though the story is, it offers some needed comic relief amid the fleshpots of Memphis, the site of some of Faulkner's wickedest humor. Miss Reba, the keeper of the bawdy house where Popeye imprisons Temple, is a madam wise in the ways of the world, who enjoys profiting from the world's oldest profession. The Snopes family begins its comic history in the pompous figure of Senator Clarence Snopes and his gullible country cousin, Virgil Snopes, who thinks Miss Reba's house of pleasure is a respectable hotel.

Faulkner wrote the novel in three weeks, then had to spend three months revising it, because his conscience wouldn't let it stand as originally written. He wanted it to be, as he later said, "something which would not shame *The Sound and The Fury* and *As I Lay Dying* too much." He needn't have worried, because by then he had become a master of fiction, who could vary the form of his novels without sacrificing any of the essentials of fiction: plot, character, and setting.

Faulkner had published two radically experimental novels in *The Sound and The Fury* and *As I Lay Dying*. Some readers found them too difficult, so he determined to make his next novel a hard-hitting, straightforward narrative that would pack an immediate punch. Some readers found the new novel too explicit, but they had no trouble understanding it. He wanted it to be sensational and he wanted it to be readable, so instead of writing another deep psychological study in stream-of-consciousness narration, he wrote a crime novel that concluded with a courtroom drama. He succeeded so well that when S*anctuary* was published in a popular Modern Library edition, he felt obliged to write a preface in which he disparaged the book as a cheap idea designed to make money. But he underestimated his talent; because his command of fictional form had matured greatly in a decade, and he had developed a prose style that seemed natural yet pulsing with rhythm. His gift for creating believable characters, real individuals rather than stereotypes, was as evident in this novel as in his earlier novels, and went far beyond the usual detective thriller. The plot is still shocking, even in our freethinking age, when freedom of speech has made obscenity commonplace. What is shocking is not the explicitness of its language, but the spectacle of innocence brutally violated. By making the conflict of good and evil central to the action, Faulkner was able to superimpose an allegorical framework on a body of naturalistic description. In its dark fatalism, *Sanctuary* is overpowering: once the action begins, the reader is catapulted irresistibly toward the impending doom.

The novel starts with a classic opening scene: "From beyond the screen of bushes which surrounded the spring, Popeye watched the man drinking." Popeye looks at Horace Benbow across a forest pool. Good meets Evil in human form. This confrontation comes at the very beginning of the novel, set in a dark wood where nature seems as menacing as man. Faulkner gave it that master touch when he revised the novel. Horace Benbow is a good man; when he hears a bird singing in the woods he wants to identify it, because nature is friendly to him, but Popeye, the evil man, is frightened by the sudden shadow of an owl flitting overhead, since to him nature is a hiding place, a "sanctuary" for his evil designs. The rest of the novel is thus foreshadowed at the start, with evil dominating over good from the very beginning. Popeye is always dressed in black, a small wiry man with a ruthless will, whose face has "that vicious depthless quality of stamped tin," lighting a match with his thumb and blowing smoke through his nostrils, his "hat slanted above his delicate hooked profile." He is clearly the devil incarnate, however impotent he turns out to be in his relations with women, who fear and despise him as inhuman. Horace is an educated man and a lawyer, well-meaning but weak, unhappily married to the former wife of another man, about to leave her when he meets Popeye in the woods as he is on his way to Jefferson. Popeye marches him off at gunpoint to the Old Frenchman Place, an abandoned plantation house in the woods, which has been transformed into a bootlegger's hideout by a motley gang from Memphis. Popeye detains Horace only briefly that night, but a few nights later he latches on to Temple Drake and will not let her go. She, an innocent young college girl who strays into his domain, becomes his victim, like a fly caught in a spider's web. The Gothic setting of the Old Frenchman Place adds to the symbolism of evil. Faulkner's allegory has started working as soon as the action begins, and it overlays all the events of his swift and violent plot.

The novel is a counterpoint of two interwoven plots. One plot is an extension of *Sartoris*, in which the main characters are Horace Benbow, his sister Narcissa,(Young Bayard's widow), her son Benbow, (nicknamed Bory), and Aunt Jenny, the sister of Col. Sartoris. Horace is ten years older than he was in *Sartoris*, and has married Belle Mitchell, whom he courted in the earlier novel, but has left her just before he encounters Popeye. The other plot concerns Temple Drake, the central figure in the whole novel, a flirtatious college co-ed who enjoys sneaking out of her dorm at night to date town boys, leading her unwittingly into a drunken adventure with Gowan Stevens, who takes her on a wild ride in his car from Oxford (the college town which Faulkner places at a distance from the county seat of Jefferson in this novel) to a football game in Starkville, but stops on the way to see a bootlegger who occupies the Old Frenchman Place in the woods. There Gowan wrecks the car, and goes with Temple to the house of the bootlegger, Lee Goodwin, who is doing his unlawful business (it is the period of Prohibition when liquor is illegal) with the help of his commonlaw wife Ruby, under the watchful eye of Popeye, the gangster boss from Memphis. Temple, daughter of a respected judge in Jefferson, has lived a sheltered life as a college girl in Oxford, and she is petrified with fear when suddenly thrown into the company of uncivilized men and a strange woman. Gowan Stevens is too drunk to protect her, leaving her to become the target of a group of predatory males, dominated by Popeye, who comes alone to her dark room where she lies paralyzed with fear on a cornshuck cot, and coldly deflowers her with a corn cob, having first murdered his feeble-minded helper Tommy. Popeye takes over Temple Drake's life and rules it ruthlessly from then on.

Faulkner alternates between two plots, going back and forth between Horace and Narcissa Benbow and Aunt Jenny and their civilized life in Jefferson, and Popeye and Temple Drake as they move from the Old Frenchman Place in the woods of Yoknapatawpha County to Miss Reba's brothel in the Red Light district of Memphis, where he abducts her after he has committed both murder and rape. Popeye installs Temple as his mistress in the seedy Memphis brothel, and keeps her there until near the end of the novel. The really shocking event is not her imprisonment but her complete and utter corruption. She can remember her formerly privileged life as the daughter of Judge Drake, when she was a popular co-ed on campus, but she willingly becomes Popeye's love-slave, a common prostitute like the other women in Miss Reba's brothel. She knows she is sinking into abject moral perversion, but she does little to resist it. She even justifies herself, recalling what one of her girl friends at college had said to them about Adam and Eve in the Garden of Eden:

> She said the Snake had been seeing Eve for several days and never noticed her until Adam made her put on a fig leaf. How do you know? they said, and she said because the Snake was there before Adam because he was the first one thrown out of heaven; he was there all the time.

Temple willingly accedes to Popeye's seduction, like Eve to Satan's seduction. She did not seek him; he sought her, but she has acquiesced in his possession and becomes his partner in crime. She feels ashamed but not really guilty of any wrongdoing, and she consents to being controlled entirely by Popeye, though she is scornful of his impotence. She calls him "Daddy," and makes herself a passive instrument of his ill will.

The two plots separate for a time between Memphis and Jefferson, but they converge again when Lee Goodwin is unjustly accused of murdering Tommy. He and Ruby come to Horace Benbow in Jefferson, to ask him if he will be their lawyer, and defend Lee from the charge of murder. Horace agrees, since he knew them earlier at the Old Frenchman Place, and believes Lee Goodwin is innocent of the murder of Tommy, despite his ugly reputation in Jefferson as a bootlegger who has already served jail time for murder. The rest of the town assumes Lee is guilty as charged, but he steadfastly declares his innocence. He refuses however to point to Popeye as the murderer, fearing that if he did he would face swifter execution than is facing him at court. Horace suspects that Popeye is the culprit, having earlier seen what a ruffian he is, and he takes on the role of Lee's lawyer and detective, determined to identify the real murderer of Tommy. Ruby has told him that there was a girl at the Old Frenchman Place who drove away in a car with Popeye, and so he goes from Jefferson to Oxford by train to look for Temple Drake. All he learns is that she has run away from college but no one knows where she has gone. He returns by train to Jefferson, and meets State Senator Clarence Snopes aboard, another link with *Sartoris*, since Faulkner had introduced the Snopes family in the earlier novel in the sinister figure of Byron Snopes, Old Bayard's cashier in the bank, who sneaks into Narcissa Benbow's room at night and steals her panties from a dresser.

Clarence is a different breed of Snopes, a country bumpkin who has been dignified by election to the state legislature. He swaggers around with a cigar in his hand, and tries to ingratiate himself with "Judge Benbow" as he calls Horace. Then another and more comical Snopes enters the scene. It is Virgil Snopes, who with his friend Fonzo goes to Memphis to attend a barber college, and they find a cheap room in a "hotel" which turns out to be Miss Reba's brothel. They are too gullible to suspect what is really going on, but the hotel is a bawdy house, and with a Snopes inside, Faulkner injects some comic relief into his sordid plot. Senator Clarence Snopes calls on Virgil, and being older and shrewder, he discovers that Judge Drake's daughter Temple is living at Miss Reba's house of ill repute. He quickly offers to sell this piece of vital information to Horace Benbow for a price. Horace pays the price, hoping to find Temple at Miss Reba's, and he does, but when he confronts her at last, he finds to his dismay she isn't interested in telling him the truth about what happened to Tommy at the Old Frenchman Place. She is so completely in thrall to Popeye that she lives most of the time in an alcoholic haze, and is unmoved by Horace's plea for help in saving Lee Goodwin's life. What she does tell him is how she spent the night at the Old Frenchman Place, lying terrified on a cot, waiting to be attacked by one of the strange men threatening her, until Popeye came and stood over her and she felt him violating her flesh with his hand. She never mentions the murder of Tommy, the one fact Horace hoped to gain from her. He goes away in disbelief, haunted by Temple's shocking story of her deflowering by Popeye—her description of "the evil, the injustice, and the tears," that she endured as "the woman motionless before him as though in a musing swoon of voluptuous ecstasy." He has come to know evil in human form, and he realizes that "there is a logical pattern to evil" that leads to moral corruption and death. What Temple Drake has shown Horace Benbow is that when evil is as potent as it is in Popeye, no ordinary human being is capable of resisting it. He carries that disillusioning discovery away with him, after his encounter with Temple Drake in a Memphis brothel.

Temple takes into her brothel boudoir a new lover named Red, an accomplice Popeye has brought in to satisfy Temple's increasingly desperate physical desires. In the most revolting scene in the novel, Popeye lies whinnying on the bed while they make love, but when he sees he is losing Temple to Red, he shoots Red in cold blood in the dance hall, out of fear that Temple might leave him. We do not see the murder. In a deliberate ellipse in the action, the scene suddenly shifts to Red's funeral, in the dance hall where he has been killed. The funeral is black comedy at its darkest, an old-fashioned wake with wild drinking and dancing which results in upsetting the casket and ejecting the corpse, which tumbles out with a bullet hole in its head. The scene shifts again to Miss Reba's brothel, where the black comedy continues. After Red's funeral the ladies go on drinking beer and gin with Miss Reba, who keeps a pet dog named Mr. Binford, another ironic touch, since it was the real name of the Commissioner of Vice in Memphis when the novel came out. One of the ladies has brought her little boy along, nicknamed Uncle Bud. While they weep over the death of Red who "looked so sweet" in his coffin, Uncle Bud steals a bottle of beer and proceeds to get drunk, whereupon the ladies send him away so that they can continue talking about Temple and Popeye and Red, relishing their gossip about the perverted love triangle that ended in murder.

The comic relief ends when the action shifts again, this time to focus on Horace Benbow, who is bravely trying to defend Lee Goodwin, but is forced to refuse payment of his fee by Ruby, who offers him her body instead of the money she doesn't have. Horace is stunned by her offer, and asks her "cant you see that a man might do something just because he knew it was right, necessary to the harmony of things that it be done?" Horace Benbow is honest and unselfish, but he hasn't the strength to combat pure evil in human form, which is embodied in Popeye. He finally loses his defense case in court, when Temple Drake takes the stand and testifies in an elaborate lie that it was Lee Goodwin who raped her with a corn cob and killed Tommy who was trying to interfere. Temple's corruption is complete. Horace sees what has become of her, and he retreats to the comfort of his wife, Belle, whom he had earlier planned to divorce. He has tried hard, but has been defeated in his attempt to save an innocent man's life, by Lee himself as well as by Temple, both of whom fear Popeye more than they fear the law. Lee is unanimously convicted by the jury and sentenced to die for his alleged crimes. The trial ends with Judge Drake solemnly entering the courtroom and taking Temple away in shame after she has testified against Lee Goodwin. The crowd which has gathered around the courthouse to hear the sentence cannot wait for him to be legally executed. They become so enraged when they hear the report of Temple's testimony that they drag Lee from the jail and burn him alive.

Popeye has been a silent witness to the trial which should have convicted him, but he is never charged with a crime and is free to go on bullying others. However, with his chief victims out of his reach, his own end comes swiftly. When he is mistakenly arrested for murdering a deputy sheriff in Birmingham, he refuses to fight the unjust charge, declines legal aid, and contemptuously dismisses the minister who comes to pray for his soul. The jury convicts him without dissent and he is sentenced to hang for his supposed crime. He is hardly innocent, since he has committed other murders, but he is executed ironically for a crime he didn't commit. He seems indifferent to this twist of fate. When the hangman puts the noose over his neck, Popeye calls out "Fix my hair, Jack." "Sure," the sheriff says "I'll fix it for you," and springs the trap that hangs him. Popeye gets exactly what he deserves, but not for the murder he committed. The novel ends with Judge Drake sitting quietly with his daughter Temple in the Luxembourg Gardens in Paris, among the statues of marble queens, "in the season of rain and death," a somber ending to a horrifying tale.

Pity and fear are the tragic emotions central to Greek tragedy, which in Aristotle's view aroused such powerful emotions that it purged the conscience of the audience, who watched it with fascination. *Sanctuary* has its full measure of pity and fear. The fear is everywhere in the novel, from beginning to end, and Popeye is the prime cause of it, from the opening scene where he confronts Horace Benbow in the woods, to the murder of Tommy, the violation and corruption of Temple Drake, and the killing of Temple's lover Red. The pity is also there, not for Temple Drake, the chief victim of Popeye's cruelty, but for Ruby, the loyal wife of Lee Goodwin, who stays with him despite his brutality to her and his infidelity with other women, and also for Horace Benbow, the good man who is too weak to defend Lee or to prevent his lynching, who cannot find a way to convict Popeye of his crimes nor to redeem Temple from her corruption. Temple's sanctuary is a brothel, and Popeye is executed for a crime he didn't commit, but their ironic fate produces some of the cathartic effect which Aristotle ascribed to Greek tragedy. When the worst that human beings are capable of seems to overwhelm the best, it is tragic, yet in the end it is the weak good that survives, not the strong bad. Faulkner's tragic view is relieved by the persistent good will of Horace Benbow even in defeat, and by many moments of dark comedy, when the enterprising Snopeses appear, and the rollicking funeral is given for Red, and Miss Reba entertains the ladies in her brothel. In the larger context of Yoknapatawpha County that surrounds the action, Faulkner has shown evil lurking along with good, criminals and prostitutes and lynch mobs mixing with the decent folks who live there, who give some balance of normality to the wilder extremes of human existence.

By the time he had finished *Sanctuary*, Faulkner had mastered the art of fiction and dealt with universal problems of human existence within his mythical Yoknapatawpha County, which had become more and more a microcosm of the world. He had made it an increasingly varied landscape of towns and villages and farms and wilderness, peopled by credible individuals both male and female, who ranged in age from the childish Vardaman Bundren to the venerable Aunt Jenny Sartoris, in mentality from the inarticulate Benjy Compson to the eloquent Quentin Compson, in morality from the vulnerable but endearing Caddy Compson and the pitifully corrupt Temple Drake to the petty, sadistic Jason Compson and the monstrously cruel Popeye. He had treated both races frankly, white along with black, and looked into the deep divide between them, marginally with Simon Strothers and his black family in the dominant white Sartoris family, centrally with the imposing figure of Dilsey Gibson, the bulwark of three generations of the white Compson family, who managed somehow to look after her own black family while attending to the needs of the white family which she loyally served. But he still had not dealt directly with the problem of racial identity, the hostility between the white and black races, which was the central concern of his next novel, *Light in August*, published in 1932.

The title is one of his most intriguing. It is not a quotation from a well-known writer, like Shakespeare in *The Sound and The Fury*, or Homer in *As I Lay Dying*, nor is it a family name like *Sartoris*, nor an ironic commentary on the plot like *Sanctuary*. The ambiguity of the word "light" in *Light in August* caused some early readers to guess that it referred to the pregnancy of Lena Grove, perhaps to the weight of her unborn illegitimate child, which she carries patiently through the novel until the end. However, that possibility was quickly ruled out by Faulkner's French translator, Maurice Coindreau, since the English word "light" has two different meanings, and Coindreau faced a dilemma in French, which has two different words for "light." Coindreau had to decide whether to translate it as "Légère en Aout," that is, lighter in August than in an earlier month, or "Lumière en Aout," describing the waning sunlight at the end of the summer. When he appealed to Faulkner for help, Faulkner told him he had the second meaning in mind, that he meant to invoke the peculiar quality of sunlight in late summer in the South. Faulkner would later elaborate it, saying that "in August in Mississippi there's a few days somewhere about the middle of the month when suddenly there's a foretaste of fall, it's cool, there's a lambency, a luminous quality to the light, as though it came not from just today but far back in old classical times. It might have fauns and satyrs and the gods and—from Greece, from Olympus in it somewhere. It lasts for just a day or two, and then it is gone... it was to me just a pleasant evocative title because it reminded me of that time, of a luminosity older than our Christian civilization." So he chose a title for his new novel that was loaded with atmosphere, giving a further symbolic overtone to his Mythical Kingdom of Yoknapatawpha, County, Mississippi, linking it to the Western literary tradition with its origins in Classical Greece.

Faulkner wanted his novels to vary in form, but to maintain continuity in their setting, with the result that the South became more and more mythical in his portrayal of it. His first two Yoknapatawpha novels, *Sartoris* and *The Sound and the Fury*, were about families much like his own, the Southern gentry who were inheritors of the slaveholding plantation society that had flourished in the South before the Civil War, who became bankers and landholders in the towns that emerged after the war. But in his third Yoknapatawpha novel, *As I Lay Dying*, he wrote about a family quite unlike his own, poor whites who settled the back country on small farms and worked the land by hard labor, ploughing with mules, employing horses for transportation. There were prominent black characters in the Sartoris and

Compson families, who were descendants of the old planters, but there are no blacks at all in *As I Lay Dying*, since the Bundrens never owned slaves and couldn't afford servants. In *As I Lay Dying* he made relatively uneducated country people think and talk as intelligently as the more sophisticated townspeople of *The Sound and the Fury*, and in *Sanctuary* there are no black people but there are criminals and outlaws, bootleggers and prostitutes living in Yoknapatawpha County and its neighboring city of Memphis. Memphis too became mythical, the chief repository of sin in Faulkner's world, implying that if evil is inherent in human nature, it is more concentrated in the city than in the town or country. Lee Goodwin the bootlegger and Ruby his commonlaw wife, Popeye the gangster and Temple Drake whom he prostituted, Miss Reba with her brothel full of ladies of the evening— these too are part of Yoknapatawpha County, though they live in an underworld disdained but patronized by law-abiding citizens, and they are as active on the fringes of society as the respectable people in the middle of it, and in a sense freer, since they aren't hampered by any moral restraints.

Faulkner went further afield with his fifth Yoknapatawpha novel, *Light in August*. He directly tackled the formidable challenge of racial hostility between whites and blacks. It was an old familiar American problem, but had been complicated in the South by prolonged slavery and segregation, and the assumption by white people that they were not just different from black people but superior to them. *Light in August* was Faulkner's attempt at racial realism, since the male protagonist, Joe Christmas, believes he is a mixture of the two races, and is therefore destined to be a pariah, a lost soul unacceptable to either race. Faulkner in his previous novels had shown how the black and white races survived the Civil War, the emancipated slaves remaining an integral part of their white families, as servants rather than slaves. The defeat of the slaveowning society of the Old South had not essentially changed the ways of the Sartorises and Compsons, who were their descendants. Blacks still had an accepted place in the postbellum society that survived the Civil War, even if an inferior one. But anyone who had the misfortune to be born of mixed race—a constant possibility when intimacy between the races was a fact of life—was ostracized from the community and had virtually no place to go. In his fifth novel, Faulkner entered the forbidden territory of racial conflict, focusing his attention on a character whose whole life was a search for identity which ended in tragedy.

We do not meet Joe Christmas at once. As with *Sanctuary*, Faulkner elected to weave together two plots, the first of which was a tale of pathos, centering on Lena Grove, the pregnant country girl from Alabama in search of the father of her unborn child, and the second was a tragedy, centering on Joe Christmas, an itinerant with no place to come from or go to, who had taken a menial job in Jefferson before Lena arrived. We start with Lena on her way to Jefferson, steadily plodding her way by wagon, who sees a plume of smoke rise as she enters the town. What the smoke might mean she does not know, and we do not learn until near the end of the novel. Lena Grove is looking for the man who abandoned her, and it takes her much of the novel to find him, and to learn that the smoke was coming from a house that Joe Christmas had set on fire.

The second plot takes up the story of Joe Christmas, who lives and works in a sawmill, beside a man who calls himself Joe Brown, but who is really Lucas Burch, the father of Lena's unborn child. The separate paths of Lena and Lucas do converge eventually, but not immediately. First we meet two other main characters: Byron Bunch, who works with Joe Christmas and Joe Brown at the planing mill, and befriends the hapless Lena as soon as she arrives in town, and Rev. Gail Hightower, a defrocked minister of the Presbyterian church in Jefferson, who is a recluse living by himself, disgraced by the wife who abandoned him, a hapless character in the tragic plot. Byron Bunch and Rev. Hightower, old friends in Jefferson, share the secret knowledge that Joe Christmas and Joe Brown, who work together at the sawmill by day, operate a thriving bootlegging business by night. Their hideout is a small cabin behind the house of a lonely spinster named Joanna Burden, another main character in the plot. She is an outsider to the people of Jefferson, having been brought there after the Civil War by her abolitionist father and uncle, victorious Yankee carpetbaggers, and she has never been part of the town, though she has lived on its outskirts most of her life. Byron tells Hightower the final devastating chapter of Joanna Burden's lonely existence. She has taken Joe Christmas as her secret lover, but in a fit of rage one night he has killed her and burned her house down. He is now a fugitive from the law, and worse, he is known to be "part nigger," which means he is certain to be lynched if he is ever found.

So we learn that Joe Christmas is a desperate man, with a guilty conscience and an inner conflict that will be tragically resolved at the end of the novel. We follow him as he runs wildly away, trying to distance himself from the scene of his crime in Jefferson. The suspense builds around him, as he is pursued by a posse of citizens led by Percy Grimm, the angry white avenger, but he loses his bearings and runs in circles, and in time he is caught inside Rev. Hightower's house where he has taken refuge, where Percy Grimm empties his revolver into him and then castrates him, a heinous form of lynching reserved for the black murderer of a white woman.

The novel as a whole starts and ends with the story of Lena Grove, but the bulk of the novel is about Joe Christmas, the man who commits murder and arson, who is an outlaw from birth, who began life as a foundling left at the door of an orphan asylum on Christmas Eve. Growing up, he is spotted by a young dietitian when he happens to observe her love affair with a doctor, and it makes him the object of her hatred, driving him out of the orphanage. He is then adopted by a farm couple named MacEachern, devout Calvinists who are determined to raise him according to their strict moral code. Joe Christmas rebels against their Puritanism and becomes the lover of Bobbie, a waitress in a small town cafe, who is the mistress as well of a gang of men from Memphis, who treat her much as Popeye treated Temple Drake in *Sanctuary*. Joe Christmas runs away one night from the MacEacherns, and goes with Bobbie to a dance hall, where he is pursued by MacEachern until Joe Christmas knocks him down with a chair, thinking he has killed his foster father. Bobbie and her men friends accuse him of murder and tell him they will have nothing to do with a "nigger bastard" which Joe believes himself to be. Actually, he does not know what his racial identity is, since he never knew his parents and was given the name Joe Christmas at the orphanage, after he was left as an infant on their doorstep at Christmas time. But he *thinks* he is a Negro, and the thought becomes an obsession which feeds a furious hatred of himself that leads him to self-destruction through sex and liquor and fighting and eventually murder and arson. The plot is as ugly as *Sanctuary*, but Joe Christmas is not Popeye. He is not intentionally cruel but he is a desperate man, who is strangely appealing in his victimhood. Faulkner was dramatizing a character so ostracized from society he felt he had a right to attack it in every possible way. He seems to seek to be punished for his crime of not knowing who he is, and he gets exactly what he wants in the end. He is a haunted figure, running away from everyone including himself. The running starts when he is only eighteen, when he leaves his mistress Bobbie and his foster parents the MacEacherns behind, and "entered the street which was to run for fifteen years." He is alone for the rest of his life and never stops running away: "From that night the thousand streets ran as one street." He runs through the oil towns of Oklahoma and the wheat fields of Kansas and even enlists in the army at one point to escape from civilization, but deserts it after four months. He sleeps with white women, and maliciously tells them he is a Negro, and he sleeps with black women, trying to feel what it is like to be a negro, "trying to breathe into himself the dark odor, the dark and inscrutable thinking and being of negroes." Eventually he wanders into Jefferson and learns that Joanna Burden is living by herself in a big house on the edge of town, shunned by whites but protected by blacks. She becomes his mistress and then his victim, for after sleeping secretly with her for months, he murders her and burns her house down, and then quickly is chased and caught by a mob and lynched at the age of only thirty-three, in a final episode of violence and self-destruction that stops his endless running away from himself.

Before he becomes a fugitive from the law, Joe Christmas lives in the cabin behind Joanna Burden's house, two miles outside of Jefferson, and works at the planing mill, eating meals alone which she supplies, and sleeping with her every night. One night she tells him the story of how she came to Jefferson to live. Her father and brother were fierce Abolitionists, who came to the South after the Civil War as carpetbaggers from the North, and were never accepted by the townspeople. She has lived as an outcast ever since her father and brother were killed by Col. Sartoris in an election dispute, (subject of an episode in a later novel, *The Unvanquished*), when black people and the white people who had emancipated them were trying to take over the South from the dominant white population. So she and Joe Christmas are alike in being estranged from the tight-knit Southern community, but instead of sympathizing with her, Joe perversely rebels against her--as he had rebelled against the dietitian at the orphanage, against Bobbie the waitress, and against the MacEacherns who adopted him--and in a fit of rage he kills her and sets her house afire. That was the plume of smoke Lena Grove had seen as she entered Jefferson at the beginning of the novel, and it brings the two plots full circle, one of them to a ghastly conclusion, the other to a further stage in a long journey.

The denouement of the tragic plot is exciting if inevitable, because we follow Joe Christmas closely in his futile attempt to escape punishment by running away, only to find he has run in a circle. He lets himself be captured in Mottstown and taken to Jefferson for trial, where he escapes from jail and runs off again, this time to Rev. Hightower's house, where he pistol whips the astonished Hightower and then hides in the house until Percy Grimm and his lynch mob catch up with him. Percy Grimm wildly empties his revolver into Joe Christmas and then castrates him, saying "Now you'll let white women alone, even in hell." It is a gruesome tale of vengeance and retribution, against a man who is guilty of a double crime and deserves to be executed, but not at the hands of a mob. The novel is as brutally naturalistic as *Sanctuary*, but it is not allegorical. It is rather about what Faulkner called in his Nobel Prize address "the human heart in conflict with itself." Joe Christmas is a man who hates himself because he thinks he is a mixture of white blood and black blood, and is driven by a self-destructive urge, an insatiable death-wish which is finally fulfilled.

The tragic plot ends with the lynching of Joe Christmas, whose grandparents, Doc Hines and his wife, have, very late in the novel, identified him as the illegitimate child of their daughter Milly, who never married his father, a Mexican circus hand who might have been black. They witness Joe's death and make the arrangements for his burial, helped by the lawyer Gavin Stevens, (related to Gowan Stevens of *Sanctuary* and a major character in the later Snopes novels). But the novel is not over, for there are two final scenes which are only remotely connected with the story of Joe Christmas. First we see Rev. Gail Hightower in his house, brooding on the lynching which has just occurred there, and thinking back to his father and even more to his grandfather, who had once been a minister like himself, and who was a Confederate officer killed by Yankees in Jefferson. He pictures his grandfather riding to defeat in battle with a blare of trumpets. His own life has been a failure, he knows, but he has an image always in his mind of the heroism of his grandfather in the Civil War, which he remembers as the young Bayard Sartoris remembers his great-grandfather, Col. John Sartoris. His grandfather had known Col. Sartoris as well as the Burden who was Joanna's father, the Yankee carpetbagger who came to Jefferson after the war was over. Hightower, alone in his house after the violent death of Joe Christmas, sits in silence, reflecting on "the lambent suspension of August into which night is about to fully come; it seems to engender and surround itself with a faint glow like a halo," thus evoking the meaning of the title, *Light in August*. Rev. Gail Hightower is one of Faulkner's most sympathetic and philosophical characters, who quotes Tennyson and Shakespeare and the Bible in his reverie, dwelling in his mind on the heroic exploits and tragic death of his grandfather in the Civil War, living more in the past than the present, much like Quentin Compson in *The Sound and The Fury*.

 The final chapter of *Light in August* returns to the frame story with which the novel begins. Lena Grove is now nursing the child she had carried in her womb from Alabama west to Mississippi, seeking its father who had abandoned her. The child was born three weeks earlier in Joe Christmas's cabin behind Joanna Burden's house, and she is taking it north to Tennessee. We see her crossing the border with the faithful Byron Bunch who is accompanying and protecting her, on the bed of a truck which picked them up in Mississippi and is carting them to Tennessee, where the truck driver lives. She had found the father of her child, Lucas Burch alias Joe Brown, but he has fled again, as he did from Alabama where he impregnated her. He had settled temporarily in Jefferson where he saw his child briefly after its birth, but he has absconded again, no one knows where, and she must rely on the companionship of Byron Bunch, a man of good will who looks after her and her child wherever they go. They are wandering like gypsies with no particular destination, but Lena is strangely content. Her last words express her patient outlook and her wonder at the vastness of the world, "My, my. A body does get around. Here we aint been coming from Alabama but two months, and now it's already Tennessee."

 Light in August is Faulkner's fourth masterpiece about Yoknapatawpha County. It is a compelling story with vividly realized characters and as always the magnetic power of his words. Many of the events are violent and repugnant, especially the lynching of Joe Christmas in Rev. Hightower's house, yet the twin plots are complementary: Lena Grove in the frame story is the opposite of Joe Christmas in the main narrative. She is placid and patient, a pregnant barefoot country girl who has become a mother without a husband, yet is confident she will somehow manage to raise her new baby with the help of Byron Bunch. She is, as surely as Dewey Dell in *As I Lay Dying*, the Earth Mother, the Eternal Feminine, fecund and enduring, a sympathetic character from beginning to end. Joe Christmas is her opposite, a rebellious character fighting himself and fighting others, self-condemned, impatient to destroy himself, hating his mixed race and uncertain parentage, cruel to those who befriend him, a loner at odds with the world. The racial conflict inside Joe Christmas is mirrored in those who try hardest to help him. The MacEacherns who adopt him are fanatical Puritans, and his grandfather, Doc Hines, is a rabid racist, bent on seeing Joe Christmas, his own grandson, lynched, as the bastard offspring of a wayward daughter, born of "Bitchery and abomination." Joanna Burden is the granddaughter of Abolitionists determined to rescue the black race from slavery, and she becomes the willing mistress of Joe Christmas, allowing him to live in a cabin behind her house and sleep with her every night, but her very kindness to him throws him into a fit of rage, until one night he wantonly kills her and burns down her house. Joe Christmas embodies the tragic fate of a man who can never be sure of his identity, and who lashes out at the world because he is desperately unhappy with himself.

Oddly, Lena Grove never meets Joe Christmas. They are both residents for a time of the little town of Jefferson, Yoknapatawpha County, Mississippi, the small world which was Faulkner's "mythical kingdom," the setting for most of his major novels and stories, but though Joe Christmas is a partner in bootlegging with Lucas Burch alias Joe Brown, the father of Lena's child, and the child is born in the cabin where they live, the two main characters of the double plot never meet. They remain separate, a peasant woman and a hobo man, victims of circumstances beyond their control. Lena is pregnant and unmarried; Joe Christmas is a thief and a murderer, yet Faulkner evokes sympathy for them both through his portrayal of their suffering. Both are acquainted with Byron Bunch, the most admirable character in the novel, the man who unselfishly befriends her and becomes her protector, willingly becoming the male companion she needs to continue her long journey from Alabama through Mississippi to Tennessee. The Russian poet and novelist Boris Pasternak had a particularly high regard for this novel, saying that "*Light in August* is a marvelous book. The character of the pregnant woman, Lena Grove, is unforgettable. As she walks from Alabama to Mississippi, something of the immensity of the South of the United States, of its essence, is captured for us who have never been there."

In Faulkner's opinion, Joe Christmas was neither good nor bad, but was driven by his fate as an orphan. Not knowing his parents' identity, he could not know his own identity, and therefore, as Faulkner said in one of his talks at the University of Virginia, (founded by Thomas Jefferson, for whom Faulkner's mythical county seat was named) "his only salvation in order to live with himself was to repudiate mankind, to live outside the human race." Joe Christmas's fate, Faulkner believed, was "the most tragic condition that an individual can have." His French translator, Maurice Coindreau, thought Faulkner understood human beings so well he knew "the secret of souls," and in his view *Light in August* was "the profoundest and richest of Faulkner's works." Faulkner may shock the reader with his violence, but he can enchant the reader with his style, his often hypnotic power with words. To Boris Pasternak, whose *Dr. Zhivago* is a novel about a poet ending with a set of poems, Faulkner's style was the epitome of verbal expression: "I believe that prose is today's medium, elaborate rich prose like Faulkner's," he said. If you enter Faulkner's fictional world by tuning your ear to his language, which reverberates throughout his work, you possess the key to his Mythical Kingdom.

CHAPTER 4

The Civil War As Tragedy and As Comedy

Faulkner's ninth published novel, *Absalom, Absalom!* was the sixth of his Yoknapatawpha novels, and to many, it is his best. Strangely, it followed publication in 1934 of one of his most forgettable novels, *Pylon*, about the newly popular flying circuses that grew out of the burgeoning aircraft industry of the 1930s. It was timely, but it lacked the character interest and stylistic distinction of his best novels. The timeliness soon faded, as flying circuses became less and less exciting and the pilots who flew them less daring and heroic, and Faulkner's storytelling powers in this minor novel did not match the gravity of major Faulkner novels. But he had not lost his touch. He was able to follow one of his weakest efforts with one of his strongest, by turning his attention from the transitory present moment to the rich historical past. *Absalom, Absalom!* is a masterpiece about the central event of Southern history, the Civil War. In it, Faulkner dramatized the gripping story of the South's defeat by centering the action on one of his aristocratic families, the Compsons, who are seen earlier than in *The Sound and the Fury*, the summer before Quentin would go to Harvard and kill himself. Remarkably, Faulkner wrote most of it not in the real South of Oxford, Mississippi, but in the fantasyland of Hollywood, California, where he had gone to earn money writing screen plays for the movies. The opportunity to write screenplays in Hollywood had come to him as a direct result of the popular success of *Sanctuary*, and he was able to turn it to his advantage as the principal financial supporter of his entire family. Faulkner wrote often for the movies during the 1930s and 1940s, and proved to have a talent for it valued by leading directors like Howard Hawks, but he didn't let it distract him from his real work, which was writing serious fiction. It was while he was working on the screenplay for a film called *Road to Glory* in 1935, that he succeeded in finishing one of his fictional masterpieces, *Absalom, Absalom!*

The novel was published in New York by Random House in1936, using a title drawn from the Bible. Faulkner had a gift for choosing titles that were arresting yet puzzling, and this title drove readers to look for the source. It was the Book of Samuel, and the exclamation comes at the end of the bloody story of King David and his rebellious son Absalom, told in five chapters of Second Samuel, a story as sensational as if Faulkner had written it. Faulkner thought of it as a parallel to the central plot of his novel, the bloody tale of Thomas Sutpen and his sons, who lived through the tragedy for the South of the Civil War. In the Old Testament story, Absalom was the favorite son of King David, who was driven to kill his brother Amnon for raping their sister Tamar. He then rebelled against his father, raising an army to oppose him, and suffered a violent death after losing the battle against his own father, when his hair became entangled in the branches of a tree. Helpless to defend himself, he was slain by the spear of Joab, a leader of the king's army, who defied the edict of King David to spare his son Absalom. When Joab reported to David that all his enemies had been slain, including Absalom, King David cried aloud: "O my son Absalom, my son, my son Absalom, would God I had died for thee, O Absalom, my son, my son!"

The title was apt, for Faulkner's tale of Thomas Sutpen, who had risen from poverty in West Virginia to build Sutpen's Hundred, a mansion and plantation in Mississippi, is about the rebellion of a son against his father. Thomas Sutpen's ambition had been to create a lasting dynasty for his family, but it is dashed by his own children, who one by one turn against him, until he loses any possibility of a lasting legacy, and dies at the hands of his own workman. Thomas Sutpen, like King David, is betrayed by his own son, and the title came to Faulkner as he was writing the novel. It was not the first title he had tried. In 1934, he wrote a letter to his previous publisher, Harrison Smith, saying he had started work on a new novel tentatively titled *Dark House*. His letter outlined the plot: "Roughly, the theme is a man who outraged the land, and the land then turned and destroyed the man's family. Quentin Compson, of *The Sound and The Fury*, tells it, or ties it together; he is the protagonist so that it is not complete apocrypha. I use him because it is just before he is to commit suicide because of his sister, and I use his bitterness which he has projected on the South as a form of hatred of it and its people to get more out of the story itself than a historical novel would be. To keep the hoop skirts and plug hats out, you might say." The Biblical title was inspired, but it came to Faulkner as a second choice, for as he put it to Smith, writing novels was like giving birth: "I believe that the book is not quite right yet, that I have not gone my nine months, you might say." He worked on it for over a year, making many corrections along the way. In the first version of *Absalom, Absalom!* he had carelessly made the date of Quentin's narration the fall of 1910, forgetting that Quentin Compson had entered Harvard in 1909 in *The Sound and The Fury*, and by the summer of 1910 he had drowned himself. Sometimes Faulkner's penchant for linking his fictional events and families in the Mythical Kingdom he created had to be checked for accuracy.

The novel eventually went to a new publisher, Random House, which bought the bankrupt firm of Smith & Haas in 1936 and became Faulkner's regular publisher. It seemed a lucky break for Random House, and it was in the end, but its first appearance proved disappointing. *Absalom, Absalom!* was published in the same year as Margaret Mitchell's all-time bestseller about the Civil War, *Gone with the Wind*, which won the Pulitzer Prize for fiction. Her novel was made into an Academy Award winning film in 1939, adding insult to injury, because the classic Hollywood film about the Civil War appeared the year after Faulkner published his second novel about the Civil War, *The Unvanquished*. Margaret Mitchell had trumped Faulkner twice on the Civil War, but her triumph was temporary. In the long run, both of Faulkner's Civil War novels have proved superior to her novel and its prizewinning movie. When Faulkner was asked whether he had ever read her then famous novel, his reply was blunt: "No story takes 1000 pages to tell."

Absalom, Absalom! occupies a central place in Faulkner's fiction, because it was the novel in which he firmly staked out his claim to be the inventor of Yoknapatawpha County, Mississippi. He drew an imaginary map of his territory and signed it "William Faulkner, Sole Owner and Proprietor." The fictional map of his Mythical Kingdom served as the end paper of his novel, bearing the names of characters and events that had appeared in earlier novels: *Sartoris, The Sound and The Fury, As I Lay Dying, Sanctuary,* and *Light in August*. As a further aid to readers, he provided a genealogy of the Sutpen family who were central to *Absalom, Absalom!* For the first time, Faulkner was trying to show his readers what he had accomplished in the seven short years between *Sartoris* and *Absalom, Absalom!* In a series of five novels he had made what amounted to a mythical history of the South. It was a mythical history containing much real history, since the Civil War figured as the most important event in the mythical as well as the factual history of the South. In his fifth novel, he lets Miss Rosa Coldfield ask Quentin Compson the crucial question about the Civil War: "Is it any wonder that Heaven saw fit to let us lose?" Quentin's answer was Faulkner's answer. It was the story of Thomas Sutpen's tragic career. It embodied the unbridled human will that built the whole plantation society of the antebellum South and foreshadowed its destruction. In this climactic novel, about his Mythical

Kingdom, Faulkner gave a fictional portrayal of how the Old South lost the war because of its own grave flaws, its share of Original Sin. The flaws were shared by the rest of the country, and could only be atoned for by the most costly war Americans ever fought, which was against themselves. The prosperity of the South had been based too much on exploitation: exploiting nature by converting the wilderness from a primeval forest into a vast cotton field, and at the same time exploiting man, dispossessing the native race of red men of their land, and importing and enslaving another race, black people imported from Africa, to work its vast plantations. Faulkner viewed the Civil War as a tragedy, in the classical Greek sense of the word, caused by excessive human pride leading inevitably to disaster and death. *Absalom, Absalom!* stands as Faulkner's most truly tragic novel.

Thomas Sutpen's life was a story of human ambition ruthlessly pursued all the way to self-destruction. He had started life as a poor young hillbilly from West Virginia, whose eyes were opened when he descended from the mountains to Tidewater Virginia. There he beheld an image of civilized grandeur such as he had never known, and he wanted to claim it for himself. He began by sailing to the Caribbean island of Haiti, where he went to work for a French planter, and in time he married the planter's daughter, but something went terribly wrong when she bore him a son. He "put her aside," as he later says, and left for the Mississippi frontier, where, with the help of an imported French architect and a band of wild Negro slaves, he bought land and built a mansion he christened Sutpen's Hundred. He then succeeded in his dream of becoming a planter in the old Virginia mold, courting and marrying a respectable daughter of Jefferson society, and hoping to found a family dynasty that would last for generations. But the dynasty did not even last his lifetime, because of his own domineering behavior. He had a legitimate son and daughter by a respectable wife in his new home, but conveniently forgot that long ago he had a son by the French planter's daughter, and that, when he discovered she was part Negro, he had "put her aside." He wanted to forget that earlier marriage, but she didn't. She plotted to send her son to claim his legacy, and sent him off to Mississippi. When the earlier son appears unexpectedly in Yoknapatawpha County, and tries to marry Thomas Sutpen's daughter, his own half-sister, her brother is appalled. He cannot believe his own half-brother would commit incest compounded by miscegenation, and the only way he can prevent the marriage is to kill his own kin.

Thomas Sutpen's grand dream had almost come true, but suddenly it came crashing down, and the person who tells Quentin Compson, in the summer before he goes to Harvard, the shocking story of what happened to the South, is someone who has personally witnessed the collapse of Thomas Sutpen's dream, who was herself a victim of Thomas Sutpen's tragic fall.

It is Miss Rosa Coldfield, the younger sister of Ellen Coldfield, who had been Thomas Sutpen's second wife and the mother of his two Mississippi children. As an old woman she calls for Quentin Compson to come to her house in "the summer of wisteria" in 1909, and hear the story of Thomas Sutpen, which to her is emblematic of what caused the South to lose the Civil War. She wants to convince Quentin that Sutpen embodied the "fatality and curse on the South and on our family as though because some ancestor of ours had elected to establish his descent in a land primed for fatality and already cursed with it." Quentin, himself the grandson of a Civil War general, listens with fascination to Rosa Coldfield's gripping tale of the rise and fall of Thomas Sutpen. He will repeat it later to Shreve McCannon, his Canadian roommate at Harvard. He recounts Rosa Coldfield's improbable tale to Shreve, to explain to this outsider what his father had told him, that "she chose you because your grandfather was the nearest thing to a friend Sutpen ever had in this county."

Quentin Compson had idolized his grandfather, General Compson, despite the defeat of the South, just as Young Bayard Sartoris, in Faulkner's first Yoknapatawpha novel, had idolized his grandfather, Col. John Sartoris. Bayard had followed the pattern of the male Sartoris line, recklessly courting death in a potentially lethal aircraft, and Quentin is on a self-destructive course toward drowning, even though both Bayard Sartoris and Quentin Compson are two generations removed from the battles of the Civil War. They are both latterday victims of the tragedy Faulkner incorporated in *Absalom, Absalom!* more than in any other of his novels: the defeat of the South in the Civil War. Faulkner saw the fatality of Greek tragedy in the history of the South. Father Compson tells Quentin that their ancestors were "people too as we are, and victims too as we are, but victims of a different circumstance, simpler and therefore, integer for integer, more heroic and the figures therefore more heroic, too, not dwarfed and involved but distinct, uncomplex who had the gift of loving once or dying once instead of being diffused and scattered creatures drawn blindly limb from limb from a grab bag and assembled, author and victim too of a thousand homicides and a thousand copulations and divorcements." The later generation of Southerners, Faulkner was saying, inherited the shame of the South's defeat without living through the heroic but vain struggle of their forefathers to defend their homeland.

Absalom, Absalom! was Faulkner's first serious venture into historical fiction. He had written about the earlier Postbellum South and the contemporary Post First World War South, but in *Absalom, Absalom!* he was dramatizing the Antebellum South as it suffered through the Civil War. He would continue to pursue it in his second Civil War novel, *The Unvanquished*, published in 1938, just two years after *Absalom, Absalom!*, though his perspective on the war had changed significantly in those two years. His first novel about the

Old South was tragic, the culmination of the Tragic Phase of Faulkner's career as a novelist, while his second novel, written two years later, was arguably comic, the beginning of what could be called his Comic Phase, which would continue through the rest of his career as a novelist. He had written his first novels about the later generation, the unhappy descendants of the plantation families, his own generation of Southerners. Their self-destructive behavior he came to see as the consequence of the defeat in the Civil War suffered by the earlier generation. He was for the first time imagining how that earlier generation had felt. In *Absalom, Absalom!* he dramatized the South in the act of trying heroically but vainly to defend itself, suffering a humiliation which would be passed down through three generations to Quentin Compson— and to Faulkner himself. The theme of *Absalom, Absalom!* was definitively tragic while the theme of *The Unvanquished* was broadly comic. Instead of continuing to suffer their humiliation and go on blaming the Yankees for it, the South in Faulkner's view had another possibility open to them: it could renounce revenge and break the cycle of self-destruction, figuratively turning the other cheek, replacing revenge with renunciation. So he wrote two successive novels about the same war, the decisive event in Southern history, and chose to see it first as a story of ambition and pride leading to a tragic fall, and second as a broadly comic story of vengeance transformed into redemption, of honor preserved by consciously refraining from violence.

To read these two novels consecutively is to see Southern history in a new light, since Faulkner's mature view of the Civil War was as *both* tragedy and comedy, the tragic ending brought about by excessive pride, by what the Greeks called ὕβρις, while the comic outcome came from a change of heart, by self-conscious restraint on the part of the survivors. The survivors were the men and women—especially the women—whom Faulkner called "the unvanquished," who relinquished revenge and remained gallant in defeat. The difference is crucial, and constitutes a turning point in Faulkner's career, just as the Civil War had been a turning point in Southern history. It makes his mythical history regenerative, because if he had once viewed it as tragically heroic, he came to see it as potentially heroic in comedy as well. Faulkner's tragic sense clearly prevails in *Absalom, Absalom!*, which chronicled the disastrous Rise and Fall of the House of Sutpen, but his comic sense prevails in *The Unvanquished*, which imagines an earlier chapter of Sartoris family history that was of a different kind, when the capacity for ending the cycle of self-destruction is dramatized, and revenge is deliberately renounced by Bayard Sartoris, whose father Col. John Sartoris has been killed by a jealous rival. It is the same Bayard Sartoris who had been Old Bayard Sartoris in Faulkner's first Yoknapatawpha novel, and thus a significant transformation of character has taken place. Faulkner often repeated characters in his fiction, sometimes as seemingly different people, but here he was allowing the same character to become more heroic, less tragic, as he aged and matured. It was exercising poetic license; making the difference between his two Civil War novels not only a matter of character but of tone. *Dark House* was his first title, but when he changed it to *Absalom, Absalom!*, he kept the darkness, infusing it into momentous and violent actions, while *The Unvanquished* seems infused with light, and punctuated by frequent flashes of humor. He wrote the two novels in sequence, and surely meant them to be read that way.

The first chapter of *Absalom, Absalom!* takes place long after the Civil War. It is the summer of 1909, when Quentin Compson is nineteen and on his way to Harvard for his freshman year. He is the same Quentin who in *The Sound and the Fury* was bent on committing suicide, but in this novel he has another concern: trying to understand why the South lost the Civil War, the ultimate cause of his death-wish in the earlier novel. He is summoned by an aging spinster, Miss Rosa Coldfield, to come to her house, so that she can tell him the true story of Thomas Sutpen, who had been a towering figure in antebellum Yoknapatawpha County at the time he arrived in Jefferson in 1833, accompanied by a French architect and a band of wild Negro slaves from Haiti. He proceeded to buy a hundred square miles of the best bottom land, and then, with the help of the French architect, to build a mansion as large as a courthouse and name it Sutpen's Hundred. Having finished that monumental task, he courted and married a highly respectable young lady in Jefferson, Ellen Coldfield, whose father was a prosperous merchant and a staunch Methodist. It was her younger sister, Rosa Coldfield, who told Quentin the story of Sutpen and brought him vividly back to life.

She was the first narrator in the novel but not the only narrator, for the novel has several narrators, including Quentin himself as he learns more and more about Thomas Sutpen and becomes fascinated with the story of his life. Sutpen had arrived in Jefferson in the summer of 1833, and had gone to work immediately, energetically working toward the grand scheme he had in mind since boyhood. One of his first acquaintances in Jefferson was Quentin's grandfather, who would later become Confederate General Compson. Quentin's father was General Compson's son; thus he can add to Rosa Coldfield's account whatever his own father had told him about Thomas Sutpen. It is a tale of grandiose ambition and diligent labor resulting in one of the largest plantations in Yoknapatawpha County. Quentin's grandfather had been in awe of Thomas Sutpen's strong will and powerful physique, his ability to command other men to do whatever he asked. In five years he built his mansion and planted his fields, filling Sutpen's Hundred with fine furniture and glass windows imported from abroad, carried by steamboat up the Mississippi River. Then he set out with equal determination to marry a respectable young lady in Jefferson, to give him the children he needed to inherit his property and perpetuate his fortune. The young lady was Ellen

Coldfield, daughter of a Jefferson merchant, a pillar of the Methodist Church, who soon gave him a son named Henry and a daughter named Judith.

He was a well-established planter when he left Jefferson and went off to war in 1861, and when he came back in 1865 as a defeated Confederate officer, he was determined to renew his dream of a dynasty. His wife Ellen had died during the war, leaving him an eligible widower, and he promptly proposed to his wife's sister Rosa to replace the wife he had lost. She accepted, and they were engaged for a time. But suddenly, she broke it off and left him, for reasons we find out later on. Before the war, his son Henry had gone away to the State University in Oxford, a town forty miles from Jefferson, where he met Charles Bon, a cultivated young man from New Orleans, and formed a close friendship. Henry brought Charles Bon home to meet his family at Christmas time, and quickly a romance developed with Henry's sister Judith. With her mother's approval, they became engaged, and Rosa Coldfield began sewing wedding garments for a wedding that would never take place. It isn't clear why it didn't take place until later in the novel, but it is clear that Charles Bon has become part of the Sutpen family and is regarded as engaged and almost married to Judith. Then the Civil War intervened. Thomas Sutpen joined the Confederacy as an officer in Col. John Sartoris' cavalry troop, and led his men so bravely in the Battle of Bull Run in Virginia that he earned a citation from none other than Robert E. Lee. He was an honored officer in the war, having already become the largest landholder in Yoknapatawpha County, where the Sutpen family was looked on as local royalty. His long friendship with General Compson had helped him secure his social standing. But tragedy began taking over the Sutpen family when Ellen Coldfield died during the war and fortunes swiftly declined throughout the South.

The general decline affects everyone, but the Sutpen fortunes have already begun declining, starting at the moment when Henry Sutpen brings home his college friend, Charles Bon. Charles Bon ingratiates himself with the family and becomes engaged to Judith Sutpen before his true identity emerges. It turns out that Charles Bon is actually the son of Thomas Sutpen by his first wife, the daughter of the French planter in Haiti, a woman Sutpen had discovered to his dismay to be of mixed blood. That was why he "put her aside" and moved to Mississippi where he married again. It is Thomas Sutpen's own sons who destroy his dream of a dynasty, just as King David's sons had aggrieved him in the Bible, and at the very moment when the South is suffering defeat in the Civil War, causing a double blow to his dream. He had been elected to replace Col. Sartoris as the head of his cavalry troop, and Henry and Charles Bon had joined the University Rifles and fought side by side for four years, but as the war grinds down to its bitter conclusion, Charles Bon writes a long letter to Judith to say they have been engaged long enough and he is returning to claim her as his bride. Charles Bon has concealed his true parentage from Henry, and worse, he has kept it a secret that he has a black wife and child in New Orleans. When Henry finds out the truth about his friend, he sees that if he were to marry Judith, it would be brother marrying sister, violating the primordial taboo against incest. And he learns it would be compounded by a later taboo of miscegenation, since Charles is partly black, and still further compounded by the legal prohibition against bigamy, since he already has a wife. Henry learns of this triple affront to family dignity a little at a time, and stays close to Charles Bon during the war, hoping he will break his engagement to Judith. But Charles Bon has come to Thomas Sutpen with one consuming ambition, to be recognized as his son, and when Thomas Sutpen refuses him that satisfaction, he refuses to give up his engagement. He rides home with Henry from the battlefield, all the way to the gate of Sutpen's Hundred, where Henry asks his brother one last time not to marry their sister. Charles refuses, and Henry shoots him in cold blood, to prevent a thrice-cursed marriage from taking place. Judith does not know what has happened, and waits inside Sutpen's Hundred with her wedding dress ready, but it is her fate to become a widow before she becomes a bride. The fourth chapter of Faulkner's novel ends with the high drama of Charles Bon's death at the hand of his half-brother, just as he is about to claim their sister as his wife.

Rosa Coldfield then comes in again as the narrator, her whole chapter printed in italics, to give Quentin her eyewitness account of the aftermath of the murder of Charles Bon by Henry Sutpen. When she hurries out to Sutpen's Hundred from Jefferson, she finds the Negro servant Clytie (Clytemnestra) guarding the room where Judith is grieving over the bloody corpse of Charles Bon. Rosa is Judith's aunt, but she is only nineteen and is four years younger than her niece, and is deeply shocked to see Judith weeping over the body of the man who was to be her husband. She asks herself why it had to happen, why the hoped-for marriage has ended in tragedy, and wonders "is that wisdom which can comprehend that there is a might-have-been which is more true than truth"? She answers her own question a little later, when she says "there is that might-have-been which is the single rock we cling to above the maelstrom of unbearable reality," realizing how much she wanted her niece to marry the man she loved, now being forced to grieve over his dead body. There are three women left at Sutpen's Hundred--Judith, Rosa, and Clytie--to wait for the return of Thomas Sutpen, sure he will "begin the Herculean task" of rebuilding his plantation. While they wait, they see the aftermath of the Civil War in lines of demoralized Confederate soldiers passing by their gate, "men who had risked and lost everything, suffered beyond endurance and had returned now to a ruined land." Thomas Sutpen returns home and proposes to Rosa

Coldfield, and she accepts, but she never marries him. Undeterred, at the age of 59, he sets about rebuilding his plantation with all "his ruthless pride, his lust for vain magnificence." Two months after Rosa accepts his proposal, he tells her he will marry her only after she produces a male child. She is so indignant that she breaks the engagement and goes back to Jefferson to live in her father's house. When Quentin hears her story, he agrees to accompany her to what is left of Sutpen's Hundred, where Henry Sutpen, the fugitive who committed fratricide, has been glimpsed moving about the empty house.

The scene of the novel shifts abruptly away from Yoknapatawpha County to Cambridge, Massachusetts, where Quentin Compson is at Harvard in the winter of 1910, reading to his Canadian roommate, Shreve McCannon, a letter which his father has sent from Jefferson, Mississippi, to tell him that Rosa Coldfield has died. When Quentin repeats to Shreve the whole story Miss Rosa told him about Thomas Sutpen, Shreve cannot believe it. He asks Quentin incredulously, "Tell about the South. What's it like there. What do they do there. Why do they live there."

The novel then shifts its focus from Thomas Sutpen to the question Shreve asks, how the South differs from the rest of the country, how it has become an isolated region outsiders cannot understand. Quentin succeeds Rosa as the narrator, telling Shreve how he went out to Sutpen's Hundred with Rosa Coldfield to see who may have been hiding there. Shreve becomes entranced, and begins sharing the narration with Quentin, guessing what happened when the aging spinster and the young college boy arrive by night at the mansion Sutpen had built, deserted now except for his illegitimate black daughter, Clytie, and his legitimate son, the elusive Henry Sutpen, a murderer who is now a fugitive and outcast. Shreve guesses what had outraged Rosa Coldfield so much, that Sutpen offered to marry her only if she produced a son, and understands why she broke off her engagement, moved back home, and from that time on followed the fortunes of Thomas Sutpen from a distance.

She knew he had committed a further outrage by seducing Milly Jones, the granddaughter of Wash Jones, Thomas Sutpen's loyal handyman, and then, when she gave birth to a baby girl rather than a boy, treating her so contemptuously that it enraged Milly's grandfather, Wash, who killed Thomas Sutpen with his scythe. He was buried next to his daughter, Judith, in a grave marked by the marble effigy he had ordered from Italy and carried back from the war. Rosa Coldfield has seen it, and has read the names on the other gravestones: Ellen Coldfield Sutpen, who had died during the war, Charles Bon, the son who had been killed by his half-brother Henry, and Charles Bon's son, Charles Étienne Saint Valéry Bon, who had been brought there as a child when his mulatto mother died in New Orleans.

Clytie, Sutpen's illegitimate daughter by a black slave, had raised the child at Sutpen's Hundred, but he had gone back to New Orleans, married a black woman, and had a son by her he named Jim Bond, the last survivor of the Sutpen line, now a sharecropper at Sutpen's Hundred. So the princely line that Thomas Sutpen dreamed of founding has faded almost completely away, and he himself has died a violent death. All this is narrated by three different men—Quentin Compson, his roommate Shreve McCannon, and Quentin's father, who reported what Gen. Compson had told him, making General Compson a fourth narrator. Faulkner ends the fifth chapter of his novel with a question: who is still living at Sutpen's Hundred?

The answer is teased out in the next chapter, in a conversation between Quentin Compson and his roommate, Shreve McCannon, at Harvard in the winter of 1910, with Shreve shivering with cold, still trying to understand this mysterious place called the South. Quentin has been trying to spell it out for him by telling him the story of Thomas Sutpen and the dynasty he dreamed of and lost. Shreve listens so eagerly he exclaims, "It's better than theatre, isn't it." It is theatre, for Thomas Sutpen is the tragic hero who realizes his high dream only to lose it all, because of his overbearing treatment of others. "He wasn't even a gentleman," Rosa Coldfield laments, as she tells Quentin about the price the South paid for its exploitation of the land and the people. The price was defeat in the Civil War, a tragedy that had to end as it did. Margaret Mitchell had written memorably about the Civil War in her more popular novel, *Gone with the Wind*, but hers was a romantic story of virtuous Southern planters vanquished by a larger and better equipped army of unmannerly Yankees, who left them defeated and desolate, resenting the loss inflicted on them through no fault of their own. *Absalom, Absalom!* is something else. It is a realistic portrayal of the *hubris* of Thomas Sutpen, who built his plantation on slave labor, destroyed the wilderness for his own profit, and destroyed himself by bullying everyone around him: his wife, his children, his workmen and his slaves. Thomas Sutpen was not an evil man, but he was one of the most rapacious of the new planters who cleared the land and established their estates all the way across the South to the Mississippi Delta. "Sutpen's trouble was innocence," Quentin's grandfather says: "he had never even heard of, never imagined, a place, a land divided up and actually owned by men who did nothing but ride over it in fine horses or sit in fine clothes on the galleries of big houses while other people worked for them." Innocence had prompted him to do what he did without regard for the consequences.

What Quentin Compson tells Shreve McCannon is that Thomas Sutpen never understood what went wrong with his plan: "I had a design," he told Gen. Compson in 1833, while they were resting from the pursuit of the escaped French architect in the woods of Sutpen's Hundred. "To accomplish it I should require money, a house, a plantation, slaves, a family—incidentally, of course, a wife. I set out to acquire these, asking no favor of any man." He confessed to Gen. Compson that he had a first wife, the daughter of a French planter in the West Indies, but she became unsuitable for his plan because she had black blood, and he "provided for her and put her aside." She had a son named Charles Bon who eventually became the Absalom who defied his father and destroyed his dream. Quentin sees in Sutpen's career what caused the South to lose the Civil War: excessive pride leading to the exploitation of man and nature. To Quentin the day of reckoning had to come: "that day when the South would realize that it was now paying the price for having erected its economic edifice not on the rock of stern morality but on the shifting sands of opportunism and moral brigandage." In *Absalom, Absalom!* Faulkner dramatized the grandeur of the South's ambition and the humiliation of its defeat, through the tragic story of a single man.

There is more to the story, for the conversation that takes place between Quentin and Shreve at Harvard is about racial identity in the South, something beyond defeat in the Civil War. Quentin tells Shreve that the murder of Charles Bon by Henry Sutpen was caused by racial differences not created nor settled by war. Eulalia Bon, the daughter of a French planter in Haiti and the first wife of Thomas Sutpen, had been "put aside" because he discovered she had black as well as white blood. She never forgave him for abandoning her, and she groomed her son Charles Bon to exact her revenge on him. She sent him to the University of Mississippi with a letter of introduction to Henry Sutpen, expecting them to become close friends. What she wished for happens, and Charles goes home with Henry to Sutpen's Hundred, where he meets Judith, falls in love with her, and becomes engaged with her mother's approval. But they are never married, because Henry learns from his father that Charles is their half-brother and is appalled to think he would commit incest. So he tries for four years, while they are serving in the University Rifles, to dissuade Charles from marrying his own sister, but Charles refuses, because he sees it as his means of forcing Thomas Sutpen to acknowledge his fatherhood. To him, Judith is the instrument of recognition; to his mother, she is the instrument of revenge. Shreve helps Quentin tell the story, guessing events before Quentin can speak them. The gripping climax of the novel, which Faulkner withholds till near the end, is the meeting between Thomas Sutpen and his son Henry on the battlefield in Virginia, as the Civil War is rapidly winding down, followed by Henry's meeting with Charles Bon. Sutpen will not give Charles the satisfaction of calling him son, but summons Henry to his tent and tells him "I have seen Charles Bon, Henry." He asks Henry to promise he will not let Charles marry Judith, but Henry refuses, until he learns the awful truth, that the marriage of Charles and Judith would be not only incest but miscegenation. "He must not marry her, Henry," Thomas Sutpen tells his son. "His mother's father told me that her mother had been a Spanish woman. I believed him; it was not until after he was born that I found out that his mother was part negro." This new knowledge has the desired effect on Henry, who makes up his mind that he will kill Charles Bon if necessary to keep him from marrying their sister. Henry is willing now to face "the acceptance of eternal damnation" with Charles Bon and his father. He sees himself headed for hell as surely as Quentin Compson was headed there in *The Sound and the Fury*. As soon as he tells Bon what his father has said, Bon sees what most offends him: "So it's the miscegenation, not the incest, which you cant bear." Charles Bon has resolved to flout the taboos against incest and miscegenation because his father has refused to recognize him as his son, and pleads with Henry, "He didn't need to tell you I am a nigger to stop me. He could have stopped me without that, Henry." Now he will not break his engagement to Judith, insisting "Unless you stop me, Henry," and offering his pistol to Henry, saying "Do it now." Henry doesn't do it, still hoping Bon will relent, and only when they reach the gate of Sutpen's Hundred does he make a final appeal before shooting his half-brother dead.

Shreve has listened to the Sutpen story, has even participated in telling it, but he is still mystified about the South, and asks Quentin in continuing disbelief:

> "I just want to understand it if I can and I don't know how to say it better. Because it's something my people haven't got... We don't live among defeated grandfathers and freed slaves (or have I got it backwards and was it your folks that were freed and the niggers that lost) and bullets in the dining room table and such, to be always reminding us never to forget. What is it? something you live and breathe in like air? a kind of wraithlike and indomitable anger and pride and glory at and in happenings that occurred and ceased fifty years ago? a kind of entailed birthright father and son and father and son of never forgiving General Sherman, so that forevermore as long as your children's children produce children you wont be anything but a descendant of a long line of colonels killed in Pickett's charge at Manassas?"

"Gettysburg," Quentin said. "You cant understand it. You would have to be born there." In exasperation, Shreve puts a final question to Quentin: "Why do you hate the South?" Quentin's reply is passionate and ambivalent. He blurts out: "I don't. I don't. I don't hate it! I don't hate it!" Quentin's last desperate words conclude Faulkner's fullest fictional treatment of the South, just as Clytie's burning down of Sutpen's Hundred concludes the story of Thomas Sutpen. Quentin has not absolved himself of the burden of guilt;

we know it will lead him to commit suicide, but Faulkner was not Quentin; he exorcised his guilt by inventing and peopling his Mythical Kingdom of Yoknapatawpha County.

In *The Unvanquished*, his second novel about the Civil War, Faulkner resurrected the Sartoris family of his first Yoknapatawpha novel, in order to redeem the sins of the South that had caused the war. Old Bayard Sartoris of *Sartoris*, the son of Col. John Sartoris, was haunted by his father's ghost and doomed to suffer sudden death as a victim of his grandson's reckless driving, but Faulkner transformed him into Young Bayard Sartoris of *The Unvanquished*, a son who was ready to suffer the death of his father without exacting revenge. He became the protagonist of a very different novel, in which Col. Sartoris was no longer a ghost but a vital living character, a hero in spite of the South's defeat, who was killed after the war by a jealous rival named Redmond. *Absalom, Absalom!* embraced three generations of the Compson family, starting and ending in 1910, but going back into history as far as 1833, whereas *The Unvanquished* embraced two generations of the Sartoris family, starting in 1863, in the middle of the Civil War, and ending in 1875, well after the war was over. *Absalom, Absalom!* was narrated by five different voices, past and present, a technique reminiscent of Joseph Conrad's multiple narrators in *Lord Jim*, while the second novel followed the example of Sherwood Anderson in *Winesburg, Ohio*, gathering a collection of short stories together as a novel. The stories had already been published separately, in the popular magazines of the 1930s, *The Saturday Evening Post* and *Scribner's*, and to make a novel of them Faulkner put them together in chronological sequence, with Col. John Sartoris and his son Bayard Sartoris as heroes in successive generations. What Faulkner produced by combining seven stories about the Sartoris family was something akin to what Germans call a *bildungsroman*, a story about growing up from boyhood to manhood. Bayard Sartoris does mature from boyhood to manhood, from childish innocence to adult knowledge. He becomes at the end a new kind of hero in Faulkner's mythical history of the South, deliberately repudiating revenge for the murder of his father. Thomas Sutpen's story had been Faulkner's way of showing that there was moral justice in the defeat of the South, which had come about chiefly because of its own tragic flaws; the story of Bayard Sartoris was his way of showing that a change of heart was possible in the survivors, "the unvanquished," who were capable, in the person of Bayard Sartoris, of absorbing the defeat and stopping further bloodshed. He was backed by his Aunt Jenny, Virginia Sartoris Dupre, who cheered him on with the Charleston smuggler's motto, "No bloody moon," and welcomed him on his return. Faulkner would later say admiringly that "The women were the ones that could bear it because they never had surrendered."

The Unvanquished begins in 1863, in the middle of the Civil War, and continues until 1875, at the end of the postbellum period the victors called Reconstruction. The novel consists of seven chapters that were originally short stories. The first, "Ambuscade," is the most humorous in its tone, signaling that though this novel is about the Civil War, it is going to be comic from the start. Two little boys, Bayard Sartoris and his black playmate Ringo (short for Marengo, the site of one of Napoleon's major battles) are playing a war game about the Civil War, now on its way to two decisive Northern victories, Gettysburg in Pennsylvania and Vicksburg on the Mississippi River, but they matter little to the young boys. Loosh, Ringo's father, asks them what they are doing, and they tell him they are besieging Vicksburg, whereupon he laughs and sweeps their dirt city away, because he knows the Battle of Vicksburg has just been won by Grant after a long siege. The date of the first episode can thus be dated as just after July 4, 1863, when the tide of war is turning against the South. Suddenly Bayard's father, Col. John Sartoris, comes riding home on his horse Jupiter, and starts building a hidden corral for horses in the meadow, to guard them against the Yankees who are reported to be on the way. When he rides off again, the boys beg Granny Millard, John Sartoris' mother-in-law, to read them a recipe for "cokynut cake" from her cookbook, because they are living on scarce provisions in the middle of the war. When they hear the Yankee troop is coming toward the Sartoris plantation, they take down a musket which Col. Sartoris had brought back two years earlier from the first Battle of Bull Run in Virginia. They load it and hide in the bushes. When the Yankees come riding up the road, the boys fire the musket at the leader and quickly run back inside the house, thinking gleefully they have killed a Yankee. They shout "We kilt the bastuhd!" to Granny, who quickly hides them under her hoop skirt. The Yankee colonel enters the house, looking for the boys who he says fired the musket and killed the best horse in his regiment. The boys, under the voluminous skirts of Granny Millard, are relieved to hear they killed a horse, not a man. Granny Millard claims there are no boys living there. The Yankee officer politely accepts her lie, knowing that it is a lie, and commands his men to stop their search and ride on to engage the Rebel troops. Granny is as relieved as the boys underneath her are, but she brings them out from under her skirt and tells them to kneel down and pray forgiveness for their profanity and her lie. Then she orders them to wash their mouths out with soap. Though the episode contains violent action, it is full of humor, and sets the tone for the rest of the novel, a new departure for Faulkner, treating the Civil War more as comedy than tragedy.

"Retreat" is a second comic episode, though it includes the violent burning down of the Sartoris mansion by the enemy, an event reminiscent of actual history, because it happens in 1864, the year when Oxford was set on fire by Yankee troops under General Smith. It introduces the McCaslin twins,

Uncle Buck (Amodeus) and Uncle Buddy (Theophilus), who are elderly citizens of Jefferson fiercely loyal to Col. John Sartoris. They are from a landed family who have a large plantation 15 miles from town, but they have chosen to move out of the mansion and let their black slaves live in it, practicing their own form of racial equality before the Civil War. Uncle Buck and Uncle Buddy will reappear in a later novel about the McCaslin family, *Go Down, Moses*, but Faulkner says in this novel they are "ahead of their time," believing that "the land did not belong to the people but that the people belonged to the land." As the Yankees near the Sartoris plantation, Granny Millard loads up her wagon with silver, hitches the mules to it and starts toward Memphis, passing Jefferson on the way, but she is stopped by a Yankee patrol, which cuts the mules loose and leaves her stranded with Joby and Loosh and Louvinia in the wagon, while Bayard and Ringo go running after the mules. They "borrow" a white horse to ride, and they run right into Col. Sartoris, in pursuit of a Yankee troop bivouacked for the night. They help him trick the Yankees into thinking he has a superior force of men, when he has only a handful of soldiers and two young boys whooping it up, and he boldly orders the Yankees to remove their clothes, then lets them sneak off at night so that he won't have the trouble of taking them captive. He returns to the Sartoris plantation, and when the Yankees appear at the gate looking for him, he disguises himself, tricks them into thinking he is someone else, and escapes on Jupiter, leaving them to burn the Sartoris mansion to the ground. It is a genuine retreat told humorously, like the Civil War itself in Faulkner's second novel about it.

The third episode, "Raid," occurs a little later in the war, when the Sartoris mansion is only a pile of ashes with the chimneys sticking up, and Granny and the boys are living in the Negro cabin with their black slaves, Joby and Louvinia. Granny Millard gets in her wagon and goes in search of the Yankee officer she met in the first chapter, hoping to recover the chest of silver and mules which her emancipated slave, Loosh, has stolen, and to return two "borrowed" horses she took from the Yankees, sending an explanatory note to the officer in charge, Col. Nathaniel G. Dick of the Ohio Cavalry. They head for Hawkhurst, a plantation in Alabama which belonged to their cousins, but it too has been burned, and the collapse of the Confederacy is clearly symbolized by the piles of ashes and solitary chimneys they pass. They see Negro slaves moving in a body toward the Tennessee River, which they call the Jordan, as if it were the Biblical Exodus, in the hope that the Yankees will emancipate them. Cousin Drusilla is found amid the ruins of Hawkhurst, a spirited young woman who has lost her fiancée in the war and is dressing and acting like a man, hoping to join John Sartoris and his Rebels to continue the fight against the Yankees. She recounts a real event, the gripping story of the Great Train Race, when a Union train chased a Confederate train on a nearby railroad, the Yankee train pursuing the Rebel train but never quite catching it. "It was like a meeting between two iron knights of the old time, not for material gain but for principle—honor denied with honor, courage denied with courage—the deed done not for the end but for the sake of the doing—put to the ultimate test and proving nothing save the finality of death and the vanity of all endeavor." Such a moment of heroism, known as the Great Railroad Chase, is still possible for the South, but there is no longer any hope of victory, because "the name for the life we had led for the last three years was hardship and suffering." The Yankees in retaliation dug up the railroad tracks and bent the rails so that no supply train could use it again. Granny Millard drives her wagon along the road to the river, which the Yankee cavalry are crossing rapidly, holding the Negroes back with force, then blowing up the bridge so that the "emancipated" Negro slaves can't follow them. Clearly, the Yankee troops don't know what to do with hundreds of Negroes begging them for freedom. Granny fords the river in her wagon and presents her request to Col. Dick for two mules and two Negroes and a chest of silver. He generously gives her a written order for 10 chests of silver, 110 mules and 110 Negroes. Surprised but undaunted, Granny takes them all back across the river and on to the Sartoris plantation, arriving there with a long train of mules and Negroes in tow. She feels a little guilty for making off with many more chests of silver and mules and Negroes than she asked for, and so she tells Bayard and Ringo to kneel down with her and pray for forgiveness. The epic journey to and from Sartoris has been exhausting, at times pathetic, yet in the end hilarious.

Granny Millard goes on trading mules and supplies with the victorious Yankees in "Riposte in Tertio" (a fencing term for "third counterthrust") as the Civil War winds down, in minor raids and skirmishes rather than pitched battles. But in her daring trades she has become involved with the slippery Ab Snopes, Father Abraham of the notorious Snopes clan, the family of opportunists introduced earlier in *Sartoris*, *As I Lay Dying*, and *Sanctuary*, and she is playing a desperate game of survival that results in her death at the hands of a merciless outlaw band who are pillaging the countryside. Ab Snopes helps her sell mules to the Yankees, stealing them and selling them back again. She has given Ab the written order for mules issued to her by Col. Dick, which he uses over and over until they are caught in the act, and Granny manages to escape into the woods with Bayard and Ringo, returning to what is left of the Sartoris plantation, vowing not to try any longer to steal mules from the Yankees. They go to church, where Granny stands up and confesses her sins, but declares publicly: "I did not sin for revenge. I defy you or anyone to say I did... I sinned for the sake of food and clothes for Your own creatures who could not help themselves—for children who had given their fathers, for wives who had given their husbands, for old people who had given their sons to a holy cause…" and she ends with a prayer that "if this be sin in Your sight, I take this on my conscience too. Amen." The Yankees recover the stolen mules she has hidden in Col. Sartoris' corral, and she realizes that Ab Snopes has told them where to look, so she now knows Ab Snopes is no longer to be trusted. She goes alone in foolhardy pursuit of horses stolen from her by Grumby's Independents, a band of marauders who are pillaging the South at the end of the war, and she finds them hiding out in an old cotton mill, but when Bayard and Ringo follow her path to the cotton mill, it is too late to rescue her: all they find is her lifeless body on the floor.

They bury her in the Jefferson cemetery, with all the townspeople and country people in attendance because she has been their benefactress, and in the fifth chapter, titled "Vendée" (after a region of France which resisted the Revolution), Bayard and Ringo, who are now fifteen (they were twelve when *The Unvanquished* began in 1863), swear vengeance for Granny's death, and with the help of Uncle Buck McCaslin they go in pursuit of Ab Snopes and Grumby, which takes them two long months, from December 1866 to February 1867, during the dead of winter. Eventually they find Ab Snopes alive but bound to a tree, with a warning sign not to pursue Grumby and his outlaws any further, but they ignore it and eventually find Grumby himself, abandoned by his men because he "got scared and killed an old woman," meaning Granny Millard. Grumby fires at Bayard and wounds him, but Bayard shoots back and kills him. Then he and Ringo carry his body to the deserted cotton mill where he had killed Granny Millard, cut off his right hand, and carry it to the Jefferson cemetery where they nail it to her tombstone. Bayard has had his bloody revenge, proving that he is capable of risking his life for the sake of vengeance. "Vendée" ends when Col. John Sartoris and Cousin Drusilla, who has been riding with his cavalry troop, come home from the war.

"Skirmish at Sartoris," the sixth chapter, occurs after the Civil War is over, when John Sartoris comes home and rebuilds his mansion. Faulkner makes clear in this episode that "the unvanquished" are the Southern women, because "the men had given in and admitted they belonged to the United States but the women never surrendered." Bayard says that "now we lived in a world of burned towns and houses and ruined plantations and fields inhabited only by women." John Sartoris is about to marry Cousin Drusilla who has fought beside him like a man, but first he has to contend with the freed slaves and carpetbaggers who are taking over the postbellum South. Ringo, who has grown up with Bayard, tells him: "I ain't a nigger any more. I done been abolished." Two Burden brothers have come from Missouri to organize the emancipated Negroes into political potency as Republicans, and John Sartoris is forced to prevent them from holding a rigged election in Jefferson. One of the Burdens is the father of Joanna Burden, the lover of Joe Christmas in *Light in August,* and when the two carpetbaggers confront Col. Sartoris, they fire first but he kills them both with two shots from his derringer. He then takes the ballot box out to the Sartoris plantation where an honest election is held, after they listen to his plea, "Don't you see we are working for peace through law and order?" The honest vote ends in a resounding "No" for the black Republican candidate, and John and Drusilla are married at last as the crowd shouts "Yaaay!" for both of them.

The final, and most telling, chapter of *The Unvanquished* is "An Odor of Verbena." Bayard Sartoris, who was only twelve when the novel began, is now 24 and is at the university in Oxford, forty miles from Jefferson, when he hears that his father, Col. John Sartoris, has been murdered by a jealous rival, and he returns to face the murderer. He has avenged the death of his grandmother at the hands of Grumby; it would be natural for him to follow with equally violent revenge on his father's killer. However, in a surprise ending, Bayard makes up his mind to renounce further violence in the Sartoris family, even though his stepmother, Cousin Drusilla, now the widow of John Sartoris, whom he calls "the Greek amphora priestess of a succinct and formal violence," offers him a pair of dueling pistols that belonged to his father. He has the backing however of his Aunt Jenny, who in the first Sartoris novel had called the male line of Sartorises "savages, all of them." Bayard listens to both of these unvanquished Sartoris women, but it is he, The Sartoris, the male heir of the Sartoris line, who renounces revenge when he goes to meet Redmond, his father's killer. He thinks it is time to stop the killing that has been going on for too long. Redmond's motive for killing his father was jealousy, since the two men had been business partners in the building of the railroad through Jefferson, but John Sartoris ran against him for a seat in the state legislature from Yoknapatawpha County, and when he won, his old friend became so enraged he murdered him in cold blood on the street of Jefferson. Thus the first William Falkner, great-grandfather of the second William Faulkner, has returned to life in fictional form.

Bayard walks alone to the town square of Jefferson, goes to the office marked "B.J. Redmond, Atty at Law" and mounts the steps to the room where he knows Ben Redmond is waiting for him. He knocks and enters, and sees Redmond seated behind his desk with a pistol resting on top of it. As he walks towards the desk, Redmond lifts the pistol and invites Bayard to draw first, then fires his pistol, but does not aim at Bayard, and Bayard does not return fire. Redmond rises, goes out the door, and boards a train "and went away from Jefferson and never came back." When Bayard leaves the office alone, onlookers think he has fired and missed, but quickly realize it was Redmond who had fired and then left town. "Well, by God," one of his friends says to him, "Maybe you're right, maybe there has been enough killing in your family," and congratulates him for his forbearance. Bayard returns home, where he is welcomed by Aunt Jenny, who tells him smilingly "So you had a perfectly splendid Saturday afternoon, didn't you?" She tells him further that Drusilla has gone back to Alabama for good—in disgust, he assumes, at his cowardice. However, when he goes up to his bedroom, he sees she has left him a souvenir: on his pillow is a sprig of verbena, which she said you could smell "above the smell of horses and courage."

It is a master touch to end the novel with a sprig of verbena, Drusilla's flower, as jasmine was Aunt Jenny's flower and the rose was Granny Millard's flower. She had worn a sprig of it from her garden in her hair, and pinned it on Bayard's coat as he left to confront his father's killer. The sprig of verbena she leaves on his pillow is a wordless acceptance of his decision not to avenge the death of Col. John Sartoris, her husband and his father. It is a silent tribute to his courage in disavowing revenge, prompted by words he remembered John Sartoris saying as he went to meet his killer, "now I shall do a little moral housecleaning. I am tired of killing men, no matter what the necessity nor the end." Faulkner's first novel about the Civil War had been tragic. His second novel about the Civil War was broadly comic, enlivened by humor, with an unexpectedly tragicomic ending. The real South had fought for a lost cause, trying to preserve its way of life by seceding from the United States, but in Faulkner's Mythical Kingdom it had symbolically stopped the fighting and rejoined the Union.

CHAPTER 5

Snopes vs. McCaslin

Between *The Unvanquished* in 1938, a minor masterpiece, and *The Hamlet* in 1940, a major masterpiece, Faulkner published an interesting but not entirely successful novel called *The Wild Palms*. It came out in 1939 to mixed reviews, the typical reaction to most of Faulkner's work up to that time. It was an experiment with form which was original, but which failed to coalesce. Faulkner thought he could interweave two short novels into one long novel, but though each of his short novels had merit in themselves, they never really meshed. Both were about the Mississippi River in flood, a headline topic in 1937, but the title novel, *The Wild Palms*, did not center on Yoknapatawpha County, which had become Faulkner's fictional home, and *Old Man,* the novel he wove into it chapter by chapter, barely touched his mythical county, focusing instead on the Mississippi Delta west of Jefferson, where the flood was raging. *Old Man* could have succeeded as a short novel: it was about a convict freed from prison to rescue victims of the Mississippi flood. It would eventually prove more effective as a short novel than as half of a longer novel. *The Wild Palms*, his title story, never succeeded in standing alone, though like *Mosquitoes*, one of the two main characters in the title story was modeled on his old flame, Helen Baird of Nashville. But Charlotte Rittenhouse, as he now called her, was much wilder, more worldly, and less sympathetic than Patricia Robyn of *Mosquitoes*, who had the appeal of a liberated but still innocent young woman, closer to the real Helen Baird Faulkner had known in New Orleans. The Mississippi flood was a violent setting for the violent romance between Charlotte Rittenhouse and Harry Wilbourne, but it was only one of many settings that took place across the country, in which the couple acted out their passionate and doomed affair. So the history of *The Wild Palms* is of an experiment that failed. It is seldom read today as a unified novel, because the two halves do not make a whole. Faulkner had been a constant experimenter with form in his novels ever since he wrote *The Sound and the Fury*, and most of his experiments worked beautifully. *The Wild Palms* was promising but it never quite worked. It was original in conception but not in execution, for Faulkner was unable to achieve the intended counterpoint he was aiming at. Alternating chapters of two very different novels about a historic flood on the Mississippi River was not enough to fuse them into a single coherent novel.

Then came *The Hamlet*, his comic masterpiece, a tall tale fit to compare with Mark Twain's *Huckleberry Finn*. Its hero is Flem Snopes, the predatory head of the Snopes family, a prolific clan of rustic entrepreneurs, and its setting is his fictional Yoknapatawpha County. This was an experiment with form that definitely worked. *The Hamlet* consists of four major sections divided into shorter chapters. Each major section is identified by a Roman number and a title--I. Flem II. Eula III. The Long Summer IV. The Peasants. The chapters are numbered separately within each section, and divided further by Arabic numbers for the shorter episodes. It is the most complex arrangement Faulkner ever tried for telling a story, and the Roman numerals and Arabic numbers are needed to help the reader understand what is going on, since it is not a plot novel with a continuous narrative, but a character novel with episodes for each of the many colorful members of the Snopes clan.

The novel is set in historical time, after the Civil War but before the First World War, about 1904, to be exact, since the St. Louis World's Fair is mentioned, which was held in that year. The geographical setting is Frenchman's Bend, a rural area south of Jefferson in Yoknapatawpha County, mentioned in earlier novels, especially *As I Lay Dying*, but not yet fully explored. Frenchman's Bend is located in the backwoods, definitely not plantation country, though the irony is that its name came from what was left of The Old Frenchman Place, once a mansion surrounded by cotton fields, now a deserted ruin, its spacious yard overgrown with dense vegetation. Faulkner had used it as the opening setting for *Sanctuary*, where it was the menacing home of a bootlegger, Lee Goodwin, and his commonlaw wife, Ruby, who provided a hideout for the gang of Memphis outlaws, led by the villainous Popeye, who captured Temple Drake there and made her his prisoner. In *Sanctuary*, The Old Frenchman Place was a Gothic setting emitting an atmosphere of horror, but in *The Hamlet* it was only part of the rustic scene surrounding the rural village called Frenchman's Bend. The dominant families were the lower class Varners and Snopeses, who made their profits by taking advantage of the decent people who lived there. The decent people were honest farmers, like the Tulls and Armstids and Bundrens of *As I Lay Dying*, who were regular customers in the Varners' general store, and gullible victims of the schemes devised by Flem and other members of the Snopes clan to extract money from them.

The Varners were the village capitalists. They owned most of the land and the store and the cotton gin in Frenchman's Bend, running the legal enterprises that served the community of small farmers in the vicinity. The Snopeses were opportunists who owned nothing, but who found ways of infiltrating the legal enterprises and taking advantage of ever-present human greed and credulity. The Snopeses had started out as sharecroppers, owning nothing, working land that belonged to others, but they were so adept at fooling the local inhabitants, terrorizing landowners by threatening to burn their barns, that in time they seemed to own everything. Abner Snopes was the patriarch of the Snopes clan, a scoundrel who wiped his muddy boots on Major De Spain's fine imported rug and ruined it. He was called Ab by those who knew him, such as Granny Millard in *The Unvanquished*, who had kept him busy stealing mules from the Yankee troops and selling them back again, as long as he could get by with it. In an unpublished story Faulkner wrote in 1925 but never published, he compared Ab Snopes to Father Abraham of the Old Testament, a stretch of imagination that was clearly meant to be comic. Ab's most honorable service had been as a foot soldier in Col. Sartoris's cavalry during the Civil War, a position he proudly claimed in *The Unvanquished*. In *The Hamlet*, he is more wily, climbing the social ladder to become a rival to Will Varner, the village chieftain, while his eldest son Flem is craftily replacing Will Varner's son Jody as heir to the Varner land and fortune.

A principal character of *The Hamlet* is V.K. Ratliff, who moves freely about Yoknapatawpha County as a sewing machine salesman and itinerant trader. He is the wry and pithy commentator on the steadily rising fortunes of the Snopeses. He stands apart from the credulous crowd, watching the machinations of Flem from a distance, and saying, with a shake of his head, "You can't beat him." But for all his shrewdness and skepticism, in the end Ratliff, too, falls prey to Flem's schemes, when he is duped into a nighttime adventure with the local farmers, Bookwright and Armstid, digging for gold that is rumored (by Flem Snopes) to be buried in the yard of the Old

Frenchman Place. Ratliff should have known better, but he is tricked by Flem like everyone else in Frenchman's Bend. Ratliff retaliates by dreaming a vivid nightmare, printed in italics at the end of the "Eula" section of the novel, that Flem descends into Hell and tricks Satan himself, who orders him to be punished for his sins, but who is dumbfounded when he discovers that Flem doesn't have a soul he can punish. Flem comes into his own as the comic villain of Faulkner's Mythical Kingdom, outwitting Will Varner and the rest of Frenchman's Bend by preying on their natural human greed while deftly satisfying his own.

Flem is the main character in the novel, and Ratliff is the principal observer and commentator. In the first section, we learn how Flem, following in the footsteps of his father Ab, skirts the law and takes advantage of everyone in Frenchman's Bend. He begins his upward mobility when he is put in charge of the country store owned by Will Varner and operated by his son Jody. Flem had cleverly used his father Ab's reputation as a barn burner to land the job, pitching it to Will Varner as a form of "fire insurance." Ab is a sharecropper on Varner land, and the Snopeses live in a Varner house, so Will Varner wants to be sure it is left standing when the Snopeses move out. Flem learns quickly how to run the store for maximum profit, even charging Will Varner for a plug of his own tobacco. Just as quickly, he brings in his cousins Eck Snopes and I.O. Snopes to run the blacksmith shop, and he personally takes over the accounts of the cotton gin. He soon earns a reputation as a young man "who never made mistakes in any matter pertaining to money." Jody Varner sees his fortune sinking with every new scheme of Flem Snopes, but all he can do is wonder helplessly "Just how much is it going to cost me to protect one goddam barn full of hay?"

By the end of the first section of the novel, Flem Snopes and his clan have taken over Frenchman's Bend from Will and Jody Varner. He has brought in cousins to run the businesses and farms, and has joined Will Varner as a landowner, riding around in a carriage to inspect the territory he has acquired. Ratliff tries to outwit Flem, extracting a note from Mink Snopes to pay for a sewing machine, but Flem refuses to acknowledge it, and Ratliff sends word to Will Varner by Mrs. Littlejohn, who runs the boarding house, that "It ain't been proved yet," that is, whether Flem has taken advantage of everyone else in Frenchman's Bend. Ratliff fears he too may be fooled—and by the end of the novel, he is. The idiot Ike Snopes appears, herding his cows dreamily, as if he had fallen in love with them, while Lump (short for Launcelot) Snopes tries to be his guardian, and I.O. Snopes angles for a job as the village schoolteacher. The Snopeses soon outwit and outnumber the Varners, and Flem becomes the principal owner of almost everything that once belonged to Will Varner.

Flem goes farther in the second section, marrying Will Varner's nubile daughter, Eula, the Earth Mother of Frenchman's Bend, who attracts men like bees to honey, and is already pregnant by another man. For his willingness to be cuckolded, Flem receives a large parcel of land from Will Varner plus a honeymoon in Texas. Eula is Faulkner's most extravagant female character, an earth goddess in rural Mississippi. She is like the mythical Venus, a temptress to every man who comes near her. One of her suitors is a country schoolteacher named Labove, a football star at the nearby university in Oxford, who has earned a bachelor's degree and a law degree, yet is not smart enough to resist Eula's charms. He waits for her in his one-room schoolhouse in Frenchman's Bend, but when he tries to embrace her, she shoves him away, sneering "Stop pawing me, you old horseman Ichabod Crane." She must have read Washington Irving's ghost story, "The Legend of Sleepy Hollow," although she is indifferent to studies, and is interested only in attracting men. Young men pursue her everywhere she goes, and one of them takes her out courting in his buggy, only to be ambushed by a crowd of jealous rivals. Her unlucky suitor escapes with only a broken arm, which the local veterinarian Will Varner manages to set for him. Despite the injury, he goes on with his courtship, finally impregnating the more than willing Eula. When Will Varner learns that Eula is carrying a child, he saves the family honor by marrying her off to Flem Snopes. Flem gets the better of the deal, since Varner bribes him with a parcel of land and a Texas honeymoon, leading the watchful observer Ratliff to marvel at how clever and ruthless Flem Snopes can be. Ratliff imagines that if Flem ever met the Prince of Darkness, he would take over the throne of Hell as he has taken over Frenchman's Bend. In his fantasy, Satan is forced to surrender his throne to Flem, and crawls away on the scorching hot floor, as Flem ascends the throne of Hell triumphantly, beating the devil at his own game. Ratliff's dream pictures Flem Snopes as a consummate charlatan who is on his way to conquering the universe.

In the third section of *The Hamlet*, we are introduced to a comical parade of the Snopes family: Lump Snopes, Ike Snopes, I.O. Snopes, Eck Snopes and his son, Wall Street Panic Snopes. Last in line is Mink Snopes, who is the meanest of the clan that has followed Flem Snopes into Frenchman's Bend. They are all adept at shady enterprises. Lump Snopes runs a peepshow right off the Jefferson town square, and makes a fairly good income from it, even though he is an embarrassment to the town. Eck Snopes runs the blacksmith shop, much in demand in a farming community dependent on mules and horses. Ike Snopes, the idiot, falls in love with one of the cows he is herding. He steals her from Jack Houston's barn and takes off with her into the countryside, milking her and thirstily drinking her milk, allowing her to defecate on him when they stop at a creek, blissfully allowing the cow to do anything it likes to him. Jack Houston misses his cow, which actually belonged to Mink Snopes, who kept it in Houston's barn to pay for letting it graze in his pasture, and Mink resents paying so much that he hides in the woods and shoots Jack Houston dead. Mink looks for a place to bury the corpse, and searches until he finds a hollow tree, which he uses to bury Jack Houston's body. When Mink learns from Lump Snopes that Jack Houston had fifty dollars in his pocket, he goes back to exhume the corpse. But Lump, who was knocked out by Mink to avoid sharing the booty, is revived by the sheriff, and together they catch Mink red-handed lugging the corpse of Jack Houston. Mink is put in jail to await trial for murder, where he is visited by his wife and children, but never by another Snopes. He thinks Flem Snopes will get back from his Texas honeymoon and post bail for him, but learns from his wife that only Eula has returned to Jefferson. Flem stays in Texas until Mink can be tried and hung for his crime, which would be a fitting end for a Snopes, but Mink is shipped off to the state prison, letting Flem come back to Frenchman's Bend.

Mink's wife survives his imprisonment by earning her living as a prostitute, Ike is cured of his bestiality by the gift of a wooden replica to replace the real cow he loves, and Eck has the bright idea of naming his son Wallstreet Panic because "I.O. read about that one in the paper. He figured if we named him Wallstreet Panic it might make him get rich like the folks that run that Wallstreet panic." I.O. has set himself up as a schoolteacher in Frenchman's Bend, but he is forced to close the school and run away from town when his lady friend returns with a child in her baby buggy. She is last seen pursuing him, one more Snopes on the run for his misdeeds, typical of the clan of outlaws Ab Snopes has imposed on Frenchman's Bend.

The fourth and final section of *The Hamlet* is called "The Peasants," and is dominated by Flem Snopes. Flem has cleverly brought back with him from Texas a band of spotted wild horses, which he means to sell to the poor farmers who flock into Frenchman's Bend to bid on them. These include the Armstids and Bookwrights and Tulls who appeared in *As I Lay Dying*. In that earlier novel, Jewel Bundren had worked nights to earn one of the spotted ponies as his mount, so that he could ride in style alongside the mule-drawn wagon carrying his mother's coffin to the Jefferson cemetery. Faulkner chose to feature the wild Texas horses, ten years after first mentioning them, in what he made into one of his fictional triumphs. It is a hilarious tall tale, a piece of frontier humor worthy of Mark Twain. (Katherine Anne Porter thought it even funnier than Mark Twain.) Flem is clever enough to auction the wild horses off to the poor farmers, who had made "a fair farm out of the bare scrap of hill land" which they "bought at less than a dollar an acre." They know how to work their meager farms, but fall for Flem Snopes's ingenious scheme, willingly spending their hard-earned dollars for untamable horses they can't catch, much less ride. Flem is fully in charge behind the scenes, but he takes no direct part in the auction. He has brought with him from Texas a veteran auctioneer named Buck, who carries a pearl-handled pistol in the back pocket of his jeans, and coolly herds the wild horses with barbed wire and staves of wood. "Them ponies is as gentle as a dove, boys," he says to the assembled crowd at Frenchman's Bend, "and when one of them tries to rush you, bust him over the head so he will understand what you mean." Flem isn't seen until after the sale is complete, but he's there to collect the money. Ratliff watches it all and shakes his head, seeing the hapless farmers as they are being bilked, and admitting balefully, "I reckon there aint nothing under the sun or in Frenchman's Bend neither that can keep you folks from giving Flem Snopes and that Texas man your money."

When Buck opens the auction, the crowd is reluctant to bid, until Buck starts the auction by giving a horse to Eck, exacting a promise from Eck that he will make the first bid. Eck keeps his promise, and when the auction is over, he is left with one dead horse and another he can't catch, a victim of Flem even though he is a Snopes. The most pathetic victim of Flem's legerdemain is poor Mrs. Armstid, who is clad in a grey dress and grey sunbonnet, her hands rolled up in her dress, who accompanies her husband Henry to the auction and entrusts him with five dollars she has earned "weaving by firelight after dark." Her husband buys a wild horse with it despite her pitiful protest, "And us not but five dollars away from the poorhouse, he aint no more despair." Henry buys the horse but breaks his leg trying to catch it, receiving a punishment he deserves. Buck soft-heartedly offers to give the five dollars back to Mrs. Armstid, but Flem Snopes suddenly appears on the scene and snatches back her money. When she timidly tries, the next day, on the porch of Varner's store, to claim it back from Flem, he gives her a five-cent bag of candy as "a little sweetening for the chaps," and coolly keeps the rest for himself. Mrs. Armstid thanks Flem, saying "You're right kind," as she goes off to Mrs. Littlejohn's boarding house to rescue her husband, in bed with a broken leg. The wild horses which have been auctioned to the gullible country folks break out of their corral and roam freely, cutting a destructive path through the whole neighborhood, until the "Texas sickness" as Ratliff calls it, "that spotted corruption of frantic and uncatchable horses, had spread as far as twenty and thirty miles."

The Spotted Horses episode ends with a series of ludicrous trials at an impromptu court held in a country store, presided over by a Justice of the Peace, "a neat, small, plump old man resembling a caricature of all grandfathers who ever breathed." He rules, in Armstid vs. Snopes, that Flem can't be held liable for damage done by horses he never owned, and that the five dollars poor Mrs. Armstid earned from weaving by lamplight, which her husband gave to the auctioneer for a horse and then broke his leg trying to catch it, was the property of the Texas man, who conveniently left town after the auction was over and hadn't been seen since. Mrs. Armstid meekly accepts the ruling and mounts her gaunt mule for the long ride home: "I better get started," she says, "It's a right fur piece." Eck Snopes, whose wild horse was killed after splitting their wagon apart and knocking Tull out, was sued for damages by the Tulls; the judge ruled that Eck had to pay them--with his dead horse. Theirs was the second case settled in the country court. The third case was against Mink Snopes for the murder of Jack Houston, which was justice long delayed. Mink has been sitting in jail for eight months, awaiting trial, expecting his cousin Flem to appear in court and bail him out. Flem is smart enough not to be seen, and Mink is convicted of second degree murder and sentenced to life imprisonment at the State Penal Farm. He is led off by the deputies, loudly cursing Flem for abandoning him. Flem has laid Frenchman's Bend waste, and is prospering at everyone else's expense, including his own relatives, the prolific clan of Snopeses.

Flem Snopes has one last triumph left in *The Hamlet*, and it is a particularly sweet one, because it involves V.K. Ratliff, the one person in Frenchman's Bend who has seemed all along to be aware of Flem's schemes and to remain outside the circle of his victims. Ratliff has been laughing while the others were fooled, but Flem has the last laugh on him. What finally hooks Ratliff is a rumor that there is gold buried on the Old Frenchman Place, property which belongs to Flem as part of the dowry he got from Will Varner for marrying his pregnant daughter, Eula. What persuades Ratliff that the rumor might be true is his knowledge that Will Varner was once the proprietor, and "he knows something's there. If there wasn't, he wouldn't never bought it." Not wanting to be seen digging for buried treasure, he goes out to the place at night, taking Bookwright and Armstid in his buckboard. Henry's broken leg has healed, but he is still goaded by "impotence and fury" at what Flem has done to him, tricking him into buying a horse that broke his leg without ever being caught. The three men dig night after night but find nothing, at first. Then, with the help of an old countryman who has a divining rod, they find a sack of coins. They are elated, and keep digging until they find two more sacks of coins. They count out their treasure in the dark and find that each sack holds twenty-five silver dollars. They are overjoyed, but are afraid that Flem as property owner might claim their buried loot, so Ratliff goes looking for Flem Snopes to ask how much he will take for the Old Frenchman Place. Flem is quite willing to sell it, but when he names the price, Ratliff snorts, "I'm just talking about them ten acres where that old house is, I aint trying to buy all Yoknapatawpha County from you." Flem holds firm on the price, and so "A little after six that evening, in the empty and locked store, Ratliff and Bookwright and Armstid bought the Old Frenchman Place from Snopes." They have mortgaged a house and restaurant to buy it, but they congratulate themselves for owning the place where they have unearthed three bags of silver coins. Now that they are homeowners, they start digging for more treasure, night after night, but never find another sack of coins. It gradually dawns on Ratliff that Flem may have tricked them. His suspicion leads them to open the sacks frantically and look at the dates on the silver dollars. They are appalled at what they see: these bags could never have been buried by the French planter who was the first owner of the property, because not a single coin had been minted before the Civil War. Henry Armstid will not accept the plain truth they have uncovered and starts digging again, but Ratliff and Bookwright are sadder and wiser and they give up the search. Flem has fooled them into buying three bags of silver dollars for the price of the Old Frenchman Place. Spectators who begin coming to watch Henry dig conclude that "Anybody might have fooled Henry Armstid. But couldn't nobody but Flem Snopes have fooled Ratliff." Enriched by the sale of property for which he paid nothing, Flem grandly loads up a wagon and moves Eula and her child from Frenchman's Bend to Jefferson, the county seat. *The Hamlet* ends with Flem Snopes on his way to higher social status and greater fortune in the capital of Yoknapatawpha County.

Faulkner's next novel, *Go Down, Moses*, published in 1942 with a title drawn from a familiar Negro spiritual, was less comic and more tragic than *The Hamlet*, but it contained another masterpiece, *The Bear*, one of the finest hunting stories ever written, centered on a family quite unlike the Snopeses. The McCaslins are in fact more like the Sartorises of his earlier Yoknapatawpha novels. They have a patriarch like the Sartorises who built a plantation in Yoknapatawpha County, and who left them a heritage that lasts through several generations. *Go Down, Moses* ranges widely in historical time, from the antebellum period when Lucius Quintus Carothers McCaslin comes from North Carolina to Mississippi, buys land from the Indians and clears it for his plantation, to the Second World War when Ike McCaslin, who was just a boy when he killed his first deer, goes on his last deer hunt as an old man. Carothers McCaslin is in the heroic mold of Col. John Sartoris, and his descendants inherit his plantation, but they also inherit an ancestral guilt that did not die with him. John Sartoris was courageous, a leader of men who inspired them in battle, but he was headstrong, inspiring some men to envy him, and he was killed by a jealous rival after surviving defeat with honor in the Civil War. He had the fault of excessive pride which brought the South to grief, but he did not have the domineering personality of Thomas Sutpen nor his weakness for the opposite sex, which produced descendants of both races who caused his downfall and theirs. The Sartoris legacy was self-destruction through reckless behavior, while the Sutpen legacy was interracial hostility and violence, father against son, brother against brother. Carothers McCaslin was really more like Thomas Sutpen than John Sartoris, since he too corrupted his own inheritance by fathering black as well as white descendants.

The McCaslin descendants however did not go on imitating their ancestor and bringing further destruction to the family. Unlike the Compson family, who degenerated from their patriarch, General Compson, later generations becoming dissolute and suicidal, unable to live up to their ancestor's example, the McCaslin family proved to be better than their patriarch, Carothers McCaslin. Of all Faulkner's principal families, the McCaslin family has the distinction of improving in later generations, and at least one of them has the will and the capacity to absolve the ancestral guilt and to redeem the family honor. The Snopeses, of course, are without honor from the first to the last generation; they lie and cheat and steal to get ahead in the world, without troubling their consciences. Flem Snopes is the comic villain of Yoknapatawpha County. He cheerfully makes fools of everyone else for his benefit. Ike McCaslin, in contrast, could be called the comic hero of Yoknapatawpha County. His actions are unselfish; he treats others honorably, doing his best to atone for the sins of his grandfather. While Flem Snopes preys on others to advance his selfish interests, Ike McCaslin repays others for his ancestor's selfishness. Flem Snopes rises in the world by tricking others and acquiring what belongs to them; Ike McCaslin chooses when he grows up to forfeit the plantation he has inherited from his grandfather, and to share the legacy Carothers McCaslin left with his black relatives, acknowledging their right to inherit some of his wealth even as he disavows his right to own the property he has inherited.

Ike McCaslin is the central character in *The Bear*, by far the longest story in *Go Down, Moses*, whose renunciation of ancestral property can best be compared with Bayard Sartoris's renunciation of violence in *The Unvanquished*. Bayard renounces revenge for his father's murder, and in so doing proves his courage while forgoing any further killing. In that sense, he redeems the Sartoris family name in an earlier generation, though it will unfortunately degenerate later. What Ike McCaslin renounces is his title to the plantation his grandfather left him, which takes a different kind of courage. It is sacrificial, an acknowledgment of the wrongs committed in the McCaslin name and a desire to set things right. *The Bear* is a tragic story in one sense, because it tells the riveting tale of a successful hunt, that brought down more than just a powerful wild animal. In the figure of Old Ben, the great bear, who is a major character in the story, death has destroyed a symbol of the wilderness, nature as it existed before men invaded and settled and tamed it. Ike McCaslin as a young hunter has the courage and acquires the skill of the older hunters, and he helps them kill Old Ben, the massive bear that has outlived so many hunters intent on killing him that he has come to seem immortal. Down with him goes Lion, the huge hunting dog that finally tracks Old Ben down, and Sam Fathers, the man of three races—red, white, and black—who knows the wilderness better than any of the hunters, and who has taught Ike how to hunt. In a memorable encounter in the woods with Ike, Sam hails the bear as "Grandfather," as if he too were descended from wild nature. Sam knows the bear must be killed, but wants it to be killed by those who respect it, to give it an honorable death. *The Bear* is tragic for Sam, Lion, and Old Ben, but it is not tragic for Ike McCaslin. Ike McCaslin is a comic hero in spite of the tragedy he witnesses and participates in as a young man. To him, the hunt is a ritual leading to a willing sacrifice of life. It isn't killing nor is it murder; it is death with honor. Ike will go on in the same spirit to sacrifice the plantation his grandfather left him believing that nature cannot be selfishly owned, that the earth belongs, not to individual human beings, but to the "communal anonymity of brotherhood," which he had experienced in hunting the bear. Ike has learned the great virtue of humility, which he will carry through the rest of his life, until he compensates for his grandfather's pride of possession by renouncing his inheritance. The McCaslin saga has elements of tragedy in it, but Ike McCaslin is a more comic than tragic hero, and he stands tall as the principal hero of the family.

Ike's story does not come first in *Go Down, Moses*, though it is the heart of the novel Faulkner put together by combining a series of separate stories. He was using the form he had developed successfully in *The Unvanquished*, putting short stories together to make a novel. Bayard Sartoris was the protagonist in a series of chronologically told stories, whereas *Go Down, Moses* is about Ike McCaslin only in part, even if the best part. We first have the story of his father, Theophilus McCaslin, "Uncle Buck," and his twin brother, Amodeus McCaslin, "Uncle Buddy." Faulkner had introduced them in *The Unvanquished* as "ahead of their time," letting their Negro slaves live in the McCaslin mansion while they lived in less spacious quarters nearby. Uncle Buck had helped Bayard Sartoris track down Granny Millard's killer in *The Unvanquished*. The twin McCaslin brothers have made the first step toward renouncing the heritage Carothers McCaslin left, which Ike will some day complete. "Was" opens *Go Down, Moses* with a comic story about the McCaslin and Beauchamp families who live on neighboring plantations and share their slaves. Uncle Buck and Uncle Buddy play a game of poker with Hubert Beauchamp to determine which of the brothers marries Hubert's sister, Sibby (Sophonsiba), and which of their plantations will be the home of their Negro slaves, Tomey's Turl and Tennie, who see each other every night but aren't allowed to live together. Tomey's Turl is a black McCaslin, the illegitimate son of Carothers McCaslin and his slave girl Tomasina; Tennie is a Beauchamp because she is a slave of Mr. Hubert. Uncle Buddy wins the poker game against Hubert, who refuses to call his hand and therefore concedes victory. The result of this gamble is that Uncle Buck McCaslin has to marry Sibby Beauchamp and to beget Ike McCaslin, who is both a Beauchamp and a McCaslin. Tomey's Turl and Tennie will live together on the McCaslin plantation because Uncle Buddy won the poker game. It is a comic story about the awful days of slavery, which in Faulkner's humorous portrayal of it, makes the relations between neighboring plantation families and their black slaves in the Old South intimate and even tolerant.

"The Fire and the Hearth," the second story in *Go Down, Moses*, takes place almost a hundred years later, when the son of Tomey's Turl and Tennie, Lucas Beauchamp, is 67 years old. He is descended from Carothers McCaslin on the male side and proud of that fact, and lives in a cabin on the McCaslin plantation, whose owner is Carothers "Roth" Edmonds, descended from Carothers McCaslin on the female side, and thus really less the proper heir of the plantation than Lucas. Lucas keeps a fire burning on the hearth of his cabin for his wife Molly, who is living in the main house as nursemaid to the Edmonds family. The story is comic, because Molly comes back to find that Lucas has foolishly bought a divining machine from a St. Louis trader, sure he will find buried gold with it. He is so addicted to nightly divining for gold that Molly threatens to divorce him, but Lucas finally agrees to give up the divining machine if Molly will agree not to divorce him. Molly is the moralist of the McCaslin family, as Dilsey was in the Compson family, raising Roth Edmonds to respect the chivalric code of the South, which Faulkner expresses in this story, "to be gentle with his inferiors, honorable with his equals, generous to the weak and considerate of the aged, courteous, truthful, and brave to all." The black McCaslins teach the white McCaslins the code of honor they should live by, and though Lucas Beauchamp seems obsessed with his divining machine, he is gentleman enough to renounce it eventually, so that Molly won't divorce him, and thus they can keep the fire burning on their hearth.

"Pantaloon in Black," the third story in *Go Down, Moses*, is not about the McCaslin family but about a black man who rents a cabin from Roth Edmonds. His name is Rider. He is so inconsolable when his wife dies that he becomes bent on destroying himself. He buries his wife and immediately goes on a rampage, buying a jug of corn liquor from a white bootlegger in the woods and getting raving drunk, then going to the sawmill where he works to join a crap game. A white man named Birdsong controls the game with a pair of concealed dice, cheating the negroes until Rider sees his trickery and challenges him. When the white man pulls out a pistol, Rider slits his throat with a razor. He is pursued and captured by the county sheriff and put in jail, but escapes from the jail by brute strength, only to be captured again by white relatives of Birdsong, who hang him by a bell-rope in a country church. The story is reminiscent of *Light in August*, exciting as a narrative from beginning to end, with an equally bloody resolution. Yet Rider, like Joe Christmas, is sympathetic though self-destructive, and heroic in his desperate grief over the death of his wife. Rider is the most violent of all Faulkner's black characters, but he is not portrayed as evil; he acts impulsively and fatally, devastated uncontrollably by the death of his wife.

"The Old People" is a prelude to *The Bear*, a fine short hunting story which introduces Ike McCaslin and Sam Fathers and defines the ritual of the hunt. Ike is a boy of twelve who kills his first deer and is blooded by Sam as an initiation into the wilderness. Hunting afterwards with Sam, Ike sees a fabulous giant stag which he refrains from shooting, though both men are carrying loaded guns. Seeing the stag unites Ike with the wilderness, a secret he shares only with Sam. The other hunters say they have seen nothing more than an ordinary deer, while Ike knows he has seen a magnificent stag. He has a conversation later with his cousin "Cass," McCaslin Edmonds, who tells Ike that Sam once showed him the same giant stag, and gave it the same salute, "Chief, Grandfather" without firing a shot. The majestic deer precedes the massive bear which Ike will pursue to its death in Faulkner's longest and finest hunting story, *The Bear*.

The Bear is a complete novel in itself, often printed separately, but Faulkner chose to incorporate it into *Go Down, Moses*, because it contains the fullest account of the McCaslin family. The novel consists of five parts, in the course of which Ike grows up, from boyhood to manhood, learns how to hunt, and inherits the McCaslin plantation which his grandfather built before the Civil War. Ike was born in 1867, two years after that war ended. He is ten years old in 1877, when he is initiated into the brotherhood of the hunters. The hunters are a mixed group of men. There is Sam Fathers, the child of an Indian chief, Ikkemotubbe, by a mulatto woman. There is Boon Hogganbeck, a half-breed, a mixture of white and red blood. There is McCaslin "Cass" Edmonds, Ike's cousin, who is like an elder brother to him, descended from Carothers McCaslin on the female side. There is Walter Ewell, champion hunter, a deadeye with a rifle. There are Major de Spain and General Compson, former Confederate officers become gentleman hunters. There is Tennie's Jim, a Negro whose mother and father were once slaves on the neighboring McCaslin and Beauchamp plantations, and Uncle Ash, the black camp cook. There is above all Ike himself, the grandson of Carothers McCaslin and the son of Uncle Buck McCaslin. Two animals are also central to the story: Old Ben, the bear they hunt to his death, and Lion, the hound they train to track Old Ben. The tragic hero of the story is really Old Ben, "the big old bear with one trap-ruined foot" about whom a legend has accumulated of "a corridor of wreckage and destruction beginning back before the boy was born, through which sped, not fast but rather with the ruthless and irresistible deliberation of a locomotive, the shaggy tremendous shape." The bear is not an evil force, but symbolizes nature in the raw, the "doomed wilderness," and when Ike joins the hunt for him, he believes "they were going not to hunt bear and deer but to keep yearly rendezvous with the bear which they did not even intend to kill."

Ike is eager to take part in "the yearly pageant-rite of the old bear's furious immortality." He first encounters the bear at the age of 10, when he waits on stand with Sam Fathers until a strange baying sound of the dogs in the woods signifies that Old Ben has come and gone, though they never see him. They know who he is, because one of the dogs has been struck by the bear and is bleeding. Sam takes Ike deep into the woods to see, next to a fallen log, "the print of the enormous warped two-toed foot." A day later, Ike hears the sound of "the big woodpecker called Lord-to-God by negroes, [as it] clattered at a dead trunk." The sound is that of the Ivory-billed Woodpecker, not yet extinct. When the pecking sound stops, Ike knows Old Ben is looking at him, and when the woodpecker starts hammering again, he knows Old Ben has departed. He now knows he must go into the wilderness alone to see the bear, first relinquishing all the tools of the hunter—gun, compass, and watch—until he loses his way in the woods. As soon as he is sure he is lost, he sees a fresh footprint filling with water, and it causes him to look up: "Then he saw the bear. It did not emerge, appear, it was just there, immobile, fixed in the green and windless noon's hot dappling, not as big as he had dreamed but as big as he had expected, bigger, dimensionless against the dappled obscurity, looking at him." Ike watches in amazement as "It crossed the glade without haste, walking for an instant into the sun's full glare and out of it, and stopped again and looked back at him across one shoulder. Then it was gone." The bear fades into the wilderness, and Ike, just ten years old, enters into the brotherhood of nature, recovering the innocence of Adam before the Fall. Unfortunately, the knowledge of good and evil after the Fall tells him the bear must be killed.

The next year is 1880 and Ike is 13, when Lion appears as a huge mastiff menacing all the farm animals. Ike has killed his first deer, been blooded by Sam Fathers with a mark on his forehead, and has killed his first bear. He is such a skilled woodsman that he can find the bedding place of a deer and wait for it to return so that he can kill it. "If Sam Fathers had been his mentor and the backyard rabbits and squirrels his kindergarten, then the wilderness the old bear ran was his college and the old male bear itself, so long unwifed and childless as to have become his own ungendered progenitor, was his alma mater." He takes a pet terrier, a fyce, with him into the woods, and ambushes Old Ben, startling him but not shooting him. Ike and Sam make a pact that Old Ben will die at their hands some day, because they share the belief that they must do the killing, not leaving it to be done by some uncaring stranger. Lion is the dog that will hunt Old Ben down. They do hunt Old Ben with Lion, until General Compson shoots him and draws blood, but the bear escapes. Ike believes that next year they will bring

Old Ben down, and he is "humble and proud that he had been found worthy to be a part of it."

The event they have been waiting for happens in the third section, in 1883, when Ike is 16, and they finally track the bear down and kill it. But first, Ike and Boon are sent to Memphis to bring back more whiskey, and there in the city, Ike dreams of the woods he has left behind: "He felt the old lift of the heart, as pristine as on the first day; he would never lose it, no matter how old in hunting and pursuit: the best, the best of all breathing, the humility and the pride." On their return, they find the camp full of people who have come to see Lion hunt down Old Ben. Ike rides Katie, the one-eyed mule that cannot be spooked by blood, given that privilege because General Compson says of him, "He's already a better woodsman than you or me either and in another ten years he'll be as good as Walter." He and Sam Fathers ride together until they confront Old Ben in a glade with his back against a tree, and Lion and Boon Hogganbeck go in for the kill. The bear catches the dog in its embrace, and in a wild attack Boon plunges his hunting knife into the bear's throat. The bear drags Boon and Lion a few steps till it crashes down. "It didn't collapse, crumble. It fell all of a piece, as a tree falls, so that all three of them, man dog and bear, seemed to bounce once." The bear is down, the dog is down, and even Sam Fathers is down, having suffered a heart attack when he sees the bear die. Ike stays loyally beside them on "one of those windless Mississippi winter days which are a sort of Indian summer's Indian summer." When they examine the carcass of the bear they find 52 bullets lodged under his skin. The great hunting story has finally been told to its dramatic ending.

The fourth and fifth sections of *The Bear* provide the aftermath, when Ike McCaslin is 21 and inherits the land his grandfather Carothers McCaslin once owned. Ike makes the momentous decision to give it up. He does so after learning about Carother McCaslins' sins of adultery and incest, fathering a child by a Negro slave named Tomasina, then fathering another child by his own daughter, driving her mother Tomasina to drown herself in shame. Ike feels his patrimony is tainted with Original Sin, and he makes up his mind to renounce it for good. His cousin Cass tries to talk him out of "relinquishing" his heritage, but Ike argues that "I can't repudiate it. It was never mine to repudiate. It was never Father's and Uncle Buddy's to bequeath me to repudiate because it was never Grandfather's to bequeath them to bequeath me to repudiate because it was never old Ikkemotubbe's to sell to Grandfather for bequeathment and repudiation." Ike's argument is based on his reading of "the Book," that is, Genesis, where after God creates the earth he creates the creatures of the earth and gives man the duty of being "overseer" for Him, "to hold the earth mutual and intact, in the communal anonymity of brotherhood, and all the fee He asked was pity and humility and sufferance and endurance and the sweat of his face for bread." So Ike takes the Fall of Man to mean that settlers in the New World have selfishly taken possession of the land which should belong to everyone. When Carothers McCaslin, Ike's grandfather, bought the land from the Indians, then drove the Indians out and enslaved Negroes to work the land, he was guilty of the Second Fall of Man. He could not own the land morally, but he could own it legally, and Ike, his heir, refuses to own it any longer. Instead, he will bequeath it to the other descendants of Carothers McCaslin, black and white, including Lucas Beauchamp, because doing so will "set my people free," true to the words of the old Negro spiritual: "Go down, Moses, /'way down in Egypt land,/ tell ol' Pharaoh/to set my people free."

Ike renounces title to the McCaslin plantation, and determines to pay each of his black cousins the thousand dollars Carothers bequeathed to them, to compensate for his double sin of fathering a daughter by one of his slaves and compounding it by committing incest with his own daughter. Ike seeks out Carothers McCaslin's three black grandchildren, Tennie's Jim, Fonsiba, and Lucas Beauchamp, to give each of them the thousand dollars Carothers has left them in his will. Lucas Beauchamp is younger than Ike by seven years and lives on the McCaslin plantation, owned by Roth Edmonds after Ike gave up his title to it. What Ike learned first by hunting the bear, and next by unearthing the record of his grandfather's sins, is that he must renounce his heritage and pay off his grandfather's debt. He knows he cannot bring about heaven on earth, but he can at least satisfy his own conscience, "because I have got myself to have to live with for the rest of my life and all I want is peace to do it in."

In the final section of *The Bear*, Faulkner goes back to the time when Ike was 18, when he made a pilgrimage to the woods, to the spot where Sam Fathers and Lion were buried with the paw of Old Ben, three noble creatures joined in death. A logging train carries him like a snake winding its way into Eden, which has been reduced to a square plot of woods surrounding the grave of Sam, Lion, and Old Ben. When he sees a real rattlesnake near the grave, a miracle occurs: the snake seems to rise up and walk away from Ike, as if Ike were Adam Before the Fall. Before the Fall of Man, the snake had not been condemned by God to crawl on its belly for tempting Eve, but could walk in the Garden of Eden with the rest of God's creation. Ike has recovered his innocence, and temporarily feels that God has restored the earth to its original goodness, at the very spot where Sam and Lion and the Bear are buried. But the feeling doesn't last. It is interrupted suddenly by the sound of someone hammering on metal, and he sees Boon Hogganbeck hammering on his gun, shouting to Ike "Get out of here! Don't touch a one of them! They're mine." He means the squirrels. Boon represents fallen man, trying to possess the earth when he should be thanking God for granting it to him. Ike's dream of Paradise is shattered, but for a moment he has communed in spirit with Sam and Lion and Ben, and so the story of *The Bear* ends happily for Ike, making him the comic hero of Yoknapatawpha County.

In "Delta Autumn," the story following *The Bear*, Ike McCaslin is an old man returning to the land he had relinquished, which is steadily succumbing to human devastation. It is 1940, and Ike is 73, aware that his time on earth is short, regretting that the woods and wild game have given way to paved roads and motor cars. He remembers that once the wilderness was only thirty miles from Jefferson, and reflects sadly that "all that remained of the old time were the Indian names," Yoknapatawpha in particular. There is little left of the land he once knew and the people he once admired, but Ike takes some comfort from thinking that "No wonder the ruined woods I used to know don't cry for retribution!...The people who have destroyed it will accomplish its revenge." Ike sees that Progress inevitably means destroying wild nature; and he knows that it was a futile gesture on his part to repudiate his inheritance, but he does not regret the sacrifice he has made.

"Go Down, Moses," the title story, is unfortunately the last and the weakest of all the stories in Faulkner's eighth Yoknapatawpha novel, but it completes the saga of the McCaslin family. It is not about the further adventures of Ike McCaslin, but about the execution of Mollie Beauchamp's grandson, Samuel Worsham Beauchamp, for murdering a policeman. He is distantly related to Ike McCaslin and is a disgrace to the family, but Molly mourns her grandson's death despite his crime, and insists on bringing the body back from Illinois where he was executed, to be buried near her in Jefferson. Ike, the hero of the McCaslin family, is left with barely a trace of the family heroism he sought to restore. The McCaslin family were redeemed for one generation, but not forever.

CHAPTER 6

The Golden Book of Yoknapatawpha County

It was in 1945 that Malcolm Cowley persuaded Faulkner to let him edit and publish a selection of stories which were a landmark in his career, because for it Faulkner updated his map of Yoknapatawpha County and added an Appendix which was an extension backwards and forwards of the Compson family, the main characters in his finest novel, *The Sound and the Fury*. Since most of his books were then out of print and his reputation was at a low point despite the masterpieces he had written ("Faulkner is finished," one critic wrote), *The Portable Faulkner* helped revive his standing among American writers, prompting a critical response from Robert Penn Warren that signaled a new assessment of his achievement.

> The study of Faulkner is the most challenging single task in contemporary American literature for criticism to undertake. Here is a novelist who, in mass of work, in scope of material, in range of effect, in reportorial accuracy and symbolic subtlety, in philosophical weight, can be put beside the masters of our own past literature.

Cowley had performed a service no critic up to that time could claim; he called attention to the continuity and integrity of Faulkner's fiction, which Faulkner himself was glad to acknowledge. Cowley had published an earlier essay on "William Faulkner's Legend of the South," and went on to assemble from his work "The first chronological picture of Faulkner's mythical county in Mississippi." Readers could see more clearly that Faulkner was a writer with an encompassing vision that informed everything he wrote. Five years later, the world recognized his achievement, when in 1950 he was awarded the Nobel Prize for Literature.

The book which propelled him to that pinnacle was his next novel, *Intruder in the Dust*, which came out in 1948, and was more favorably reviewed than anything he had published before. The next year it was made into a movie, which was filmed in and around Oxford, Mississippi, and became the best movie to be made from a Faulkner novel. He was paid $50,000 for the screen rights, making him financially independent for the first time in his life. He did not write the screenplay, but agreed to serve as a consultant, pointing out places where the cameramen could find authentic scenery. The premiere was held in Oxford in October, 1949, and Faulkner was talked into attending it with family and friends.

He resisted further publicity, however. When Hamilton Basso, a novelist who knew Faulkner in New Orleans in the 1920s, asked if he could write a *New Yorker* profile of him, Faulkner said "Hell, no!" and added: "I am working tooth and nail at my lifetime ambition to be the last private individual on earth. I expect every success since apparently there is no competition for the place." Malcolm Cowley asked Faulkner if he could write something for *Life* magazine, but though Faulkner was staying with him in New York at the time and had been glad to let Cowley edit *The Portable Faulkner* a few years earlier, he gave the same response. "It is my ambition to be, as a private individual, abolished and voided from history, leaving no refuse save the printed books."

Yet *Intruder in the Dust* was the book that brought Faulkner to world attention more than any he had published, and it was his fourteenth novel. It was a worthy successor to his thirteenth novel, *Go Down, Moses*, though nothing in the new novel bore genuine comparison to *The Bear*. It was nevertheless a continuation of the McCaslin family saga, centering on Lucas Beauchamp, one of the black descendants of Carothers McCaslin. As a detective novel, it bore some resemblance to *Sanctuary* but wasn't nearly as shocking. It was in the broad sense another comic novel, a continuation of the Comic Phase of his work which began with *The Unvanquished*. Lucas Beauchamp was as racially mixed as Joe Christmas, but he was no lost soul in search of his identity. Quite the contrary, Lucas was proud of his identity, since what mattered most to him was that he was the grandson of Carothers McCaslin. He was also the child of Tomey's Turl and Tennie, who had been slaves of the McCaslins and the Beauchamps, a fact that made him the target of racial hatred and led to his being accused of murdering a white man. Things look bad for Lucas, who is arrested with a smoking gun near where Vinson Gowrie has been shot in the back. And it happens in Beat Four, a notoriously hostile section of Yoknapatawpha County. Lucas knows he is innocent, but he bears the murder charge manfully and goes to jail in Jefferson, expecting to be vindicated eventually. He is vindicated, but it takes the combined efforts of three white citizens of Jefferson, a boy of sixteen named Chick Mallison, his uncle, Gavin Stevens, a lawyer, and Miss Habersham, a public-spirited spinster, to prove that Vinson Gowrie was murdered by his own brother, Crawford Gowrie, not by Lucas Beauchamp, who was framed to look like the murderer.

Lucas had befriended Chick Mallison as a young boy when he fell in an icy creek and had to be rescued, and he calls on him to come to the jail and help him prove his innocence. He knows that Chick's uncle is a respected lawyer in town, and sure enough, Chick quickly enlists Gavin Stevens in the defense of Lucas Beauchamp. They go to see Lucas in jail, and Gavin Stevens agrees to defend him, though he assumes Lucas is guilty as charged and all he can do is try to avoid the death penalty. Chick believes in his innocence, however, and Lucas asks if he will do him a favor. He wants Chick to go out to the cemetery where Vinson Gowrie is buried, dig up his coffin, and prove that the bullet which killed him did not come from Lucas's gun, a "fawty-one Colt," but from another man's gun. Chick is dumbfounded to be asked to go out at night to the cemetery where the Gowries bury their kin, dig up a fresh grave, and ask the sheriff to identify the bullet that killed Vinson Gowrie. Nevertheless, he says he'll try to do it and get back to the jail in time to keep the Gowrie clan from lynching him. Lucas tells him calmly, "I'll try to wait."

Miss Habersham volunteers to go with them in search of the real killer, because she was raised with Molly, the wife of Lucas Beauchamp, and feels a natural sympathy for him. She has a pickup truck which she offers for the trip to the cemetery, and she takes Chick Mallison and his black friend, Aleck Sanders, out to the churchyard at night, where they dig up Vinson Gowrie's fresh grave. To their surprise, they find it occupied by the body of another man, Jake Montgomery, and the plot thickens. Chick goes back to see his uncle, and they enlist the help of the sheriff, since Gavin Stevens is now as convinced as his nephew that Lucas is innocent. He believes someone else has murdered

Vinson Gowrie and they must find the culprit. The sheriff goes with them to the cemetery and has the grave dug up again, only to find it empty. No Vinson Gowrie, no Jake Montgomery, just an empty coffin. They are baffled now and begin plotting a trap for the real murderer, whose identity is still a mystery.

Intruder in the Dust, like a good detective novel, has its aura of suspense, while the lawyer and the sheriff work feverishly to free Lucas Beauchamp before he can be lynched by the Gowries and their kin in Beat Four. They go back to the cemetery and find a mule track leading from the grave down to a creek, where they discover the body of Jake Montgomery in a fresh mound of earth, and soon after, the body of Vinson Gowrie in the creek in a bed of quicksand. It is apparent that the murderer could not have been Lucas Beauchamp, who has been in jail all this time. Gradually they piece together the motive for the murder, and the later movement of the bodies. Crawford Gowrie, brother of Vinson, has been stealing lumber from his brother's yard and has been seen in the act by Lucas Beauchamp. So Crawford devises a plan that will get rid of both men, arranging for Lucas to be having target practice with his gun near the country store where he will shoot his own brother Vinson in the back. He assumes that Lucas will be jailed and executed for the crime, and he will have eliminated both men. But Jake Montgomery intervenes, because he suspects Crawford of the murder, and he digs up the body of Vinson Gowrie while Crawford is watching him in the dark. Crawford hits him over the head, crushing his skull, and buries him in Vinson's grave, thinking no one will know. He then takes Vinson's body to the creek and dumps it in quicksand. But when he sees that others have come to dig up the grave again, he quickly exhumes Jake Montgomery's body and hastily buries it near the creek where Vinson is buried deep in quicksand. The pursuers now know who the real murderer is, and to prove it is Crawford, the sheriff releases Lucas Beauchamp from jail and baits a trap for Crawford, sending word that Lucas is on his way home. Crawford appears and is about to shoot Lucas when he is apprehended by the sheriff and put in jail in place of Lucas. The mob that has come to see Lucas lynched is shamed and leaves Jefferson sheepishly, "They ran," Chick says to his uncle. In the final episode, Lucas comes to Gavin Stevens's office to pay him a fee, but Gavin says it was his nephew Chick who proved his innocence, and he will only accept $2 for his broken fountain pen. Lucas laboriously counts the money out, pays him the $2 in small coins, and Gavin tells him he should also take a bouquet of flowers to Miss Habersham, who kept the lynch mob at bay while he was waiting to be absolved of the crime. He agrees, but doesn't leave the office, and Gavin asks Lucas what he is still waiting for. "My receipt" are his last words, as the novel ends with a show of Lucas's pride.

The novel is effective as a detective story, keeping suspense alive with the twists of plot, but it seldom rises to the eloquence of Faulkner's best novels.

Lucas Beauchamp is the most admirable character in the novel, and he is a McCaslin, but he is not Ike McCaslin. His pride and his patience sustain him as Gavin Stevens and Miss Habersham and Chick Mallison prove his innocence, and shame those who would judge him automatically guilty just because he is black. It has at least one passage worthy of Faulkner at his best, giving proof late in the novel that he hadn't forgotten how to write a memorable passage:

> A small voice, a sound sensitive lady poet of the time of my youth said *the scattered tea goes with the leaves and every day a sunset dies:* a poet's extravagance which as quite often mirrors truth but upside down and backward since the mirror's unwitting manipulator busy in his preoccupation has forgotten that the back of it is glass too: because if they only did, instead of which yesterday's sunset and yesterday's tea both are inextricable from the scattered indestructible uninfusable grounds blown through the endless corridors of tomorrow, into the shoes we will have to walk in and even the sheets we will have (or try) to sleep between: because you escape nothing, you flee nothing; the pursuer is what is doing the running and tomorrow night is nothing but one long sleepless wrestle with yesterday's omissions and regrets.

If *Intruder in the Dust* had been full of passages of such power and eloquence it would have been another of Faulkner's masterpieces, but it does stand as a gripping detective novel that brought Faulkner to national and international attention in 1948 and 1949, just before he was awarded the Nobel Prize for Literature in 1950.

Faulkner published his last masterpiece, *The Bear*, in 1942, eight years before he went to Sweden in 1950 to receive the 1949 Nobel Prize for Literature (the Swedish Academy had delayed awarding it, because a year earlier they couldn't agree on a recipient). He hadn't completed his work, however, because he had said earlier "My last book will be the Doomsday Book, the Golden Book of Yoknapatawpha County. Then I shall break the pencil and I'll have to stop." He declared his work complete in 1960, when he published *The Mansion*, the last of the Snopes trilogy, but in fact he had one novel left in him. It was *The Reivers*, published in 1962, the year of his death, which won a posthumous Pulitzer Prize. By then every book he wrote was a bestseller; he had won his first Pulitzer Prize with *A Fable* in 1954. The last ten years of Faulkner's career brought him the recognition he had long deserved, while he still had time to enjoy it. He became a celebrity, making State Department trips to farflung places like Japan and Venezuela, Athens and Paris, accepting appointment as Writer in Residence at the University of

Virginia, and being singled out by President Eisenhower to head the Writers' Group of his People-to-People program, a public role he accepted gladly and carried out conscientiously. The Nobel Prize had changed a man who jealously guarded his privacy into a man who smiled for photographers and even began answering questions about his books.

In 1951, he published *Requiem for a Nun*, as a sequel to *Sanctuary*, the scandalous novel he had published two decades earlier. That novel was a commercial success, which brought him the wider audience he sought, but he felt apologetic about it, and a need to redeem Temple Drake some day from the moral corruption into which she had sunk under Popeye's evil guardianship. Faulkner's new novel was another of his experiments in form, but less like *Sanctuary*, a straightforward narrative, than like *The Wild Palms*, a double-barreled plot that never quite held together. This time he tried seeing whether he could combine fiction with drama. He did it, but combining different literary forms worked no better than juxtaposing two different short novels.

Requiem for a Nun did, however, add a few touches to the legend he had been developing for more than two decades. It starts with a chapter called "The Courthouse," which is a fictional portrait of early Jefferson, going back to its establishment as a trading post in Indian territory, and then to the first major land purchase from the Chickasaw chief, Ikkemotubbe, of the original square mile of woods that became the center of Yoknapatawpha County's rich and varied life. The purchaser is a white settler named Compson, progenitor of one of Faulkner's princely lines, which came to include a governor and a general, although it decayed badly in later generations, as we know from *The Sound and the Fury* and *Absalom, Absalom!* The first Compson in this new territory swapped a horse for a square mile of land, a lopsided barter worthy of a Snopes. He then erected in the center of it the first courthouse, assisted by a French settler named Louis Grenier, who would build a home in the woods nearby which became the celebrated Old Frenchman Place of *Sanctuary* and *The Hamlet*. A town square quickly sprang up around the courthouse, shops appeared facing it, and houses spread out in all directions, as the wilderness, the deep woods, steadily disappeared.

From this early fictional history of what became of the virgin Mississippi forest, Faulkner leapt to a courtroom drama in the thriving town of Jefferson, now in the twentieth century, and what had started as a novel takes the form of a play, complete with stage directions and dialogue. A Negress named Nancy Mannigoe is being charged with the murder of Temple Drake's baby, her child by Gowan Stevens, the man who had abandoned her to Popeye's fatherly care. The slatternly Temple Drake has become the respectable Mrs. Gowan Stevens, in an ironic aftermath of the events in *Sanctuary*, but she is not a good mother. Her self-indulgent neglect of her child distresses her black maid so much that she smothers the infant in a kind of mercy killing.

The rest of the story concerns Temple's vain attempt to obtain clemency for Nancy, who is no paragon herself, since she is the same Nancy who was the central figure of Faulkner's superb story, "That Evening Sun," waiting in her cabin, terrified with fear that her husband Jesus would return and kill her for adultery. He didn't, but having been a fallen woman herself, she survived to become a believing Christian. She is the "nun" of Faulkner's title, who wants to convert the fallen Temple to her faith and save her tarnished soul. Temple is no nun, but she is trying to be a better woman, and she goes with her husband's uncle, lawyer Gavin Stevens, to "The Golden Dome," the capitol in Jackson, to beg the governor to pardon Nancy. It would be the one redeeming act of her dissolute life, but it fails, and in the end Nancy is to be executed for the mercy killing of Temple's baby. Nancy is in "The Jail," the third fictional part of the novel, under a death sentence, but she still pleads with Temple to "believe" as she does, to become like her a redeemed sinner. Faulkner is too much the realist to carry off a deathbed conversion, but though the plot is interesting, it is not convincing, either as novel or as play, nor are the characters as believable as they had been in their earlier incarnations. Thus *Requiem for a Nun* is not a worthy sequel to *Sanctuary*, which had been a much more brutal but much more effective novel. To a large extent, however, it set the pattern for the novels Faulkner wrote in his last decade, which borrowed heavily from his earlier, better fiction.

Faulkner had been sharing his work on *Requiem for a Nun* with a young woman from Memphis named Joan Williams, who came to him for encouragement as a writer and became his secret mistress. It was not his first extramarital affair, but he fell so much in love with her that he gave her as a present his most valuable possession, the original manuscript of *The Sound and the Fury*. To express further how much he cared for her, in 1953 he wrote her one of his most revealing confessional letters, in which he invited her to look back with him over his whole professional career:

> And now, at last, I have some perspective on all I have done. I mean, the work apart from me, the work which I did, apart from what I am…And now I realize for the first time what an amazing gift I had: uneducated in every formal sense, without even very literate, let alone literary, companions, yet to have made the things I have made. I don't know where it came from. I don't know why God or gods or whoever it was, selected me to be the vessel. Believe me, this is not humility, false modesty: it is simply amazement. I wonder if you have ever had that thought about the work and the country man whom you know as Bill Faulkner—what little connection there seems to be between them. (*Selected Letters of William Faulkner*, ed. by Joseph Blotner, page 348)

Faulkner, in his fifties and world-famous, was admitting in this very personal letter that his early period of inspiration, which lasted from *Sartoris* in 1929 to *The Bear* in 1942, was through, and the books he was now writing would not and could not equal the level of greatness he had once achieved.

But he still had the ambition to equal it, and he tried again with *A Fable*, which he published with much fanfare in 1954. The idea for the novel came to him while he was in Hollywood, from a film producer he knew. The fellow spoke enthusiastically about having Christ and his apostles come to earth during the First World War and bring about a brief period of peace, known historically as "the false armistice." Faulkner fell for the idea, and wrote a screenplay about it, then, when it was rejected, wrote *A Fable*, clearly meant to be allegorical. That was its chief fault. It was too obviously a Christian morality play about the First World War, in which a French corporal and his eleven followers try to stop the fighting, with a brief cease-fire, but the corporal is eventually killed and the war goes on. By then Faulkner's fame guaranteed that any novel he wrote would be successful, and *A Fable* won him his first Pulitzer Prize, though it won him little else, since most critics held it to be one of his least successful novels. Allen Tate, who credited Faulkner with writing more masterpieces than any American novelist, called *A Fable* his only failure. It continues to have a measure of fame, partly because visitors to Oxford are shown the outline of the novel exactly where Faulkner wrote it, in big letters on the walls of his office at Rowan Oak. Faulkner was free to admit that the idea was not his originally, that it had come from a movie producer he knew. However, he had taken it seriously enough to make a "research" trip to France, to see the battlefields of the First World War, in particular the field where some of the worst fighting took place at Verdun, an indecisive battle that produced a huge number of casualties on both sides. That exploratory trip was made in 1951, after he had received the Nobel Prize in Sweden, when he went to Paris to attend a party given by his French publisher, Gallimard, proof that Faulkner was now the toast of France. He would later be given the French Legion of Honor in New Orleans.

Publicity mounted quickly when *A Fable* came out, and Bennett Cerf wanted Faulkner to let *Time* do a cover story on him, which would have further solidified the American audience for his work. But characteristically, Faulkner declined, telling his publisher at Random House: "Let me write the books; let someone who wants it do the publicity." He was always railing against journalists, deploring "one of the most fearful things in modern American life: the Freedom of the Press." He managed to discourage *Time*, but he couldn't stave off *Newsweek*, which did a story on him even after he was rude to their reporter. Though Faulkner quoted some of the affirmative language of his Nobel Prize Acceptance Speech in the novel, and mistakenly thought *A Fable* was his best book at the time he published it, he had second thoughts about it later, and when he was Writer in Residence at the University of Virginia, he returned to his earlier judgment about his fiction, affirming once again that *The Sound and The Fury* was his favorite.

In 1957, as Faulkner was finishing the spring term as Writer in Residence at the University of Virginia, he published *The Town*, the second of his Snopes novels, which had been written more or less on the run in Oxford, Charlottesville, Washington, and New York, between November 1955 and September 1956. It too was an instant bestseller, although the reviews of it were mixed, and were mostly unfavorable. It begins with a link, not to *The Hamlet*, but to *Intruder in the Dust*, in the person of Chick Mallison, an amateur detective in the earlier novel, the initial narrator here. His uncle is the lawyer, Gavin Stevens, who shares the role of narrator with his nephew, and becomes the main commentator on the Snopes fortunes, which are still rising in Jefferson. Ratliff, the canny sewing machine salesman who had been the main observer of Snopes behavior and misbehavior in *The Hamlet*, is a third narrator in this novel, but Gavin Stevens provides a more educated perspective on the Snopeses, though he is too often the long-winded moralist who talks too much, not the wise-cracking, pungent country philosopher, Ratliff. All three narrators, different as they are, are aware that Flem Snopes is on his way up. He has become superintendent of the power plant in Jefferson, appointed by the mayor, Major de Spain (one of the hunters in *The Bear*), who is enjoying a liaison with Eula Varner Snopes, Flem's unfaithful wife. Flem is always ready to sacrifice principle to get ahead.

The other Snopeses are also flourishing, since Eck has become manager of the hotel on the town square, Byron is cashier in the Sartoris bank, Wall Street Panic Snopes owns a little grocery store, and Montgomery Ward Snopes is a pornographic photographer in town, having successfully managed an army canteen in the best French style, not only offering refreshment to soldiers on leave, but a back room where they can be "entertained" by ladies. As Chick Mallison comments, "Snopeses had to be watched like an invasion of snakes or wildcats." Flem, the family entrepreneur who brought them to town in the first place, quietly and shrewdly buys stock in the Sartoris bank to become its vice-president, reaching a higher rung on the local social ladder. He manages to undercut Major de Spain, the bank president as well as the mayor, by putting all his money in the rival Jefferson bank, while being the major stockholder in his own bank, and his wife Eula, who had cuckolded Flem Snopes twice, is so outdone with him she commits suicide in desperation. True to form, Flem and her daughter Linda Snopes order a marble monument from Italy to be erected over her grave with a fitting inscription: "Eula Varner Snopes, 1889–1927, A Virtuous Wife Is a Crown to Her Husband, Her Children Rise and Call her Blessed." Flem never misses a chance for glory, and sends his daughter off to college in New York as the novel ends.

Faulkner began writing *The Mansion*, third and last of the Snopes novels, in the fall of 1958 at Charlottesville, where he was no longer Writer in Residence but had become "consultant in contemporary literature" at the Alderman Library of the University of Virginia. That library today houses most of Faulkner's original manuscripts and papers, and while he was there he was given a faculty study where he did much of his writing. *The Mansion* was published in 1960 to the usual raving reviews, though with some expressions of misgiving about his later writings. He himself called it "the final chapter and summation of a work conceived in 1925," and testified that he had been living with some of the characters for thirty-four years, and knew them better than when he invented them, because he claims "the author has learned more about the human heart" than when he started writing. *The Mansion* is not the equal of *The Hamlet*, but it does compare favorably with *The Town*, and it does finish the Snopes saga with a flourish. The flourish is the death of Flem Snopes, the backwoods entrepreneur who rose to be president of the Sartoris bank in Jefferson and to own the largest home in town. Flem's end is fitting: he is shot dead in his mansion by his mean cousin Mink Snopes, who has languished in prison after being convicted of murder, and who never forgave Flem for failing to come and bail him out. With Flem dead, Faulkner had nothing more to say about the Snopeses. Gavin Stevens, one of the narrators in *The Town*, delivers more longwinded sermons, but the novel is structured more like *The Hamlet*, each section devoted to one of three main Snopeses: first Mink, Flem's murderous cousin, then Linda Snopes, the socially activist daughter of Eula but not of Flem, and Flem himself. But though it is not one of Faulkner's best novels, it served his larger purpose, completing the family saga that he began with "Father Abraham" in 1925, the initial episode of the long and colorful history of the Snopeses, his name for the family of predatory schemers determined to get ahead in the world. The Snopeses were a family full of crude and clever con men who made fools of others for their advancement, and were quite ready to betray their own kin if necessary. When he wrote the novel, Faulkner had moved from Mississippi to Virginia to be near his daughter Jill, and once a dinner companion in Charlottesville asked him whether he had encountered any Snopeses in Virginia. He said yes, he saw them every day. *The Mansion* was proof he could write about them as easily in Virginia as in Mississippi.

Faulkner's last novel was a worthier end to his career than his Snopes trilogy. It was a folk comedy he began writing in the summer of 1961, tentatively titled *The Horse-Stealers: A Reminiscence*. That title was too explicit to last. He first changed it to *The Reavers*, a synonym for Robbers, but chose to make it more mysterious by spelling it the Scottish way, *The Reivers*.

Faulkner had a definite knack for giving his books titles that were intriguing and memorable. The narrator is named Lucius Priest, aged 67 years and a grandfather, but his tale is retrospective, going back to the time when he was 11 years old, in 1905. Since Faulkner wrote it in 1961, when he was 64, Lucius Priest could have been his fictional alter ego. The date of the story is close to the date of *The Hamlet*, which was 1904. Oddly enough, no mention is made of motor cars in *The Hamlet*, where all transportation is by horse and mule, just as it was in *As I Lay Dying*. But in *The Reivers*, the central event is a trip from Jefferson to Memphis in one of the first automobiles to be seen in Jefferson. The owner of this antique car was the narrator's grandfather, also named Lucius Priest, and so there is a remote connection with the patriarch of the McCaslin family, Lucius Quintus Carothers McCaslin. *The Reivers* is set in past time, but ranges over the history of Yoknapatawpha County, mentioning many of the families that figure prominently in Faulkner's fiction: the Sartorises, the Compsons, the McCaslins, and the Edmonds. Ike McCaslin is a cousin of the narrator, and has given the plantation he inherited from his grandfather to his cousin, Cass Edmonds, choosing to live modestly above the hardware store he owns in Jefferson.

The main character in the novel is Boon Hogganbeck, Ike McCaslin's old hunting companion, the burly half-breed who killed the bear with his hunting knife, last seen hunting squirrels when Ike McCaslin made his pilgrimage to the graves of Old Ben, Lion, and Sam Fathers. Boon was an exuberant, rough-hewn character in *The Bear*, and was much the same when Faulkner reintroduced him as the protagonist of *The Reivers*. "He was tough, faithful, brave and completely unreliable; he was six feet four inches tall and weighed two hundred and forty pounds and had the mentality of a child." He starts the action when he "borrows" the automobile of Lucius Priest's grandfather, The Boss, with the excuse of taking the Boss's eleven-year-old grandson to Memphis. The adventures on the road with one of the first motor cars is the heart of the plot. The boy who tells the story is young but not innocent, for as Faulkner observes "There is no crime which a boy of eleven had not envisaged long ago." Boon is a child of nature and a hunter, but he has fallen in love with the new-fangled automobile, and he takes young Lucius on a wild ride over muddy roads from Jefferson to Memphis to see his lady friend, Corrie, one of the call girls in Miss Reba's brothel. We know Miss Reba and her seedy boarding house from *Sanctuary*, where Popeye kept Temple Drake as his mistress, but in *The Reivers* it is more like a house of pleasure, and Corrie is a fun-loving prostitute who is happy to accommodate Boon Hogganbeck when he comes to town. Lucius Priest is much too young to understand how she makes her living, but he falls in love with her, and Corrie is so flattered by the young boy's frank admiration that she gives up her profession and marries Boon Hogganbeck at the end of the novel. The love story of Boon and Corrie gives the novel half its appeal.

The other half comes from the story about a race horse named Lightning, a stolen thoroughbred that Lucius rides to victory in a race to win back the automobile which their black traveling companion, Ned, has traded for a horse. Boon Hogganbeck stole the Boss's automobile while he was out of town attending a funeral, and drives it to Memphis with young Lucius Priest, but discovers on the way they have a stowaway passenger who came along for the ride. Ned emerges from under a tarpaulin in the back seat, and when they get to Memphis, he complicates their escapade considerably by trading the automobile for a horse. He is no sucker; he knows how to make Lightning run fast enough to win races, and the outcome is comic. When the Boss, who is Lucius Priest's grandfather, suddenly appears, he has already won the race on Lightning, and they recover the automobile and drive back to Jefferson together. Ned has had a secret method of winning horse races: he knows that Lightning has a craving for canned sardines, and he waves one in front of him as Lucius rides him down the home stretch. The novel deftly interweaves the love story between Boon and Corrie with an adventure story about a young boy's fling in an automobile and on a horse. Young Lucius Priest rides to Memphis in his grandfather's newfangled motor car, then rides to victory in a horse race, ably assisted by his black friend Ned. Faulkner's last novel is his most light-hearted, a pure old-fashioned comedy, which was made into a colorful movie starring Steve McQueen, a box office favorite.

The Reivers is also one of Faulkner's most readable novels, a distinction it shares with *Sanctuary*, *The Unvanquished*, and *Intruder in the Dust*. It is a piece of fictional nostalgia that he clearly enjoyed writing. When he took the manuscript into Gathright-Reed drugstore in 1962, to have it wrapped for mailing to the publisher, he remarked to his old friend Mac Reed, "I bin aimin' to quit this foolishness." It was good fun for him, and his reputation was so high that it was immediately chosen as a Book-of-the-Month-Club selection, later awarded a second, but posthumous, Pulitzer Prize for Fiction. Irving Howe, who wrote an early critical study of Faulkner, said that *The Reivers* was to *The Bear* what *Tom Sawyer* was to *Huckleberry Finn*. He had a point, because Mark Twain wrote two closely connected books, one for boys and another for readers of all ages. *The Reivers* is about a boy, as were Twain's two novels, but it is not written for boys. Faulkner greatly admired Mark Twain but he was a more sophisticated writer; all of his fiction is written for adults. In *The Reivers* he was at his most playful; it was Faulkner's exit from the world laughing, a final comic episode in the chronicle of Yoknapatawpha County, and a humorous postscript to his Snopes trilogy.

Faulkner's South has come to mean more than the actual South, because he translated the actual South into literature. And literature, as Aristotle argued, is truer than history, because history only tells us what was, while literature tells us what might be. At his best, Faulkner made history into myth. His Mythical Kingdom is Yoknapatawpha County, Mississippi. It became so real to him that he drew a map of it, and signed it "William Faulkner, sole owner and proprietor." It closely resembled the real Lafayette County, Mississippi, where Faulkner lived, so closely that a French photographer made a book of photographs of it which he called *Yoknapatawpha, Le Pays de Faulkner* ("Yoknapatawpha, Faulkner Country"). But to it he added new places like Jefferson and invented characters with colorful names like Col. John Sartoris, CSA, Bayard Sartoris (the older and the younger), Miss Jenny Sartoris Du Pre, Miss Rosa Millard, Miss Rosa Coldfield, the innumerable Snopeses--Flem, Mink, I.O., Eck, Ike, Col. Sartoris, Admiral Benbow, Wall Street Panic, Montgomery Ward--and all the Compson family, Benjy, Quentin (male and female), Jason (father and son) and Caddy, as well as Popeye, Miss Reba, Temple Drake, Joe Christmas, Rev. Gail Hightower, Thomas Sutpen, Ike McCaslin and Lucas Beauchamp. The list is endless, and Faulkner's characters all seem so real that a fellow novelist, John Dos Passos, gave him credit for creating more believable characters than any modern novelist.

The South of his fiction is not Lafayette County. It is Yoknapatawpha County, Mississippi, which first materialized in the pages of *Sartoris* in 1929. That was his third published novel, but he had not yet named it. Only in his fifth novel, *As I Lay Dying*, did he name it Yoknapatawpha County, and only in his ninth novel, *Absalom, Absalom!* did he draw his map. By the time he published his last novel, *The Reivers*, in 1962, the year of his death, he had made the South into a new territory of the mind recognized all over the world. The Swedish Academy, in awarding him the Nobel Prize for Literature in 1950, had called him "the epic writer of the American South." It was true then. It is still true now.

EPILOGUE

Reading Faulkner

Why read Faulkner? For the same reason we read Shakespeare, or Henry James, or Mark Twain, because different as they were from each other, they are classic authors whose work is essential to our understanding of the nature of man. That means understanding ourselves, a challenge repeated in every generation. Faulkner schooled himself on such writers, and during the course of his career he proved he had gifts great enough to become one of them himself. He knew he had a gift, but he didn't know how great it was, until he was able in his lifetime to make it manifest. It took him thirty years to discover what he could do and thirty more years to do it, but in the end he succeeded in writing a number of works of fiction that are of lasting, perhaps everlasting, value. Much of what he wrote will never be forgotten. It will endure as all major classics endure, because they are unforgettable.

Faulkner's ambition, he vowed early in his life, was to be forgotten as a man and remembered only as a writer. That's easier to do with Shakespeare than it is with Faulkner, because we know so little about Shakespeare's private life. We know much more about Faulkner's private life, but we will never know the secret of his genius. Nor did he know: he called himself a "failed poet," and said that none of his works had lived up to the dream he had in his mind when he wrote them. What he shared with Shakespeare was not the way he lived but the capacity he had to make history into myth by the power of his imagination. We read Shakespeare and Faulkner and other great writers to learn what human experience never was but conceivably could be—at its worst as well as its best. Great writers like Shakespeare and Faulkner make us aware of the full scope and depth of human experience; they open us up to a knowledge of man that is beyond our sight but not beyond our imagination.

Faulkner discovered this knowledge himself by reading the classics, which taught him that "when a man learns to read, he learns of the tragedy and despair of his own kind which he himself may suffer." On the whole, it is true that when you read Faulkner you see that honorable men and women like the Sartorises, who lead others because of their virtues, are often the tragic heroes and heroines of his stories, while unscrupulous scoundrels like the Snopeses, who profit by preying on the weakness and susceptibility of others, are the comic villains. "You can't beat him," Ratliff, the canny sewing machine salesman who is one of Faulkner's storytellers, says of Flem Snopes. He knows what a clever con man Flem Snopes is, but that doesn't keep him from becoming one of Flem's victims at the end of *The Hamlet*. That the comic villains should prevail over the tragic heroes is one measure of Faulkner's judgment about people.

Allen Tate, a poet and novelist as well as a critic, credited Faulkner with creating more masterpieces than any American novelist, at least five by his count: *The Sound and the Fury*, *As I Lay Dying*, *Sanctuary*, *Light in August* and *The Hamlet*. Tate thought Mark Twain, long recognized as a classic American author, wrote only one and a half masterpieces: *Huckleberry Finn* and the first volume of *Life on the Mississippi*. I think Tate was right, and I would add two more Faulkner masterpieces to Tate's list: *Absalom, Absalom!* and *The Bear*. That makes a total of seven masterpieces in all. How many of the world's great writers have matched his achievement? The majority of Faulkner's masterpieces are indeed tragic, though they are replete with comic episodes. *The Hamlet* is a comic masterpiece, and it is the first of the Snopes trilogy, the comic sequence which he completed with *The Town* and *The Mansion*. There are also a number of comic short stories in Faulkner's fictional repertoire, like "Mule in the Yard" and "A Courtship" and the story with his longest title, "My Grandmother Millard and General Bedford Forrest and the Battle of Harrykin Creek." It can be said of Faulkner, as of Shakespeare, that in the long view tragedy does take precedence over comedy, because tragedy is profounder than comedy and truer to life. Comedy often ends in a happy marriage, while tragedy inevitably ends in death. Faulkner may be said to have wept his way through the first half of his career, which was mainly tragic, but made up his mind to laugh his way through the last half of it, which was mainly comic. Faulkner like Shakespeare could write both tragedy and comedy, and they have few rivals. Socrates, in the Symposium, argued that a great poet should be able to write both tragedy and comedy, but we know of no Greek poet who accomplished that remarkable feat.

Many people feel challenged the first time they read a Faulkner novel. It was a challenge he must have sought, since it is clear he never meant his books to be easy reading. He wrote not merely to entertain his readers, but to mystify and intrigue them, to confront them with stories and novels whose very titles implied they were meant to be puzzling. He succeeded so well when he wrote *The Sound and the Fury* that many readers felt stymied, yet it was his own favorite among his novels, as it is with most expert readers, who are undaunted by any barriers to comprehension they might encounter and determined to overcome them. Katherine Anne Porter, a Southern novelist herself, said she liked a challenge when she read a book or story, and she became an early champion of Faulkner's fictional technique. She was aware that from the beginning of his career Faulkner identified himself as a Modernist, bound to be original at any cost, who used a variety of techniques to catch a reader's attention and hold him spellbound. He might do it by means of elliptical narratives, deliberately bypassing the main events of a story to make the reader guess what is happening, by stringing his sentences out page after page till you wonder if they will ever stop, by introducing obsolete words, dialect words, phonetic spellings that drive you to distraction or to the dictionary, often mixing fact with fiction so that you are never quite sure which is which.

To many American readers, Faulkner remains a household name whose work is more admired than read. Most of them know he won a Nobel Prize for Literature, but so did Sinclair Lewis and Pearl Buck and other American writers now largely forgotten. Oprah Winfrey boldly urged millions who belonged to her popular Book Club to spend a Summer of Reading Faulkner, and many took the cue. Her enthusiasm was surprising, since Faulkner used the forbidden word "nigger" repeatedly in his works. Nor, apparently, was Barack Obama bothered by it. He quoted Faulkner favorably during his successful campaign to be the first black President of the United States, in a speech he made in Philadelphia that centered on racial politics in America. Clearly, Faulkner's work appeals to black as well as white readers, and his novels are taught regularly in courses in American literature, whether in high school or in college. Yet in spite of his fame, his works have never become widely popular. Many Americans have read very little of his fiction; few have read all of it.

There are understandable reasons why even serious readers resist reading Faulkner. During his lifetime, many of his friends and fellow citizens in Oxford, Mississippi, refused to read him, because they thought he was besmirching the town's reputation, with his wild tales of immoral, freakish, violent behavior in Yoknapatawpha County, clearly modeled on Lafayette County where they lived. They found it hard to believe he could be awarded a major international prize in a foreign country, when some American critics denounced his work, arguing that his characters were too abnormal, his settings too menacing, and his style too verbose for a writer of genuine talent. Alfred Kazin was one of the reputable critics who wrote a skeptical essay as late as 1942 called "Faulkner: The Rhetoric and the Agony." Faulkner was often compared with Erskine Caldwell, author of *Tobacco Road*, a popular scandalous novel about the rural South. Many readers avoided Faulkner simply because they found him too difficult, dismissing him as not worth their time and effort. I have met educated people who confessed they tried to read a Faulkner novel but were unable to finish it. Often it was *The Sound and the Fury* which stopped them, since it is both his greatest novel and the hardest to understand.

Because Faulkner wrote mainly about the South, some were quick to place him as another regional American writer whose provincialism limited his appeal. But Faulkner wrote about his native region so perceptively that it became universal, like Hawthorne's Puritan New England, or the wide open spaces of Mark Twain's West. Faulkner's South is not a geographical place that can be located on a map: it is a territory of the imagination. He called it his Mythical Kingdom of Yoknapatawpha County, Mississippi, and he acquired international stature by translating the place where he lived into believable fictional reality. He accomplished this remarkable feat in thirty years, starting with *Sartoris* in 1929 and ending with *The Reivers* in 1962, overcoming much local prejudice along the way. Most of his fellow citizens in Oxford, Mississippi, continued to look down on him until late in his life. They knew him well but they could not understand what he did for a living. Faulkner outlived their scorn: he made the town famous all over the world when he won the Nobel Prize for Literature in 1950, and many of its citizens became aware that his work was being taken more seriously in far-off places than in his own home town.

What I know about Faulkner I got largely from reading him, not from meeting him. I learned little from what he said to me seventy years ago, and what he said to my uncle was not what I hoped to hear. I saw that he wanted to talk, not about his writing, but about the people he knew in Oxford, who were the same people my uncle knew. Yet that was worth something; it taught me that Faulkner liked to talk about the people of Oxford as much as they liked to talk about him, and he knew much more about them than they knew about him. Hearing him talk to my uncle made me realize that great writers learn all they need to know from ordinary people, whoever they are or wherever they happen to live. Many people in Oxford thought he was writing about them and they resented it; they didn't see that he was transforming the lives of ordinary human beings into extraordinary characters you would never meet anywhere except in his fiction.

Faulkner was self-educated; he had little use for formal education. It was clearly his choice to learn on his own. There were plenty of opportunities in a college town to become an educated man, yet he never finished high school, and though he took a few college courses, they were his own choice, none of them leading toward a degree. To a Japanese audience on a State Department tour in 1955, Faulkner confessed freely that "I have had no education. I never did like school and I have had to teach myself my trade." He taught himself by being a prodigious reader of everything from literary classics to detective novels, and he learned the use of the English language so well that he knew how to break all the rules of grammar and diction with impunity. His style is idiosyncratic and odd; it takes some getting used to, since it varies from the formal and archaic to the colloquial and dialectal, and he was forever trying out new forms of narration that didn't always work. There is meaning in them, even when it seems elusive; all he asks of his readers is the patience and perseverance to filter the meaning out.

The world Faulkner created by the power of his imagination would never have existed without him. You cannot find Faulkner's South on any map because he created it himself, out of the real South in which he lived. He eventually gained international stature by translating his home, the very place where he lived, into a new, fictional reality. To read the whole work of Faulkner is to become immersed in a mythical region, all of it derived from his own surroundings, which is peopled by individuals whose names and characters he fashioned from ordinary human beings he knew. Faulkner was a realist; he was not a sentimentalist or a reformer. He took a critical but sympathetic view of the world and its inhabitants, not trying to make them any better or worse than they were, not idealizing but humanizing them. There is as much good and evil in the people of Faulkner's fiction as there was in real people he knew, but he refined and concentrated the contrasting elements, testing the reader's judgment to the limits in the process. We get to know his Satorises and his Snopeses and all the gradations of personality between them better than we know our fellow human beings. To read Faulkner is to make yourself a better judge of human nature than you would have been without sharing his keen insight, as he probed deeply into characters created by his own imagination. Faulkner wrote, in *As I Lay Dying*, that Darl Bundren's inner thoughts go so far into the minds of others that his father Anse declares with amazement: "It's like he had got to the inside of you, some way." The same might be said of Faulkner, that he could be a mind-reader, especially when he was inspired to write such multiple stream-of-consciousness novels as this one.

John Dos Passos, a contemporary American novelist sometimes compared with Faulkner, credited him with creating a greater number of believable characters than any American novelist. There is really only one other American novelist who can be compared with Faulkner for the magnitude of his accomplishment, and that is Henry James, a very different kind of writer. James can be credited with writing as many masterpieces of short and long fiction as Faulkner, but his setting was transatlantic, the International Scene, European as well as American, while Faulkner's Mythical Kingdom was only the South, a distinctly American region, bounded on the north by the Ohio River, on the west by the Mississippi River, on the east by the Atlantic Ocean, and on the south by the Gulf of Mexico.

He gave this fictional place a name for the first time in *As I Lay Dying*, his fifth novel in order of publication. It is Yoknapatawpha County, Mississippi, consisting of deep woods, small farms, large plantations, and rustic villages, surrounding the county seat of Jefferson, a Southern town without a university. It is populated mainly by two races, black and white, who live together as close-knit families often related by blood, though the blacks were once slaves who became servants to the whites after the Civil War. Most of his characters, both black and white, are unhappy, self-destructive people, born to be no one but themselves even if it means death rather than life. Faulkner was the South's greatest writer and its most severe critic. He saw the South was in decline and he mirrored it in his works, but he also saw its virtues, its chivalric code of courtesy, honor and courage, and didn't want them to be forgotten. He loved Mississippi, he said, "not for its virtues but despite its faults." He thought the South deserved to lose the Civil War because of its faults, which were shared by all Americans but were greater in the South: despoiling the pristine wilderness, treating nature as a commodity for human use, dispossessing native red men and importing black slaves from Africa to work its plantations. It was not a happy story and Faulkner told it as it was, with realism but with grace. Katherine Anne Porter called Faulkner's work "Dionysian," as if inspired by the Greek god of wine and drama, "the world of illogic and human feeling and of complete giving over, I should say, to emotion rather than reason." She said many of Faulkner's characters willingly chose death in preference to dishonor. She called him a "superlative" writer and said she was quite willing to read one of his books five times if necessary in order to understand it. When he wrote about the Civil War, as he often did, he was writing about the generation of men who died in a valiant but vain attempt to defend their homeland from the equally valiant and victorious Yankees, and when he wrote about their descendants, it often seemed they were bent on dying by their own hands, out of the shame of defeat they had inherited from the earlier generation. The novelist and critic, André Malraux, in a preface to the French translation of *Sanctuary* in 1932, went so far as to say that Faulkner's novel marked "the intrusion of Greek tragedy into detective fiction," because his families appear to bear an inherited curse which they must expiate even if it means they too are doomed. A later French novelist and critic, Marcel Brion, in an obituary tribute to Faulkner at the time of his death in 1962, called him "the white spiritualist of the Negro race."

It is true that Faulkner's work was largely sombre and tragic as he began, and it is also true that it became lighter and more comic later on. Katherine Anne Porter thought that he always wrote on a hairline between tragedy and comedy, and might go either way in any story or novel. She considered *The Bear* his supreme masterpiece, a tragic hunting story that ends in multiple deaths, but she thought the "Spotted Horses" episode in *The Hamlet*, a comic story of a country auction that goes wildly wrong, funnier than Mark Twain. *The Hamlet* is all about the Snopes family, who are as their name suggests the white trash of his fictional South, a vulgar and ambitious clan opposed to the courtly and aristocratic Sartorises, whose name suggests the chivalric code they try to live by. The Snopeses come out of the backwoods into Jefferson and outwit the Sartorises by hook and by crook. In his final novel about them, *The Mansion,* the Snopeses have taken over the town of Jefferson from the Sartorises, and are running it for their own profit. His first Snopes was not comic; he was a sinister character named Byron Snopes who works as a cashier in Old Bayard Sartoris's bank and is a peeping tom. But ten years after writing *Sartoris* Faulkner turned his full attention to the Snopes clan, and introduced Flem Snopes as his principal comic villain. Flem is the crafty son of the scheming Ab Snopes, the Father Abraham of a degenerate clan, and it is Flem who in *The Hamlet* auctions off a band of wild horses from Texas to the gullible country people of Frenchman's Bend, who own them but are unable to capture them and keep the spotted ponies from breaking out of their corral and rampaging like demons over the whole of Yoknapatawpha County. Flem auctions off the horses he has brought from Texas while managing the more respectable job of clerking in a general store. His numerous kin have invaded Frenchman's Bend, bringing increasingly colorful names, such as Ike Snopes and Lump Snopes and I.O. Snopes and Eck Snopes and Mink Snopes and St. Elmo Snopes and Colonel Sartoris Snopes and Admiral Benbow Snopes and Wall Street Panic Snopes and Montgomery Ward Snopes. Prolific and acquisitive, they are able to get ahead under Flem's skilful guidance, and Flem himself rises to be president of the Sartoris bank. He has his comeuppance, though, from another Snopes. He has failed to post bail for his mean cousin Mink, who gets out of prison and murders him at the peak of his power. It is not tragic. It is exactly what he deserves.

The more you read Faulkner, the more deeply you become involved in his imaginative world. He can be relentlessly naturalistic at times, when he is describing some gruesome rape or murder that is integral to the tale he is telling, and there is much in Faulkner that is deliberately repugnant, yet there is a magnetic power in his writing that draws you to him, even while you watch with horrified fascination as some inevitable tragedy unfolds, or pursue a wildly comic scene to an unexpected but hilarious outcome. Faulkner goes to extremes of violence and brutality that are shocking to any reader—but so does the Bible, and Faulkner was forever quoting the Bible--yet the effect of reading him is that of feeling curiously satisfied. The feeling is comparable to the cathartic effect Aristotle thought Greek tragedy had on its audience, purging them of the pity and fear generated by the plot and action on stage. The Greek audience, like Shakespeare's English audience, could behold a stage piled high with corpses, and feel relieved not to be one of them. The same holds true for Faulkner. If a Faulkner story or novel baffles you or disgusts you the first time you read it, try reading it a second or third time and see if you don't begin to like it. The best reason for reading Faulkner is re-reading him. You can start wherever you like, you can continue where you left off, but there is one thing you should always keep in mind: the first time will only be the beginning.

APPENDIX

French tribute to Faulkner

Obituary by Marcel Brion, French novelist and critic, published in Le Monde, *Paris, July 8–9, 1962.*

The death of William Faulkner plunges the whole literary world into mourning. It forces us suddenly to take stock of an achievement in the contemporary novel which is, in the true sense of the word, monumental. This achievement, nearly as vast as Balzac's *Human Comedy*, was apparently complete at his death, for the author wrote, as he began his novel, *The Mansion* (published in French some months ago): "This book is the final chapter and the consummation of a work conceived and begun in 1925."

It was thirty-five years ago, in fact, that Faulkner began to paint his extraordinary portrait of American society in the Southern States, and in time he became so fascinated with the characters which his imagination produced that he could not separate himself from them, for when the heroes of a novel are truly living, they seem to go on developing into indefinite, and perhaps infinite, time.

What interested him, even more than the description of a particular society, was the development of characters into full human existence, over a long succession of generations. From volume to volume of Faulkner's work, individual destinies become entangled, and, as the work progresses, new complications develop, linking father and son through the operation of an implacable fate, which seems to hang suspended over the family. Ancestral hatreds smoulder for a long time, then burst suddenly into brutal flames, and things that seemed forgotten or ignored suddenly reappear, in a blinding flash of revelation.

Even the trance-like passivity of certain of his characters is only a patient sufferance of will, waiting for that instant when the soul will finally take possession of its total existence, and join the other souls who have already reached their full evolution, and mix its fate indissolubly with theirs.

William Faulkner was truly a novelist of temperament, who so identified himself with his characters that he seemed incapable of detaching himself from them, or they from him, before they attained the third dimension of reality, the fullest reality possible to characters in fiction. This complete involvement with the characters is what a reader submits to as soon as he opens one of Faulkner's books. Faulkner himself was the first to submit to it.

His imagination had the constructive power to invent an entire region, and then define it so well and will it so powerfully that the myth became reality, and the whole region became fully present: the Country of Faulkner. The fields of cotton, the wide rivers colored by the dawn or by the clay, the little towns alternately burning and slumbering beside them, with their Negroes, their poor whites, their plantation-owners proud of their recent ancestors and their new-won prosperity--all these things live as clearly and vividly in the reader's mind as does the province of Balzac's novels, with its lawyers, its old women, and its fanciful children.

Faulkner forces his reader to take for truth whatever it pleased him to invent. The almost fatal fascination of his work arises, no doubt, from an extraordinary poetic quality in the style, which serves to illuminate secret passions, consuming hatreds, suppressed longings of the soul, until even the shadows seem to glow with a strange light. Instinctively rejecting older forms of character analysis, he directed his interest--and that of his reader--to the intermediate stages between crime and folly, into which men seem led by some obscure evil genius. Because his characters lack the moral force necessary to subdue the vital energy of their passions, they willingly follow the darker impulses of their minds, without regard for the normal pattern of conduct required by civilized society--and for that, Faulkner was often criticized.

It remains true, however, that Faulkner's novels, when taken as a whole, form not only a saga, but a full-scale myth--in fact, many myths. His total work, in its sweeping architecture, comprises an epic, describing the eternal struggle between life and death, between being and non-being, within society and within the individuals that compose it, stretching all the way from *Sanctuary* to *The Mansion*. The spirits that he summoned from the shade return to the shade, facing their destiny with the sort of cold arrogance that one recalls in the heroes of Homer. Indeed, if comparisons must be sought for this American novelist, who yesterday went to join the shades in the country of shades, his nearest kin will be found among the tragic poets of Greece, rather than among his countrymen and contemporaries, such as Dos Passos, Steinbeck, or Hemingway, for like the Greeks he discerned the imminence of doom behind the drama of everyday life.

Not that the Fate of the House of Atreus bears any historical resemblance to that of the House of Sartoris. The Faulknerian world is clearly modern, clearly of its own time and place. But hovering over his work is an anguish of being and an anxiety of becoming which has not yet, I think, been measured to the full extent of its divine or diabolic power. The unfracturable solidity of his work, the balance he achieved between flesh and spirit, assure him of a universal permanence.

--Translated by William Pratt.

The Nobel Prize and other prizes

1. Faulkner won many prizes for his writing, most of them after he won the greatest among them, the Nobel Prize for Literature, in 1950. Before then, his only honor had been election to the American Academy of Arts and Letters in 1948. The 1949 Nobel Prize for Literature, belatedly awarded to him on Dec. 10, 1950, was presented by King Gustaf of Sweden in Stockholm. Further honors included:
2. William Dean Howells Medal, 1950
3. National Book Award for Most Distinguished Book of Fiction, 1950
4. Officer of the French Legion of Honor, 1951 (presented at the French consulate in New Orleans)
5. Newspaper Guild Award of New York, April 13, 1951
6. Verdun Medal, 1951
7. National Book Award for *The Collected Stories of William Faulkner* in 1951
8. Pulitzer Prize for Fiction for *A Fable* (1955)
9. Silver Medal of the Athens Academy, 1957 (on a State Department visit to Greece)
10. Order of Andrew Bello (on a State Department visit to Venezuela in 1961)
11. Gold Medal of the National Institute of Arts and Letters, May 24, 1962 (the year of his death)
12. Pulitzer Prize for Fiction for *The Reivers*, 1963 (awarded posthumously)

Three orders of Faulkner's novels

Faulkner's nineteen novels can reasonably be arranged in three distinct orders: the Order of Publication, the Order of History, and the Order of Artistry. The first order is simply the order in which he wrote and published them, though Faulkner would later claim they formed a coherent whole in his mind as early as 1925. They comprise what became his Mythical Kingdom of Yoknapatawpha County, Mississippi. The second order is the chronological order of the novels if the events had happened in historical sequence, from the antebellum South before the Civil War to the contemporary South of Faulkner's lifetime. But the most important order of all is the Order of

Artistry, the order of merit that originates in every reader's critical judgment of Faulkner's work, taken novel by novel. The resulting consensus, whenever it occurs, will become a permanent tradition surrounding Faulkner's fiction.

Order of Publication:	Order of History	Order of Artistry
Soldier's Pay 1926	Absalom, Absalom! 1936	The Sound and the Fury
Mosquitoes 1927	The Unvanquished 1938	Absalom, Absalom!
Sartoris 1929	Go Down, Moses 1942	As I Lay Dying
The Sound and The Fury 1929	The Hamlet 1940	Light in August
As I Lay Dying 1930	The Reivers 1962	The Hamlet
Sanctuary 1931	As I Lay Dying 1930	Go Down, Moses (The Bear)
Light in August 1932	A Fable 1954	Sanctuary
Pylon 1934	Soldier's Pay 1926	Sartoris
Absalom, Absalom! 1936	Sartoris 1929	The Unvanquished
The Unvanquished 1938	Mosquitoes 1927	Intruder in the Dust
The Wild Palms 1939	The Sound and The Fury 1929	The Reivers
The Hamlet 1940	Sanctuary 1931	Mosquitoes
Go Down, Moses 1942	Light in August 1932	The Town
Intruder in the Dust 1948	Pylon 1934	The Mansion
Requiem for a Nun 1952	The Town 1956	Soldier's Pay
A Fable 1954	The Wild Palms 1939	The Wild Palms
The Town 1956	Intruder in the Dust 1948	A Fable
The Mansion 1959	Requiem for a Nun 1952	Requiem for a Nun
The Reivers 1962	The Mansion 1959	Pylon

Comparing these three very different orders of his work lends credence to Faulkner's own belief that time is a fluid medium, in which there is no "was," only "is'—that the present constantly recapitulates the past, human memory mirroring all experience, past and present, individually or collectively. Faulkner was an Existentialist as well as a Modernist in his fiction, since he clearly thought that present consciousness contains potentially all the possibilities of human existence. Human nature in his view was unchanging, though the circumstances of life changed within a lifetime and throughout history. His family dynasties and his recurrent characters prove that he thought human beings are destined to be what they are, to live in the past as much as the present, to act as honorably or dishonorably as each individual has the impulse to act, and to be responsible for whatever good or evil he felt impelled to commit during his lifetime. Temple Drake in *Sanctuary* believes that the Snake was in the Garden of Eden before Adam and Eve, and in her willing innocence she becomes the victim of Popeye's ruthless will; Flem Snopes, in Ratliff's wildly imaginative dream in *The Hamlet*, goes down to Hell and outwits Satan, because he has no soul to suffer punishment. The tragic or comic outcomes in the lives of Faulkner's characters seem more a matter of destiny than of choice; each one without choosing is "condemned to be free," a paradox of fate and free will which the French novelist-philosopher Jean-Paul Sartre held to be true of all human beings. Sartre, like most French readers, greatly admired Faulkner, though he criticized Faulkner for creating too many characters like Quentin Compson, who saw life as if through a rearview mirror, and lived more in the past than the present. All of Faulkner's characters, not just Quentin, have their own personal fate. They are what they are, for better or worse. André Malraux, after reading the French translation of *Sanctuary* published in 1932, famously wrote that it signaled "the intrusion of Greek tragedy into the detective novel." It may be said that Malraux understood Faulkner's achievement better than Sartre, placing it where it belongs, in the long Western literary tradition inherited from the Greeks. Faulkner became a classic in the minds of French readers before he was a classic in the minds of American and English readers and shares with Edgar Allan Poe the distinction of being an American writer whose entire work is published in the renowned Pléiade edition of classic French writers.

www.ingramcontent.com/pod-product-compliance
Lightning Source LLC
Chambersburg PA
CBHW060946230426
43665CB00015B/2086